I0605615

"Gerald Bray's book provides an impressive, integrative historical overview of the relationship between theology and philosophy. Bray displays a good deal of self-discipline by not getting bogged down by rabbit trails and unnecessary details. And while readers may disagree here or there, the larger project is impressive. The book's good pace and flow and sufficient depth provide a valuable survey on the important question about the relationship between Athens and Jerusalem."

—PAUL COPAN, Pledger Family Chair of Philosophy and Ethics, Palm Beach Atlantic University; author of *A Little Book for New Philosophers* and coauthor of *An Introduction to Biblical Ethics: Walking in the Way of Wisdom*

"In this daring study Gerald Bray paints on a wide canvas—nothing less than the entire Christian tradition—as he traces the subtle connections and stark differences between faith and reason, philosophy and theology, human learning and divine wisdom. Well conceived and well written, this book encourages us to think, and teaches us how."

—TIMOTHY GEORGE, Beeson Divinity School, Samford University

"Bray presents the complex range of ways that pagan philosophy ('Athens') has been variously engaged within Christian theology ('Jerusalem'), from the pre-Christian era to post-Christian New Atheism. With a disarmingly clear style, Bray skips across the Western world-map and throughout the centuries. Highly recommended for ambitious lay study, college students, and clergy alike. Two thumbs up!"

—KATHRYN GREENE-MCCREIGHT, priest affiliate, Christ Church New Haven, Connecticut

"Far more than a history of the interaction between Athens and Jerusalem, Bray's well-written and researched book offers a history of the interaction between philosophy and theology, Catholicism and Protestantism, traditional and modern, religion and science, Christian orthodoxy and Enlightenment deism. Though I did not agree with all of his conclusions, I appreciated the dialogue, the clarity, and the sincerity."

—LOUIS MARKOS, professor in English and scholar in residence at Houston Christian University; author of *From Plato to Christ: How Platonic Thought Shaped the Christian Faith*

"In the midst of modern attempts at retrieving the Christian tradition's exegetical and theological heritage, a deeper understanding of the variegated philosophical and contextual worlds of our forebears is sorely needed. *Athens and Jerusalem* helps to fill this gap in classic Gerald Bray form: by drawing together swaths of lofty ideas and historical characters into a readable, coherent, and enjoyable narrative. The result is a book that both summarizes prevailing narratives while also challenging them."

—BRANDON D. SMITH, chair of the Hobbs School of Theology and Ministry and associate professor of theology and early Christianity, Oklahoma Baptist University; cofounder of the Center for Baptist Renewal

ATHENS & JERUSALEM

Philosophy, Theology, and the Mind of Christ

ATHENS & JERUSALEM

Philosophy, Theology, and the Mind of Christ

Gerald Bray

LEXHAM PRESS

Athens and Jerusalem: Philosophy, Theology, and the Mind of Christ

Lexham Press, 1313 Commercial St., Bellingham, WA 98225
LexhamPress.com

Print ISBN 9781683597728
Digital ISBN 9781683597735
Library of Congress Control Number 2024930867

Lexham Editorial: Todd Hains, Elliot Ritzema, Katrina Smith, Mandi Newell
Cover Design: Sarah Brossow
Typesetting: Justin Marr

24 25 26 27 28 29 30 / TR / 12 11 10 9 8 7 6 5 4 3 2 1

O Almighty God, you make the minds of all faithful believers to be of one will; grant that your people may love what you command and desire what you promise, so that despite the many and varied changes of the world, our hearts may be fixed where true joys are to be found, through Jesus Christ our Lord. Amen.

—Adapted from the collect for the Fourth Sunday after Easter in the *Book of Common Prayer* (1549)

CONTENTS

1

A TALE OF TWO CITIES

Sometime around the year AD 200, Tertullian of Carthage (ca. 160–ca. 220), a convert to Christianity who became one of its greatest apologists, wrote in exasperation: "What has Athens got to do with Jerusalem?"[1] Tertullian was a master of the pithy statement, and his outburst has become famous over time. For him "Athens," the university town of ancient Greece, stood for philosophy in all its many shapes and sizes. Not all the Greek philosophers came from Athens, and many never went there, but the city was famous as the meeting place of ideas. The New Testament (NT) writer Luke captured its aura very well when he wrote: "All the Athenians and the foreigners who lived there would spend their time in nothing except telling or hearing something new" (Acts 17:21). The occasion was the visit of the apostle Paul to the city, when he was able to present the gospel of Christ to an eager crowd of listeners on the Areopagus (Mars Hill), the ancient equivalent of the courthouse. Paul had no trouble at all in getting an audience and nobody tried to drive him away, which is more than can be said of his attempts to preach in most other places. The Athenians were remarkably polite and inquisitive, but at the same time they were also noncommittal. To them, Paul was just one more eccentric who had come to share his ideas with people who would listen to anything—and believe nothing. The visit was not entirely fruitless, but neither was it a great success. In other places,

1. Tertullian, *De praescriptione haereticorum* 7.9. The complete quotation is: *Quid Athenis Hierosolymis? Quid academiae et ecclesiae? Quid haereticis et Christianis?* ("What therefore has Athens got to do with Jerusalem? What does the academy have to do with the church? What do heretics have to do with Christians?")

like Thessalonica, Corinth, and Philippi, Paul had left a thriving church behind, but in Athens there were only a handful of converts—Dionysius, who was a lawyer on the Areopagus, a woman called Damaris, and a handful of others whom Luke does not name (Acts 17:34).

Jerusalem, on the other hand, was a completely different story. For Paul, it was the center of his cultural universe, the ancestral capital of Israel, the site of the temple, which lay at the heart of Jewish worship, and the place where Jesus of Nazareth had been crucified. Even when he was wandering around Greece, Paul's thoughts were never far from the place where Christianity had originated, and one of his last recorded journeys was largely devoted to raising funds for the support of the local church there. It was in Jerusalem that Paul had been educated at the feet of Gamaliel, one of the great rabbis of his time, and it was there that he was arrested, put on trial, and eventually dispatched to Rome on appeal. But to the wider world, Jerusalem was a provincial backwater. The Greco-Roman world was a maritime civilization, linked by great port cities that hugged the Mediterranean shoreline. But Jerusalem was inland, high up in the mountains, and largely cut off from the great trade routes that bound the Roman Empire together. By Tertullian's day it had been razed to the ground—not once but twice—and its Jewish character had been obliterated. It continued to exist under the name Aelia Capitolina, but as a religious and cultural center it survived mainly in the imagination of both Jews and Christians, whose holy writings made it out to be a kind of foretaste of the kingdom of heaven on earth.

By Tertullian's time, while Athens too had long since lost its political significance, the monuments of its ancient glory were still there to be seen and it continued to attract intellectuals from all over the Roman world. Jerusalem, by contrast, had already become something of a myth—idealized in prophecy and poetry but a small town that few people visited and that had almost nothing to show for its illustrious past. Yet Tertullian was in no doubt about which of the two was more important. Not only did he think it fitting to compare the two cities, apparently so different from one another, but his preference (as a Christian) was clearly for Jerusalem. He never went to either place, but that did not matter to him. As far as he was concerned, Athens represented the crowning achievement of Greek culture, the *de facto* capital of civilization. But Jerusalem was the place where God had revealed himself to humanity and where he had come down to earth in the person of Jesus Christ.[2] For Tertullian there was no contest—Jerusalem won hands down. His contemporaries must have thought it was an odd choice, and Tertullian knew that he was confronting the main intellectual currents of his time, but history was on his side. It would take some time, but in AD 529 the Emperor Justinian I (527–565) closed the philosophical schools in Athens because they were the last remaining source of opposition to Christianity. In the meantime, Jerusalem had come back from oblivion and was home to one of the five patriarchal churches of the Roman world, alongside Rome, Constantinople, Alexandria, and Antioch.[3]

The contrasting fortunes of the two cities mirrors the relationship between Christianity and Greek philosophy in the early centuries of the church's existence. As geographical locations, neither one plays a significant role in Western intellectual thought nowadays, but in metaphorical terms—which was the dimension that appealed to Tertullian—their names are still instantly recognizable and they continue to symbolize two very different approaches to human life and thought. At times it has seemed that one has virtually absorbed the other, while at other times they have appeared to be in conflict. Both have exerted a powerful influence on the world, and modern civilization cannot be understood if one of them is disregarded. The two strands belong together, however much purist devotees might try to separate them and (usually) emphasize one at the expense of the other. Can they live in harmony with one another, or must we conclude, as Tertullian did, that they are mutually incompatible?

Different answers to that question have been given in the course of time, though it must be said that few Christians have adopted Tertullian's position, which they have usually regarded as extreme. Broadly speaking, most observers would probably agree that the Roman Catholic and Eastern Orthodox traditions place a greater emphasis on philosophy, and

2. It is true that Jesus was born in Bethlehem, a village just outside Jerusalem, and that he grew up in Nazareth, but Jerusalem was the center of his ministry in the sense that it was there that he died and rose again from the grave. His earthly career was an extended journey from the provinces to the capital, where he was tried before the leaders of his people and crowned King of the Jews by the man to whom those leaders had consigned him for punishment.

3. Its primacy was recognized at the first Council of Ephesus in 431, but Justinian was the first emperor to refer to it as a patriarchal see, which he did exactly a century later.

especially on Greco-Roman philosophy, than most Protestants do, but this broad characterization must be treated with caution. It is not true to say that the Protestant Reformation was a revolt from the side of Jerusalem against a church that had fallen captive to Athens. None of the magisterial Reformers (or their opponents) thought in that way. Both sides regarded the Bible and the theological tradition that had grown up as a means of interpreting it as primary for the doctrine and worship of the church, and it was because the Reformers believed that the church had gone astray on significant theological matters that they protested in the way they did. As far as philosophy was concerned, both were ready to use Greek categories of thought, derived mainly from Aristotle, but with strong elements of Plato as well, as the framework for expressing their ideas.

This meant that in a real sense they were speaking the same language and could express their differences in ways that made it possible for debate to take place. The significance of this can be seen when we consider the effect that the Reformation had on the Eastern Orthodox churches, which had not experienced the revival of Aristotelianism that had so affected the medieval West. The Eastern churches did not know how to respond to the Reformation because they did not understand the concepts that were being debated. This did not mean that the Reformation passed them by completely, though. In fact, what happened was that the Eastern churches developed a pattern of theological education that was closely modeled on that of the West and learned to express their own theology in essentially Aristotelian categories. Sometimes this led them in the direction of Protestantism, in particular a Protestantism of the Reformed (Calvinist) type, but more often the Easterners were shaped by Roman Catholicism, to the extent that many Protestants came to perceive them as little more than "Catholics with beards."

In the twentieth century there was a reaction in the Eastern churches against this, but it is one that has divided the Orthodox world. The theological academies have leaned more toward Protestantism, particularly of the liberal German variety, but there has also been a powerful movement seeking to recover what is perceived as the authentic tradition of the early church. In practice, this has led to a new emphasis on mystical theology, which has been (wrongly) celebrated as the essence of Eastern Orthodoxy in contrast to the more academic approach of the

West. This claim has even influenced some Westerners who are dissatisfied with the approach taken by their own theological traditions to turn to Orthodoxy, which they imagine is somehow more spiritual and therefore more authentic.

In reality, the Eastern churches are divided between those who continue to revere the Greek philosophical tradition and those who reject it. The chief proponent of the former was Georges Florovsky (1893–1979), who went so far as to write a detailed history of ancient Greek theology in order to emphasize the importance of what he called "Hellenism" for understanding it. The Hellenism of which he spoke was what we would call Neoplatonism (not Aristotelianism), which meant that while it could be seen as a break with the more recent Orthodox past, it remained within the parameters of the classical philosophical tradition. Much more recently, the Protestant theologian Hans Boersma (1961–) has claimed that Christianity would not exist in its present form without the input of what he calls "Christian Platonism," and has even gone so far as to say that without it the Bible cannot be properly understood.[4] He thinks that biblical scholars generally, and Protestant ones in particular, have discounted the importance of philosophy for understanding the Bible and wants them to be more open to what amounts to an allegorical reading of the text.

Not surprisingly, this suggestion has not made much of an impression on biblical scholars, nor is it likely to. Boersma cites a number of ancient Christian writers in support of his thesis, but ignores the evidence that disagrees with it. Justin Martyr (100–165), for example, was a critic of the philosophers, in particular of Plato, whom he regarded as a brilliant but blind guide to the truth, but Boersma does not mention this. He does, however, quote Origen (185–254) with approval, though Origen was eventually repudiated and even condemned as a heretic for his rather too enthusiastic willingness to accept certain philosophical principles for the interpretation of Christian theology. Neither Justin nor the accusers of Origen went as far as Tertullian, but they were more sympathetic to his position than proponents of a "Hellenic" Christianity are prepared to admit.

4. Hans Boersma, *Five Things Theologians Wish Biblical Scholars Knew* (Downers Grove, IL: IVP Academic, 2021). See especially pp. 39–63.

Who is right? What options are open to us, and which should we prefer? Are different choices equally valid? Whether we like it or not, we live in a world where a plurality of voices on this subject can be heard and where it is rare to find people who are genuinely willing to consider options other than their own. A book like this one can hardly aim to provide definitive answers to a question that is now nearly two millennia old, but at least I can try to clear the air and provide a guide, if not a generally agreed solution, to the problems involved in reconciling philosophy and theology to each other.

SUMMARY

1. In ancient times, Athens and Jerusalem were the recognized centers of Greek philosophy and Jewish religion, respectively. Their names were first used metaphorically by the Christian writer Tertullian and are still encountered today as symbols of philosophy and theology generally.

2. Christians have long had an ambiguous relationship to "Athens." Everyone agrees that philosophy, and especially classical Greek philosophy, has influenced Christianity, but there are different interpretations of what this means. Some regard its influence on the church as pernicious and a few have tried to dispense with it altogether. Others see it as essential for the construction of Christian theology, which they believe must be described in basically philosophical terms. Most people are somewhere in the middle—they recognize that philosophy and theology have many things in common, but also that there are important differences between them that should not be underestimated or neglected.

II

ATHENS

What exactly is philosophy, and where did it come from? The word itself is Greek for "love of wisdom," and most accounts trace its origin to about 700 BC. Many societies in human history have had their wise people who have occupied a special position. Very often they have been what we would now call magicians, claiming the ability to control the elements for the benefit of the tribe of country to which they belonged. In many cases, they were religious leaders who professed a knowledge of the supernatural that they could use to frighten people into submission. In some cases, they were able to develop genuine skills that served to develop what we would now call civilization. In ancient China and Babylonia, elite groups of wise men acquired a knowledge of astronomy that made it possible for them to predict the movement of the stars, which they believed influenced human destiny. Some developed mathematical abilities that they put to good use in geometry, leading to the development of architectural skills that continue to impress us today as we contemplate the magnificent structures that they left behind. Over time, they accumulated a store of learning that they passed on to their successors, both orally and in writing. It is in the latter form that most of what we know about them has been preserved. Much of it is what we would now call practical information, including incantations and rituals that were supposed to produce the desired effects. Sometimes their wisdom was condensed into proverbs—pithy sayings that were designed to impart wisdom to the young as they sought to master the secrets of a good and successful life.[1]

Wisdom of this kind is known to have flourished in many different places, including China and India as well as Mesopotamia and Egypt. The first two of these had great influence in south and east Asia, but were largely unknown to the rest of the world until relatively recent times. The ancient lore of Mesopotamia and Egypt, however, spread across the Mediterranean, where it was absorbed and transformed as it went. A good indication of this is the system of writing that originated in Egypt as hieroglyphics, was simplified in western Asia into phonetic symbols, and migrated from there to Greece, where it developed into the alphabet as we know it. For centuries, writing was a skill mastered by only a few, and those who were capable of it were regarded as especially gifted. In China, writing never really got past the hieroglyphic stage, and even today the Chinese use a complex system of characters that bears no relation to the sounds of their language. Elsewhere, in India they developed various scripts that were based on syllables rather than simple sounds, and in the Middle East the Egyptian hieroglyphs were turned into consonants that were written without the accompanying vowels.

It was in the Greek world that a truly phonetic alphabet was first produced, allowing the language to be recorded in a way that was relatively easy for most people to master. That does not mean that literacy was widespread, but writing was no longer a sacred mystery reserved to a few. The acquisition and transmission of learning was democratized to a previously unknown degree, and although there were still oracles and religious officials who claimed to possess superior intelligence and to have access to hidden knowledge, they were no longer unique. People with inquiring minds could develop intellectual skills on their own and transmit them to others as part of a common fund of human wisdom. Those who did this were few in number, and at first not many people appreciated their significance, but their approach bore fruit in the form of mental constructions that they promoted as the key to understanding the world around them. As always, some people were better at doing this than others, and their

1. We are most familiar with them from the OT book of Proverbs, a collection attributed to King Solomon (tenth century BC).

thoughts and sayings were copied and handed on, sometimes by disciples who formed a school to perpetuate their memory and study their ways of thinking. These men were the first who can properly be called philosophers.

Where they got their knowledge from is not easy to determine. They undoubtedly observed the world around them and drew conclusions from what they saw as to how it operated, but they did not usually go beyond observation to experiment. In other words, they produced theories about how the world works without testing them to see whether they were right. Instead, they preferred to use their minds to create logical paradigms that they imagined were the foundation of reality. They were particularly good at mathematics, a discipline that requires great mental agility and is relatively free of the need to experiment. In their heads they could create squares, triangles, and circles that did not exist as such in the material world, and with those shapes in mind they could refashion matter and subdue it.

Mind over matter was what it was all about, and in some cases it worked fairly well. Stones could be cut into cubes and used for building, and mathematical calculations enabled people to create complex structures, using columns and the like. Eventually they were able to perfect the dome, the single most outstanding achievement of ancient architecture. They were even able to speculate about the possibility of flying, but they never got beyond thinking about it, and it was not until modern times that their theories were turned into realities. One outstanding example of this tendency was Democritus, who lived in the fifth century BC. Democritus is famous today because he believed that the universe was composed of atoms, a theory that he got from his teacher Leucippus that has turned out to be true. But Democritus and Leucippus were only guessing at that, and for centuries their beliefs remained just one possibility among many—nobody did anything to try to figure out whether they were right! They had no way of demonstrating that their theory was correct, and so we should not be surprised that they were largely ignored in ancient times. After all, why should anyone take seriously something that claimed to be both material and invisible at the same time? It was only when modern scientists discovered atomic theory that Democritus was remembered—and credited by some with a genius that he did not really possess.[2]

2. Leucippus has unfortunately gone unrecognized, both in ancient and in modern times.

Democritus was one of a group of thinkers who were making their mark in the years before 400 BC. Very little is known about them because their teachings have survived only in fragmentary quotes, often in the writings of people who wanted to refute their ideas. As far as we can tell, the earliest of these thinkers was Thales of Miletus, who lived more than a century before Democritus. He was supposed to have predicted the eclipse of the sun that occurred on May 28, 585 BC, which he could only have done by a sophisticated use of astronomy and mathematics. Where did Thales get that knowledge? Some of it may have come from Babylon, but most scholars think Egypt was the more likely source. According to later legend, Thales went there and learned the art of geometry from the Egyptians. He is said to have calculated the height of the pyramids by measuring the shadow they cast at the time of day when the length of his own shadow was equal to his height. Whether that is true or not, Thales is credited with having been the first Greek to have rejected the myths of ancient tradition in favor of what we would now call scientific experiment, and for that reason he has often been hailed as the "father of modern science."

Thales seems to have believed that the world was made up of four elements—earth, air, fire, and water—and that water was the first and most important of these.[3] Other thinkers agreed with him in principle but debated which of the four elements was the most important. Anaximenes, one of Thales's disciples, apparently tried to move beyond this debate by suggesting that all four elements held together in a kind of proportional balance, which he suggested was the basis of cosmic justice, whatever that was supposed to be. Neither Anaximenes nor anyone else could say for sure, but what mattered for subsequent thought was that he connected the structure of the universe with the concepts of right and wrong. To understand how the world worked was the basis for knowing how to live in it, and to go against its supposedly natural laws was to court disaster. The order of nature was not arbitrary, and could not be, because if it were, life on earth would be impossible. There would be no good and bad, no principle of existence against which everything could be measured. It

3. The first clear indication of this division of the elements comes from Empedocles (497–437 BC), but the scheme is probably considerably older.

was the task of the philosophers to find out what that principle was and to apply it to the needs of everyday life. One way or another, the whole of classical philosophy can be understood as an attempt to answer that quest for meaning in the universe.

One important though little-known figure in this quest was Xenophanes (sixth century BC), who seems to have been the first Greek thinker to challenge the traditional view of the gods. Xenophanes realized that the Greeks, like other peoples, had created a pantheon in their own image. The gods of Olympus and of the great Homeric poems (the *Iliad* and the *Odyssey*) were superhuman figures but they were just like the Greeks themselves—brilliant in some ways but highly immoral and untrustworthy in others. He knew that this had to be wrong, if only because every other nation did the same thing, with the result that the gods of one people reflected its particular characteristics and none of them could claim to be truly transcendent. To resolve this problem, Xenophanes came up with the idea that there is only one supreme God, who is completely detached from the world as we know it. This detachment was necessary, Xenophanes thought, because if God were involved with the world he would be taking sides in any number of conflicts and would lose any claim to be an absolute, independent sovereign. Apparently, Xenophanes believed that his God had only one thing in common with humanity—the power to think. Of course, he had no idea what God would be thinking about, except that whatever it was, it would be quite unlike any form of human thought.[4]

The difficulty with Xenophanes's assertion was that although his hunch about God was logical, there was no way he could prove it. A God who was completely cut off from the world could not be known at all, and so what Xenophanes had to say about him (or it?) was essentially meaningless. It was pure speculation on his part, as his many critics were quick to point out. Today we may be impressed by his intelligence, but his contemporaries were not. To them, a theory that was unprovable by definition could not be the basis for rational argument and so it was dismissed, even by people who might in principle have been sympathetic to it. It

4. Compare Isa 55:8–9, where God says: "My thoughts are not your thoughts, neither are my ways your ways. ... For as the heavens are higher than the earth, so are my ways higher than your ways and my thoughts than your thoughts." Xenophanes would doubtless have agreed with that.

was not the end of the search for a single ultimate Being who lies beyond the material universe, but later generations would try to explain how that Being could be known, if only to a limited degree, and so Xenophanes's basic assumption would of necessity be discarded.

A generation or so after Thales, there appeared another gifted mathematician called Pythagoras. He lived in the latter half of the sixth century BC, but almost everything we know about him comes from Plato (427–347 BC), who was writing more than a century after Pythagoras's death. Whether Pythagoras knew of Thales is uncertain, though if he came from the island of Samos, which is near Miletus, he probably did. Like Thales, he is also supposed to have absorbed Babylonian and Egyptian learning, though how that came to him is unknown. At some point, Pythagoras left his homeland and went to Croton (Crotona), one of the Greek colonies in southern Italy, where he rose to prominence before being driven out by a popular revolt. He ended his days in an obscure place called Metapontion or Metapont(i)um, also in southern Italy, but not before he had founded a guild of mathematicians who preserved both his memory and his theorems.

Pythagoras was convinced that numbers were the key to understanding reality. Earlier thinkers had used mathematics as a tool for understanding matter, but Pythagoras turned their theories on their head by claiming that numbers *are* reality. He began with the number one, which he called the Monad, and which formed the basis of everything else that exists. Reproducing the Monad led to the existence of two principles, or the Dyad, from which everything else derived. Putting the Monad and the Dyad together resulted in the Triad, which led naturally to the construction of a triangle. Thanks to the famous theorem that says that the square of the hypotenuse of a right-angled triangle is equal to the square of the opposite two sides, Pythagoras came to be recognized as the founder of geometry, even if it is far from certain that he invented the theorem. Pythagoras, or at least those who called themselves Pythagoreans, did not stop there, but added a fourth principle, which stood above the other three and formed a pyramid. His followers later named this the Tetrad, which they claimed was indicative of the perfect harmony that can be found in the world around us—examples of this are the musical scale, which contains four intervals, and the four seasons of the year.

Pythagoras's reputation as a mathematician and theorist of music remains high to this day, even if little of what he supposedly taught actually goes back to him, but his belief in numerology has fallen victim to widespread skepticism.[5] Nevertheless, Pythagoreanism did not carry all before it in his own time, and had Plato not drawn attention to it, it is possible that little or nothing of Pythagoras's achievement would have survived. The problem was that for the Greeks, the ideas of men like Thales, Xenophanes, and Pythagoras had to be accepted as articles of faith—or not at all. Other opinions were equally possible and were put forward by different thinkers whose theories were just as credible—or incredible—as those of their contemporaries.

One of the most important of these was Heraclitus (535–465 BC), whose view of things was completely different from anything that Thales or Pythagoras would have recognized. Heraclitus had no interest in finding a fixed principle around which a coherent vision of reality could be constructed. As far as he was concerned, order and stability did not exist. His famous motto was *panta rhei* ("all things are in flux"). To his mind, permanent, never-ending change was the order of the day, and conflict between moving objects was inevitable—the very stuff of life, in fact. Notions of good and evil were entirely relative. Those who went with the flow found it good, whereas those who were overwhelmed by it did not. If this view sounds curiously modern in some respects, it is because Heraclitus's approach to reality was revived in the late nineteenth century by Friedrich Nietzsche (1844–1900), who regarded him as the greatest philosopher of antiquity. To "go with the flow" has become a commonplace expression and reflects the sort of relativism that is often associated with Nietzsche, but how far it represents the view of Heraclitus is another question entirely.

Heraclitus believed that there was a fundamental principle underlying material reality, without being part of it. This principle he called the *logos*, a Greek word that is notoriously difficult to translate but that was to become one of the most important terms of both classical philosophy

5. It should be noted, however, that the advent of the digital age has given Pythagoras's ideas greater currency than they previously had. His form of numerology might be naive and simplistic, but the importance of numbers for our understanding of reality is more popular now that it was for a very long time.

and Christian theology. *Logos* conveys a range of meanings, from speech to reason. It is the subject of the prologue to John's Gospel, where it is normally translated as "Word," but it is Word with a mind and a purpose and not just a collection of sounds and syllables (John 1:1–14). Like John, Heraclitus believed that the *logos* inhabits every human being and that it can be relied on to guide us through the ever-changing ups and downs of life. If we rely on it, instead of on material objects (including wealth, fame, power, and so on), we shall be unsettled by nothing. The *logos* will give us understanding, and with understanding will come peace of mind. It is this aspect of his teaching that differs most strikingly from Nietzsche and from the nihilism of modern times, and makes an appeal to Heraclitus as the father of modern relativism difficult to justify.

Heraclitus was strikingly different from Pythagoras, but he was not alone in that. Another contemporary thinker, Parmenides (fl. ca. 515–485 BC), also rejected the mathematical approach but did so in a completely different way. Whereas Heraclitus thought that stability was an illusion, Parmenides said the exact opposite. To analyze reality into the four elements of earth, air, fire, and water was a mistake, he claimed, because ultimately all four are the same. What we perceive as change is just another window revealing the underlying permanence of reality. To put it in scientific terms, matter can neither be created nor destroyed. It is always there in its basic sameness because it belongs to the fundamental reality of Being. Change is therefore an illusion—it is just a reordering of what is permanent and therefore real. Where Heraclitus and Parmenides are at one is in their belief that we cannot base our lives on what we see around us. Those who put their trust in material objects will either be swept away by the forces of change (Heraclitus) or be forced to watch as their perception dissolves into a different form of reality (Parmenides). Either way, the only permanence that can be relied on is something metaphysical, whether we call it the *logos* or not. We have to stand back from what we see around us, rise above it and live our lives in relation to a principle that transcends it. Whether we can *escape* from the illusions that surround us is another matter entirely. Physically speaking, that may be impossible, but in the mind it can (and must) be done.

This is the legacy that these early Greek philosophers left to their successors. The quest for meaning in life would still be pursued, but answers would not be forthcoming within the parameters of the visible, material world that we see around us. How we can (or should) resolve the problem of our own finitude remained an unanswered question, but it would not sit still for long. Within a generation, a new breed of philosopher would appear, and it is with them that the history of classical philosophy may properly be said to begin.

PLATO

By common consent, the man who marked the transition from the early stage of Greek philosophy to its more mature flowering was Socrates (470–399 BC), the notorious "gadfly" (his own self-description) who self-consciously tormented the Athenian elite during the difficult days of the Peloponnesian War and its aftermath, when a defeated Athens was casting around for a scapegoat on whom it could lay the blame for the catastrophe. Socrates, who had little time for the Greek gods, was duly accused of atheism and of corrupting the youth of the city, and was sentenced to death by drinking poisonous hemlock.

Socrates has often been compared to Jesus, and there are indeed some similarities between them. Both men were at odds with the leadership of their society. Both criticized the hypocrisy that they saw in official religion. Both gathered disciples whom they taught to think in a different way—an activity that could easily be interpreted by their opponents as a form of sedition. Neither one wrote anything, but their character and teaching has come down to us from a variety of witnesses, giving us a fair impression of what they were like and how they affected those with whom they came into contact. The similarities are striking, but they are also superficial. Socrates questioned everything about his society and taught others to do the same. He stirred things up but had no real answer to what he perceived to be wrong with Athens. Jesus denounced the priests and religious leaders of his time, but he did not leave his disciples without an alternative. "I am the way, the truth and the life," he said (John 14:6). Those who followed him would not walk in the darkness but have the light of eternal life. In sharp contrast to that, Socrates had nothing comparable to offer—his horizons were limited to this world.

Socrates attributed his thinking to what he called his inner *daimōn*, a word that has come into English as "demon" but should probably be translated as "conscience" or something like it. Whether this *daimōn* can be identified as a divine power akin to what Christians would call "God" is an interesting question, and perhaps it can be. But if Socrates believed in a Supreme Being with which he had direct contact, he never explained how it related to the world in which he lived. Jesus said that he had come to do the will of his Father who had sent him, and who was clearly to be identified with the God of Israel, who was also the Creator of the universe. There was no inner *daimōn* in his life, guiding him as he went along, but rather a clear mandate with a set purpose that was known from the beginning. Both men were unjustly condemned to death, but Socrates's last moments were pure theater, clearly designed for posterity and remembered by his disciples as such. Jesus was taken away to be crucified when his disciples had run away. There was no staged dialogue about the meaning of life, only the agony of a death made necessary in order to atone for the sins of the world—a dimension utterly foreign to Socrates and his companions. Above all, there was no coming back from the dead in Socrates's case, and no ongoing movement dedicated to propagating his mission. Socrates was remembered, to be sure, but his disciples moved on and Plato (at least) formed a school to propagate *his* ideas, not those of his master. Jesus's disciples did more than remember him—they proclaimed that he was still alive in their midst and preached that those who believed in him would be united with him in eternity. Today, Socrates is a name known to a relative few and his teachings remain obscure even to most of them, whereas Jesus is worshiped as God by perhaps a third of the human race and his teaching has spread even further than that.[6] In that respect, there is no similarity between the two men at all.

Our portrait of Socrates is mostly filtered through the lens of Plato, to the extent that it is difficult to know what comes from him and what has been put in his mouth by his most prominent disciple. Even if Plato's reporting is basically accurate, it is also doctored in ways that suit what he wanted to say. Socrates was probably far less organized and systematic than Plato made him out to be, but that hardly matters now. What has come down to us may ultimately derive from Socrates, but it is

6. That is admittedly a very generous estimate, but the difference is nevertheless considerable.

undoubtedly the teaching of Plato, and it is as Platonism that Socrates's thought is generally expounded today.

From the standpoint of his philosophical inheritance, Plato may be said to have reconciled Heraclitus and Parmenides in an overarching synthesis. Heraclitus described the world of existence in which we live. It is constantly changing. Parmenides therefore looked beyond it to find a deeper stability, which Plato conceived as the world of Being. The link between them was the human soul (*psychē*), which was more or less the equivalent of Heraclitus's *logos*. According to Plato, the rational soul (*logikē psychē*) is present in every human being and gives us our identity. It is the tool we must use to probe the secrets of the universe and come to terms with them. In a word, it is the presence of Being in the realm of Existence. The duty of the philosopher is to explain how we can rise above the limitations of Existence and experience pure Being. To illustrate this, Plato came up with the idea that human beings are imprisoned in a cave, where there is little light and things appear only in shadows. These shadows represent something that is real, but the darkness of the cave prevents us from gaining access to that reality.

If we are to see what the shadows represent, we have to come into the light, but as anyone who has emerged from a cave can testify, that is not easy. Far from giving us knowledge, the light blinds us because we are not used to it. We may adjust to it in time, but many people do not want to make that effort. They prefer to live in the darkness and not ask too many questions. But for the few who persevere with the light, the experience is transformative. No longer are they content to live in the shadows. They want to explore the light in all its many possibilities, rising from the objects on which its rays shine to the source of light itself. Just as no one can look straight at the sun, so no one can achieve perfect knowledge in this life, but the philosopher can come close. At least he knows what the source of light is, even if he cannot perceive it directly. This is the way of enlightenment to which the true philosopher aspires.

In the realm of light, the shadows of the cave take on clearly defined shapes. These are what Plato called the "forms." These forms are not material objects but ideas that only the rational soul can perceive. Plato did not know how many forms or ideas there are, but he was convinced that everything we perceive in the world of Existence has its prototype in the realm of pure light. Sometimes they take on a particular shape, and we identify them as visible objects—tables, for example, or human beings. But often they retain their abstract character, even in our material universe. This is true of things like justice, beauty, honesty, and so on. We have some notion of what these are, even though we cannot see them or isolate them as such. It is relatively easy to identify a table, a tree, or a man, but whether I think something is just or beautiful depends entirely on my mental judgment. That in turn is shaped by my knowledge of the realm of light. If I have perceived the forms of justice and beauty in the abstract, then I have a standard by which to measure what I see around me.

Most importantly, these abstractions can be graded. Some actions are more just than others; some phenomena are more beautiful than others. Plato did not believe that beauty is in the eye of the beholder, as we might say today. If a man thinks that something is beautiful when in fact it is not, it is because he lacks the understanding that knowledge of the idea of beauty gives. Most of us have a sliding scale of beauty, which we apply to different objects. For example, I might think that a hammer is beautiful but that a rose is more beautiful, and that a newborn child is the most beautiful of all. This gradation of beauty is not a personal prejudice but an evaluation of different things according to a scale of values known only in the realm of light. A hammer may be beautiful because it is useful, but a rose is more beautiful because of its color and the complexity of its design, which no human being can imitate. A child is more beautiful still because a child possesses a rational soul, even if that is not immediately apparent, and is therefore potentially able to ascend to the form that gives beauty its meaning.

The highest of all the forms is the Good. All the other forms point toward it and illustrate particular aspects of it, but in themselves they are not the ultimate Good. Indeed, the Good may be practically unknowable. Like the sun, we know it is there but cannot perceive it directly because its light is too bright for us. But at the same time, we are well aware of the gradations of goodness that we perceive all around us. Some things are better than others, and we are all looking for the best insofar as we can find it. This is especially true in human life. I may be a competent ice skater, for example, and that is good. But there is always room for improvement, and when I watch figure skating competitions I realize that in my case, the best is still a long way off. Every once in a while, a figure skater will master the technique so skillfully that the judges will give his performance ten out of ten—as near to perfection as it is possible to get. Whether that is really true, though is open to doubt, since the most accomplished athletes know that an even higher achievement is possible and will aim for that, but the judges (who after all are limited, finite human beings) find that hard to imagine. As far as they are concerned, perfection, or the next thing to it, has been realized and that is good—good enough for them at least, and certainly more than good enough for me.

The ultimate Good is perfect—that is what makes it good. In the world of Existence, perfection is unattainable because our knowledge is always partial and incomplete. But perfection is also unattainable because it is One, and we live in a plural universe. The only way we could ever achieve perfect goodness would be by losing our identity as distinct individuals and dissolving our particularity into the one Supreme Being. Whether that is possible or not does not really matter, because if it is, we shall lose any consciousness of our own being and the philosophical quest will be over.

Plato believed that all human beings have a rational soul, but where did that come from and how did it operate? It was clearly not part of the material universe but shared something in common with the realm of light. As Plato understood it, the human soul originates in that realm and comes into particular human beings at birth. When we die, our soul goes back to where it came from and gets recycled in another human being who comes along after us. We are familiar with this as reincarnation, which is the belief of certain Eastern religions. The Dalai Lama, for example, is thought to be the reincarnation of the previous one, who died at the moment of his birth. When a Dalai Lama passes away, Tibetans go searching for a newly born infant who has inherited his soul, and so the line of lamas carries on through time. Plato's vision was similar to this, though it was not so specific. After Socrates died, Plato did not go looking for a reincarnation of his master but thought only that his soul would return—in whom or to what purpose he could not say. Thus it is better to speak of his view as the transmigration of souls rather than as reincarnation in the strict sense, although the underlying principle is much the same.

If the soul of every child is the soul of an adult who has died, it follows that the knowledge of that adult is present in the child, even though the child is not naturally capable of expressing it. For that reason, the dormant knowledge has to be teased out of him by a process that we still call "education," a word that literally means "leading out." By a series of questions and tests, the child is challenged to become conscious of what he already knows and to reveal it. Education is therefore a kind of tug-of-war between the questioning teacher and the questioned student, the object of which is to extract as much hidden knowledge from the latter as possible. The great weakness of this approach is that, according to it, there is no such thing as progress because there is no new knowledge. Everything is simply recycled from one generation to the next. Our knowledge can be truncated by poor education and thus lost as far as we are concerned, but it can never be increased beyond what is already there. There is quite literally nothing new under the sun, and to go in pursuit of the unknown is a delusional waste of time. The ancient Greeks and Romans had no conception of the Americas, for example, but sailing west to see what might be there was pointless. As far as they were concerned, there was nothing to be discovered, and so they did not bother!

Plato was well aware that the quest for enlightenment was a minority interest, but he did not think that philosophers should live in isolation from the rest of society. On the contrary, he believed that they were the natural rulers of the state, an intellectual aristocracy whose special gift was to guide everyone else in the way of justice and truth. This view was a hard sell in Athens, where every citizen had a voice in the city's government whether he was educated or not. Plato's vision was only practicable in a place where one man, or perhaps a small oligarchy, already controlled the levers of government. He found what he wanted in Syracuse, a Greek colony in Sicily; he went there at the invitation of Dionysius I, the city's dictator, or "tyrant" as the Greeks called such people. Plato made a great impression on Dionysius's brother-in-law Dion, but that merely made Dionysius jealous. He had Plato arrested and sold into slavery, though Dion was able to rescue him and send him back to Athens. After Dionysius's death, his son and successor Dionysius II, tutored by his uncle Dion, was set to become the philosopher-king of Plato's dreams, and Plato went back again to supervise the operation. But it turned out badly once more, and the experiment had to be abandoned.

That might have been the end of it, but Plato was a gifted writer, and thanks to his books, theories that were inapplicable in practice became widely accepted. In his *Republic* and again in his *Laws*, Plato laid out the principles by which he believed society ought to be governed. Despite their idealism, both books (but especially the *Republic*) have become classics of world literature and have influenced countless generations of statesmen through the ages. It was in these works that Plato got to grips with the problem of religion. Earlier philosophers had rejected the myths of the gods as recounted by poets like Homer, but they generally avoided the subject because it was too dangerous. Socrates, after all, was put to death because he was an atheist who rejected the Athenian gods, and few people wanted to share his fate. Plato did not have to worry about that—the death of Socrates was such a scandal, and Plato's hero worship of his master was so influential, that nobody would have dared to subject him to trial and execution for his beliefs.

But Plato was no less critical of the gods than Socrates and others had been. Like his predecessors, he rejected popular religious practices, which he regarded as superstitious and ignorant. But unlike them, he sought to explain the traditional stories of the gods in a way that made some kind of sense. It was he who invented the term *theologia*, the study of the gods, which we would do better to translate as "mythology" rather than "theology" in the modern sense.[7] The myths of Greece and of other nations were attempts to explain how the world works to people who were incapable of pure rational thought. They needed stories to help them understand, and stories were what they got. They were far from perfect, of course, but unenlightened people could hardly be expected to rise above them. In a state run by philosophers, mythology and religion would be redundant because logical explanation would suffice to explain everything. That in itself would not be enough to get rid of religion, so in the *Laws* Plato advocated banning it altogether. People who clung to their outdated myths would have to be coerced into accepting the unvarnished truth, and the whole panoply of rites, sacrifices, and temple worship would be dismantled. Once all that was out of the way, nobody would have a choice. Reason would rule them, and those who could not (or would not) accept

7. Plato, *Republic*, 379a.

it would be punished for their recalcitrance. That this was undemocratic did not bother Plato in the slightest—democracy was not conducive to science as he conceived it. Nor was he worried that religion might address questions that surpassed the competence of reason, because there was no such thing. Reason was the entry into the realm of light, and anything else was a dangerous distraction from the pursuit of truth.

Modern readers are familiar with Plato's attacks on religion because they were recycled by atheist governments in the twentieth century in their attempts to suppress traditional religious observances. But it would be a great mistake to conclude from this that Plato was an atheist in the modern sense. He portrayed Socrates as a man who believed in a transcendent Deity who dwelt in the realm of the forms and ideas. That realm was akin to the rational soul and was necessary in order to make sense of the transmigration of souls in which Plato believed. How much of this goes back to Socrates is impossible to say for sure, but it seems clear that the charge of "atheism" leveled against him was false—at least from a modern perspective. Whatever we think about that, there is no reason to doubt that Plato believed what he put in the mouth of Socrates, and the charge of atheism cannot be made against him.

More importantly, there is evidence that Plato had a vision of the Deity that went well beyond anything Socrates might have thought and that comes close in many respects to what Jews and Christians believe about God. The main source for our knowledge of this is the *Timaeus*, one of Plato's later dialogues that reflects the time he spent in southern Italy and Sicily. The fictional Timaeus was portrayed as an Italian Greek, more attuned to the ideas of Pythagoras than to those of Socrates or anyone else. Plato used Timaeus to expound his own adoption of Pythagorean numerology as the basis of the entire universe.[8] What he came up with was the picture of a Supreme Creator (*dēmiourgos*), who used the forms/ideas as a kind of blueprint to fashion our world. These forms/ideas were not created by him but already existed as numbers. Nor could the Creator invent or even modify the four elements, which also predated his activity. He created by reproducing himself, the only way that he could ensure that

8. It should be said that Timaeus is a substitute for Plato's friend Archytas, who was very much a real person.

his creation would be as perfect as possible. From there, Plato followed Pythagoras's geometry and produced a scheme that embraced the four traditional elements. The triangle, which was the basis of the pyramid, was also the shape of fire. The cube (four squares or eight triangles) was earth, the octahedron (eight squares) was air, and finally the twenty-sided icosahedron—an elaborate combination of squares and triangles—was water.

In addition to these four "solids," as Plato called them, there was a fifth, which was the twelve-sided dodecahedron. This was not made from triangles but from what Pythagoras called the pentagon, a device by which he could shape squares and triangles into spheres—the perfect shapes, which the Creator, operating through his agents the Olympian gods, used to build both heaven and earth. The result was a universe that is a perfect mathematical construction. Moreover, it is the only universe that can exist, since it is modeled on the image of the Creator himself. The spheres move (or stay put) in different measures, but there is a perfect harmony among them, which later generations would call "the music of the spheres." The Creator of this perfect system dwells above and beyond it, but presides over it and maintains it in being. Matter has no significance in itself unless and until the rational Creator sets to work on it. That is what gives it its meaning, and when we study it that is what we should be looking for. In line with what Heraclitus had said, the world that appears to us to be constantly changing is in fact a unity that does not change but stays eternally the same. Our senses do not perceive this, but by the use of our reason we can attain to that knowledge and be at peace with the universe.

The *Timaeus* was the one dialogue of Plato's that was translated (badly and only partially) into Latin and was read in Western Europe throughout the Middle Ages.[9] Christian theologians and philosophers naturally interpreted it in the light of the Bible. Not surprisingly, Plato seemed to them to be a kind of Christian before the coming of Christ, one of the few gentiles on whom the light of truth had shone. There is indeed a remarkable similarity between much of what Plato said and what the Bible teaches, but there are also differences that cannot be ignored. The Platonic Creator was not the originator of all things—both the forms and

9. The others were rediscovered at the time of the Renaissance when they were translated from the original Greek.

the matter on which he worked were already in existence and their limitations constrained his activity to a large extent. Even more importantly, Plato's Creator was not a person with whom it was possible to have a relationship. The Platonic Creator certainly acted in what to us would be personal ways, so it is easy for us to think in those terms, but Plato did not. Whatever the Creator was, he (or it) operated exclusively through mathematical reason. The Creator had no love or emotion, and no interaction with the created order of the kind that we find in the Bible. At best, the Creator might be equated with the God of natural theology, but not with the Father of Jesus Christ, who sacrificed himself for the sins of the world. That was a dimension of divine activity that was alien to Plato and remains problematic for all forms of Platonism, including Christian ones that try to harmonize his views with those of the apostles and prophets in the Holy Scriptures. But whatever conclusions we come to about that, it is safe to say that Plato was not an atheist and that claims to that effect, based on his opposition to religion, are wide of the mark.

ARISTOTLE

Plato's most famous pupil was Aristotle (384–322 BC), a Greek from the borders of Macedonia in the north who came to Athens to sit at his feet. Aristotle learned a good deal from Plato, and his thought reflects his master in many ways, but he is famous not because he was Plato's disciple but because he rejected many of the principles that Plato taught and went a different way. As a result, students of the history of Western philosophy are accustomed to dividing the subject into contrasting emphases, the Platonic and the Aristotelian—and in the minds of many, never the twain shall meet. This is an exaggeration, because there is much that unites the two men and their ways of thinking. They both based their interpretation of the world on reason. They agreed that the material world is shaped by immutable, eternal forms that transcend matter. But where Plato thought that those forms had to be found above and beyond matter, Aristotle insisted that they only had meaning within it. To put it a different way, for Plato the world we see around us was always under judgment from a higher authority. For Aristotle, it was under investigation instead.

Legend tells us that Plato and Aristotle fell out while the latter was the former's student, but that does not appear to have been the case.

Most likely it was only after Plato's death that Aristotle went his own way, though doubtless the seeds of disagreement with his master were being sown long before that. Aristotle accepted the Pythagorean notion that mathematics is a logically pure and exact science, and that philosophical principles ought likewise to be logically consistent, but he did not conclude from this that philosophy is a form of mathematics. If it were, as Plato thought, then a proposition could be shown to be true without experiment—mathematical certainty would allow us to predict what the outcome of our experience would be, and if things did not add up the way they should, the fault would be in us and not in the theory that governed our calculations. Aristotle rejected that. He said that reality is what we see around us and that its meaning and coherence had to be discovered by experiment. Only once the experiment has been conducted and its results analyzed could a theory be constructed that would explain the process at work. By following this method, Aristotle was able to classify different species of creatures and examine their interrelationships.

Because of his approach, Aristotle can claim to have been the inventor of the scientific method, and therefore of science itself. Almost every "-ology" that we can think of was invented by him—biology, entomology, ichthyology, zoology, meteorology, and gerontology, to name but a few. Add to them such things as logic, physics, and astronomy, and we have an encyclopedia of scientific knowledge whose framework has stood the test of time. Later generations would surpass Aristotle's knowledge and falsify much of what he believed, but it would do so by using his fundamental methods. We can therefore say, with little exaggeration, that the natural sciences as we know them are Aristotelian in their conception, if not in their conclusions. We can further add that their conception is more important because it stays the same. All scientists are trying to falsify their theories in order to attain to a deeper understanding of the way things work—nothing in their mental universe is ever fixed and unalterable. But that conviction stays the same and makes it possible for the sciences to advance in the way that they do. The last thing a scientist wants (or needs) is to be tied down to an immutable formula that can never be questioned. Ideologies that try to do that—like Marxism, for example—hinder freedom of inquiry and are therefore the enemies of the science on which they claim to be based. When the theories undergirding Marxism were discredited, Marxism ceased to be a living philosophy and could only be maintained by force.[10] This was the real tragedy of the Soviet Union and its dependencies, which trumpeted scientific progress even as they stifled scientific creativity. This inner contradiction led eventually to collapse as the Aristotelian method asserted its primacy over the (essentially Platonic) desire for an intellectual certainty grounded in ideas rather than in empirical facts.

One important feature of Aristotle's scientific method is that it allowed for change and development in a way that Plato did not. For Plato, reality was an abstract idea that could only be deformed and corrupted in the material universe, so all change was in fact a form of disintegration. For Aristotle, on the other hand, every material object was real in itself, and change was part of a natural process. A baby does not stay a baby forever, or even for very long. It grows into an adult, who then ages and eventually dies. But as a material object, the human being stays the same—the newborn baby is the same individual who will die eighty or ninety years later. This sameness is what Aristotle called "substance" (*hypokeimenon*). At that level, the level of species (*genos*), all human beings are the same. Their differences can be accounted for by natural evolution, not from one species to another (as in later Darwinism) but within a single species. The result is that we have male and female, black and white, tall and short, etc. All these variables Aristotle called "accidents" (*symbebēkota*) because they do not alter the underlying substance. They can be explained, not as corruptions of a hypothetical ideal, but as natural outgrowths influenced by external phenomena and other causes that can be investigated and classified.

Differentiation is therefore something to be expected and regarded positively (or at least neutrally), not as something that would not happen in a perfect world and therefore ought to be resisted as much as possible. We see the effects of this most clearly in the way Plato and Aristotle used the word "being" (*ousia*). For Plato, Being is One, eternal, and unchanging. Everything else is mere existence (*hyparxis*), which is a pale copy and

10. This was demonstrated by Leszek Kołakowski, *Main Currents of Marxism*, 3 vols. (Oxford: Oxford University Press, 1978), who dated the breakdown of Marxism as a philosophy to the Russian Revolution in 1917.

basically a deformation of true Being. But for Aristotle, beings are plural, as in the phrase "human beings." The ultimate source of all things is the Supreme Being, to be sure, but that is not the *only* being. For Aristotle, Being and Existence are not opposites, but virtually synonymous, as they have become in most modern languages. The Supreme Being is the First Cause or Prime Mover of everything else—the one that sets the ball rolling, as it were—but here Aristotle's experimental logic failed him. He knew that such a cause had to exist, since otherwise life as we observe it could not be explained, but what it was, how it came into being, and whether it could be known or identified as such, he could not say. Did the First Cause have a cause of its own, or was it just the product of an unending cycle of change that periodically returned to the starting point before launching off again? There was no way of knowing that, so in the end Aristotle's science broke down just when it hoped to attain its goal.

For Aristotle, the concept of "cause" had four distinct, though related, aspects to it. First came the *material* cause, which in the case of human beings is our flesh and blood. Without them, we would simply not exist. Next came the *efficient* cause, which in the human case is the man and woman who procreate a child. Again, if they do not do that, the human in question will not exist. Third there is the *formal* cause, by which is meant our bodily shape, or form. Procreation does not produce just anything at random, but a particular thing than can be perceived and identified as such. Last, there is the *final* cause, which is the purpose for which the being in question has come into existence. In the case of humans, this can get quite complicated because there can be many reasons why human beings exist, but the reason given in Genesis 1:28 will do as well as any—humankind was created in order to fill the earth and have dominion over it. Aristotle did not put things as succinctly as that, but he would no doubt have concurred with the biblical statement as far as it goes.

Modern people restrict the notion of cause to what Aristotle called the efficient cause and ignore the purpose behind it, but he thought differently. For him, the most important thing was the final cause—the reason for, and meaning of, our existence. He believed that everything in the world was moving toward union with the Prime Mover. That was Aristotle's God. The Prime Mover was itself unmoved and was incapable of inner change or development. Unlike the rest of the world, it had no potential (*dynamis*) because its power (*energeia*) was fully realized. The world moves because it thinks, but the Prime Mover can have no contact with it because contact would impair its perfection. The Prime Mover thinks only about itself and is totally self-absorbed, since that is the only way that its perfection can be protected. Here again, there is a contradiction that seems to have escaped Aristotle but that makes modern people reject his theory. If the Prime Mover affects the world by its thoughts, how can it be said to think of nothing but itself? Does not *any* involvement, however minimal or notional, with something outside itself diminish its perfection? How can we, who live in the world, be influenced by something with which we have no contact? There is a gap here that cannot be filled, an abyss that cannot be crossed.

Aristotle's vision of reality does, however, have a positive aspect to it: it looks to the future. This is the inevitable result of his theory of evolution or development. We do not have to worry too much about the past, because we cannot return to it, though we can learn from its mistakes and try to avoid them in the future. What we must do is plan for what is coming, and we do this best by learning certain habits that will govern our behavior throughout our lives. For example, we learn that it is better to tell the truth than to lie. It is better to preserve life than to destroy it. It is right to use the gifts that we have and wrong to covet those of others. Put together, this all adds up to an ethics of enlightened self-interest—we shall do better if those around us do better, and those around us will do better if we treat them as we would want to be treated ourselves—in other words, justly. Of course, this can get complicated at times. For example, it would normally be wrong to steal another man's bottle of wine, but if that man is an alcoholic, it might be the kindest thing that we can do for him. Moral judgments are not absolute, but must be decided by circumstances, always bearing in mind that what we want is the selfless good of the other person and of the whole society, knowing that in that way we shall be doing the greatest good to ourselves as well.

It will therefore come as no surprise to discover that Aristotle's vision of a just society is totally different from Plato's. Plato believed in enlightened despotism because only someone with his transcendent knowledge of right and wrong is really capable of governing. This philosopher-king will inevitably appear to some people as a tyrant because he will be doing not what they want, but what is good for them. The mass of humanity is ignorant and incorrigible and the only way to ensure peace, order, and good government is by repressing their baser instincts—in other words, by telling them what to do. Aristotle, on the other hand, saw the need for greater individual freedom and responsibility. The philosopher-king did not discuss with his subjects—he dictated to them. But the scientific experimenter had to be free to make mistakes, to discuss with others what the best way forward might be, and to cooperate in the outworking of collective projects. He had to be able to adapt his methods to fit changing circumstances and to abandon theories if they clearly did not work. The goal was to achieve the perfection inherent in the Prime Mover, but this required a lengthy process of discussion, debate, and even a measure of democracy, provided that it was restricted to those who knew what they were talking about. Aristotle believed that people were basically good and that they wanted the best for themselves and for everyone else, and he thought that this could eventually be achieved by a process of moral education that would persuade people that doing good is the most rational course of action.

The social implications of this can be seen quite clearly in the United States. Thomas Jefferson (1743–1826) thought that it was self-evident that all men had been created equal, and that they had been endowed by their Creator with the right to life, liberty, and the pursuit of happiness. Of course, there was nothing "self-evident" about that at all, and Jefferson himself did not believe it, unless "all men" is taken to mean white males who agreed politically with him. Non-whites, women, and those who did not want to rebel against the colonial government were out of luck in Jefferson's Platonic vision of the better life. Later on, more Aristotelian heads prevailed, and the American Constitution was designed to accommodate reality, with checks and balances to offset natural selfishness. But the ideal was never lost sight of—the goal of American society was to achieve a "more perfect union," as it still is, at least in the rhetoric of politicians. That is pure Aristotle—recognize that we must live with imperfections for the time being but work toward eliminating them over time by educating people in the habit of doing good. The fact that "affirmative action" of this kind may lead to other evils is a problem that is often ignored but that will never go away. The good Aristotelian must believe that things are getting better all the time, because if the principles he laid down are followed, that is what will happen. The evidence that this does not work is simply airbrushed out of the narrative, and the futile pursuit of perfection continues unchecked.

LATER GREEK PHILOSOPHERS

Plato and Aristotle are the unchallenged giants of Greek philosophy, and their schools of thought have persisted, with many variations, to the present time. But they were by no means alone in the Hellenic world. Already in the time of Plato, a poor man named Antisthenes (446–366 BC) had gathered disciples around him at the Cynosarges, a gymnasium in Athens, and taught them to renounce all worldly possessions. This extreme form of asceticism, known as Cynicism from the name of the gymnasium, would never become popular, but it fascinated people who did not buy into it and challenged their value systems.[11] Its most famous practitioner was Diogenes (412–323 BC), who lived naked in a broken water jar and begged for his living. Diogenes was so outrageous in his behavior that he feared nothing and nobody, including his admirer Alexander the Great, who supposedly met him on one occasion only to be insulted and rejected by the object of his admiration. Diogenes got away with his rudeness because his approach was a radical critique of human nature that struck a chord with those who saw and heard him. He believed that only if we are stripped of all that we own and cherish in this world can we be made ready to receive the light of truth. In that respect, Diogenes was a disciple of Socrates, whose views he took to their logical conclusion. Asceticism would struggle to survive in the ancient world, but the advent of Christianity gave it a new lease of life in the form of monasticism. The early hermits and monks of Egypt were scarcely less extreme than Diogenes, even though they were not his followers. Nor could they be called Cynics, with the disdain for the things of this world that the name implies. Christian monasticism was different from Cynicism because it practiced asceticism for the purpose of drawing closer to God, a dimension that was essentially foreign to Diogenes and his admirers.

---

11. It is not clear whether Antisthenes would have recognized himself as a "Cynic," but that does not matter much for our purposes.

Similar to the Cynics were the skeptics, who believed that it was impossible to know anything for certain. Given that all knowledge in the ancient world was essentially a form of speculation with little or no objective basis that could withstand criticism, skepticism was a thoroughly rational approach—on the assumption that every assertion was guesswork, skepticism almost imposed itself. There is a sense in which the early Christians could be called skeptics—not that they doubted the possibility of knowing anything at all, but that they agreed that true knowledge was impossible if the methods of the Greek philosophers were used to obtain it. When the apostle Paul spoke about vain philosophies or when Luke described the schools of Athens as pointless talking shops, they could have been taking a leaf out of the skeptics' book, because that is exactly what they would have said, too (Col 2:8; Acts 17:21). The difference was that Paul and Luke had something positive to offer instead, which the skeptics did not.

In 311 BC, more than a decade after the death of Aristotle, a man called Zeno (336–265 BC), a Phoenician from Cyprus, turned up in Athens and began lecturing in a covered arcade (*stoa*) in the marketplace (*agora*). Zeno was an early example of what would become a standard phenomenon of the ancient world. He was a "barbarian" who had adopted Greek culture and was accepted as an equal by the Greeks. Like many peoples before and since, the Greeks despised foreigners, whose incomprehensible babbling they mocked as *bar-bar* ("blah-blah"). But they were not racists in the modern sense. They were intellectual snobs, and if a barbarian learned their language and adopted their ways he was treated as an equal. It was a trait that would endure for centuries, becoming one of the hallmarks of the medieval Byzantine Empire just as much as it had been of ancient Athens. In this sense, Zeno was a pioneer whose influence would transform the world of the Greek city-states and make Hellenic culture universal.

Zeno was basically a disciple of Plato who took one aspect of his teaching to an extreme. This was Plato's belief in the need to live a virtuous life as the only path to true happiness. The Stoics, as his followers were called from the *stoa* where they met, did not renounce worldly goods and pleasures in the way that the Cynics did, but they were indifferent to them. A Stoic endured pain and experienced pleasure in equal measure because he was indifferent to such things. We may find it hard to believe the legends that are told of some Stoics, with their superhuman feats of endurance, but the sense of detachment from worldly concerns was certainly a main feature of their outlook. It had a particular appeal to aristocratic Romans, many of whom looked back with longing to the simpler days of their early republic, when heroic self-sacrifice and patriotism had been the supreme virtues. The expansion of the empire had diluted these to the point where Rome was in constant danger of collapsing under the weight of luxury and corruption, a perception that only made Stoicism seem even more attractive. Stoicism was the philosophy of Seneca (4 BC–AD 65), the tutor of the notorious Emperor Nero (54–68), who knew more than most just how deceptive worldly power and influence could be. It was also the worldview of the Emperor Marcus Aurelius (161–180), who escaped from the burden of ruling the most powerful state on earth by meditating on the value of virtuous living.

Unusually for an ancient philosophy, Stoicism was materialistic. The Stoics denied the existence of "spirit" as a non-material substance and claimed that what we define by that term is in fact highly refined matter. But, odd as it may seem to us, this material universe was suffused with a divine power that controlled it and determined everything that might happen in it. To the Stoics, this offered reassurance because they believed that nothing occurs by chance. Human beings are neither to be praised if things turn out well for them, nor are they to be blamed if they do not. It might seem as though people were just the playthings of a blind force that decided their destiny, but it was not as simple as that. The Stoics also believed that human beings had the capacity to understand the way of the world and to live in accordance with its nature. Nobody is wise enough to succeed at this completely, but some do so more than others. They cannot alter their fate, but by accepting it willingly, this elite becomes better, and is therefore superior to everyone else. Their end may be tragic, but if it is endured without complaint they have achieved heroic virtue.

This ethic had an appeal to some early Christians, who resonated with the idea of determinism, which they interpreted as divine providence, and appreciated the apparent willingness of the Stoics to embrace martyrdom, as many Christians were forced to do. Tertullian, for example, was attracted to Stoicism and even went so far as to say that Seneca often sounded like a Christian, though of course he was not one.[12] There is even an apocryphal

12. Tertullian, *De anima,* 20: "Seneca saepe noster est."

correspondence between Seneca and the apostle Paul, which makes much the same claim.[13] Stoicism went into decline after AD 200 and ceased to have much influence as a distinctive school of thought, though the doctrine of its resilience in the face of pain and suffering has continued to attract both admirers and imitators from that day to this. Its weakness was its fundamental pessimism. The Stoics acknowledged no God above and beyond the material universe who could intervene and overcome the relentless path of determinism. The world was a torture chamber that had to be endured, but there was no way out. Like Sydney Carton in Charles Dickens's *A Tale of Two Cities*, the virtuous man would justify himself by a heroic and self-sacrificial death, but that was the end of the story—there was no redemption and no resurrection.

Finally, in 306 BC, a man named Epicurus (341–270 BC) turned up in Athens with an entirely new philosophy based on the principle that the chief aim of a good life was to seek pleasure and avoid pain. Odd though it must seem, this was really just an extreme interpretation of Aristotle's belief that our senses, not our minds, are the source of all knowledge. Aristotle would never have concluded that seeking pleasure was the logical outcome of that belief, but that was what Epicurus taught. "Eat, drink, and be merry, for tomorrow we die" was his watchword, and not surprisingly, it proved to be far more popular than the asceticism of the Cynics or the self-sacrifice of the Stoics. Epicureanism has had its devotees in every generation, whether they recognize the name or not, and it is still very popular today, as anyone who watches television or reads glossy magazines can testify.

At the same time, Epicureanism has provoked strenuous opposition, not least from Christians, who have habitually regarded it as immoral. Winning the lottery may be a pleasant sensation, but it is achieved at the cost of taking money from thousands of people, many of whom may not be able to afford it and some of whom could be compulsive gamblers. Is that really a source of satisfaction to the lucky winner? Considerations of that kind have dogged the Epicureans for centuries, but they have also led to a situation in which their critics have been portrayed as world-denying misanthropes.

13. Seneca and Paul were almost exact contemporaries, and were probably in Rome at the same time in the early 60s AD. They could have met, and it is quite likely that Paul knew who Seneca was (though not the other way around), but there is no evidence that they ever exchanged views, either in writing or in person.

No doubt some of them are, though that is hardly a fair characterization of them. Epicureanism's great weakness is its lack of purpose. Seeking pleasure may be fine as far as it goes, but pleasure is fleeting. If it is an end in itself, it leads nowhere. Its devotees expend their energy for a mirage that as often as not produces a hangover the morning after. It is hardly surprising, therefore, that its reputation among intellectuals has never been high, and that its enemies have been so fierce and so numerous, not least in the Christian church.

SUMMARY

1. The Greek philosophical tradition began sometime around 700 BC, probably under Egyptian influence, and its first great representative was Thales of Miletus, who lived about a century after that. Its major centers were the eastern Aegean region (Ionia) and southern Italy, including Sicily. A wide range of philosophers appeared, with some very different and often contrasting ideas, but most of what we know about them has been filtered through later writers, making their views often difficult to reconstruct accurately.

2. The relationship of the earliest Greek philosophers to religion is unclear, but it seems that Xenophanes, who lived in the sixth century BC, questioned the existence of the Greek gods and opted for a form of monotheism instead. Another important person of this period was Pythagoras, who migrated from Ionia to Southern Italy. He became famous for his interest in numbers and mathematics, but it is not clear how much of what is attributed to him actually originated with his disciples. The opinions of these men were based on speculation, not experiment, which meant that one man's opinion was as good as another's—they were never tested to see whether they were true or not.

3. In the generation after Pythagoras, alternative theories were put forward by Heraclitus and his younger contemporary Parmenides. Heraclitus believed that the world had no stability—everything was in constant flux. Parmenides went to the

opposite extreme and regarded all change as illusory because in his mind, there was a single and simple reality that underlay everything that we perceive to be different. This underlying reality was a metaphysical principle that the human mind had to discover in order to understand the world.

4. Socrates of Athens is credited with having been the true founder of the classical Greek philosophical tradition, though he wrote nothing himself and most of what we know about his thought comes from his disciple Plato. Plato was a prolific author who borrowed extensively from some of the pre-Socratic philosophers, especially Pythagoras and his disciples. In later times, Jews and others claimed that Plato had got his best ideas from Moses and the Jewish Torah, though that is unlikely and modern scholars reject this theory.

5. In some ways, Socrates was like Jesus, but the resemblances are superficial and misleading. He believed that he possessed an inner spiritual power that guided his thinking and can best be compared to our idea of the conscience. This power was in some sense divine, but it was completely different from popular notions of the gods, which Socrates rejected. For that reason, he was condemned for "atheism" and forced to commit suicide.

6. Plato reconciled the approaches of Heraclitus and Parmenides by saying that the former spoke of the world of Existence, where things are constantly changing, whereas the latter focused on Being, the permanent reality that undergirds the universe. Most people live in the realm of Existence only, but the philosopher goes beyond that to seek out the principles of Being, of which the Good is the highest and most desirable.

7. Plato believed that human souls are reincarnations of earlier people whose beliefs have been transferred to us. Because of this, knowledge is essentially a recollection of what our souls have always known but have forgotten in the process of reincarnation. Plato was against pagan religion as much as Socrates was and wanted it to be banned from the ideal state, but he was

not an atheist. He believed that the world had been created by divine Reason, a portion of which has been implanted in the soul of every human being. Reason has produced ideas that are manifested in forms, which philosophers can perceive and use to govern the world.

8. Aristotle, the other great name in ancient Greek philosophy, was a pupil of Plato's who eventually diverged from his master on a number of significant points. Aristotle was pragmatic in a way that Plato was not, and he is usually credited with having inaugurated the natural sciences by dividing the study of the universe into particular categories, or species. Aristotle distinguished between the substance of a thing, which is permanent, and its "accidents," or particular characteristics that can be altered without affecting the substance.

9. Aristotle distinguished between a thing's potential and its realization. Progression from one to the other explains the phenomenon of change and gives it a sense of purpose. He believed that there is a great chain of being set in motion by the Prime Mover, who alone is unchanging and who is therefore "God." Aristotelianism was absorbed by the early Christians and became the basis of classical "Christian" philosophy in the Middle Ages.

10. Later Greek thinkers started new schools of philosophical thought, which we know as Stoicism, Epicureanism, and Cynicism, among others. Elements of these philosophies were later absorbed into the Platonic and Aristotelian traditions and some of their ideas have percolated down to modern times, even though the schools they created have disappeared. Many early Christians admired the Stoics because of their steadfastness in the face of suffering and failure, which seemed to them to be akin to martyrdom. They were also generally opposed to Epicureanism, which they interpreted as a godless enjoyment of the good things of this life to the neglect of spiritual values.

III

JERUSALEM

Anyone surveying the ancient Mediterranean world in the time of Jesus would have concluded that Greek culture had conquered it. Rome might have been the supreme political power, but culturally it was the Greeks who were ascendant. The Romans copied them, even if they preferred to use their native Latin to do so, and the venerable civilizations of Egypt and Babylonia were in eclipse. Other people groups existed, but none of them could measure up to the Greeks. The Celts of the West were still in a primitive stage of development and could not compete with Rome, let alone with Greece. The Persians had never really recovered from the conquest of Alexander the Great, and although they avoided the embrace of Rome, Greek culture tended to dominate among them and its influence could be felt as far as India, where there were Greek kingdoms that survived for centuries.

The only partial exception to this overwhelming cultural dominance was the nation of the Jews. Politically, they counted for very little. For centuries they had been subject to the Assyrians, the Babylonians, the Persians, and the Greeks. Around 160 BC, they wrested their independence from the declining Greek empire of Syria, but a century later they fell under the sway of Rome, from which they were not to emerge. The Romans granted them a good deal of local autonomy but Hellenic influence was strong, even in their Palestinian homeland, where Greek cities dotted the landscape. More importantly, the Jews themselves started to migrate across the Mediterranean, and by the time of Jesus there were significant Jewish colonies in a number of Greek cities. Of these, the most numerous was in Alexandria, the capital of Egypt, where they may have constituted as much as a quarter of the total population. They soon adopted Greek as their daily language, but they never integrated into the Hellenic world. Greek religion remained anathema to them, and although some dabbled in Greek athletics and philosophy, the community as a whole never took those things on board. The Jews remained an alien presence in a world that tolerated them but did not understand them.

At the same time, a few gentiles (as they called non-Jews) took an interest in Jewish beliefs and adopted them to varying degrees—a concession to "barbarism" that was practically unique in the Greek world. In the NT they appear as the "God-fearers," people who attended Jewish synagogues but sat at the back, as it were. The Jews could not turn them away (nor is there any indication that they wanted to), but they did not know what to do with them. Jews were descended from the ancient patriarchs Abraham, Isaac, and Jacob and were proud of it, but they had little thought of absorbing other nations into theirs in the way that both the Greeks and the Romans did. Conversion to Judaism was not impossible, but it was very rare and discouraged—on both sides. The price of Jewish survival was segregation, and for the most part it worked. But how had this extraordinary situation come about?

The origins of Israel go back to about 2000 BC, when a man called Abram (later Abraham) was told to leave his home in Mesopotamia and travel westward to an unknown country, where he would settle and become the ancestor of a great nation. Two generations later, his family migrated to Egypt in order to escape a famine and stayed there for over four hundred years. During that time, they increased in number and became a threat to the rulers of Egypt, who enslaved them. Finally, under the leadership of a man named Moses, they escaped from Egypt and, after a generation of wandering in the desert, found their way back to the land that had originally been promised to Abraham. They were forced to conquer it from its inhabitants, but once that was accomplished they settled there and eventually founded a state that achieved a modest degree of unity and prosperity under the rule of King David and his son Solomon. It did not last, and after Solomon's death it split into two kingdoms: one (Judah) centered on David's capital of Jerusalem and continuing his legacy, and the other to the north (Israel). By then, Solomon had built a temple in Jerusalem that became and remained the center of Israelite worship, even for those in the northern kingdom, despite their kings' attempts to set up rival places of worship.

The northern kingdom was conquered by Assyria in 722 BC and its inhabitants were deported, but Judah survived until 587 BC, when it too was destroyed by the Babylonians, who had conquered Assyria a generation earlier. Its inhabitants, or most of them, were taken to Babylon, where they remained for two generations. After Babylon was conquered by the Persians in 539 BC, the Jews (as the inhabitants of Judah were now called) were allowed to return to their homeland, and many did so. They remained under Persian rule, but in many respects they enjoyed religious and cultural autonomy. It was during this time that most of them adopted Aramaic, a language closely related to their native Hebrew, as their mother tongue, and that remained the case for the next thousand years.

Throughout this time, the Jewish people were held together by a small body of literature that we know today as the Old Testament (OT) or Hebrew Bible. It contained the Law of Moses, the writings of the Israelite prophets, a number of historical books that were also mainly concerned with the prophets and kings of the pre-exilic period, and some miscellaneous writings, including psalms, proverbs, and books of "wisdom." These books have been pored over by generations of scholars who have advanced many theories about their origins, all of which are of necessity speculative and reliant on internal evidence. The truth is that nobody really knows where they came from or who put them together in what is now their traditional form, but one thing is certain: in spite of all the internal differences that scholars claim they manifest, and regardless of the many sects and interest groups into which the nation of Israel was divided, there was only one collection of books that united them all.

It is true that there were different editions with variant readings in some of these books, and the Samaritans, whom most Jews regarded as a deviant sect, preserved a version of the Law of Moses that occasionally differs from the standard Hebrew text, but these variations are minor and do not constitute an independent intellectual or religious tradition. There may have been disputes between the priests of the temple and the prophets, or between Jews and Samaritans, but these were not remotely comparable to the differences between Plato and Aristotle, for example, not to mention the many other schools of Greek philosophy. However different they were, all Jews clung to the same set of books, although the Samaritans recognized only the Law of Moses and the book of Joshua, and the Christians (much later) would add a second collection that they called the NT. But even then, Christians continued to accept the Hebrew Bible (as we still do) and claimed to be the true heirs of the ancient Israelites. The core texts, few in number though they were, remained authoritative for everyone, giving them a sense of intellectual unity that was completely foreign to the Greeks. In the end, this unity, despite its slender base, would be enough to challenge the philosophical inheritance of the Greeks and replace their many schools of thought with one all-embracing worldview.

A RELIGION OF THE BOOK

It seems to have been the Arabian "prophet" Muhammad (ca. 570–632) who first put his finger on the strength of Judaism and Christianity more than five hundred years after the time of Jesus. Seeking to establish a religion of his own, he considered the two main monotheistic faiths of his time, one of which (Christianity) had recently taken over the Roman Empire, and he concluded that they had survived and succeeded because they were religions of the book. So taken was he by this that he produced a book of his own (the Qur'an) which is even more central to his religion of Islam than the Bible is to either Jews or Christians. Islam claims for the Qur'an all that Jews and Christians claim for their Scriptures—and more. Jews and Christians do not believe, as Muslims do, that the Bible came down from heaven as the direct word of God. They do not believe that it was given in Hebrew and Greek to the extent that no translation into other languages is possible—indeed, much of the NT is already a translation from the Aramaic spoken by Jesus and his disciples into the common Greek of their time. They certainly do not believe that mutilating or destroying a Bible is an act of blasphemy punishable by death, though they deplore such practices when they occur. In these and other similar respects, Muslims appear to Jews and Christians to be taking their beliefs to an unwarranted extreme, though in fairness to them, Muslims often regard the Jewish and Christian approach to such things as a sign that they are less serious about their faith than they themselves are. To their minds, if Jews and Christians really believed what they claim to believe, they would be just as determined to exalt and defend their sacred texts as Muslims are. We must therefore look very carefully at what Jews and Christians actually think about the Bible before we move on to consider its place in Judaism and Christianity.

Jews and Christians both believe that the Bible is the written word of God. It was not given to one person, as Muslims claim the Qur'an was given to Muhammad, but to a number of people, many of whom are unknown to us. For example, nobody knows who wrote the OT books from Joshua to 2 Chronicles, but their status as divinely inspired books of Holy Scripture has never been questioned. The first five books of the OT—Genesis to Deuteronomy—are traditionally ascribed to Moses, but we cannot say what his true relationship to them was. Genesis recounts events that took place at least five hundred years before Moses's time, so even if Moses wrote it he must have got the information from somewhere—but from where? Did he use oral traditions that had been handed down through the generations? Did God reveal the material to him directly? Were the stories made up later on, sewn together in their present form and then attributed to Moses? Theories of all kinds abound, but the only thing we know for sure is that the text as it stands has always been accepted as God's word and that as such, it has enjoyed a unique authority in Israel.

Even the prophetic books, which contain the sayings of particular people whose historical context is to some extent recoverable, tell us less than we might like to know about their origins. The main exception to this is Jeremiah, which has come down to us in different recensions, at least some of which were probably written by the scribe Baruch, who is known to have collaborated closely with the prophet. Was Jeremiah a writer? We do not know. What about the other prophets? Scholars have dissected Isaiah in search of multiple authors but with meager results. Unlike Jeremiah, there is only one recension of the text, and we cannot say who was responsible for it. How much of it goes back to Isaiah himself is uncertain, but so is the contribution of later compilers and editors. Who did what? Once again, we do not know.

This story can be repeated with variations for virtually the whole of the OT. The Psalms are somehow connected with David, though we know from internal evidence that he did not write them all himself. The so-called wisdom literature (Job, Proverbs, Ecclesiastes, Song of Songs) is likewise associated with Solomon, but precisely how, nobody can say. That David and Solomon were patrons of the arts is quite possible, and they may have been personally involved in the production of at least some of the writings attributed to them, but it is equally likely that their example was an inspiration to others who claimed to stand in their tradition even if they lived centuries later. Here too we are left with an insoluble mystery, despite the many hypotheses that have been advanced to explain it.

This situation is all the more remarkable in that Israel was a small and relatively centralized society. Members of the literary class would certainly have known one another, as would the priests of the Jerusalem temple, who must have played a central role in the preservation of the written texts, if not in their original composition. All we can say for sure is that the end result was a small but remarkably uniform body of writings that all Jews accepted as authoritative, whatever their personal beliefs or preferences may have been. In the time of Jesus there were sects of Pharisees, Sadducees, Essenes, and others who disagreed about many things, but on the canon of Scripture they were at one.

When we turn to the NT, the situation is somewhat clearer but still markedly different from the Qur'an. The teaching and life of Jesus have come down to us in four different versions, three of which (Matthew, Mark, and Luke) are quite similar. They tell the same story but independently. Scholars analyze every word to try to piece together how they are related to each other and which of them is more authentic, but the results are inconclusive. The Pauline Epistles come closest to being texts with a known author and context, but even many of them have given rise to various theories of authorship. We know that Paul relied on secretaries to pen what he had to say, but although one or two of these are known to us, we have no idea how much influence they had over the final text. Did they correct Paul's grammar, or suggest words to convey his thoughts? We do not know.

Luke wrote both his Gospel and the Acts of the Apostles at the behest of Theophilus (Luke 1:3; Acts 1:1), but who was he? Was he a particular individual, or is Theophilus a generic name for "God lover," and therefore a literary device used to refer to any believer? And who was John? Did the apostle of that name write all five books attributed to "John," or were there different people who shared what was, after all, a very common name? The Epistle to the Hebrews is another mystery—it must have been written by a Jew who moved in circles close to those of the apostle Paul, but beyond that we cannot go. Some modern scholars have posited the existence of different groups in the early church who sponsored the writing of particular books—a "Johannine circle," for example, or a "Matthean community" at Antioch, but beyond their imaginations there is no evidence to support their attempted reconstructions. Whatever tendencies there may have been toward creating factions among the first Christians were nipped in the bud, as we can see from Paul's rebuke to the Corinthians who were attributing their baptism to different apostles (1 Cor 1:12–17). Pseudepigraphal gospels and epistles there certainly were, along with false apostles and deviant teachers of various kinds, but the early church retained a remarkable sense of unity, despite its lack of any central authority and the fact that it had to operate outside the law for nearly three centuries. The twenty-seven books of our NT were effectively canonized by the fourth century, with only very marginal doubts remaining, and they have held their own ever since.

From the standpoint of human authorship, there is much about the Bible that is opaque. The canon came together almost imperceptibly, and it was being widely used long before anybody thought to make it official.[1] What held it together was the conviction that these books were inspired by God. This conviction came from the books themselves, which were used for preaching, teaching, and discerning God's will for his people. In the case of 2 Peter, for example, where there were serious doubts about who the author was, it was the fact that the epistle was being used to win people for Christ that persuaded the church to accept its canonicity.

Attempts to impose canonical status on certain writings were also made, but they failed. The most obvious example of this is the inclusion of a number of books in the Greek OT (commonly known as the Septuagint and abbreviated as LXX) that are not found in the Hebrew text.[2] The translators evidently thought that these books, known to us

1. The first official statements defining the canon did not appear until after the sixteenth-century Reformation.

2. This translation was made from the third century BC onward and had become commonly accepted in the Jewish diaspora by the time of Jesus. Its name comes from the legend that it was

as the Apocrypha, belonged in the OT, but Jews generally rejected them and Christians did not use them. Not one of them is quoted in the NT, nor were commentaries written on them—a sure sign that they did not figure much in the preaching of the early church. In the fourth century, the Latin scholar Jerome (ca. 342–420) argued for their exclusion from the Christian Scriptures, though he was unsuccessful. His objections to them resurfaced at the time of the Reformation, when the Protestants removed them from the canon, and today everyone accepts that they are of secondary status. Hardly anyone ever preaches on them, nor are they used to determine the church's doctrine—not because anyone has proved that they are false or pseudepigraphal, but because they have failed to demonstrate any divine origin or seal of approval in the life of the Christian community.

By now it will be obvious that the Christian view of divine inspiration is much more subtle and complex than the Islamic one is, but that only strengthens its credibility. The authority of the Scriptures does not rest on the say-so of one man, not even Jesus. It is true, of course, that Jesus regarded the OT as divinely inspired and used it as such, but he did not invent that idea—it was the common belief of all Jews and always had been. Nor did Jesus commission his followers to write the NT, at least not directly. The NT writers occasionally speak about the divine inspiration of the OT, but they say remarkably little about it. Peter tells us that the writers "spoke from God, as they were carried along by the Holy Spirit," and Paul adds that the God-breathed texts are "profitable for teaching, for reproof, for correction, and for training in righteousness," but neither apostle was saying anything that could not have been said equally well by any Jewish teacher of their day (2 Pet 1:21; 2 Tim 3:16). Peter also tells us that Paul's epistles were treated as Scripture, but mainly because they contain things "that are hard to understand, which the ignorant and unstable twist to their own destruction" (2 Pet 3:16). The underlying assumption is that only those who are solidly grounded in the knowledge of the Holy Spirit will read the texts correctly. Those who lack that knowledge but

translated by seventy (Latin: *Septuaginta*) or perhaps seventy-two scholars who worked independently but produced identical translations.

who attempt to make sense of them will not simply be left bemused—they will be condemned to destruction. Such is the power of the word of God.

THE COVENANT CONTEXT

Jews and Christians do not believe that the Bible is a divine artifact like the Qur'an or the Book of Mormon, which supposedly came down from heaven on golden plates already written in mock-Tudor English. Nor do they believe that Moses or Jesus were great teachers whose thoughts were transcribed by loyal disciples who wanted to preserve their message. Still less do they think of particular books as having been written to correct (or contradict) other accounts of the same events. For example, it has never been suggested that the author of 1–2 Chronicles was trying to put the record of Genesis–2 Kings straight. In the NT, Luke tells us that he consulted many sources before writing his Gospel, but his intention was not to amend Matthew or Mark (assuming that he had read them), nor did John write in order to give the church a more accurate picture of Jesus than the one(s) found in the other Gospels. Paul's relationship to Jesus was not like Plato's to Socrates, nor can his dispute with Peter over the place of gentiles in the church be compared to the differences between Plato and Aristotle, or between the Stoics and the Epicureans. However distinctive they may have been, they were not rivals competing for attention. On the contrary, they were all proclaiming the same message, and their witness has survived as a common confession of faith that unites Christians everywhere. Their perspectives and emphases may differ to some extent, but the underlying message is the same.

The reason for this is that all the biblical writers operated within the context of God's covenant with Israel. Not every book of the Bible speaks about this with equal clarity, but it is the assumption that undergirds the whole and predates even the most ancient biblical text. Some scholars make much of the idea that Christians do not worship a book but a person—a half-truth that nevertheless makes an important point. There is no contradiction between the person of Jesus and the book he regarded as the word of God because the book bears witness to him—that is its purpose. But it is also true that God had people who worshiped him long before there ever was a Bible, and that the written text points beyond itself to a relationship with him that modern Christians are meant to enjoy just as much as Abraham, Isaac, and Jacob did—if not more, because the revelation given to us is more extensive than what was given to them.

The first point that must be made about this relationship is that it was initiated by God, not by Abraham (Gen 12:1). Abraham (or Abram, as he was still known) was not looking for God and perhaps had no idea about him until God spoke to him. We do not know how God communicated with Abram—was it in a dream or by some inner movement of Abram's mind? Nor is there any sign that God introduced himself or explained who he was and what he was like. All we know is that he told Abram to leave his homeland for a distant country of which Abram had never heard and that there God would make him the father of a great nation. From the vantage point of four thousand years we can see how that eventually happened, but Abram was not so privileged. He did as he was told, but he died without ever seeing the promises made to him fulfilled. As later generations understood it, he acted in faith (Heb 11:8–10). Faith, or trust in God, was the bond that created the relationship and that sustained it through all the ups and downs of the succeeding centuries. Those who shared that faith were included as heirs of the promise, while those who did not were cast aside.

Abram was not the first person to have faith in God, as the Epistle to the Hebrews reminds us, but he was the first person who was given a promise that he was expected to pass on to his descendants. With Abram, God was doing something new—he was establishing a covenant with a particular man that he expected would bear fruit over many generations. Neither Abram nor any of his descendants had a choice about this—they were called by God whether they wanted to be or not, and the only question was whether they would obey his voice. Abram passed that test, even to the point where he was willing to sacrifice his son Isaac if that was what God wanted, and for that reason his calling and covenant were confirmed (Gen 22:1–18). His name had already been changed to Abraham as a sign of that covenant, and it was by that name that he would ever after be known (Gen 17:5).

Why did God choose Abraham rather than someone else? Indeed, why did God choose any particular individual at all? This is a question that cannot be answered. Moses alluded to it when he told the Israelites:

"It was not because you were more in number than any other people that the LORD set his love on you and chose you, for you were the fewest of all peoples, but it is because the LORD loves you and is keeping the oath that he swore to your fathers" (Deut 7:7–8). There was no other explanation, and none would be forthcoming. But not only was this question never to be answered, it should not even have been asked in the first place. The apostle Paul made that clear in his Epistle to the Romans: "Who are you, O man, to answer back to God? Will what is molded say to its molder, 'Why have you made me like this?' Has the potter no right over the clay?" (Rom 9:20–21). It would be hard to think of anything further from the spirit of philosophical inquiry than this!

The second thing about the relationship between God and Israel is that it was not a relationship of natural equals. God is the Creator, and everything else is a creature of one kind or another. The entire human race was made in his image and likeness, which was a great privilege, but it was also a heavy responsibility, because when that race rebelled against him it incurred condemnation (Gen 1:26–27; 3:22–24). The covenant God made with Abraham was a covenant made with a sinner who was in rebellion against him. Being chosen did not automatically relieve Abraham of that burden, but it provided a way out in the form of atoning sacrifice. The sins of Israel were not blotted out or disregarded; they were paid for. For centuries the payment was made annually in the form of a spotless lamb that was sacrificed for the sins of the people, but this was a temporary expedient. In the fulness of time, God sent his Son to become the eternal Paschal Lamb, whose one sacrifice of himself once offered would make atonement for the sins of the whole world, past, present, and future.

The Greek philosophers had a concept of sin, but they saw it differently. For them, sin was ignorance and the failure that naturally came with that. The cure was knowledge, although that knowledge went beyond the capacity of most people to absorb and led those who acquired it to distance themselves from the uncomprehending world around them. With Israel, it was quite different. Sin was not the fruit of ignorance but of rebellion against a God who was known. Even non-Israelites knew about him, although they did their best to suppress that knowledge and live as though God did not exist (Rom 1:18–23). Atonement was not a matter of increasing knowledge but of offering forgiveness, and it applied equally to all who were within the bounds of the covenant, regardless of their intellectual ability or inclination.

This understanding of sin went hand in hand with a corresponding view of evil. Many non-Israelites thought of evil as something inherent in matter, or else as the absence of being—evil was literally "no thing." But Israel learned that evil was a spiritual force in rebellion against God. This force was not part of the material creation but of a spiritual realm that lies somewhere between God and the world. It is populated by spiritual creatures whom we call angels, and it was some of these who rebelled against the Creator. Because the rebellious angels are eternal, they did not die when they sinned but became what we call "demons"—that is to say, angels who are at war with God. These rebellious angels, or demons, are headed by Satan, whose sin was pride—he thought he could be his own god and live independently of his Creator. When God created humanity, Satan tempted humans to follow him by promising them that if they did so, they would become like God. The first human beings succumbed to the temptation and were subsequently trapped as servants of Satan, which they still are. Because Satan's rebellion was personal, he did not suffer in any material way, so that there is no natural defect in him that would put people off. On the contrary, Satan can (and does) appear as an "angel of light," which is how he managed to deceive human beings in the first place and how he is still able to control them (2 Cor 11:14).

In the Jewish and Christian worldview, sin and evil are not corruptions of the created order, which remains good in itself, since that is how God made it. They are, rather, mental and spiritual perversions brought on by pride and rebellion against the Creator. A sinful man is not mentally or physically handicapped. He can use his God-given faculties just as well as anyone else. The problem is that the fundamental orientation of his life is one of opposition to God. This does not necessarily result in Satan worship, something that is in fact quite rare, but in self-worship. To put it a different way, fallen human beings do not normally worship Satan as if he were God, but copy Satan by worshiping themselves. "Man is the measure of all things" becomes their motto, and the deceived person looks no further than himself as the judge of universal reality. For this reason, the first step toward God is not the acquisition of knowledge but the self-abasement of the person concerned, who must recognize that he is incapable of knowing himself as he ought and therefore equally incapable of saving himself from what has gone wrong.

The third thing about the relationship between God and Israel is that it was intensely relational. God called Israel by its name—indeed, he *gave* it its name. When Jacob was returning to the promised land after many years spent with his uncle in a kind of self-imposed exile, God met with him in the night and wrestled with him until daybreak. At that point, while Jacob was still hanging on to the fight despite his obvious inferiority, God said to him: "Your name shall no longer be called Jacob, but Israel, for you have striven with God and with men, *and have prevailed*" (Gen 32:28, italics mine). This is an astonishing statement—Jacob had somehow prevailed against God! Of course, things were not that simple, because when Jacob asked God to tell him his name, he was rebuffed. It was then that Jacob realized that he had been struggling with God, and that God had honored him by accepting him as a kind of equal, not in objective terms but in relational ones.[3]

In biblical language, Jacob had seen God "face to face," and yet his life had been spared. It is this "face to face" that constitutes the personal relationship with God that allows a man to address his Creator on terms of *de facto* equality—to plead with God, to intercede with God, even to express anger against God. The "face to face" encounter was rare in ancient Israel. Moses knew God in that way but those who came after him did not (see Deut 34:10–12). But it is this degree of intimacy with God that is promised to Christians, as the apostle Paul told the Corinthians: "Now we see in a mirror dimly, but then face to face. Now I know in part; then I shall know fully, even as I have been fully known" (1 Cor 13:12). The Greek word for "face" is *prosōpon,* translated into Latin as *persona*. To know God "face to face" is to have a personal relationship with him, to be able to communicate with him in a way that is denied to all other creatures, including the angels. Indeed, in the very same epistle Paul told the astonished

3. Later on, we are told that God did reveal his name to Moses as YHWH. It appears in the Hebrew Bible without vowels, but in the NT and in translations of the OT, including the LXX, it is usually rendered as LORD, capitalized in English so as to alert the reader to the underlying Hebrew text. This is done because pious Jews refused to pronounce God's name, even though it had been revealed to them.

Corinthians that one day they would judge the angels, an event that would clearly demonstrate their superiority to and authority over them (1 Cor 6:3).

The personal relationship that God established with Israel granted the latter a kind of equality with him, but this must not be misunderstood. Israel received this status not by any kind of entitlement but by grace—it was God's pleasure to allow Israel to approach him and not something that Israel possessed by right. Furthermore, it was a relationship based on Israel's obedience to God's law. Jesus later told his disciples that they were his friends if they did whatever he commanded them to do, which is essentially the same thing (John 15:14). This is a far cry from the kind of friendship found in the Greek philosophical schools, where everyone was seeking after truth. In Israel, God (and later Jesus) *was* the truth—all they had to do was accept that and act accordingly.

One interesting (and important) point about God is that he was above the law and from time to time commanded that his followers should ignore it. This happened when King Saul was told to kill the Amalekites and destroy all their possessions, but Saul refused to do so (1 Sam 15:1–35). He meant well, sparing the Amalekite king's life and keeping Amalekite animals for sacrifice to Israel's God, but that is not what God had commanded him to do, and so he was rejected. As the prophet Samuel told him, "To obey is better than sacrifice ... rebellion is as the sin of divination and presumption is as iniquity and idolatry" (1 Sam 15:22–23). Claiming to know better than God was not an option for his servants, even if the intentions were good. Later on, the prophet Hosea was told to marry a prostitute in order to teach Israel a lesson about its own behavior toward God, even though the Law of Moses expressly forbade such a thing (Hos 1:2; see Lev 21:7). The teaching of Jesus is full of such examples, as he regularly overturned the law in the interest of a higher principle. The Ten Commandments had enjoined observance of the Sabbath day, but Jesus said that "the Sabbath was made for man, not man for the Sabbath" and effectively dispensed with Jewish observances (Mark 2:27). He did the same with the food laws, pointing out that what defiles a person is not what goes into him but what comes out—from the rebellious heart and disobedient soul (Matt 15:11; Mark 7:20). The law was given by God and was good in itself, but its goodness was relative, and when God so chose, he could (and did) overrule it.

The fourth thing about the relationship between God and Israel was that it was exclusive. The first of the Ten Commandments is very explicit about this: "I am the LORD your God ... you shall have no other gods before me" (Exod 20:2–3). Israel lived in a polytheistic world, where every other nation worshiped a pantheon of deities, but that option was not open to them. There were many times, especially under the monarchy, when foreign gods were introduced into Israel, often by women who married its kings, but this was severely condemned and after the exile the practice ceased. Did the Israelites believe that these other gods existed? The OT addresses the question in a roundabout way. What it says is that the gods of the other nations have no power. People can pray to them, their priests can sacrifice to them, and their prophets can speak in their name, but it means nothing. The classic case of confrontation between the God of Israel and the gods of other nations was the encounter of Elijah with the prophets of Baal on Mount Carmel (1 Kgs 18:20–40). Elijah challenged his opponents to a kind of spiritual duel. They were both to build an altar on which to offer sacrifice, and ask for their god to come down and consume it with fire. The prophets of Baal failed but Elijah succeeded, after making the whole thing more difficult by first dousing his sacrifice in water to protect it from burning.

That incident proved what the Israelites believed. Their God could do anything anywhere at any time, whereas the gods of the other nations were impotent, even at the best of times. Further discussion was unnecessary. It was useless having a god who was powerless, and as far as the Israelites were concerned, such a deity might as well not have existed. The Israelites habitually mocked the surrounding peoples for making idols out of wood and stone and then bowing down to them—it was obvious to them that spiritual power could not be created in that way. In the NT we see a similar approach. When the apostle Paul went to Athens, he remarked that the Athenians were very pious, worshiping many gods, but he made no effort to denounce that practice. Instead, he focused on an altar he had seen that was dedicated to the "unknown" god and told his hearers that that was the God of Israel, whom he described as the Creator of all things (Acts 17:24–25). He hardly needed to add that this unknown god was the only true God—the logic of his argument spoke for itself.

BEYOND THE COVENANT

How did Israel view the world beyond the bounds of its covenant with God? As far as the natural order is concerned, there seems to be no doubt that it saw God's hand at work in everything, as indeed it must have been if the creation was to have any meaning. God made the world out of nothing and was therefore involved in every part of it. The winds and the seas obeyed his voice. There was nowhere in heaven or earth where he was not present. The stars in heaven, including the sun and the moon, obeyed his will. Other nations saw natural forces as gods in their own right, but Israel never did. Natural disasters, as we would understand them, were not the result of opposing forces but phenomena that God controlled. Noah's flood, for example, was sent by God and lasted for as long as God intended it to. Noah himself was saved from destruction because he obeyed God and built an ark to protect him and his family, not to mention scores of animals. The flood did not destroy the human race because God did not want it to—its purpose was to punish the sins of humanity and make a fresh start, even if sinfulness was not eliminated and sin soon returned.

Later on, God demonstrated his power over the natural order by sending a series of plagues on the Egyptians, and the Israelites had complete confidence in his ability to do whatever he chose. He parted the waters of the Red Sea so that they could escape the armies of Pharaoh, but then the waters returned and drowned the Egyptians, which was also God's doing. The entire book of Job is a study in God's power over his creation, and Job is praised for accepting the worst disasters that could befall him as the will of a holy and righteous God. The chosen people were not exempt from suffering, which they were expected to see as part of God's plan for them, however hard it might be to understand. This dimension of the covenant relationship set Israel apart from the surrounding nations, all of whom regarded their gods as being there to help them, and nothing else. The idea that a god might punish them for their own good, or to draw them nearer to himself, was foreign to their understanding, and of course it was meaningless to those philosophers who had a negative view of religion to begin with.

How the Israelites perceived the connection between God and the other nations is another question. In principle, they believed all human beings were created by him in his image and likeness, and that all had fallen into sin and disobedience. Some of the nations mentioned in the OT were closely related to Israel and were expected to act accordingly. This was particularly true of the Edomites, who were the descendants of Jacob's brother Esau and whose unwillingness to help their kinsmen in their distress was particularly resented (Num 20:14–21).[4] In the time of Jesus the Herodian family, which occupied the puppet throne of Judea, was Edomite (Idumaean) and the Herodians regarded themselves as Jewish.[5]

That God ruled the affairs of the other nations was made clear by the prophets, some of whom devoted considerable time to examining their affairs and pronouncing judgment on them. Every once in a while we hear of individuals who aligned themselves with Israel and were accepted as members of the covenant community. Ruth the Moabitess was an outstanding example of that—she insisted on going to Israel with her mother-in-law after her husband's death, and in due course she was rewarded for her faith. Naaman the Syrian general was also accepted as a worshiper of the true God, though for obvious reasons he could not immigrate (2 Kgs 5)! More remarkable still was the mission of Jonah to Nineveh, as a result of which an entire city repented and turned to God, though we know that it did not last—and also that Jonah was upset that his mission was as successful as it was. His attitude toward the Ninevites was unfortunately typical of Jews generally. They were not particularly interested in sharing their covenant blessings with others, even though they recognized that a time would come when the nations would look to Jerusalem (Zion) for their salvation. It was all there in theory, but practice was another thing, and nobody really expected (or sought) mass conversions of gentiles to Judaism.

It was on this point that Christians were radically different from Jews in their understanding of the covenant. They accepted that in Jesus Christ, the Son of God had come to his own people and died for them, but they also knew that he had come to die for the sins of the whole world. This did not mean that all human beings would be saved, but that the covenant relationship that the Jews had enjoyed was made available to everyone

4. See also the short book of Obadiah, which mentions the failure of Edom to come to Judah's aid.

5. Interestingly, the Jews never rejected them because of their Edomite background, which makes a sharp contrast with the Samaritans. The difference seems to have been that the Edomites did not attempt to establish a rival form of worship.

who believed, whether they were Jews by ethnic origin or not. This awareness was also the spur to evangelism. If anyone could become a child of God, then it was incumbent on those who knew that they were to preach this good news ("gospel") to everyone. From the beginning, the Christian church was outward looking in a way that the Jewish people generally were not, and the NT tells us of the tensions that caused between converted Jews and gentiles. Many Jewish Christians were prepared to accept gentile converts as long as they became Jews first, but the apostle Paul insisted that that was not necessary, and it was his view that won the day. As a result, within a couple of generations the church was largely gentile in composition and expanding to the point where it eventually took over the Roman Empire.

It might be argued that the early Christians constituted a spiritual elite and that they were aware of that fact, since the apostle Peter said, "You are a chosen race, a royal priesthood, a holy nation, a people for his [God's] own possession" (1 Pet 2:9). But if there is some truth in that characterization, it is also true that Christians had no reason to boast of their good fortune or to feel superior to anyone else. After telling the Corinthians that immoral people and others like them would not inherit the kingdom of God, the apostle Paul added, "and such were some of you" (1 Cor 6:11). Those who came to Christ came from a background of sinfulness from which they had been rescued, and that was through no merit of their own. But just as importantly, they were called to go out and seek the lost, so that they too might be saved. Whatever knowledge they possessed or whatever blessings they enjoyed were to be shared with others until all God's chosen people were drawn in. They were an elite, perhaps, but they were not elitist in their mentality. The word of God was sent to all people everywhere, whether they accepted it or not.

Jesus told his disciples that he was "the way, and the truth, and the life," and that no one could come to the Father (God) except through him (John 14:6). It was this intensely personal union with Christ that made all the difference. It was sealed, not by some higher knowledge, but by the indwelling presence of the Holy Spirit, who would lead them into all truth (John 16:7–15; see also Gal 4:6). Christians had no further need of enlightenment. They could wander the earth, knowing that God was with them and that they would be provided with whatever they needed to glorify him. They did not have to worry if they were arrested, condemned, and even put to death, because the Holy Spirit would give them the words to say when the need arose (Luke 12:12). They would be God's witnesses in Jerusalem, Samaria, and to the ends of the earth, and their message would be the same wherever they went (Acts 1:8).

DOES THE BIBLE CONTAIN A PHILOSOPHY?

The singularity and the universality of the message proclaimed by the early Christians shows that they believed that what they had to say was enough to teach people everywhere how they ought to live. Their belief in a Creator God, who made heaven and earth, proclaimed the essential unity of all things. The problem of evil was explained, if not resolved, by saying that evil was not a thing inherent in any part of creation but a spiritual attitude—one of disobedience to the word of God. Every conceivable aspect of reality was contained within this vision, making it, if anything, more comprehensive than any known philosophy of the time. But does this make the Bible and its worldview a philosophy in its own right? The early Christians did not think so. They were aware of the philosophies that were circulating in the Greco-Roman world, but they never thought of their faith as one of them. On the few occasions that the NT mentions Greek philosophy, it presents it as something fundamentally alien and relatively worthless. Speculating about the nature of reality was a pointless exercise when all the reality that anyone needed to know was openly declared in the word of God. There was more to the universe than that, to be sure, but what remained hidden from human eyes was meant to stay that way for the time being. All would be revealed in due course, at the end of time, but until then there was no need to inquire any further. Is this a form of philosophy or is it an alternative to it?

Tertullian clearly thought that the Christian message was an alternative to philosophy, which is why he said that Athens has nothing to do with Jerusalem. To his mind, if you choose one you cannot have the other, since nobody can be in two places at the same time. Many Christians have agreed with him about this, and so have a lot of philosophers, though they come at it from the opposite angle. To the Christian mind, the world cannot be explained apart from God, and some have concluded from that that if you know him you have no need to bother with anything else. On the other hand, to many philosophers, "the proper study of mankind is man."[6] To go beyond the physical world is to get lost in a maze of theory and speculation, none of which can be proved, even if it exists. God is at best a distraction; at worst, an irrelevance. Is one of these positions what a comparison of the biblical worldview with different schools of philosophy is bound to lead us to?

Most Christians, for most of the time, have refused to be forced into one or other of these opposing views. Some biblical books deal with philosophical questions, though whether they can be considered "philosophy" is more doubtful. The book of Job, for instance, is an extended discussion of the nature of good and evil. Proverbs is a collection of wise sayings, not unlike the aphorisms of some of the lesser-known Greek philosophers. And Ecclesiastes has often been read as the meditation of a philosopher who has concluded that the quest for wisdom is all pretty much a waste of time! The Bible is not a book of philosophy as such, but it presents a coherent view of the universe, which is what most philosophies strive to achieve. It does not classify material things to any great extent, though some awareness of different species can be gleaned from Genesis 1 and elsewhere. There is no attempt to analyze the created order in the way that Aristotle did, though the Bible says nothing that would prevent the human mind from thinking in terms of biology, mathematics, ethics, and so on. These categories of human thought are compatible with a biblical worldview, even if the Bible says nothing about them.

Where the Bible differs most obviously from any form of philosophy is the way that it deals with what philosophers call theology. To them, theology, the study of God, is one intellectual discipline alongside the others. In the biblical perspective, however, what philosophers would call "theology" is something else altogether. The Bible does not study God—it reveals him. Theology is not a branch of philosophy but its fundamental component. In theory it could exist without any philosophy whatsoever, and in a sense that is what happens in the Bible, which is no more a book of theology than it is a book of philosophy. But as soon as we try to make sense of the biblical worldview, to see God in all the coherence of his

6. A well-known saying of Alexander Pope (1688–1744), taken from his *Essay on Man*, first published in 1733.

self-revelation, something approaching philosophy is bound to come into view. Theology is systematic, and a system relies on logic for its meaning. Some things make sense, but others do not. For example, God is above and beyond his creation, so he cannot be portrayed by created objects. Idolatry is therefore ruled out, and the Bible corroborates that. At the same time, God cannot be both good and evil, even though good and evil both exist in the world he has made. This is a paradox, until we realize that evil is not a created thing in itself, nor is it inherent in creation. It is a spiritual rebellion against the Creator and cannot be understood in any other way.

The existence of sin and evil requires a complete reordering of our understanding of the created order. We are forced to go beyond pure materialism and consider a different dimension to reality, a dimension that introduces the concept of the person—which does not exist in classical philosophy—and the idea of love, which binds one person to another. The Bible says that God is love, a statement that would be meaningless to a Greek philosopher. He might accept that God is indifferent to human concerns, that God is spiritual, beyond our comprehension, and so on. But love? And not just love in the abstract, but love in the form of a crucified, dead, and risen Son, fully God and fully man? This is beyond the scope of any form of classical philosophy, and makes the Christian message something quite different from what the Platonists or the Stoics had to say.

To put it a different way, classical philosophy is an exercise in observation, contemplation, and separation. It is the observation of the world, the contemplation of its structure and meaning, and the mental separation or distancing of the observer from the things he observes. The biblical worldview, by contrast is observation and contemplation, to be sure, but it is not separation—it is involvement. A Christian cannot sit idly by, contemplating the folly of humankind. A Christian must be engaged with that folly—analyzing it as sin, condemning it as alienation from God, and confronting it with a gospel of redemption and salvation. The world is not there merely to be observed and contemplated. It is there to be transformed into the likeness of what God wants it to be. That transformation will not be fully accomplished until the end of time, but in his love, God has graciously reached out to us and given us what the Bible calls the "firstfruits" of that redemption—the enjoyment of a personal relationship with him that integrates us into his inner life as a community of Persons

(Father, Son, and Holy Spirit) and opens up his mind to us. In that sense, it is the goal of the philosopher's striving, the answer to the questions that he is eternally asking but never truly resolving. As the medieval thinkers used to say, philosophy is the handmaid of theology, a means to the end to which all lovers of wisdom aspire.

THE CREATOR AND THE CREATION

The triumph of Christianity over its pagan rivals in the ancient world had many facets, but at the heart of them all lay the distinction between the Creator and the creation. The pagan philosophers had never managed to establish a proper balance between these two factors and had frequently confused them with one another, but for Christians there was a clear difference between the two. So much so, in fact, that when Arius (256–336) tried to maintain that the Son of God was a creature (*ktisma*) his teaching split the church. If the Son of God was God, then he was the Creator; if he was a creature, then he was not God at all. That was the doctrine maintained by the orthodox party at the First Council of Nicaea (325) and defended for centuries against anyone who sought to find a compromise between these two opposing principles.

It is not often realized now, but the portion of the Bible most frequently commented on in the fourth and fifth centuries was the creation narrative in Genesis 1–3. Christians tackled it from every conceivable angle. Some interpreted it literally, but most resorted to allegory of one kind or another because they realized that the story was laden with symbolism. They did not deny its fundamental truth, though. God may have accommodated his revelation to the understanding of unsophisticated nomads, but the substance of what he said was clear—he had created a good world for the benefit of humankind, but it had been ruined by the intrusion of sin.

Where sin and evil came from and how powerful they were became matters of central importance to the early Christians. Some people were attracted to the dualist ideas that came from Persia, most notably in the teaching of Mani (216–276), a prophet who believed that the force of Good and the force of Evil contended with each other for mastery of the world. Manichaeism, as this view is generally known, held little appeal as long as the ancient pagan philosophies were dominant because they could not conceive of evil as a coherent power in its own right. But as

Judeo-Christian monotheism gained in popularity, it was tempting to think of evil as a similarly monotheistic power that was opposed to the God of the Bible. Of course, as many people soon realized, dualism is not really viable as a philosophical theory. For a start, where did these two opposing forces originally come from? Did one create the other? If not, how did they ever come into contact with each other, let alone conflict? If Good and Evil were equal, why should anyone choose one over the other? Indeed, why would one of them be labelled "Good" and the other "Evil" in the first place?

The result, as Augustine of Hippo (354–430) discovered, was that the Manichees had no morality at all. They preached and sometimes practiced a form of asceticism, at least on the surface, but underneath they surrendered to the worst kind of debauchery, because it was ultimately just as justifiable as the alternative. Here pagan thinkers and Christians were at one. They might have different conceptions of morality, but they all believed that there was a Good that was far superior to any form of Evil. Manichaeism fell apart at the seams, and although it was popular in intellectual circles for a time, it did not survive as a serious option for very long.[7]

The biblical doctrine of creation made it clear that God made everything that exists, and that everything he made is fundamentally good. Evil is not an opposing force of equal strength, nor is it the result of something defective in God's handiwork, as the second-century Gnostics had usually maintained. Evil was not an objective thing at all but a spiritual attitude. It was not a legitimate alternative to the work of God but a rebellion against him, initiated by Satan. The Bible says little about Satan, but his existence and his rebellion against God are clear from the beginning. Christians generally assumed that it was pride that caused him to rebel—Satan was such a strong angel that he thought he could dispense with God and rule the world on his own. It was in this spirit of rebellion that he approached Adam and Eve, the first human beings, and tempted them away from God by promising them that, if they followed him, they would become gods themselves. It was a trap. Human beings acquired the knowledge of good

7. Forms of it did, however, resurface in the Middle Ages: first as Bogomilism in Bulgaria and then as Albigensianism in the south of France. It was not finally extinguished until the thirteenth century.

and evil, which they had not previously had, but as a consequence they were denied access to eternal life—death was to be the wages of their sin.

But God did not create the world in order to see it condemned to death. The rebellion of Satan and the resulting sin of Adam and Eve was the consequence of granting them the free will to disobey him, but it was not his intention. As an immortal creature, Satan could not die, and so he continued in existence, but God made it plain to him that he could not have unfettered domination over the world. What God chose to do instead was to rescue his human creatures from Satan's power, and thereby deliver them from death. In the first instance, he chose a particular people—Israel—to be the bearers of that message. Israel was given the law of God to show them what God expected of them, and that law set them apart from the rest of humanity. But the law was a message of righteousness, not of salvation, and non-Israelites (the so-called gentiles) were not totally excluded from his plan of redemption. Even in the OT, there were prophecies concerning them, and the book of Jonah testified that when the message of repentance was preached to them, they might well respond, even if they were the sworn enemies of Israel.

The law was not a message of salvation, but it was a promise that one day salvation would come. In the fullness of time, God sent his Son into the world as Jesus Christ. This was far and away the most momentous event in human history, one that is universally recognized as a turning point in the way in which we measure time—Before Christ (BC) and *Anno Domini* (AD, "in the year of the Lord"). The incarnation of the Son of God had enormous philosophical implications. First of all, it demonstrated that God is not a remote deity unconcerned with human affairs, which is what many pagan philosophers thought. He is concerned with our destiny and is deeply involved with it. Second, it shows that evil has nothing to do with matter. If it had, the Son of God could not have become a man at all. Sin is therefore not inherent in created human nature—it is a distortion of God's will for us, brought about by spiritual rebellion against him.

In the third place, what human beings do matters. God could presumably have wiped away sin, but if he had done so, the human race would have been wiped away with it. But human beings are too important for that. Their sin must be paid for, and that is what the Son of God came to do. The wages of sin is death, and so the Son died on our behalf. Because he was in the right relationship with his Father, and therefore had not sinned, he could die for our sins without having to pay for any of his own. Because of that, he was not overcome by death but rose again to become the first example of what the NT calls the new creation. By being united to him in faith, believers could trust that this new creation would extend to them also, not because of any fundamental change in their nature, but by virtue of a union with Christ that made a new and superior life possible. Christians still have to die in their earthly bodies, but like Christ they will rise again from the dead and live with him in eternity. This is the hope that is held out to them, giving their faith content and purpose.

But there is still more. The coming of the Son revealed that God is not a single person in the strict sense. The Son identifies himself in relation to the Father who sent him, and both are equally and eternally God. Furthermore, the return of the Son to his heavenly glory at the Father's right hand was not the end of the story. Having gone away, the Son sent a replacement, his Holy Spirit, who dwells in the hearts of believers and makes it possible for us to know the Father in a way that parallels the relationship that the Son has with him, even if it is not identical (Gal 4:6). To put it bluntly, what the Son is by his divine nature, believers become by the outpouring of divine grace, in the person of the Holy Spirit.

The presence of the Holy Spirit in the life of believers changes everything. We remain sinners in the descent of Adam and Eve, but we have been given new life in our union with the Son. This means that we have the mind of Christ, which gives us the ability to think and act in a way that conforms to God's will and is therefore pleasing to him. The moral life enjoined by the law, and advocated in different ways by most pagan philosophers, is transcended by a higher principle—the presence of the Lawgiver himself, dwelling in our hearts and minds. Christians are not judged by whether or not they keep the precepts of the law of Moses, which is ultimately impossible, but by the spiritual attitude they have toward God and his plan of salvation. In our behavior we are bound to fall short in many ways, but our faith is measured by the way in which we acknowledge that and react to it by seeking repentance and forgiveness. Where the mind of Christ is not present, there is no repentance, and therefore no forgiveness either. But where his Spirit informs our thoughts, we are led to confess our own powerlessness and to turn to him for the gift of salvation, which is ours by his grace. In theory, it is all very simple—the message of Christ's salvation (the "gospel") is not a riddle that only brilliant minds can solve. But in practice it is very difficult, because the pride that led to our rebellion continues to attract us and to make us think that we can somehow solve our problems on our own. That is a fatal mistake, and the ultimate reason why so many people never enjoy the blessing that God holds out to us in Christ.

For a Christian who is born again by faith to a new hope, the world becomes a different place. On the one hand, we see it as the work of an Almighty and beneficent Creator. In recent years, some people have been tempted to deny the omnipotence of God, preferring to see him as a deity who identifies with us by embracing our weakness and suffering. This is a heresy, but like all good heresies, it contains enough truth to make it seem plausible. God does indeed enter into our suffering, but his purpose is not primarily to identify himself with that. On the contrary, his goal is to overcome that suffering and to set us free from sin and death. Christians are those who understand that and who embrace it as God's will for them. Our primary orientation must therefore be toward God, who has delivered us from evil and given us the opportunity to live—for him in this life and with him in the next.

Once we understand that, the next step is to apply our minds to the world around us. This takes two distinct, though not unrelated, forms. The first is that we are called to treat our fellow human beings as we want to be treated ourselves (Luke 6:31). In effect, this means that they are just as important as we are, and what we think, say, and do must always bear that in mind. The second is that we must take up God's command to "be fruitful and multiply and fill the earth and subdue it"—the creation mandate given to Adam and Eve but compromised by their disobedience (Gen 1:28). This means that we are called to use the resources of this world responsibly, for the upbuilding of the human race to the glory of God. It is not a mandate for indiscriminate exploitation but a challenge to us to use what we have intelligently and for the common good. One consequence of this is that the material world must be "desacralized" in our minds. The notion that divinity infuses the earth, that inert objects have some kind of spiritual power or that certain places must be recognized as "holy" in a way that others are not—all these fantasies must be rejected. Doing that alters our perception of what matter is and what it is for. Modern science would not have developed in the way that it has if that principle had not been accepted, because the idea that some things are off limits to human investigation would have prevented it from doing so.

At the same time, this freedom to explore the universe must be balanced by acknowledging the sovereignty of God over all things. We may have the ability to blow the world up with nuclear weapons, but that does not justify our doing so. That may be an extreme case, but it illustrates the principle that what is possible is not necessarily right. The Christian view is that the more things become possible, the greater is our responsibility to decide which of them are legitimate exercises of human power. Far from making God redundant, the achievements of modern science have made him more necessary than ever, if we are not to destroy ourselves and fulfill the wishes of the Satan who deceived our remote ancestors by his false promises of pseudo-divinity. What has become clear in our day could not have been foreseen in ancient times, at least not in detail, but the basic principles have been there from the beginning. The world in which we live has changed in many ways, but Jerusalem stays the same forever.

SUMMARY

1. The dominance of Greek culture in the ancient Mediterranean world was resisted by the Jews, who refused to integrate into it, though they often learned Greek and translated their sacred Scriptures into that language.

2. Jews traced their origins back to Abraham and established their identity around the OT or Hebrew Bible, which was the core of their religious beliefs and practices. This gave them a cohesion that no philosophical school had.

3. Jews believed that they were a people chosen by God who lived in a covenant relationship with him. That relationship expressed itself in laws that focused on worship and ethical behavior, rather than on speculative theology.

4. Jews understood sin and evil as the result of rebellion against God, not as something inherent in the created order. God ruled the entire universe, but other nations were not in covenant with him and so did not share in the blessings and promises that were given only to Jews.

5. Jews believed that keeping the law revealed to them in the Bible was all the philosophy they needed. Some biblical books, in particular the Wisdom literature (*e.g.*, Job, Ecclesiastes) dealt with philosophical questions, but in the context of the law of God and his sovereign rule, which they could not question. Insofar as they had a philosophy, it was bound up with the laws of their religion and could only be understood in that context.

6. The Bible draws an absolute distinction between the Creator and the creation, making it sinful to worship the latter instead of the former. This ruled out other religions, with their widespread idolatry, as alternative ways to God. At the same time, it desacralized the material world, a move that would eventually make scientific research and discovery possible because it did not impinge on the divine.

7. Jews taught that rebellion against God is universal in the human race, but God has not left us without a way of escape. Jews were promised salvation from sin by keeping the covenant law of Moses, and Christians believed that the promise made to them had been fulfilled in the life, death, and resurrection of Jesus Christ. This offer of salvation was not confined to the Jews but was extended to the whole world, making Christianity a universal religion and not a national one, as Judaism was. This forced Christians to confront the Greek world in a way that Jews had never done.

IV

ATHENS MEETS JERUSALEM

When did the philosophical tradition(s) of ancient Greece first come into contact with Israel? According to some Jews and Christians, this happened very early—indeed, in their minds, the philosophical inheritance of Greece was borrowed and adapted from the Jews from the very beginning. In chronological terms, that is by no means impossible. By the time the Greeks got going, the kingdoms of Israel and Judah had already fallen to the Assyrians and Babylonians, so there is no doubt that the Israelite tradition was much older than anything the Greeks produced. We know that the early Greek philosophers borrowed from Egypt, and the Greek alphabet is a variant of the Phoenician one, which is similar to that of Hebrew, so written contact between Palestine and the Aegean world cannot be ruled out entirely.[1] It is at least possible that Plato could have read Moses and adapted the Torah for Greek consumption, as Justin Martyr (100–165) believed, though Plato never mentioned it and modern scholars dismiss the claim as idle speculation.[2]

What is more likely is that the two traditions first met in Alexandria in the third century BC, when translation of the Hebrew Bible into Greek began, and that the influence, such as it was, flowed the other way—from the Greeks to the increasingly Hellenized Jews. The first example of this comes from the surviving fragments of a Jewish teacher called Aristobulus

1. The Hebrew and Greek alphabets are distantly related, as can be seen from the names of the letters. Compare aleph, beth, gimel, daleth (Hebrew) with alpha, beta, gamma, delta (Greek)—they are the same.

2. Justin Martyr, *First Apology*, 59.

(fl. ca. 180–160 BC) who interpreted the Pentateuch in the form of a dialogue with King Ptolemy VI (184–145 BC). Aristobulus seems to have been heavily influenced by Stoicism and interpreted the Bible in a way that was consonant with it.

Later on, this technique became much more highly developed. In seeking to prove that Plato was dependent on Moses, the Jewish exegete Philo of Alexandria (20 BC–AD 50) almost did the opposite—showing how the Pentateuch could be interpreted in ways that were compatible with Plato and his disciples. Thus, for example, Philo had an interest in numerology that smacks of Pythagoras, when he saw the "perfect" numbers three and seven associated with God in the OT. God the Creator rested on the seventh day when his work was finished (and therefore perfect), and he appeared to Abraham as three men, whom Abraham addressed in the singular as "Lord" (Gen 18:1–21). It was in commenting on that episode that Philo became the first person to use the word *trias* (Trinity) of God, a circumstance that later Christians were not slow to seize on. Even today, one of the most famous Russian Orthodox icons is that of the so-called OT Trinity by Andrei Rublëv (1360/70–1427/30), which is frequently reproduced on the cover of books about the Triune God.[3]

Philo's ambiguous relationship to Greek philosophy certainly helped the early Christians to adopt a more positive attitude toward the latter than they might otherwise have done, but it was some centuries after the coming of Christ before this was felt to any serious extent. One thing that Philo did manage to achieve was to persuade many of his fellow Jews, and later many Christians as well, that the different schools of Greek philosophy were fundamentally the same because they were all attempts to interpret Moses in a gentile context. It was therefore possible to find echoes of the OT in almost every form of pagan philosophy without becoming attached to any one school in particular. This interpretation would later allow Christians to engage with philosophical thought but at the same time to transcend it, because even the most sophisticated philosophy was still no more than a partial appropriation of the biblical revelation. To

3. It should be said that this incident is never mentioned in the NT nor was it used to defend the Christian doctrine of the Trinity in the classic fourth and fifth century debates on the subject.

paraphrase the apostle Paul, Philo could be a Platonist to the Platonists, a Stoic to the Stoics, an Aristotelian to the Aristotelians, without being bound by any of them because his ultimate allegiance was to a God who was far superior to them all (see 1 Cor 9:19–20).

At one time it was common to say that the use of the term *logos* in the Fourth Gospel reflected Greek influence, but that view is no longer widely held and seems rather unlikely. Paul's encounter with philosophers in Athens was episodic in nature and had no real influence on his thought—he was in the city to evangelize, not to harmonize his view of God with that of the Greeks.[4] He warned Christians not to become entangled with Greek philosophy, though his words are too vague to enable us to trace any real connection between it and the church. In general, therefore, we can say that there was little or no contact between the Greek philosophers and the first generation of Christians. Nor should that surprise us. The Christians were mostly traders and humble people scattered across the eastern Mediterranean, whereas the philosophers were a self-appointed intellectual elite concentrated in Athens, Alexandria, and Rome. Their worlds did not normally overlap, let alone collide.

It is only in the second century that we begin to detect a more serious engagement between Christians and Greek philosophy, and it appears to have been of two kinds. Tertullian believed that the heresies that had appeared in the church were the direct result of syncretism between would-be "Christian thinkers" and pagan Greeks, and he was very precise in naming them. According to him, Valentinus was a Platonist and Marcion was a Stoic, though both men drew eclectically on Epicurus, Heraclitus, and Aristotle, with the inevitable result that their attempts to expound Christianity were an incomprehensible mish-mash.[5]

From a different perspective, the theologically orthodox Justin Martyr expounded the Christian faith from the standpoint of a gentile who had initially been attracted to philosophy but had later abandoned it for the

4. Attempts have sometimes been made to find connections between Paul and the leading philosophers of antiquity, but although it is certainly true that he dealt with some of the same subjects as they did (slavery, family relationships, etc.) it cannot really be said that there was any dialogue between them. See Joseph R. Dodson and David E. Briones, *Paul and the Giants of Philosophy: Reading the Apostle in Greco-Roman Context* (Downers Grove, IL: IVP Academic, 2019).

5. Tertullian, *De praescriptione haereticorum*, 7.3–6.

church's interpretation of the Hebrew Bible. Unlike Tertullian, he was quite complimentary of the philosophers of antiquity:

> Philosophy is, in fact, the greatest possession, and most honorable before God, to whom it leads us and alone commends us; and these are truly holy men who have bestowed attention on philosophy. What philosophy is, however, and the reason why it has been sent down to men, have escaped the observation of most; for there would be neither Platonists, nor Stoics, nor Peripatetics [Aristotelians], nor Theoretics, nor Pythagoreans, this knowledge being one. I wish to tell you why it has become many-headed.[6]

As Justin understood it, the truth of God was partially known to the philosophers, but each of them latched onto particular aspects of it, which they then developed into dogmas that were distortions of the truth. Justin also believed that different philosophers had done this with varying degrees of error. To his mind, the worst were the Stoics, because they made no claim to know the divine at all. Next came the Peripatetics (Aristotelians), who were discredited in Justin's eyes because they charged for sharing their "wisdom," which he thought ought to be the common property of humanity. After that came the Pythagoreans, who demanded a thorough knowledge of music, astronomy, and geometry before advancing to the contemplation of the divine. Finally, he hit on the Platonists, who seemed to come closer to the Christian ideal than any of the others. As he wrote:

> I spent as much time as I could with [a Platonist] who had recently settled in our city ... and I progressed, and made the greatest improvements daily. And the perception of immaterial things quite overpowered me, and the contemplation of ideas furnished my mind with wings, so that in a little while I supposed that I had become wise; and such was my stupidity, I expected immediately to look upon God, for this is the purpose of Plato's philosophy.[7]

6. Justin Martyr, *Dialogue with Trypho*, 2.
7. Justin Martyr, *Dialogue with Trypho*, 2.

Justin's preference for Plato over and above the others was to find considerable echo in later Christian writings, but he was still well aware of Plato's inadequacies. As he put it,

> I confess that I both boast and with all my strength strive to be found a Christian; not because the teachings of Plato are different from those of Christ, but because they are not in all respects similar. ... Whatever things were rightly said among all men, are the property of us Christians.[8]

Here we find a theme that would recur in later centuries and can still be encountered among Christian apologists. This is the conviction that all truth is God's truth. Therefore, if a non-Christian says something that is true, Christians can appropriate it because (in effect) these unbelievers have stumbled upon something that belongs to God, and therefore also to Christians. Unbelievers may not recognize it as such and will not attribute it to a God whom they do not acknowledge, but that does not matter to Christians, because they detect the truth wherever it is to be found and in appropriating it are doing no more than reclaiming what belongs to them already.

What finally turned Justin away from Platonism was his realization that the Platonic doctrine of the immortality of the soul cannot be correct. The human soul is part of the world of death and decay, which is why it sins. If it were immortal, it would be like God and therefore sinless. A sinful soul that is nevertheless immortal is a contradiction in terms, but Plato failed to perceive that. The life of the soul, such as it is, is a gift from God who allows the soul to share in something that does not properly belong to it. It was because they knew this that the Christians were not afraid of death. They were unjustly slandered by pagans who did not understand them because the Christians were living for God and not for their own pleasure.[9]

It was this realization that led Justin to consider something in the Jewish tradition that was lacking among the Greeks—prophecy. By this, Justin meant not just foretelling the future, though that was part of it, but the proclamation of a morally upright life lived in conscious dependence

8. Justin Martyr, *Second Apology*, 13.

9. Justin Martyr, *Second Apology*, 12.

on God. The prophets did not waste their time speculating about the structure of the universe but concentrated on the responsibility of each person to live in the way that the Creator had ordained. Justin admitted that some types of philosophy, notably Stoicism, promoted virtuous living and that the Stoics suffered martyrdom as a result, but the absence of a divine dimension robbed virtue of its meaning by denying that it had a purpose. What was the point of sacrificing everything for nothing? Christian suffering led not only to death but to resurrection, the belief that Paul's philosophers on the Areopagus found so incredible but that lies at the very heart of the Christian message. No philosophy can lead to life after death, but Jesus Christ had come back from the grave and had promised a new and eternal life to those who believed in him. Socrates had grasped at the truth to a limited extent, but no one put their faith in him because he had no power over death. Only in Christ was the great enemy of humankind defeated, and only in and through him was it possible to come to a fully satisfying knowledge of God.[10]

INTELLECTUAL ENGAGEMENT

The second Christian century saw an outpouring of Christian writings whose aim was to persuade the Greco-Roman world of the truth of Christianity. Couched in terms of respect for the Roman Empire, and often addressed to the emperor himself, these writings are collectively known as Explanations, or to use the Greek term, Apologies, after the title of Justin Martyr's two works. It is doubtful whether the emperors ever read them or even knew of their existence. The most intellectual of them, Marcus Aurelius (161–180), seems to have been completely ignorant of them, even though their subject matter would have interested him and he was well aware of the growing influence of Christians in his empire. Marcus Aurelius was a Stoic philosopher with strong Platonic leanings, which might have made him sympathetic to Christian ideas, but it did not. On the contrary, he was one of the most savage persecutors of the church, displaying a hostility to what he saw as superstition that had not been seen for two generations.[11]

---

10. Justin Martyr, *Second Apology*, 10.

11. The first persecution of Christians occurred after the great fire of Rome in AD 64 and the second in the reign of Domitian (81–96). There was no further outbreak of general persecution until Marcus Aurelius issued his decree in AD 177, after which the phenomenon became more common.

It was around the time of this persecution that the first pagan refutation of Christianity saw the light of day. It was called *Ho alēthēs Logos* (The true Logos), in a conscious reference to John's Gospel, and was the work of Celsus (fl. ca. 178), a pagan polemicist who had a remarkably broad grasp of both Jewish and Christian beliefs. Celsus is known to us now only because his work was refuted at great length by the Christian theologian, biblical scholar, and part-time philosopher Origen (ca. 185–254). Origen wrote his great work *Contra Celsum* about two generations after Celsus, whom he seems to have confused with an Epicurean philosopher of the same name. In fact, Celsus was more of a Platonist than anything else, which may be why his work was perceived to be so dangerous to the Christian cause. Celsus believed that he had demolished the claims of Christianity, and many of his arguments against it were so powerful that they would reappear, sometimes in modified forms, in later centuries, and a few can still be heard today.

So serious was the challenge presented by Celsus that Origen felt bound to refute it point by point. He quoted Celsus at considerable length and (it is generally agreed) with great accuracy, so that we can reconstruct his polemic without much difficulty. It seems likely that Celsus had read Justin Martyr and that he was reacting to his arguments in favor of Christianity, which he obviously thought demanded a response. That in itself is enlightening. Celsus had no time for the new religion, but he could not ignore it. More tellingly, Celsus's arguments show that he accepted the basic premises of Christianity regarding the nature of reality but contended that the Christians had given bad answers to real questions. In other words, Christians and pagan philosophers started from the same intellectual positions, but it was the latter who came up with the better solutions because they were grounded in reason, not in superstition.

It was this contrast that irritated Celsus and drove him to write. As he saw it, Christianity, and its parent Judaism, were irrational and therefore absurd. Moses had broken with the universal wisdom of his time by rejecting pagan notions of divinity and insisting on the worship of one God. Even worse, he and his followers taught that this one God had revealed himself exclusively to Israel. This led to the claim that a small and insignificant barbarian nation knew the secrets of the universe that were hidden from great and highly cultured peoples like the Egyptians and the Greeks. Christians took this absurdity to a whole new level by claiming that God had come to earth and embraced both sin and death in order to deliver humanity from their curse. Had Jesus been a moral teacher put to death by an ignorant mob that saw him as a threat, Celsus might have sympathized with his followers, but they went much further than that. To them, Jesus was not just a teacher but a savior who had solved the problem of evil, not by ignoring and transcending it in the philosophical manner, but by confronting it and defeating it by his death and resurrection. This made no sense to Celsus, and he railed against it with all the invective at his command.

In defense of Celsus, from his point of view he had a case that is still heard today. If God is the supreme Good, all powerful and loving, why did he not simply abolish evil by decree and restore humanity to its predestined glory? How could the perfect spiritual Being get involved with matter to the point of becoming a man himself, being born, as the apostle Paul put it, "in the likeness of sinful flesh"? (Rom 8:3) Similar criticisms are heard today from people who say that if God is a God of love, how could he have consigned his Son to a cruel and unjust death? The gospel of Christ makes no more sense to them than it did to Celsus—it simply does not stand to reason! Then as now, the answer to this is that the God of the critics is too small, and their notion of love is truncated. Celsus had a picture of abstract perfection that he assumed must be God and saw any deviation from that ideal as irrational and immoral—and therefore impossible. Christians do not reject reason or morality, but they put such things in their place. The God of the Bible transcends pure reason and defines morality as obedience to his will, not as subservience to an artificial code of values enshrined in laws that cannot be broken.

Celsus had no concept of a personal God who enters into a relationship of love with his creatures, or at least with some of them, whom he has chosen for eternal life. It is this aspect of exclusiveness that is so hard for non-Christians to accept, and understandably so. Why does God choose some people and reject others? There is no answer to that question, but simple observation shows that it is so. It is not merely that not everyone has heard the gospel message, though that is true, but that many of those who have heard it have either rejected it or failed to understand it. It is the parable of the sower and the seed all over again (Matt

13:1–9, 18–23). The seed is the same wherever it is sown, but the ground on which it lands is different. In some cases, the seed never takes root at all. In others, it grows for a time but the growth is eventually choked by weeds or restricted by stones in the way. Only in the fertile soil does it bear fruit, and even then to varying degrees. Why God should have planned it this way is unknown to us, and we have no right to question his judgment. The proper response of the Christian is to be grateful for the gift of salvation, and to recognize that it is indeed a gift and not a right or an entitlement. The rational mind cannot get its head around this, and so we find people like Celsus and those who think like him rejecting a message that makes no sense to them.

Put as starkly as this, it would seem that there is no reconciliation possible between a philosophy based on reason and a religion based on faith. But is it necessary to conclude that we must accept one extreme or the other? In the time of Celsus, it must have appeared like that. Only a few years after he wrote, Tertullian was saying as much from the Christian point of view. He had probably never read Celsus or even heard of him, but his words could serve as a fitting rebuttal: "The Son of God died—it is [utterly] credible because it is unfitting. And he was buried and rose again; it is certain, because it is impossible."[12]

Tertullian was not saying that the death and resurrection of Christ the Son of God made no sense, as some modern critics have alleged, but challenging the assumptions of the intelligentsia of his time. God is not obliged to conform to human notions of what is fitting or possible, and the fact that he did not do so is proof of his superiority to the limitations of the human mind.

Seen in this light, it is hard not to conclude that no relationship is possible between a philosophy grounded in human reason and a religion based on faith. Tertullian and Celsus would have agreed on that, though the choice each of them made was completely different. But is it necessary to make such a sharp distinction? Neither Tertullian nor Celsus would live to see it, but in fact there would be an evolution in the philosophical

12. Tertullian, *De carne Christi*, 5.4. The Latin text is: *Et mortuus est Dei Filius; [prorsus] credibile est quia ineptum est; et sepultus resurrexit; certum est quia impossibile.* In modern times, this famous phrase has often been abbreviated and misinterpreted as "I believe because it is absurd" (*Credo quia absurdum est*), which, as endless scholars have pointed out, Tertullian never said.

world that would bring at least one strand of philosophical thought closer to Christianity—so close, in fact, that later generations of Christians would struggle to see any difference between it and what they themselves believed.

The development in question was the work of Plotinus (ca. 204–270), an Egyptian Greek who studied in Alexandria and later went to Rome, where he set up a school whose teaching would rival that of the Academy in Athens and eventually take it over. Plotinus was a Platonist of sorts, but he diverged from the master in important ways that were to transform the whole notion of Platonism. Where Plato had thought of spirit and matter as incompatible realities that could never meet or mingle with each other, Plotinus conceived of them as complementary parts of a single universe of Being. He believed that there was a continuum from the source of all Being, which he called the One, right down to the lowest form of existence. He did not reject the notion of a hierarchy, which later came to be called the Great Chain of Being, and he insisted that everything was connected to everything else. Not only did this provide a principle of unity that bound the different aspects of reality together, but it allowed for communication from one level of being to another. Most importantly, it provided a way for those lower down the scale (or chain) to rise higher, and even to come into the presence of the One itself.

Movement of this kind, where human beings were concerned, was a kind of mystical experience that could be assimilated to the Christian knowledge of God. According to Plotinus, the One gave birth to the Mind (Nous), which in turn generated the Soul (Psyche), through which the rest of Being was produced. There is a remarkable parallelism between this conception of reality and the Christian doctrine of the Trinity:

PLOTINUS	CHRISTIANITY
One	Father
Nous	Logos ("Word")
Psyche	Spirit

The parallelism is even more striking when we realize that Plotinus's One (*to on*) is matched by the Christian form (*ho ōn*), the difference being that Plotinus's concept is expressed in the neuter, whereas the Christian equivalent is in the masculine, indicating a person instead of an abstraction. Furthermore, the Christian *ho ōn* can be applied to the Son (as it regularly is in Greek Orthodox icons, for example) as well as to the Father. Can this coincidence be accidental?

Most modern commentators assume that similarities of this kind are likely to derive from Christian appropriation of Platonic philosophical concepts, but in this instance that cannot be the case. The Christian *ho ōn* comes from Revelation 1:8 and so can be dated to the late first century, whereas the Plotinian equivalent first appears at least two hundred years later. Did Plotinus get the idea from the Christians?

Plotinus nowhere spoke about Christianity, and nowadays it is generally assumed that he had no contact with it, but that is not self-evident. There is an ancient tradition that says that he professed Christianity as a young man but then abandoned it for the pursuit of philosophy, which is certainly possible. But even if that was not the case, it is hard to believe that Plotinus had no knowledge of Christianity at all. His teacher in Alexandria was Ammonius Saccas, who twenty years earlier had been the instructor of the Christian Origen.[13] Plotinus and Origen probably never met each other, but they had the same teacher and therefore would have moved in similar circles. Origen was already a Christian when he studied with Ammonius, who must have known what his pupil believed and had at least some affinity with it. There is much that we do not know about their relationships, but in the intellectual world of Alexandria it would be surprising if Christianity was completely unknown in the early third century. It is far more likely that it exercised a covert but significant influence on the philosophical climate in general, as pagan thinkers strove to find ways to absorb attractive aspects of Christian teaching into their own systems.

What we do know is that Plotinus read and attacked a number of Gnostic thinkers, who (for the most part) were attempting a synthesis of pagan philosophy and Christianity, so it is highly improbable that he would have been completely ignorant of the new faith. Plotinus does not admit it, and perhaps much of what he taught was the product of subconscious

13. This is not absolutely certain. It is known that Ammonius Saccas had a pupil called Origenes, but he may have been someone else.

osmosis, but is there a better explanation for his radical reshaping of traditional Platonism? Whether he desired it or not, Plotinus revamped Plato's ideas in a way that made them more acceptable to Christians, who were not slow to perceive the connections. This Neoplatonism, as we now call it, would exert a powerful influence on Christian thought in the fourth century and later, and the possibility that it was Christianity that played a role in the transformation of Platonism should not be dismissed out of hand.

In some respects, Plotinus transformed Plato's understanding of reality, often in ways that appealed to Christians. For example, where Plato conceived of a Creator who had to work with pre-existing forms and matter, Plotinus said that the forms belonged to the Nous and that the Creator was the One from which the Nous derived its existence. Plotinus also had a more refined concept of evil than Plato had. To his mind, all Being was good by definition, and evil only entered the world because parts of it—including the human race—were not fully developed. In other words, their Being was inadequate or faulty in some respects. It was as if Being were a kind of cheese with holes in it, or perhaps a doughnut with its center missing. Because of that, Plotinus thought of evil as non-Being (*to mē on*), an idea that was to have considerable attraction to later generations of Christians, even though it is not found in the Bible.

It is important to understand that when Plotinus spoke about evil he was thinking primarily about physical defects, not moral ones. As he understood it, the material universe was entirely good, not because it is modeled on Plato's forms, but because it was made with the help of the gods, whom he believed were benevolent. He rejected both Stoic materialism and Stoic determinism, which he regarded as traps that would inevitably lead the unwary into believing that evil has real existence, because the world as we see it is so obviously imperfect. Instead of that, like a good Platonist, Plotinus insisted that our true nature is spiritual, not material. If we concentrate on that, we can come to the realization that even apparently bad things like poverty and disease work to our benefit, because they teach us not to be enthralled by the pleasures of this life.

Matter, according to Plotinus, is inherently defective, making imperfection inevitable. The gods can try to apply the forms to it, but the forms have to work within the limitations imposed by the nature of the matter on which they operate. Without the forms, matter has no real existence—it is in fact a kind of non-Being in itself. In a sense, it was not unlike the description found in Genesis 1:2: "The earth was without form and void, and darkness was over the face of the deep." The difference between Plotinus and Genesis is that in the Genesis account, matter *does* exist and is good, because it was made by the Creator God—it is not eternal as it was in the minds of Platonists. Plotinus had no real explanation for the origin of matter. He refused to see it as an evil power in opposition to the Good, because that would result in what philosophers call "dualism," the belief that there are two principles in the universe that are diametrically opposed to one another. That belief was entertained by the Gnostic sects and was common among the Persians, but it went against the Neoplatonist conception of the One that rules all things, and so it had to be rejected. The only alternative was to suggest that matter somehow escaped from Good, perhaps because the Soul, having already emanated from the One and the Nous, no longer had the energy to reproduce itself. Just as light fades the further it gets from its source, so the essential goodness of all things weakened as it passed through the different emanations, leaving us with a world that was overcome by the surrounding darkness. It was a very unsatisfactory explanation, and Christians rejected it outright. According to the apostle John: "The light shines in the darkness, and the darkness has not overcome it" (John 1:5). That was a message of hope, an affirmation of the goodness of all things, including matter, that Plotinus could never bring himself to accept, and that ultimately ensured that his renovated form of Platonism would fail to displace Christianity in the struggle for hearts and minds.

CONFRONTATION

Plotinus lived in the last generation of pagan antiquity in which it was unnecessary to grapple seriously with Christianity. His disciple Porphyry (234–305) was not so fortunate. By the time he took over from Plotinus, Christians were too numerous to be ignored, and Porphyry launched a series of attacks on them. These anti-Christian writings were destroyed after Christianity became the official state religion, so we do not know as much about them as we would like, but it seems from quotations and rebuttals of his views in other works that his general lines of objection were similar to those of Celsus. Oddly, though, Porphyry was respectful of Judaism, probably because it was an ancient religion and ethnically based in a way that made it no real threat to him. Perhaps even more strangely, he was frequently quoted by Christian writers who borrowed many of his ideas, though they were forced to refute his attacks on them.

After Porphyry's time the Neoplatonists moved off in a direction that took them further away from Christianity than ever. The leader of this reaction was Iamblichus (245–325), who succeeded Porphyry as the leading champion of Neoplatonism and completed its transformation into a religion. Far from recognizing that Platonism would have benefitted from adopting the main outlines of the Christian doctrine of God, Iamblichus preferred to resuscitate ancient pagan practices, believing that animal sacrifices, for example, could be efficacious in persuading the gods to adopt a positive attitude to their worshipers and help them in their sufferings, just as the God of the Bible was expected to help his followers. Iamblichus lived long enough to see the end of the persecution of Christians and their emergence into the public sphere, but this did nothing to moderate his approach. On the contrary, he and his successors dug their heels in and did what they could to develop an alternative theology based on a fusion of paganism with their philosophy—a combination that would have seemed strange to earlier generations of Platonists, to put it mildly.

One positive development of this was the growing tendency among pagan philosophers, led by Porphyry, to bury their differences and seek to harmonize Plato with Aristotle and the Stoics, in particular. Plato naturally dominated this movement because both Aristotelianism and Stoicism were in some sense outgrowths of his ideas, but the result was a kind of fusion between idealism, pragmatism, and the pursuit of a virtuous life that could offer a plausible alternative to Christianity. It was this sort of combination that appealed to a man like Julian the Apostate (331–363), who was brought up as a Christian but who renounced his faith when he reached adulthood. By dynastic chance he became emperor in 361 and did what he could to restore paganism as the state religion. He was not on the throne long enough for his policy to take effect, and it would probably have failed anyway because the paganism that he professed was a Neoplatonic concoction that bore only a superficial resemblance to anything that real pagans believed.

The truth was that paganism could not be systematized in the way that the Neoplatonists thought. It might appeal to a few intellectuals but would never touch the bulk of the population, who could neither appreciate nor adopt what was essentially an abstract system of ideas. Christianity, by contrast, was never an elitist belief, inaccessible to the masses. From the beginning it had appealed to a wide spectrum of people, ranging from the well-educated to the ignorant—indeed, that was one of the reasons why the philosophical establishment had opposed it as strongly as it did. When pagan philosophers tried to replicate this broad appeal, they were bound to fail because their whole approach was inimical to that of the Christians, who treated all human beings alike.

The hostility that developed between the pagan philosophical establishment and the Christians continued for two centuries following the legalization of the church. At times there were attempts to reach out to Christians, and many pagan teachers had Christian pupils. Sometimes they tolerated them because they had little choice, but on occasion they seem to have made a genuine effort to reach out across the ideological divide. But however hard they may have tried to do that now and again, they never succeeded in adopting Christianity or integrating it into their own philosophical projects. They remained fundamentally hostile and irreconcilable, until finally, in AD 529, the Emperor Justinian I (527–565) was prevailed upon by Christians to close down the philosophical schools. Many of the remaining pagans chose Persian exile over conversion to Christianity, and although some later returned to the Roman Empire, they were never again able to mount serious opposition to the new religion.

From the Christian side, awareness of the Greek philosophical schools was widespread from the beginning, and serious engagement with them was characteristic of the second-century apologists, as we have already seen. Open confrontation, though, was slower to develop. For the most part, Christians believed that they had no need of Greek philosophy, because whatever was true in it had already been revealed by God to the OT prophets. Most of them were inclined to agree with Jews that Plato and his colleagues read Moses and borrowed their best ideas from him, so why should Christians bother with them? It was only when the pagans started to attack Christianity that they felt the need to respond in kind, which is what Origen did in his great work *Against Celsus*. But even then, Origen wrote about seventy years after Celsus, so it can hardly be said that there was a debate between them. Origen was almost certainly writing to reassure Christians that they had nothing to fear from pagan opponents, of whom Celsus was a prime example, not to confront Celsus (or any followers whom he may have had) directly.

Even after Christianity was legalized and Christians began to occupy important posts in the imperial administration, their leading thinkers were more concerned to defend Christian doctrine against heretics who claimed to belong to the church, rather than against outsiders. There are any number of fourth- and fifth-century treatises directed against the teaching of men like Arius, Apollonarius, and Nestorius, not to mention Donatus and Pelagius in the Latin-speaking West, but none that were specifically aimed at Plotinus. Porphyry was a different story. At least thirty Christian writers took up their pens to refute him, and it is largely thanks to them that we know as much as we do about what he had to say. Like most of his fellow pagans, Porphyry rejected Christianity on the ground that it was irrational. According to him, virgins do not give birth, nor do men rise from the dead—two key Christian beliefs that make the faith incredible. There was much more than this, of course, but if the central teachings of the church could not be accepted, then the rest would naturally fall away as well.

The most effective rebuttal of Porphyry came from Lactantius (ca. 250–ca. 325), a pagan convert to Christianity, whose great work, the *Divine Institutes*, was expressly intended to be a philosophically based defense of Christian teaching in answer to men like him. Starting with the charge of irrationality, Lactantius turned it on its head and used it to attack the entire pagan philosophical tradition. Even someone like Socrates was not spared because, as Lactantius reminded his readers, his dying request was that a rooster should be sacrificed to the god Asclepius, which is about as irrational an act as it is possible to imagine.[14] The only philosophers who came off lightly were the skeptics, precisely because they were critical of the knowledge that their colleagues claimed to have. But even the skeptics must be faulted because, in their reaction to the irrational beliefs of pagan philosophy and religion, they went to the opposite extreme and denied that any knowledge was possible. That was absurd, said Lactantius, because even to deny the possibility of knowing anything was to assert a kind of knowledge—the claim was self-contradictory.

14. Lactantius, *Divine Institutes*, 3.20.

What Lactantius proposed instead was a middle way—not knowledge as such, but wisdom. The one who possesses wisdom will have discernment and be able to judge what is more likely to be true, without pretending to have the kind of absolute certainty that knowledge implies. Here we are reminded of the words that William Shakespeare (1564–1616) put into the mouth of Hamlet: "There are more things in heaven and earth, Horatio, than are dreamt of in your philosophy."[15] That, in a nutshell, was the approach taken by Lactantius.

Lactantius also differed from the common Platonic and Stoic belief that knowledge and virtue are the same thing. Like the apostle Paul, he maintained that it is possible to know what is right but not to do it (Rom 7:15–20). Wrongdoing is not the fruit of ignorance but of disobedience to the commands of God, a disobedience that is the result of our rebellion against him. As far as Lactantius was concerned, no amount of studying the world could solve this problem. The only way to escape evil and to live a life pleasing to God is to turn to him in repentance and faith. Knowledge of the truth is important, but it is only effective if it is applied in the context of a right relationship with God, and it was here that the pagans failed most spectacularly. They could not be in that right relationship because they did not acknowledge God as he has revealed himself in the Bible and in Christ, who is the key to understanding what the Bible means. Furthermore, said Lactantius, a virtuous life in this world could never be more than a preparation for eternal life in heaven. The reason for that is obvious. Even the most virtuous man will not live forever, and his virtue will die with him. In other words, concentrating on virtue in this life is itself ultimately irrational because it misses the point of human existence. We are pilgrims on a journey to another world, and it is only in that context that our present behavior makes any sense.

The arguments advanced by Lactantius were picked up and developed further by Ambrose of Milan (339–397) and his famous pupil Augustine of Hippo (354–430), and thus became fundamental to the Christian tradition, at least in the Latin-speaking world. They undercut the philosophical belief that education would inevitably improve human behavior and focused attention on something much deeper and more intractable. Whereas the philosophers had tended to think of evil in physical terms—earthquakes, disease, and so

---

15. William Shakespeare, *Hamlet*, 1.5.166–67.

on—Christians shifted the discussion to the state of the soul in the presence of God. Natural disasters were certainly unfortunate, but they were not "evil" in the true sense of the word. Much worse, and much more common, was the alienation of the human spirit from the mind and purpose of its Creator. That alienation could not be wished away, even if it was recognized. Only divine intervention could do what was necessary, and that led naturally to God's self-revelation, first in the Law of Moses and then supremely in the life, death, and resurrection of Jesus Christ, the Son of God become man.

Seen from that angle, the virgin birth and the resurrection were not irrational at all. On the contrary, they were necessary for the redemption of the human race to be possible. In the end, according to these Christian thinkers, pagan philosophy was superficial. The more intelligent pagans realized that something was wrong, but they lacked the philosophical framework required to explain how it could be put right. That framework was revealed to the church. As the apostle Paul put it when speaking to the Corinthians: "We have the mind of Christ" (1 Cor 2:16). What was a stumbling block to the Jews and folly to the Greeks was the power and wisdom of God, which was far stronger than anything a mere human mind could devise (1 Cor 1:23–25). Against that, pagans like Porphyry had no answer that would carry conviction.

The intellectual failure of ancient paganism did not mean that its last defenders did not go down fighting. They did, but increasingly they had to appear in a kind of pseudo-Christian guise and try to justify their pagan beliefs as acceptable substitutes for what soon became the official religion of the Roman Empire.[16] The outstanding representative of this last gasp of pagan philosophy was Proclus (412–485), whose biographer Macrinus portrayed him as a man of strong religious conviction and unimpeachable virtue—not unlike a Christian saint. Equally telling is the fact that Proclus interpreted all reality, including the Platonic forms, as having a triadic structure. He saw that as going back to the Pythagoreans and their devotion to the triangle, but it was no coincidence that the idea was revived in the fifth century just as Christians were debating the contours of the Trinity. He

16. Christianity achieved that status on February 27, 380, when the Emperor Theodosius I (378–395) issued a decree to that effect. It led to a rapid suppression of venerable pagan institutions and the widespread conversion of pagan temples into churches.

was of course a polytheist, but he ranked the gods in a hierarchy of three orders—the lowest being that of the intellective gods, that is to say, the gods who contemplated their superiors, who were classified as "intelligible." In between these were gods who were both contemplating and contemplated, and they formed the necessary link between the other two. This is not the same as saying that the Holy Spirit dwells in our hearts by faith and leads us to worship the Father by making him "intelligible" to us through the mediation of the Son, who is both worshiper (of the Father) and worshiped, but the parallel is uncanny and must surely be due to underlying Christian influence.

Proclus also broke with the Platonic tradition in asserting, as Christians did, that matter is essentially good and so cannot be regarded as the inevitable source of evil. But as he had no doctrine of sin as the fruit of disobedience, Proclus was forced to conclude that evil is the result of a clash between two good things. Water is good in itself, and essential to life, but a person can also drown in it. Likewise, fire brings heat and light, but also destruction if it is allowed to rage unchecked. How this happens in a world that is permeated with the divine at every level and is basically good, Proclus could not explain. As with his fellow pagans, he found it hard to conceive of evil in moral terms and relied instead on what we would think of as natural disasters. From the Christian point of view this was self-contradictory—since it could not be that two good things would clash with evil results—and also superficial. As Jesus told the Pharisees of his day, evil comes not from outside a man but from inside, from the thoughts of the heart that is turned away from God (Matt 15:11; Mark 7:20). Proclus, for all his similarity to Christians, never managed to absorb that fundamental point.

The inability of pagan philosophers to distinguish clearly between the divine and the material world was to dog them to the very end. We see this clearly in the work of John Philoponus (490–570), a Christian from Alexandria who was mentored by a pupil of Proclus and was thus very familiar with late Neoplatonism. Around the time that Justinian closed the philosophical schools of Athens, Philoponus wrote a lengthy treatise *Against Proclus*, in which he demolished the latter's arguments that the material world must be eternal. Proclus had claimed that because the Creator does not change, his creation does not change either, nor was there ever a time when it had not existed. Those familiar with the Christian heresy of Arianism will recognize this argument, which was used by the opponents of Arius to say that the Father cannot have existed before the Son, since if he had, he would not have been eternal, at least not as Father.

Philoponus's task was made somewhat easier by the fact that Plato had not taught that the universe was eternal—that was the doctrine of Aristotle. He thus decoupled Plato from Aristotle, reversing (or at least contesting) a trend that had been developing since Porphyry's time, and launched into a criticism of Aristotelianism that was at least as telling as his denunciation of Proclus. Aristotle had found it hard to explain how change could occur in a world where matter was eternal, and had resolved this problem by saying that the changes we observe are changes of form, not of substance. In other words, matter assumes different shapes and sizes but stays fundamentally the same. Philoponus, however, wanted to insist that God made the world out of nothing. He understood motion (and thus change) as something inherent in the objects that God created. In this way he developed an early form of the theory of dynamics, which was not appreciated in his day but has survived to become one of the fundamental ingredients of modern physics.

Interestingly, though not surprisingly, Philoponus's theory was supported by Galileo (1564–1642), who had his own objections to Aristotelianism. Unfortunately, Philoponus was far ahead of his time and, like Galileo, he suffered for it. He was condemned at the Third Council of Constantinople (680–681) and would have passed into oblivion had his writings not been rescued by scholars in the then rapidly expanding Islamic world. Unhindered by ecclesiastical anathemas, Christians living in Muslim lands were able to preserve his writings and to translate many of them into Syriac and Arabic, thus ensuring their survival. But Philoponus himself was not a Muslim, not least because he died in the year that Muhammad was born. He was a Christian who used Christian principles to defeat paganism on its own ground, and so comprehensive and compelling were his arguments that his opponents were never again able to mount a coherent counter-attack. The contest between Athens and Jerusalem was dead, at least in its classical form and for the time being, and Jerusalem had come out as the undoubted victor in the struggle.

CONCLUSION

There is no doubt that ancient pagan philosophy came off worse in the encounter with Christianity, at least in the short term. The writings of Plato and Aristotle would survive, but for centuries they were barely known in

Western Europe. Things were different in the Greek-speaking world of the Byzantine Empire and also among the Arabs, where the Greeks were translated and studied, and it is largely thanks to them that they were preserved, but even there their influence was filtered through the prism of monotheistic religion—Christianity in Byzantium, Judaism and Islam in the Middle East, North Africa, and Spain. The polytheism of the ancient world was definitively rejected and never resurfaced in a serious way. Even when the ancients were used in later times as a means of escaping from the hegemony of the church, that aspect of their thought remained a dead letter. The French revolutionaries, for example, erected statues to the goddess of Reason, drawing on classical models, but nobody seriously thought of reviving the cult of the Olympian gods. Idolatry, pederasty, and animal sacrifice, which seemed natural to the historical Plato and Aristotle, were gone for good.

Much the same can be said of the other schools of philosophy like Stoicism and Epicureanism. The memory of them lingered on in the literary works their devotees produced—Seneca, Marcus Aurelius, and Lucretius continued to be read, as of course did Cicero—but their thoughts were filtered through a Christian prism and adapted to a different intellectual climate. Christianity would be challenged, often by using these ancient writers as ammunition, but they were used selectively and the schools to which they originally belonged were not revived. The demise of pagan philosophy in AD 529 was permanent, and the world would never be the same again.

SUMMARY

1. Jews and Greeks had a limited knowledge of one another before the late fourth century BC, but serious interaction between them did not begin until after 300 BC, when Alexandria in Egypt became a major center of both Greek and Jewish culture.

2. Greek-speaking Jews in Alexandria tried to harmonize their Scriptures with Greek thought. The most important of these was Philo, a contemporary of Jesus and the apostle Paul, who believed that the best Greek philosophy was merely an adaptation of Hebrew thought to an alien environment. In fact, Philo was interpreting the Hebrew Bible along Greek (and especially Platonic) lines. His work would eventually become influential

among Christians, but it does not seem to have influenced the writers of the NT.

3. Christians began to engage with Greek philosophy in the second century AD, and tended to regard Plato as the philosopher whose beliefs were closest to theirs, though they did not hesitate to differ from Plato when necessary and regarded him as blind to the truth of the Christian gospel, despite his undoubted brilliance.

4. The first Greek philosopher to take Christianity seriously was Celsus, who wrote in the late second century AD. A generation later his work was refuted point by point by Origen, in a great work that has been preserved to the present time. Celsus claimed that Christianity was a logical absurdity, a charge that Origen denied.

5. Origen's younger contemporary Plotinus transformed classical Platonism into a kind of religion, which we now call Neoplatonism. It parallels Christianity in some important ways and in the next generation it was used by Porphyry, one of Plotinus's disciples, to attack the Christians, who did not hesitate to fight back with intellectual arguments of their own.

6. The fourth century witnessed the consolidation of Greek philosophy around Neoplatonic ideas and the development of Christian theology within the church. Many intellectual Christians had received a pagan philosophical education and did not hesitate to borrow Greek vocabulary and thought patterns to express their own beliefs. This stimulated both Christian and Greek thinkers, but did not lead to a fusion of Christianity with Neoplatonism or any other kind of Greek philosophy.

7. Greek philosophers were among the last holdouts against the spread of Christianity, which they resisted to the end. Christians did not absorb the philosophical traditions of ancient Greece but rejected them, and in AD 529 Emperor Justinian I closed the philosophical schools of Athens.

V

JERUSALEM TRIUMPHANT

The closure of the philosophical schools of Athens in AD 529 marks the symbolic end of the confrontation between pagan Greek philosophy and the Christian faith, but the direction of travel had been clear for some time before that. Christians were already confronting attempts to synthesize biblical and philosophical ideas in the time of Irenaeus of Lyons (d. 202), who wrote extensively against what he saw as heresy. Today we group these tendencies under the heading of "Gnosticism" because it appears to us, or at least it appeared to Christians in the late nineteenth century, that these writers were trying to interpret the Bible in the light of theories of knowledge based on pagan speculations. In particular, the Gnostics believed that God the Father of Jesus Christ was a higher deity than the Creator (*demiurge*), who had made an imperfect world. Some of these Gnostics identified this Creator with the God of the OT and used this identification to dismiss Judaism as an inferior religion. The most extreme case of that was attributed to Marcion (second century), a Greek from Pontus who migrated to Rome. Marcion was not a typical Gnostic, but his dismissal of the OT (and most of the NT, which shared its worldview) was unacceptable to the church and forced Christians to explain how the Creator and the Redeemer God were one and the same. Christians could not accept that the created order was faulty by design, and that inevitably led to confrontation.

By the time Christianity became a legal religion in the Roman Empire (AD 313), Gnosticism had been overcome and little more was heard of it.

The battle had shifted elsewhere, to the incarnation of the Son and the revelation of God as a Trinity of persons. These two things were distinct but closely interrelated, as the debates of the fourth and fifth centuries were to show. There would never be complete agreement among Christians about either of these doctrines, but when we look at them today, it is not always clear how much of the controversy was a matter of terminology and how much involved real substance. At the council of Chalcedon in 451, the majority view was that Jesus Christ was the divine Son of God in two natures, one divine and the other human. In themselves, these natures were incompatible, and they coexisted in the incarnate Christ without confusion, alteration, division, or separation.

This formula was uncongenial to the church of Alexandria, which was wedded to the belief that the incarnate Christ had only one nature and that the two-nature formula effectively created two different beings—Jesus of Nazareth the man and the Son of God. It was also uncongenial to the followers of Nestorius, who had been deposed as bishop (patriarch) of Constantinople in 431, for the opposite reason. The Nestorians thought that by confessing the incarnate Christ as a single divine person the humanity of Jesus was being compromised. Today, most people have come to accept that this was largely a question of terminology. The Alexandrians were using "nature" (*physis*) in a sense that was different from that of the Chalcedonians, and the Nestorians were unable to see that the word "person" (*prosōpon*) was being interpreted as equivalent to "identity" (*hypostasis*), which meant that there could only be one of them in Christ. Neither of these objections was surprising at the time, because the church had not yet defined its theological vocabulary with sufficient precision and could hardly be expected to do so overnight. In matters of substance, however, Nestorians, Monophysites (or Miaphysites), and Chalcedonians professed what was essentially the same belief, even if a common expression of it eluded them.

The christological disputes that erupted between 325 and 787 were not originally conceived in philosophical terms, but they had deep philosophical implications. In the ancient pagan world, terms like *ousia* ("being"), *hypostasis* ("substance," "identity"), *physis* ("nature"), and so on were used by different philosophical schools, but often in a fairly loose way. *Prosōpon* ("person") on the other hand, came from the theater originally and was a term unknown in philosophical discourse. When Christians had to explain who Jesus was, they had recourse to this vocabulary, but that did not mean that their beliefs were suddenly Hellenized.[1] What happened is that terms that had previously been somewhat vague were defined more closely in direct relation to Jesus Christ. In the process, the meaning of words like "God" and "man" were also defined more carefully than they had ever been before. Was it possible to be a man without having a human will, for example? No, was the answer, so Christ had two wills in accordance with his two natures. Could God take on human flesh without a human mind or soul and still be a genuine man? No. A real human being must have a rational soul, and so the incarnate Son of God had one, too.

But could a man die and return to life with a new nature? Here the answer was yes, because a man is a person, and a person controls its nature—not the other way around. Just as the Son of God could take on a second nature (his human one) without losing or compromising his first (divine) one, so he could die in that second nature and return from the dead without ceasing to be himself. Furthermore, what was possible for him is possible for us, too, because like him we are also persons. The implications of this for anthropology were enormous. Human beings do not cease to exist when their bodies die because as persons they continue into the next life. Some will go to heaven to live forever in the presence of God, while others will be cast into hell where they will be cut off from him, but either way they will continue to exist.

Furthermore, those who are destined for eternal salvation will not live independent lives of their own. They will be united with the Son in and by the Holy Spirit, and thus enjoy the fellowship of the three persons of the Godhead, though without becoming divine themselves. How this will work out in practice is a mystery, but it is the promise of Christ, who has gone ahead to prepare a place for those who follow him.

As far as the doctrine of the Trinity was concerned, it appeared that all parties in the ancient christological disputes were agreed that God is

1. That was the claim put forward by a number of nineteenth-century German theologians, developed most famously by Adolf von Harnack (1851–1930). It still resurfaces from time to time, though it has been decisively refuted by H. E. W. Turner in *The Pattern of Christian Truth: A Study in the Relations Between Orthodoxy and Heresy in the Early Church* (London: Mowbray, 1954).

three persons in one divine substance or being (*ousia*). The Father *begets* the Son, but in eternity, which effectively eliminates the temporal dimension inherent in the term "generation," and the Holy Spirit "proceeds" from the Father (John 15:26) in a way that makes him a distinct person and not the Son's twin brother. What the church did not determine was how the Son and the Holy Spirit were related to each other. They were both "consubstantial" (*homoousios*) with the Father, and therefore identical in that respect, but did the Spirit "proceed" from the Son as well as from the Father? That was the view held by Augustine of Hippo, and it became standard in the Western (Latin) church while remaining virtually unknown in the East. The doctrine of the "double procession" of the Holy Spirit eventually found its way into the Latin text of the Creed of Nicaea-Constantinople in the form of the word *Filioque* ("and from the Son"), which the Eastern churches have never accepted.[2]

How serious the *Filioque* dispute really is has been debated for centuries. The Western churches (Catholic and Protestant) have tended to regard it as secondary—a matter of terminology as much as anything else. But the Eastern churches are less sure about that. Some have emphasized the fact that the addition to the creed has never received conciliar assent, even if it may be true, whereas others—the majority—have been inclined to see in it a fundamentally different concept of God. If that is correct, then the superficially similar doctrine of the Trinity professed across the Christian world conceals two different ways of looking at reality and therefore two different ways of relating to God. Such a difference would have serious philosophical implications, which is why an apparently obscure theological controversy has been so intractable.

The doctrine of the double procession of the Holy Spirit may have been emerging even before Augustine, as something like it appears in the Pauline commentaries of the anonymous Ambrosiaster (fl. ca. 366–384), but it was Augustine who developed it and integrated it into his wider

2. This process was a long, drawn-out one. The word *Filioque* first appeared in the late sixth century (though it was not introduced at the Third Council of Toledo in 589, as is commonly alleged), and was accepted in most of western Europe during the reign of Charlemagne (768–814), though Rome apparently did not register it until about 1014. By then it had become a matter of controversy between East and West, as it still is a thousand years later.

theology.[3] For Augustine, God is love (1 John 4:15) and the persons of the Trinity represent this. The Father is the one who loves, the Son is the beloved, and the Holy Spirit is the love that flows between them and binds them together. In such a picture, the love of the Son for the Father must equal that of the Father for the Son, since otherwise it would be imbalanced. Logically, therefore, the Holy Spirit must proceed from both equally. In essence, this has been the doctrine of the Western churches ever since. The Eastern churches object to this interpretation because to their minds it obscures the principle of the oneness of deity, a principle that is manifested in and by the Father alone. They have never defined how the Spirit relates to the Son, but when asked this question, Eastern theologians have often referred to the baptism of Jesus as the model for understanding it (Matt 3:16–17; Mark 1:10–11: Luke 3:21–22; John 1:32–33). The Holy Spirit, they say, proceeds from the Father and *rests* on the Son, illuminating his true nature and revealing him to the world.

Whether these different approaches can be reconciled is one of the great challenges facing ecumenical dialogue between East and West. An attempt to do so was made at the Council of Florence in 1439 by saying that the Holy Spirit proceeds *principally* from the Father and *through* the Son, which agrees with the thought of Augustine, but this solution was rejected in the East. Modern ecumenical discussion has nevertheless usually developed along similar lines, though with particular nuances. For example, the German theologian Jürgen Moltmann (1926–) has suggested that we could say that the Holy Spirit proceeds from the Father *of* the Son, thereby acknowledging the Son's existence without involving him directly in the procession of the Holy Spirit.[4] This proposal appears to be a concession to the Eastern viewpoint, though Moltmann is careful to state that the Spirit "receives" from the Son, which is the reverse of what many Eastern theologians have claimed and may be regarded as an attempt to retrieve at least something of the traditional Western doctrine of the *Filioque*. Perhaps unsurprisingly, this way of thinking has so far not

3. See Ambrosiaster's commentary on Eph 3:17 in Ambrosiaster, *Commentaries on Galatians-Philemon*, ed. Gerald L. Bray, Ancient Christian Texts (Downers Grove, IL: InterVarsity Press, 2009), 45. It should be stressed that Ambrosiaster *hinted* at a double procession but did not explicitly affirm it.

4. Jürgen Moltmann, *The Trinity and the Kingdom: The Doctrine of God* (London: SCM Press, 1981), 182–87.

had much positive impact on either the East or the West, though if the dispute is ever to be overcome something along these lines would probably have to be the formula finally accepted.

From a philosophical standpoint, it is easy to see that the Eastern position is grounded in a concept of monotheism that insists that all things must derive from a single source—in this case, the Father. It is not an adoption of any particular philosophical doctrine but is intelligible to anyone schooled in Neoplatonism. The Western view is more complex. It does not deny monotheism but maintains that the one God is a community of persons into which those who are saved are integrated. The Eastern view emphasizes the role of the Father as Creator, though without denying that this role is shared with the Son and the Holy Spirit. By contrast, the Western approach emphasizes the Father as Redeemer, though again without denying the participation of the Son and the Holy Spirit in the work of redemption. The practical result of this is that Eastern theological thought concentrates on the concept of what has come to be called *theōsis* ("deification"), which involves a transformation of human nature into something approximating to the divine, whereas the Western equivalent focuses on "justification." This means that the Father accepts sinners as they are, without any transformation of their nature, because their sins have been paid for by the atoning blood of Christ.

Neither side totally excludes the other—the death and resurrection of the Son plays a central role in Eastern theology, just as "sanctification" in the Christian life is a rough equivalent of "deification," but the emphasis is different. As a result, the essentially mystical theology of the East remains alien to the consciousness of the West, despite occasional attempts to understand and absorb it, just as the great Western debates over the atoning work of Christ and justification by faith and not by works employ a theological language that the East finds hard to appreciate. Resolving the *Filioque* question would not change that overnight, but it is important for those engaged in such discussions to realize what their wider implications are.

Augustine extended his understanding of the Trinity as a fellowship of mutual love that produces perfect unity much farther than the doctrine itself would warrant. Basing himself on the statement in Genesis 1:26–27 that human beings have been created in the image and likeness of God, he sought to find evidence of a trinity in the human mind. What he came up with was a picture of the mind as a combination of memory, intellect, and will. Each of these things is distinct from the others, as we can see from the fact that one of them can be lost (or severely damaged) without destroying the mind as a whole. Each of them occupies the whole "space" of the mind, just as each of the persons of the Trinity is coterminous with the divine nature, and when the mind is functioning properly they work together in harmony, producing single, coherent actions. Augustine knew this was speculation on his part, but he believed it flowed logically from the biblical revelation of the divine image.

By developing this idea, Augustine virtually invented what we recognize as the discipline of psychology and fundamentally altered the ancient perception of reality. Future generations of philosophers would focus less on the nature of the external forces that shape our world and more on the inner state of the mind and its relationship to reality in general. In particular, questions of evil and suffering would concentrate less on material things like hunger and disease and more on thoughts and mental states like depression. The shift of emphasis was not total, and the earlier approach continues to find a place in modern debates, but it no longer dominates the discussion as it once did. We can see this clearly when we come to the question of God's impassibility. The classical mind thought of impassibility in terms of God's immunity to external influences—he could not be swayed or harmed by any power outside himself. But today, most people who think about impassibility view the question as one that affects the internal being of God. It is not so much a matter of whether God can suffer pain himself as whether he can feel our pain. If he can, then it seems natural to say that he suffers, not physically but mentally and spiritually. That is the modern approach, and in essence it can be traced back to Augustine.

Augustine died before the main outlines of Christian orthodoxy had been defined, which helps to explain why he appears to have been less dogmatic about the meaning of a term like "person" than would have been the case if he had written after the Council of Chalcedon. But later generations were able to read him in the light of subsequent developments, and it is only in modern times that greater historical awareness has led to a serious reassessment of his role in the definition of Christian orthodoxy.

What was happening during his lifetime, and what we can now see more clearly than those who were living through the process could, is that orthodoxy was taking on somewhat different forms. The Western Latin tradition was dominated by Augustine almost completely, but his works were not translated into Greek and remained largely unknown in the East. The Greek-speaking world was dividing into what would become Chalcedonian and non-Chalcedonian segments, only the first of which would be accepted as "orthodox" in the Roman world.

The non-Chalcedonians were divided into Monophysites and Nestorians, who were diametrically opposed to one another and incapable of forming a common front over against the Chalcedonians. For a while, they seriously disrupted the politics of the Eastern Roman Empire, but then an unprecedented and external force intervened to cut them off from it. This was the new religion of Islam, which first appeared in the early seventh century and very quickly overran the regions in which non-Chalcedonian Christianity was dominant. It would be some time before this new force settled down, but when it did it was clear that the change it had brought to the ancient world was permanent. Muslims, as the followers of Islam were called, found some aspects of ancient Greek philosophy very attractive, but they had to rely on non-Chalcedonian Christians as intermediaries who could (and did) translate that philosophy, first into Syriac (a form of Aramaic closely related to Hebrew) and then into Arabic. A new chapter in the history of both philosophy and theology was about to begin.

CHRISTIAN ORTHODOXY AND HELLENIC PHILOSOPHY

It took the church many centuries to refine its conception of orthodox belief, but Christians never doubted its existence because it was rooted not in intellectual arguments but in a personal, spiritual experience of God that in the final analysis could not be adequately defined in words. What the early church councils tried to do was avoid falling into error, with the result that there was much that they did not say at all. For example, they were adamant in affirming the doctrine of the essential goodness of creation but did not go into detail about the origin and nature of evil because the Bible did not do so. But in confronting Hellenic philosophy, Christians had to say something about it in order to defend biblical teaching. Inevitably, they would find themselves using the terminology of Hellenism in order to make themselves understood by their opponents, but in the process they would transform its meaning in ways that the surviving Hellenists would reject as a perversion of their beliefs.

This process has been interpreted in different ways, but it has never really been studied in depth. For at least two hundred years, the dominant view has been that Christianity was Hellenized by the massive importation of philosophical ideas that distorted the original Judeo-Christian faith. In the nineteenth century, it was sometimes claimed by apologists for the Roman Catholic church like John Henry Newman (1801–1890), that this was a positive development because it gave Christianity a framework that enabled it to conquer the intellectual bastions of antiquity and erect a new civilization in Europe, which came to be called "Catholicism." In contrast to that, there were many who protested that this evolution was negative and that Christian faith needed to be purified by returning to the Bible alone and rejecting all traces of Hellenism, which included the standard formulations of Christian orthodoxy in the ancient creeds. This negative approach to Hellenism came to be understood as "Protestantism" and was articulated by men like Adolf von Harnack (1851–1930). It has been strongly criticized and refuted in detail, but the broad outlines of this analysis are still commonly met with in general introductions to the subject and have contributed to popular misconceptions of both major strands of Western Christianity.

More recently, this way of looking at the subject has been challenged, not least by a revival of interest in the Eastern Christian tradition. The Latin-speaking world had never really absorbed the philosophical spirit of the Greeks and often found it difficult to translate their concepts. But Greek-speaking Christians could not get away from their language and found themselves using much the same vocabulary to express very different ideas. An obvious case in point is the word *logos* ("word"), which Plato had used in the sense of an impersonal mind that derived from the ultimate One, but which Christians applied directly to the Son of God, who is not only a person but an integral part of the divine Being. Another word that Christians used in a different sense was *ousia* ("being"), which was not objective in the way that it was in most Hellenistic thought. Christians could call the God of the Bible the "Supreme Being" if they wanted to, but the term did not come naturally to them. Once again, the reason was that, for the philosophers, the "Supreme Being" was an abstract principle, whereas for Christians God is both personal and directly present in the lives of his creatures.

The result was that Christians used terms like *logos* and *ousia* in ways that pagan intellectuals could not accept. Modern scholars usually agree that the pagans were right to protest, and some of them criticize Christian apologists for misrepresenting their opponents. But from the Christians' point of view, pagan beliefs were a caricature of the truth that comes from God. Men like Plato and Aristotle got it wrong because they lacked the faith that would make sense of biblical teaching. It was therefore up to Christians to unscramble their misunderstandings and restructure pagan philosophical notions so that they would be compatible with revealed truth. In their own eyes, the Christians were not dismissing ancient philosophy but rescuing it (insofar as that was possible) by stripping it of alien accretions. In the words of Niketas Siniossoglou, commenting on the strategy of Theodoret of Cyrrhus (393–458) in dealing with the philosophers:

> Theodoret's hybridizing of Plato and Moses requires the *ad hoc* abandonment of important structural elements and conceptual components of Plato's philosophy. Plato is treated as authoritative only to the extent that he agrees with Moses and Judaeo-Christianity. A predetermined reading of Plato is the inevitable consequence, and anything diverging from that is immediately condemned as Hellenic. ... The only criterion used for justifying either the assimilation or the condemnation of philosophical notions is compatibility with Christian "orthodoxy."[5]

There may have been arguments over some of the details, but the broad outlines are clear. For Christian apologists like Theodoret, the Bible was the non-negotiable starting point for our understanding of truth, and Plato was acceptable only to the extent that his views could be made to comply with the sacred text. Theodoret's somewhat older contemporary

---

5. Niketas Siniossoglou, *Plato and Theodoret: The Christian Appropriation of Platonic Philosophy and the Hellenic Intellectual Resistance* (Cambridge: Cambridge University Press, 2008), 22.

Augustine said exactly the same thing: "If those who are called philosophers happen to have said anything that is true, and agreeable to our faith, the Platonists above all, not only should we not be afraid of them, but we should even claim back for our own use what they have said, as from its unjust possessors."[6]

Theodoret and Augustine were both writing at a time when Christianity was in the ascendant but pagan philosophies were still tolerated by the state and embraced by a significant number of intellectuals to whom they had to make a case for their position. A century later, that was no longer true. In the Latin West, the breakdown of the Roman Empire had dealt a mortal blow to the tradition of classical education, though it took a generation or more to die out completely. Its last significant representative was Boethius (477–524), a Roman aristocrat who served the Ostrogothic king Theodoric (454–526) but tragically fell foul of him and was unjustly put to death. While he was in prison awaiting execution, Boethius composed his great work *De consolatione philosophiae* (*On the Consolation of Philosophy*), which was to become a classic in the Middle Ages. Boethius was an orthodox Christian who wrote on the Trinity and other theological subjects, but in the face of death he turned not to the Bible but to the heritage of ancient philosophy on which he had been brought up. He knew that he belonged to the last generation in the Latin West who could read the complete works of Plato and Aristotle in the original, and he feared that as they were lost, society and civilization would break down irretrievably. Keeping them alive and passing their wisdom on became the preoccupation of his last days, and although he was unable to complete his project of translating everything the great philosophers wrote into Latin, what he did manage to produce became the foundation of Western philosophical thought for the next millennium.

Why did a Christian like Boethius turn to philosophy? It was not that he doubted the teaching of Christ, but that he realized that something more was needed. Theodoric the Ostrogoth was a Christian (if an Arian one), but he was also an uncivilized barbarian. He could get to heaven, perhaps, but lacked the education he needed to live a good life on earth.

6. Augustine of Hippo, *De doctrina Christiana*, 2.60, trans. by Edmund Hill as *Teaching Christianity* (New York: New City Press, 1996), 159.

For that, Boethius turned first to Plato, and then—more significantly—to Aristotle. Plato taught Boethius to be courageous in the face of an undeserved death, just as Plato's hero Socrates had been. Socrates could not defeat his enemies physically any more than Boethius could, but he could triumph over them spiritually by clinging to the higher vision of life that Plato had him espouse—and that was most fully expressed in the *Timaeus*. But the practical tools needed for living in the world could only come from Aristotle, who had reduced the mysteries of creation to the power of logic. It was Aristotle's systematic pursuit of logic that attracted Boethius and led him to translate some of the master's basic works on the subject into Latin.

One of the great beauties of Aristotle, as far as Boethius was concerned, was that he did not contradict the Bible (as Neoplatonist philosophy did) but complemented it. The book of Genesis tells us that God created heaven and earth; Aristotle explained how the mechanisms of that creation actually worked. Had Boethius lived to complete his translations, the history of Western Europe might have been very different, but what he achieved was still enough to keep the idea of a rationally ordered secular culture alive. Best of all, the application of Aristotelian principles of logic to theology enabled Boethius to resolve questions that had eluded the grasp even of the great Augustine. In particular, he was able to appropriate Aristotle's analysis of both simplicity and relation(ship) and use them to explain the Trinity. On the one hand, God is simple in his nature, not composed of distinct parts, so that Father, Son, and Holy Spirit all share the same essence. But it is possible for a single essence to exhibit relations, even with itself, and this is what God does. He relates to himself in forms of self-identity without changing in his essence. Indeed, he *cannot* change in his essence, because if he could, he would no longer be relating to the same thing and the relationship would be compromised.

Aristotle's distinction between the absolute and the relative also made it possible for Boethius to explain how created things can be good (in a relative sense) without being part of the Good (in the absolute sense). Goodness can be predicated of both God and any of his creatures, but it is not a thing it itself, since if it were, creatures would also be divine. It is rather an attribute that must be understood in relation to the nature of the thing it is describing. When this principle is applied to the distinction between eternity and time, it becomes possible to understand how, in God's eyes, what happens in time is not eternal in itself, but eternally present (as opposed to past or future). In other words, what we experience as the "present" is eternity in the context of time. God can (and does) reveal himself as "I am" both because that is eternally true and because it is a truth that is accessible to us here and now, just as it always has been and always will be.

Boethius did not write what we would call systematic theology, but by his understanding of the principles of logic and of their compatibility with biblical revelation he laid the groundwork for the discipline that would emerge several centuries later. Systematic theology in the Christian sense was alien to ancient Greek philosophy, but thanks to Boethius and those who followed him it became a natural component of later Christian thought—philosophy, as medieval writers taught, was indeed to become the handmaid of theology.

The potential of Boethius would remain unrealized in Western Europe for nearly a thousand years because, although his works were read and copied assiduously, the conditions required for applying his ideas systematically were nonexistent. The Eastern Christian world knew nothing of him, of course, but there the legacy of ancient philosophy was preserved by an entirely different route that would come to influence the West centuries later and eventually provide the impetus for activating what Boethius had long before seen.

The key figure in the Eastern Church was an unknown writer who passed himself off as Dionysius the Areopagite, one of the few converts to Christianity at the time of the apostle Paul's visit to Athens (Acts 17:34). It would be nice to think that this identification was an accident, caused perhaps by a confusion between someone called Dionysius who may have come from Athens hundreds of years later, but unfortunately that is not the case. Pseudo-Dionysius, as he is now known, deliberately adopted the persona of this ancient convert in order to deceive his readers. We know this because among his writings are a series of letters, one of which was addressed to the apostle John, that contain statements to the effect that he was an eyewitness to events in the life of Jesus. Who he really was is unknown, but he was well-versed in the Neoplatonism of Proclus, whose works he freely plagiarizes. He may have been a student in the Athens

Academy shortly before its closure in 529, but whether he was or not, he was certainly determined to preserve its legacy in Christian dress.

Pseudo-Dionysius had no alternative but to present his philosophy in a Christian form, but it is not easy to tell how sincere his faith was. It is hard to see why, if he were a genuine Christian, he would have felt the need to conceal his true identity, but it has to be admitted that his deception was remarkably successful. Doubts were certainly expressed from time to time, and people like John Calvin (1509–1564) were unimpressed by his writings, but it was not until the nineteenth century that the forgery was finally exposed.[7] Long before that, his writings were used by many Christian apologists as evidence for the exact opposite of the truth—namely, that the Neoplatonists had copied Dionysius (and therefore the apostle Paul), not the other way around. When the truth was finally revealed, scholars hostile to Christianity pounced on the Dionysian corpus as the perfect example of the Hellenization of Christianity in late antiquity and used it to discredit much of the subsequent medieval tradition that had accepted it as genuine.

At first sight, it is easy to see how this judgment has been arrived at. Like the Neoplatonists, but unlike almost all other Christian writers of the period, Pseudo-Dionysius presented a complex series of orders leading from the everyday worshiper right up to God himself. He divided these orders into two sections—the "ecclesiastical" (on earth) and the "celestial" (in heaven)—and called them hierarchies, a word that he seems to have invented. The ecclesiastical hierarchy was a mirror image of the celestial one, and each rung of the ladder brought the believer closer to the presence of God. The celestial hierarchy consisted of angels and archangels, each of whom had an assigned place in the divine economy.[8]

Closely connected to this were the divine names by which God is known to those to whom he has revealed himself. It would normally be expected that a Christian writer would concentrate on the Trinity, but although Pseudo-Dionysius mentioned it, he did not dwell on it. His focus was on what we would call the attributes common to the divine

---

7. For Calvin's critique, see *Institutes of the Christian Religion*, 1.14.4.

8. Echoes of this survive in the Book of Common Prayer, where it is "with angels and archangels, and with all the company of heaven" that "we laud and magnify" the glorious name of God.

nature—goodness, holiness, and so on. This, too, reflects a Neoplatonist outlook, but there is an important difference. Whereas the Neoplatonists believed that it was possible to obtain a knowledge of perfect (or near-perfect) goodness, Pseudo-Dionysius denied that. As far as he was concerned, even the closest approximation to absolute goodness of which the human mind is capable still falls far short of the divine reality, which is beyond human understanding. Unlike pagan philosophers, the Christian theologian is reduced to silence in the presence of God, whose greatness surpasses anything that can be expressed in human words.

In theological terms, this approach is called "apophatic" ("negative") because it denies the possibility of defining God. The opposite approach, adopted by the philosophers and to some extent by many theologians as well, is called "cataphatic" ("positive") because it stresses the possibility of expressing truths about God that may have to be understood by analogy with human life, rather than as directly comparable, but are nevertheless made possible by the nature of divine revelation in the Bible. Systematic theology as we understand it is cataphatic; apophatic theology, by contrast, is what we would now call mysticism.

"Cataphatic" and "apophatic" describe different approaches, not closed systems of thought, and any given writer will use elements of both. Mystical theologians are supposed to promote silence in the face of the grandeur of God, but that does not stop them from expounding their principles at great length, as their critics have not been slow to point out. Similarly, even the most cataphatic theologian will admit that the essence of God is beyond human understanding and ultimately inexpressible ("ineffable") in human language. But if this distinction is of limited usefulness in Christian theology, it registers an important difference between theology and philosophy. The philosopher has no recourse to the apophatic, and this was particularly true of the Neoplatonists. Pseudo-Dionysius may have adopted a Neoplatonic framework for his thought, but in doing so he went beyond it and effectively relativized it as an analysis of reality.

We can see this most clearly if we consider the meaning of the term "non-being" (*to mē on*). To the Platonist, this was the absence of being, a void that constitutes evil, in contrast to "good," which is pure being. But to Pseudo-Dionysius and his followers, "non-being" is something else altogether. It is not the absence of being but the transcendence of it. To rise to the level of "non-being" is to go beyond mere being to a higher level of consciousness, which is the ultimate experience of reality. Nothing like this can be found in classical philosophy, but it does occur in the NT. The apostle Paul wrote,

> I know a man in Christ who fourteen years ago was caught up to the third heaven—whether in the body or out of the body I do not know, God knows. And I know that this man was caught up into paradise ... and he heard things that cannot be told, which man may not utter. (2 Cor 12:2–4)

Something similar can be read out of the accounts of the transfiguration of the incarnate Christ in the presence of Peter, James, and John (Matt 17:1–8; Mark 9:2–8; Luke 9:28–36). Theologians and commentators in the cataphatic tradition have never found it easy to interpret these passages, but it is obvious to those with an apophatic background what they are referring to. The difficulty with mystical experiences is that it is virtually impossible to evaluate them. Anyone can say almost anything and claim it as a mystical revelation from God, but how can we know that they are right? Such occurrences can be recorded, as they are in the Bible, but by their very nature they cannot be held up as models for others to follow. As a result, they usually play only a subordinate role in Christian teaching, though they cannot be denied completely.

Given that for Pseudo-Dionysius the mystical experience of God was the ultimate goal, it might be thought that he would have abandoned philosophy altogether, but that was not the case. What he did was relativize it. Philosophy (and, indeed, cataphatic theology) was an important, even a necessary, preparation for knowing God. It trains the mind to think straight, to analyze reality in a coherent way and to seek continually for greater and deeper understanding. Properly understood and used, philosophy points beyond itself and gives the intellect a thirst for the knowledge of God that can only come through revelation. In this respect, the apophatic approach of Pseudo-Dionysius represented a turning point in the relationship between theology and philosophy that is still of fundamental significance today.

On the one hand, it frees Christians from having to depend on any one type of philosophy in order to explain their faith and allows them to use different methods in order to achieve the same ultimate goal. On the other hand, it makes room for philosophical thought, which it accepts as a preparation for the gospel in much the same way that the apostle Paul saw the law of Moses as a preparation for the coming of Christ (Gal 3:19–26).

Neither is essential—gentiles can become Christians without the law, and everyone can become a believer without having to follow a course of philosophy first. But the person whose mind has been formed by philosophical thinking has much the same advantage, when coming to the gospel, as the Jew who was trained in the law. In both cases, the ground has been prepared for a person to receive Christ, and those who do so benefit accordingly. Judged alongside the church fathers of his own time and before, Pseudo-Dionysius cannot claim to have been a great exponent of the gospel, but in his own way he put philosophy in its proper place and his legacy, in however attenuated a form, is with us still.

The understanding of the relationship between philosophy and theology that Pseudo-Dionysius developed might have remained obscure and largely unapplied to Christian experience had it not been for the need to clarify the doctrine of the incarnation of Christ. The Council of Chalcedon (AD 451) had decreed that Christ was one divine person in two natures—one divine and the other human. This definition was not without its critics, and it split the Eastern Church into three—those who accepted the Chalcedonian formula (as all Western Christians did), those who insisted that the incarnate Christ had only one nature after his incarnation (the Monophysites, or Miaphysites) and those who insisted that each nature was complete in itself and so the unity of person in Christ was a conjunction of two essentially independent natures (the Nestorians). The difference between these non-Chalcedonians was that the Monophysites rejected the idea that Christ could be a complete human being apart from his divinity, whereas the Nestorians insisted that he could—and indeed did, when he died on the cross. As they saw it, the Son of God abandoned the man Jesus of Nazareth when he was crucified, and reunited with him in the resurrection, a belief that they thought was necessary in order to preserve the impassibility of the Son.[9]

Working out the finer details of the Chalcedonian definition took a couple of centuries, and the results were to be of prime importance for

9. This was how they interpreted Matt 27:46 and Mark 15:34.

theology and its relationship to philosophy. The fathers of Chalcedon may not have fully realized it, but in defining the incarnation the way they did they turned their traditional theological approach on its head and distanced it from any form of pagan philosophy. This was because, instead of seeing the person (*hypostasis*) of the incarnate Christ as the manifestation of an underlying divine and/or human nature, they said that the person was an independent agent who possessed his nature(s) and could dispose of them as he chose. In his incarnation, the divine Son of God took on a second (human) nature and gave it its *hypostasis*, or identity. This doctrine, known as *enhypostasia*, was refined by pro-Chalcedonian writers in the generations after the council, and it is generally agreed today that the greatest of these was an otherwise unknown monk called Leontius of Jerusalem, who lived in the first half of the sixth century.[10]

The implications of *enhypostasia* for our understanding of humanity extend beyond the incarnation of Christ because Christians confess that something similar happens to us as well. Human beings are persons (*hypostases*) with a human nature, but after we die we shall be resurrected with a spiritual nature that is quite different from the one we now have (1 Cor 15:35–58). But we shall still be the same persons, since if we are not, salvation would have no meaning. In other words, our persons, while not divine in the absolute sense, share something of God's nature in being immortal and capable of enhypostasizing themselves in a new nature after the death of the first one. Nothing like this was even conceivable to pagan philosophers, which is why Paul's teaching about the resurrection was foolishness to the Greeks and provoked a mocking reaction when he expounded it at Athens (Acts 17:32; see also 1 Cor 1:23).

Their doctrine of the incarnation of Christ made it necessary for Chalcedonian theologians to define what was divine about him and what was human, as well as how these two mutually incompatible natures could coexist in a single person. Not surprisingly, the question came down to the nonmaterial parts of his human nature, and in particular his "rational soul." Did Jesus have a human soul, and if he did, what did it do that his

10. Leontius of Jerusalem has been hopelessly confused in the tradition with his contemporary, Leontius of Byzantium, who said much the same thing. For a recent assessment of their work, see Angelo Di Berardino, ed., *Patrology: The Eastern Fathers from the Council of Chalcedon (451) to John of Damascus (†750)* (Cambridge: James Clarke and Co., 2006), 285–90.

divine nature did not do better? Could he have sinned as a human being? This was tricky. As a man, Jesus could have sinned, since if he could not, his temptations would have made no sense (see Matt 4:1–11).[11] But if he had sinned as a man, he would have denied his divine nature and there would have been no real incarnation at all.

In the end, this came down to an argument over the will. Did Christ's will belong to his (divine and/or human) nature, or was it purely divine? The Monophysites argued that Christ had only one will—they were in effect Monothelites. But the Chalcedonians insisted that he had two wills, corresponding to each of his two natures. This was the view defended by Maximus the Confessor (580–662) who, more than anyone else, was responsible for grounding Pseudo-Dionysius's apophatic theology in the church's teaching about Christ. Maximus made himself unpopular, so unpopular in fact that he was severely tortured and died of his wounds, but he persevered, and at the Third Council of Constantinople (680–681) his position was justified. What Maximus said was that the essence of God, present in Christ as the Son, is unknowable, but that God's actions can be seen in the universe. Maximus called these actions his "energies" (*energeiai*) and claimed that they were visible throughout creation, but supremely in the incarnate Christ. It was there, to a degree unknown elsewhere, that the divine actions were made visible, and that they were revealed to humankind in and through the human nature of the Son. Thus it was that the power of God could be seen and known in the life, death, and resurrection of Jesus Christ. His human will was by nature incompatible with his divine one, but by the agency of his divine person it could be brought into submission to the divine will, which would then act through his humanity to reveal the *energeia* of God. In this way, a human will that was naturally sinful would never actually sin, because the divine will was always (and fully) active in and on it.

Equally important, what was true of Jesus in his humanity is also true of us insofar as we are submitted to his divine will. As the apostle Paul put it, "We have the mind of Christ," and by the power of his Holy Spirit at work in us, we can accomplish his will—not perfectly, and certainly not

11. Note that the temptations of Jesus were temptations of God, not of man, as he himself pointed out to Satan.

through any merit of our own, but in a way that is consonant with the will of God himself (1 Cor 2:16). The idea that God's essence can be present (though hidden and incomprehensible) in our humanity, and that the effects of this can be seen in our actions, transformed everything. Unlike pagans, Christians do not have to go looking for wisdom, because it is already present inside us. What is needed is obedience to that wisdom on our part and the outworking of it by the action of the Holy Spirit on our minds and wills. That in turn justifies and empowers our behavior toward God, toward our neighbors, and toward the world over which we have been given dominion. We are fully entitled to use the resources of human logic to work this out under the guidance of the Spirit, because this is what God has made us for.

In many respects this conforms to the teaching of Aristotle, in particular, and his insights can be recovered for Christian use, but they do not have to be followed in every detail as if they have been revealed by God. Where Aristotle went wrong—and it was clear that, as a pagan, he had gone wrong in many respects—he had to be corrected, but that too was possible by the indwelling power of the Spirit. The result was that sinful human beings, limited by our natural finitude and our rebelliousness, can be brought into harmony with the will of God and accomplish it with his help. Part of that process involves philosophy—right thinking about what action is required in any given circumstance, plus the will to put that thinking into action. It would take many centuries for the implications of this to be worked out, but the seeds were sown in the ancient controversy about the human will of Christ, and the fruit is there for us to see all around us.

The final act in the post-Chalcedonian drama occurred in the eighth century, when elements in the Eastern church objected to the idea that the divine could be portrayed in visual images. They based this objection on the prohibition of such images in the Second Commandment, which they claimed applied to all pictorial representations of Christ (Exod 20:4–6). The problem with that was that, in his incarnation, the Son of God was made visible. The NT does not contain any physical description of Jesus, but there is no doubt that he was seen by his contemporaries and that he did not strike them as odd or supernatural. Drawing a picture of him must therefore have been possible, even if nobody did so at the time. The theological question raised by this was apparently simple—would such a picture be a picture of

God or not? It could not have been an image of the divine nature, which is invisible, but according to the doctrine of *enhypostasia* it would have been a picture of the divine person of the Son in his human nature.

What made that conceivable was the distinction between the essence of God (invisible) and his energies, which can be seen at work all around us. The difference with the incarnate Christ is that these divine energies were perfect manifestations of his divine essence, which in itself could not be portrayed. Arguments about this continued for over a hundred years and were not finally resolved until 843, when it was decreed in Constantinople that it was lawful to paint images of the incarnate Christ. These images, or icons as we usually call them, became an integral part of worship in the Eastern churches, and have remained such until the present time, though they have never caught on in the West. This is not because of any disagreement in theological principle but because too much has been claimed for the images by those who support them. Nobody doubts that God can and has worked through the incarnate Christ and (in a different way) through his followers, but this is something that is true of them personally, not of images made to remind us of them. Unfortunately, the Eastern churches have accepted the idea that the divine energies can operate in and through icons, some of which are claimed to be miracle-working! That is going too far, and the Western churches have stopped well short of following their Eastern counterparts in this respect.

It was one of the leading critics of iconoclasm (as the movement to destroy icons is known) who would produce what would become the definitive exposition of Eastern Christian theology. This was John of Damascus (675–750), who lived under Muslim rule in Syria and Palestine, but who was free to write as a Chalcedonian theologian. John was not an original thinker in the true sense of the word, but he was a brilliant compiler and synthesizer of the tradition that he inherited. He was the first person to write what we would now recognize as systematic theology, and in that respect his work has remained paradigmatic. From the standpoint of philosophy, what is so interesting about him is that he was able to use the categories of Aristotelian logic to expound the Christian doctrine of God, which in the philosophical context must be largely apophatic. He listed no fewer than eighteen attributes of God, subdivided according to time, space, being, and nature.[12] Every one of the attributes he lists begins with the Greek letter alpha, usually (though not invariably) because it is a negative, as apophatic theology demands. John's classification is the most sophisticated analysis of the divine attributes that has ever been produced, so much so that some of the words he uses have never found an adequate Latin (or English) equivalent. Given this circumstance, we must look at them as John did and try to appreciate the greatness of his achievement.

TIME-RELATED ATTRIBUTES	
anarchos	[without beginning]
aktistos	uncreated
agennētos	unbegotten, ungenerated
anolethros	imperishable
athanatos	immortal
aiōnios	eternal
SPACE-RELATED ATTRIBUTES	
apeiros	infinite
aperigraptos	uncircumscribed
aperioristos	unbounded
apeirodynamos	[of unlimited power]
BEING-RELATED ATTRIBUTES	
haplēs [13]	simple
asynthetos	uncompounded
asōmatos	incorporeal
arrheustos	[without flux]
NATURE-RELATED ATTRIBUTES	
apathēs	impassible
atreptos	immutable
analloiōtos	inalterable
aoratos	invisible

12. John of Damascus, *De fide orthodoxa*, 1.8.

13. The initial "h" is not a letter in Greek but a breathing mark over the a. It was no longer pronounced in John's day.

True to his gift for compilation and synthesis, John gave a number of definitions of the word "philosophy," but the one that stands out as most faithful to his own approach says that "philosophy is love of wisdom, and true wisdom is God; therefore the love of God is the true philosophy."[14] That sums it up beautifully and sets the stage for the way in which theology and philosophy were to relate to one another throughout the history of the Eastern churches, and by extension, to much of the medieval Western church as well. The wise man would seek to know God, and as the wise men of Matthew's Gospel demonstrated, to know God was to go to Jerusalem and find out there where he was to be born (Matt 2:1–2).

THE RULE OF LAW

The encounter between Christianity and secular learning in the Latin-speaking part of the Roman Empire was in some ways similar to that in the East, but there were important differences, too. The Latins[15] were deeply impregnated with the culture of Roman law, which gave their debates a more down-to-earth character than was usual among the Greeks. They were less inclined to debate the status of angels or the hierarchy of heaven and more likely to concentrate on things like inheritance, property laws, and criminal procedures. But as anyone who has studied law will know, that does not mean that they were not capable of subtle hair-splitting and even fantasizing. It was common for law professors to make up test cases and get their students to resolve them by applying the appropriate legal principles. For example, if a caged animal escaped and mauled someone to death, would the animal's owner be held liable? (The answer was no, because the animal would have returned to its naturally wild state for which the owner was not responsible.)

With this kind of mindset at work, it is easy to see how the question of evil could become very complicated. Everyone agreed that sin was wrong and that crimes should be punished, but were sins and crimes the same thing? In Christian terms, they were not. Sin was the result of our first ancestors' disobedience to God and was universal—everyone suffers the consequence of death, regardless of how many actual sins he or she may

14. John of Damascus, *Dialectica*, 136–37.

15. This term is preferable to "Romans" because the Greek-speakers of the East also called themselves "Romans."

have committed. Sin, or more properly sinfulness (for which Latin lacked a separate word, though "concupiscence" comes close), leads to perverse thoughts in the mind, to corrupt wills, and eventually to criminal acts. But it is only the last of these that the law can punish, because the other two are not open to external investigation. But one of the clearest teachings of Jesus was that the thoughts of the heart are just as bad as any criminal act that may result from them, even if those thoughts escape the notice of others (see Matt 5:27–30; John 7:53–8:11).

Sinfulness is a common condition that produces a standard punishment, but crimes are more complicated. We can understand why a murderer might be executed as a just recompense for his act, but if all someone did was steal a loaf of bread, such a punishment would seem to most people to be extreme and unjustified. Somehow or other, a scale of relative values would have to be adopted, and that would inevitably lead to complex discussions about right and wrong. Before the legalization of Christianity, Christians could be put to death for failing to worship the pagan gods, but later on the opposite would become more likely, particularly if the "worship of pagan gods" took the form of witchcraft, which it often did. But who would decide what punishment fitted which crime? Could such decisions be justified on some objective basis, like the so-called law of nature, or were they purely arbitrary, to be determined by the customs and prejudices of any given society?

In working this out, the Bible was of only limited usefulness. General principles could be deduced from the Ten Commandments perhaps, but applying them to particular circumstances was a different matter. The Pentateuch contained numerous case studies, but these were taken from the experience of a small tribal society and did not cover a lot of things. Maritime trade, for example, was almost completely absent from the OT because the ancient Israelites were not sailors and did not need to develop a law of the sea. It soon became clear that Christians would have to elaborate their own laws based on moral and philosophical principles that might not be covered in the Bible. Could such laws be regarded as the commandments of God? That would depend on the nature of the powers given to the lawgivers, who would have to be legitimated by a competent authority, which in this instance would almost certainly have to be the leadership of the church. In this way, popes and bishops came to be recognized as the sources of moral and spiritual legitimacy, which could be granted (and, more importantly, withdrawn) by them at their discretion. That discretion was not supposed to be arbitrary but based on the teaching of the Bible and the doctrines of the church, though how they were to be interpreted was by no means clear.

Bringing the laws of the state into line with the principles of the church was no easy task, and it took Christians a long time to achieve even modest results. One area in which they had some success was matrimony, when it was decided that the consent of the parties was required for a marriage to be valid. In a world where it was usually expected that people would marry those whom their parents had chosen for them, that was a revolutionary step. Attempts to limit and even abolish slavery, on the other hand, generally failed. In the end, it was agreed that Christians could not enslave other Christians (Englishmen could not enslave Frenchmen, for example), but they could go outside the Christian world and enslave those who had not been baptized. For a while this meant that they could go to Eastern Europe and capture Slavs, who did not become Christians in large numbers until the tenth century. (Indeed, our word "slave" is taken from them!) Later on, that door was shut and slave traders had to go elsewhere, notably to sub-Saharan Africa, where the black people who lived there had not been converted to Christianity. Thus was born the kind of race-based slavery we are familiar with today—which came into being precisely because the church had managed to exclude the trade from Christian Europe!

The slavery issue was to prove intractable until the Industrial Revolution made it possible to replace human beings with machines, but long before that, the theological and philosophical questions surrounding it had received a full airing. For a start, were slaves human beings in the full sense of the word? Was it right to treat them as property, buying and selling them as if they were horses? It seemed obvious that a man who was enslaved did not cease to be human, nor did he gain human status when he was set free. But what was it that united him with other human beings? Is there such a thing as "humanity" that we all share in common? Or is humanity merely an abstraction, created by analysts who needed a word to describe the similarities that they noticed between different individuals? How can human diversity be accounted for? If we are basically the same, why are we not all alike? And if we are primarily individuals, how is it that we have so much in common?

These basic differences in approach reflect Platonism, on the one hand, and Aristotelianism on the other, but in medieval terms they are usually known as realism and nominalism. A realist believed that there is such a thing as humanity that actually exists, and that particular people manifest that in different ways.[16] A nominalist, on the other hand, believed that "humanity" is a term given to a group of similar beings, but that there is no generic human who is a model for the rest. We encounter only particular people, not a universal Human. Both sides in this argument contain an element of truth. At some level there is a common humanity, even though it cannot be isolated or observed independently of particular individuals. But there is also great diversity, and there is no reason to suppose that one individual is more human than another.

The Bible approaches the universal/diversity debate by saying that all human beings descend from a common ancestor, whom it calls Adam. This ancestor was male, but the female was taken out of him and so shares his humanity. Over time, these humans reproduced and subdivided into the different nations that we know today, but there is no real explanation of the diversity that has resulted other than to say that the different human languages came into being in order to prevent humans from uniting in rebellion against God (Gen 11:1–9). There is no discussion of what we would call "race," nor is there any explanation given as to why some people are tall, others short, and so on. Diversity, such as it is, is the consequence of the multiplication of Adam's descendants, who remain fundamentally related and equally sinful in the eyes of God.

The choice of Israel, and later of the church, as a holy people set apart for the worship of God has created an important distinction between two kinds of human beings, but that distinction is primarily spiritual, not physical. Admittedly, the choice of Israel had a physical dimension to it, but it was not absolute, and when the Christian church came along it disappeared. The real difference between the chosen people and the rest is that the chosen ones had received the promise of salvation from the

16. It is indicative of the gulf that separates modern thought from its medieval ancestor that the word "real" and its derivatives now mean more or less the opposite of what they meant then. We would probably call medieval "realism" "idealism" today.

sinfulness into which they had fallen as a result of Adam's disobedience. This promise was contained in the law of Moses, which had been given to Israel in order to mark it out from the rest of humanity. But although Jews and Christians were privileged in that way, the law they received was not really different from the laws that govern the universe in general. The law of Moses said that it was wrong to kill, commit adultery, or steal, but these prohibitions were hardly unique. One way or another, all human societies had similar values, and all human beings have a conscience that operates to make them at least nominally obedient to them. This principle was clearly enunciated in the NT. The apostle Paul praised the Jewish law and held it up as God's revelation, but at the same time he insisted that non-Jews held to the same basic principles, even though they lacked the precise form of Moses's words:

> When the Gentiles, who do not have the law, by nature do what the law requires, they are a law to themselves, even though they do not have the law. They show that the work of the law is written on their hearts, while their conscience also bears witness, and their conflicting thoughts accuse or even excuse them. (Rom 2:14–15)

From there it is a short step to saying that the universe is governed by the "natural" law of God, which is made explicit in the Bible but can be found everywhere. This justified Christians, not only when they sought to align secular laws with biblical principles, but also when they ventured to uncover the secrets of nature in what we now call the natural sciences. It is ironic that nowadays we often hear secular commentators talk about "mother nature," an invented fantasy that merely hides the truth—"mother nature" is in fact God, the God of the Bible, acting beyond the confines of his verbal revelation.

Once medieval thinkers reached this conclusion, which they could easily do by reading the Bible itself, the way was open to constructing a complete worldview that would be valid for everyone, Christian and non-Christian alike. Given that the Bible expressed the principles of this worldview in a clear and authoritative manner, those whose job it was to preserve and interpret it—the clergy—were the natural rulers of society and everyone else would be expected to follow their guidance. But not everyone was called to be ordained in the service of the church, and there was room for disciplines other than theology, notably law and medicine, to flourish alongside it, as they did. Gradually, the number and sphere of these disciplines multiplied, not least under the mantle of Aristotle, whose scientific categories now came into their own. Eventually, they would give rise to universities, which first appeared about 1200 and have grown to become the leading organs of human knowledge ever since.

Before that happened, there was an intermediate stage of development best represented by the work of Anselm of Canterbury (1033–1109), the first real philosopher-theologian of the Western Middle Ages and the forerunner of what would later become "Scholasticism," *schola* ("school") being the term for the faculties that would make up the nascent universities. Anselm was the great exponent of the belief that the law of God is the truth that unites what is revealed in the Bible with what is discoverable in nature. Both the Bible and the "book of nature" address human reason, but in different ways. The Bible speaks to our minds directly—it is the word (*logos*) of God. "Nature" does the same, but indirectly, not in words but in observable phenomena that can be analyzed and examined by our minds. Because of this fundamental congruence, Anselm believed that it was possible to demonstrate the existence of God by using the resources of natural human reason alone, without recourse to revelation, and this is what he set out to prove.

Anselm began with the reasonable assumption that the world exists independently of our imaginations. It is built around the notion of being, which we encounter at many different levels. A rock, for example, is a being because it exists, and in itself it is "good," because it is what God intended it to be. But a tree is also a being, and is a higher being than a rock, because it is alive. Going further up the scale, an animal is a higher being than a tree, because not only is it alive, but it can move and function independently. Finally, there is the human being, who is still higher up the scale because, in addition to possessing all the basic qualities of an animal, the human also has the gift of reason, which makes it possible for him to think about the possibility of the existence of God. Humans are not the highest form of being, though. There are spiritual creatures like angels and demons who surpass them because they are non-material, so we cannot stop with ourselves. But how high can we go?

Anselm says that we can go as high as our minds can take us. All existing beings, however good they may be in themselves, have their limitations, as the above examples demonstrate. Even the angels and demons are finite and have to operate in a universe that is bigger than they are. But having got that far, argued Anselm, there must be a Being who surpasses all limitation, a Being who is so great that nothing greater can be imagined. This, he said, is God. Anselm's argument is called the "ontological proof" for the existence of God, and it proved very attractive, though even in his own time it did not command universal assent. Why not? For a start, it is possible to imagine things far greater than we are that do not in fact exist—science fiction is almost entirely based on that principle. Furthermore, to dream up the ultimate being is not the same thing as proving that such a being actually exists, and so the "proof" turns out to be hollow.

At the same time, Christians will sympathize with Anselm because, of course, it is impossible to imagine any being higher than God. But the reason for this is not that our minds have reached up as high as they can and discovered him. The reason for our conviction is that God has revealed himself to us. Whether he can properly be called a "being" like other beings is a matter of debate, because as the Creator he is quite unlike any of his creatures. That in itself makes it impossible for us to discover him by looking only at his creation, even if we can suspect that there must be something behind the universe. What Anselm did, and indeed what he is famous for, was to start with faith and work from there toward understanding the nature of reality. It was *fides quaerens intellectum* ("faith seeking understanding"). His proof for God's existence will not persuade those who have no faith to begin with, but it will reassure believers that their convictions are rational and coherent with the nature of the universe. In that respect, and to that extent, his approach remains attractive to Christians today and his greatness as a philosophical theologian is assured.

Another question that arises from all this concerns the relationship between God and the world that he has made. To put it briefly, the world exists in time and space, but God transcends them. Unlike Aristotle, who believed that the transcendent deity had nothing to do with the world of time and space, Christians believe that he does, which creates the problem of trying to explain how that can be so. If God is directly involved in my life, but dwells outside the time and space framework in which I am forced to live, what does he see when he looks at me? Does he know what I shall do tomorrow, for example, or when (and how) I shall die? To go the other way, can he reach back into my past and change it, if he is eternally present in everything and the "past" has no meaning for him? Is what I think has happened already definitive and unalterable? And if it is, does that limit the power of God to govern his creation?

In theological terms, this is the great question of predestination, and it has been answered in many different ways. The Bible states quite clearly that God made the world and that he is sovereign over it—nothing happens without him knowing about it. But is that all there is to it? Does God's knowledge (or what we would call "foreknowledge" with respect to what we think of as the "future") stop at the level of information—he knows what has happened and what will happen—or does it go further than that? If it is true that "for those who love God all things work together for good," God must be in control of events, since otherwise that would not necessarily be the case, and that is indeed what Paul says in the same passage (Rom 8:28). Indeed, Paul went further than that. When speaking of his early days as a persecutor of the church, he was bold enough to claim that God had set him apart from before he was born, and eventually called him by his grace and appointed him to preach the gospel of salvation to the gentiles (Gal 1:15–16). This, we might say, is predestination with a vengeance! But if it is true that God calls his people before they are born, he must be in control of everything, even of the times before those who have been so chosen actually come to faith. Does this mean that God is somehow also in control of evil? And if he is, can he be said to have created that evil in the first place?

At the heart of the debates over predestination was the question of free will. Do human beings have the freedom to choose good and/or evil, and if they do not, can they be blamed for the situation they find themselves in? The Bible is quite clear about this, at least up to a point. "All have sinned and fall short of the glory of God" (Rom 3:23). This does not mean that every human being has committed actual sin(s), but that everyone is born into a state of sinfulness, brought about by the sin of our first parents. Nobody chooses whether to be a sinner—that is a given. Nor can sinners choose to be perfect, even if it is possible to know what perfection is (or might be). As Paul put it: "We know that the law is spiritual, but I am of the flesh, sold under sin. For I do not understand my own actions. For I do not do what I want, but I do the very thing I hate" (Rom 7:14–15). Freedom of the will is not freedom to choose, but freedom to do what is right. That is the kind of freedom that only God has by nature, but that he makes available to those who are born again in Christ.

This would appear on the surface to be a simple and straightforward position, but it has met with great opposition. Some people want to say that God foreknows what will happen but does not cause it, and so is not responsible for what might go wrong. Others say that he predestines some to eternal life but leaves the rest to their own devices. Neither of these positions makes any sense, at least not if we are prepared to accept divine sovereignty over creation. Either he is in control or he is not God in the biblical sense, and so logic compels us to accept that everything that happens, good or bad, is somehow the fruit of his will. At the same time, God hates nothing that he has made, and he does not force his creatures to act against his will. The terrible truth is that we are naturally rebellious and deserve only condemnation. The idea that going to heaven is some form of entitlement, which so many today seem to think, is completely alien to the Bible, which teaches that our salvation is an act of God's grace, extended to those whom he has chosen for reasons that are beyond our understanding.

It is at this point that the gospel contradicts every human religion and philosophy. Faith is an act of God's grace, manifested first in conviction of sin and then in forgiveness of it. Both of these transcend the rule of law as we usually understand it and introduce the rule of a higher principle—the principle of love. Only God can love sinners, and he does so because he made them originally sinless and wants to return them to that state. Why he chooses some and not others is unknown to us, but it is a fact that we observe all around us and can do nothing to change. To those who object to this, Paul said: "Who are you, O man, to answer back to God? Will what is molded say to its molder, 'Why have you made me like this?' Has the potter no right over the clay, to make out of the same lump one vessel for honorable use and another for dishonorable use?" (Rom 9:20–21).

It is at this point that the Christian message parts company with any form of religion or philosophy that tries to find a way to reach God. It is he who must come to us, not the other way around, and unless we die to self, we shall not (and cannot) be born again into new and eternal life.

GETTING CLOSER TO GOD?

Before we move on to the next stage in the development of the relationship between theology and philosophy, there is one further aspect of medieval thought and practice that we must consider. Medieval thinkers correctly saw that the problem of sin was deeper than anything the law could resolve. Behind the acts of the sinful person were the desires of the sinful will and the thoughts of the sinful heart. As the apostle Paul knew, the realization of this leads to a kind of spiritual trauma: "I delight in the law of God, in my inner being, but I see in my members another law waging war against the law of my mind and making me captive to the law of sin that dwells in my members. Wretched man that I am! Who will deliver me from this body of death?" (Rom 7:22–24).

Medieval thinkers were only too well aware of this dilemma, but they tried to resolve it in a way that failed to grasp the radical nature of the problem and went against Paul's teaching on this all-important subject. Instead of accepting the situation and turning to the grace of God for forgiveness and restoration, they devised a series of ways in which they thought they could overcome the "desires of the flesh." Taken together, these ways were what we would call asceticism. Asceticism is the practice of self-denial, and it was the belief of those who advocated it that they could overcome the power of sin in their bodies. To some extent, we can see where they got this idea from, because the Bible uses the word "flesh" to denote everything in us that is opposed to the will of God. "Flesh" in this sense is not meant to mean the body, but the rebellious human mind that uses the desires of the body as a means of turning people away from God. Gluttony is a sin of the flesh, but it must be placed alongside less material thinks like pride, jealousy, and greed. Ascetics turned to abstinence from food and sex in the hope of killing their desire for these things, little realizing that this way of thinking might easily lead to pride, which was the worst sin of all.

The difficulty with asceticism, as with most things, is that there is an element of truth in it. Moderate consumption of food and drink as well as sexual self-discipline are good and healthy habits that ought to be encouraged. But the results of such activities are confined to the body; they do not by themselves bring us any closer to God. On the contrary, it is as we get closer to God that we will see the benefits in adopting a balanced lifestyle and be moved to do so. This is what the ascetics failed to grasp. Instead, they fasted for weeks on end, beat themselves with whips, and endured all kinds of physical torment and deprivation in order to beat the devil out of themselves, as they saw it. The young Martin Luther (1483–1546) was a notorious case in point. In fact, he was so extreme in his asceticism that his superiors in the friary forced him to leave and take up a university post where he would be unable to punish himself in ways that would bring not only his health but also his life into danger. Luther's great spiritual breakthrough came not when he realized the futility of what he was doing but when he saw that the goal he was seeking lay somewhere else altogether.

Luther discovered by reading the Bible that the way out of his dilemma was not by increased asceticism but by faith in the power of God to forgive and restore him. He could not claim any reward from God on the strength of his own actions, however dedicated and even praiseworthy they might be. He could only be justified before God by faith, and not by anything he might do to earn it, which he called "works." Justification by faith alone was what he called the "article of a standing or falling church," which means that the true profession of Christianity depends entirely on trusting God to do what he has promised to do in Christ and what Christ accomplished in his death on the cross. What Luther could not do for himself, Christ had done for him, and for every believer. This was the key that opened the gate of the kingdom of heaven.

Luther's great discovery seems obvious from hindsight, but it evoked strenuous opposition at the time. Many people could not believe that good works were useless as far as getting closer to God was concerned. They misread Luther and accused him of saying that such works were unnecessary, and even sinful. Of course, that is not what Luther meant at all. He believed that good works are necessary, but that they are the *fruit* of justification and not the *cause* of it. Someone who has been justified by faith will do good works as a matter of course, not to obtain a reward but to demonstrate what new life in the freedom of Christ looks like. Those who have seen the light of Christ will not walk in darkness, nor will they want to. On the contrary, they will want to spread the light as far as they can, because it is in that light that they can see the glory of God and of the world he has made for the first time. In other words, what philosophers tried to discover by mental exercises, believers could know and experience by a change of life. Christians are not people who sit and argue about the right way to follow—they are people who have found the way to go and who are on pilgrimage to the promised land.

One of the problems with asceticism is that it appears to suggest that the material world is evil. That is not Christian teaching, of course, but it has left a legacy in the popular mind that is very hard to shake. Christians are often portrayed as puritanical killjoys because they refrain from indulging in certain activities, which is grossly unfair but reflects this ancient tradition. What is particularly curious is that in medieval times there was a countervailing tendency that exalted matter and gave it a status that risked exalting it above the created order. This can be seen most clearly in the development of the sacraments. Baptism and the Lord's Supper, to name the most important of these, go back to the NT and were regularly observed throughout the history of the church, but before the twelfth century there was no classification of "sacrament" in the modern sense. That was the work of Hugh of St. Victor (1096–1141), which was then codified by his contemporary Peter Lombard (1090–1160) and became standard church teaching for several centuries afterward. Lombard was particularly famous for producing a four-volume systematic theology called the *Sentences*, which became the standard textbook for the next four hundred years. Those who wanted to teach theology in a university had to defend a dissertation based on some part of the *Sentences* before they could obtain a license to do so. Dozens of these defenses still survive, including one by the young Martin Luther, who could not teach at the University of Wittenberg until he had defended one.[17]

The basic belief was that God appointed certain rites as means by which he offered his grace to believers. Baptism, by which a person entered the church, was obviously the first of these. It had always been understood as symbolizing the transition from the life of this world to the life of the next—the process of regeneration, or new birth—but the exact relationship between the two was left undefined. Could the rite of baptism itself guarantee entry into the kingdom of heaven? By the twelfth century,

17. Luther commented on *Sentences* 1.17. See Paul Vignaux, *Luther: Commentateur des Sentences* (Paris: Librairie Philosophique J. Vrin, 1935).

virtually everybody in Western Europe had been baptized in infancy and was therefore considered to be a member of the church. At a time when infant mortality rates were extremely high, this was a great comfort to parents who lost a child, because they could be assured that their offspring had gone to be with the Lord. The requirement of faith that ought to precede baptism was not forgotten, but it was assumed that parents and sponsors (godparents) could pledge this on behalf of their children, who were obviously incapable of doing it themselves. That pledge would later be ratified by the rite of confirmation, which could be seen either as the completion of baptism or as a distinct sacrament in its own right.[18]

What happened in the twelfth century and later was that traditional beliefs and customs were systematized according to principles that ultimately derived from Aristotle, though that was never admitted and probably not often fully recognized either. In the case of baptism, it was stated that when the water was consecrated by a priest the grace of God flowed into it, turning it into an agent of spiritual regeneration. The effects of this were twofold. First of all, grace came to be understood as a substance that could unite with water in much the same way as detergent powder can. The water was still there, but it was permeated by something else that transformed it into a cleansing power. Second, it reduced the role of faith. If the sacrament operated automatically (*ex opere operato*), it made no difference whether the recipient believed in Christ. Rather like a vaccine, baptism did its work regardless, and the person baptized was born again whether he understood that or not.

The flaws with this doctrine somehow seem to have escaped general notice. For a start, it was still possible for laypeople to baptize, which often happened in cases of emergency, but laypeople did not have the power of consecration. Then, too, it was impossible to verify whether the promised regeneration was actually effective. There were plenty of adults who had been baptized in infancy but who showed no regard for the Christian faith, and nobody quite knew what to do with them. Were they Christians or not? In the end, a new category of the "lapsed" was invented to deal with them. The problem was not as serious as it might

18. This question is still a matter of discussion today, as confirmation has been described as "a sacrament in search of a theology."

appear because the church was able to construct a system of penance, which in most cases would extend even beyond death to a place of supernatural cleansing ("purgatory") that was conjured up for the purpose. There was no evidence for any of this in the Bible or in the practice of the early church, but the logic of sacramental theology made it necessary, and so it came into being.

Penance was in practice the application of the law to the life of the Christian. Penitents were expected to confess their sins to a priest, who would then assign an appropriate punishment, after which the offender would be forgiven and admitted to Holy Communion. Like crimes in the secular sphere, sins were graded according to their seriousness and the punishments varied accordingly. Once again, there were flaws in the system that had to be addressed. Most of us commit sins of which we are unaware, and so we do not confess them. Some people know only too well what they have done wrong, but for a variety of reasons they are unwilling to confess them. The result is that most people die with unconfessed sins and the church was left with a dilemma. Such people were obviously not good enough to go to heaven, but were they bad enough to be consigned to hell? The answer was that they should be given a second chance to put matters right. After death, the spiritual issues would be clear, and sinners would have no objection to being offered a chance to make up for their delinquency. This was the origin and the logic behind purgatory, a place where basically well-meaning people could work off their remaining debt of sin in preparation for life in the kingdom of heaven.[19]

Purgatory was a clever invention, but inevitably there would be attempts to reduce the time that a given individual would have to spend there. The church devised means of getting time off from purgatory, either by doing more penance than was necessary ("works of supererogation") or by obtaining an indulgence, which in later times could even be purchased. It was the sale of these indulgences that finally prompted Martin Luther to revolt and set off what became the Protestant Reformation. Underlying all this was a deeper legal and philosophical question: Could an earthly authority like the church or the papacy exercise jurisdiction

19. On the origin of purgatory, see J. LeGoff, *The Birth of Purgatory* (Chicago: University of Chicago Press, 1984), originally published as *La naissance du purgatoire* (Paris: Gallimard, 1981).

over Christians after their death? Did the pope's writ extend into the afterlife? This affected not only purgatory, but also heaven, since the church took it upon itself to canonize saints whose presence in heaven was guaranteed. The great benefit of these saints was that it was possible to approach them and ask them to intercede with God on our behalf. In some cases, saints became patrons of entire countries, and others were held to specialize in particular causes for which their assistance could be solicited. None of this has any backing in the Bible or in the practice of the early church, but in medieval times claims of this kind became standard.

Matters came to a head and were most openly debated with respect to the Lord's Supper. The reasons for this were not hard to understand. Only those who had been baptized and been absolved from the need to do penance were admitted to the Supper, but it was celebrated on a regular basis—weekly and even daily—and was the "normal" form of public worship. It therefore touched everyone who went to church and was a matter of personal concern to virtually the entire population. It was also possible to be excluded from this sacrament for failing to observe the rules and regulations of the church—the phenomenon we know as "excommunication." The consequences of that could be serious, since excommunicates were not only barred from the Lord's Table but were often shunned by the community in which they lived, since everyone was expected to respect the condemnation of the church authorities.

At the heart of this was the growing belief that the bread and wine offered up in celebration of the broken body and shed blood of Christ underwent a change of substance when they were consecrated by the priest. Unlike baptism, the Lord's Supper could not be celebrated by a layperson, or even by a clergyman who was not in priest's orders, so this gave extraordinary spiritual power to a small group of specially privileged people.[20] Were they gifted in a way that others were not? The answer to that had to be that they were—holy orders were therefore also regarded as a sacrament, and men who received them received a corresponding portion of divine grace, so that they could perform the tasks allotted to them.

20. There were eight orders in the medieval church, of which bishops and priests were the highest. After that came deacons, subdeacons, and a number of others. After 1123, celibacy was imposed on both bishops and priests in order to set them apart from the rest of the church, but those in the lower orders were still allowed to marry.

Transubstantiation, as the change in the bread and wine of the Supper was known, depended on an Aristotelian interpretation of material reality. According to that, everything that exists can be analyzed into the categories of "substance" and "accidents." In the case of bread, for example, there is supposed to be a substance that goes by that name. This substance does not exist in everyday life, but it underlies everything that we recognize as bread. What we see is the substance as it comes to us with its various accidents, which include such things as size, taste, color, weight, etc. These accidents are what we would call variables—they can and do change, but the substance of the bread remains the same. There is nothing supernatural about changing accidents, which happens all the time, but a change of substance is only possible by a miracle of divine intervention. That is what supposedly happens in transubstantiation. When the priest takes the bread and wine and consecrates them, the accidents remain the same but the underlying substance is changed into the body and blood of Christ. The person who then receives these consecrated elements receives something that looks like bread (or wine), tastes like bread, feels like bread, and so on, but is in fact the body of Christ.

By the fourteenth century, this had been refined still further, as the church began to withdraw the wine ("the cup") from laypeople, giving them only the bread. The reasons for that are not clear, and may have had something to do with hygiene in times of plague, but the practice was generalized and defended on the ground that bodies contain blood, so that the blood of Christ was already present in the consecrated bread, making the "cup" redundant. At the same time, the priest continued to drink from the cup on behalf of the congregation, thereby presenting himself as a kind of mediator between them and God, a human icon of Christ himself.

Once again, we are faced with a situation that has no precedent in the Bible or in the early church, but that had become the norm in medieval times. There were protests against this but they were unsuccessful, and the right of the church to legislate for things not contained in the Bible or in the church's earlier tradition was upheld. What could possibly justify this? The answer was that the church was authorized to dispense the grace of God to the world. The sacraments were "means of grace," ways in which the gift of God's salvation was extended to believers. Grace was conceived as a substance in its own right, created by God, to be sure, but manifesting his presence in the world.

The invention of a concept of created grace as a substance led inevitably to a reconsideration of the material world. For centuries, it had been assumed among Christians that the physical universe was good and that things had gone wrong because of humanity's disobedience. But in the fourteenth century this perception began to change, albeit subtly. "Nature" came to refer to creation in its fallen state, not in the condition in which it had originally been made. Thus, for example, where the early Christians described the fallen Adam as "unnatural" because his created nature had been corrupted by his sin, medieval thinkers began to speak of him as "natural." The lingering effects of this can be seen in the translation of 1 Corinthians 2:14, where the Greek *psychikos anthrōpos* was rendered as "natural man" in the KJV (1611) and is now "natural person" in the ESV. Paul's meaning is perfectly clear in the Greek—he was speaking about the human being who does not have the Spirit of God, but English lacks an adequate term for describing this. To say that a sinful man is "natural" is to deny the authentic humanity of Jesus Christ, because Jesus is a natural man in the created sense, but he is not sinful. This unfortunate misreading of the Greek must be ascribed to the way in which the word "natural" changed its meaning as the implications of "created grace" began to make themselves felt.

The formula that was eventually devised to explain how nature and grace are related was that "grace does not destroy nature but perfects it," a phrase taken from the *Summa Theologica* of Thomas Aquinas (1225–1274).[21] The sacraments were the supreme manifestations of grace at work in this way, but they were not the only ones. Prayer, spiritual exercises, and preaching were all means of grace in their different ways, and they were encouraged just as much as participation in the sacramental life of the church was. The men who promoted this new way of thinking were mostly "friars," a word derived from the Latin *fratres* ("brothers"), who lived on the fringes of the institutional church and in many ways acted as a counterculture to it. By about 1200, it was becoming clear that the ancient monasteries had lost much of their original vision and were no longer schools of poverty,

21. Thomas Aquinas, *Summa Theologica*, 1.1.8, response to question 2.

chastity, and obedience in the way that they professed to be. Men like Francis of Assisi (1180–1226) in Italy and Dominic Guzmán (1170–1221) in Spain were disturbed by this and gathered men around them who would live off the land by begging—putting the monastic ideals into practice and avoiding institutionalization as much as possible.[22]

The visions of Francis and Dominic could not be realized in practice, at least not for very long, but the Franciscans and Dominicans, as their followers were called, were at least partially successful in resisting the temptation to become just another monastic order. They banded together in houses, and soon found themselves teaching in the universities that were developing at the same time as they were. It was in this role that they engaged in the theological disputations for which Scholasticism became famous. Questions like "How many angels can stand on the head of a pin?" were debated at length in order to elucidate what the relationship between the spiritual and the material worlds is.[23] Arguments of this kind are ultimately futile because the spiritual and the material are two different and ultimately incompatible dimensions of reality, but in a climate where it was important to determine how spiritual grace can interact with material nature, it is easy to see why they were debated.

From the standpoint of centuries of hindsight, we can see what the outcome was. Pins can be measured but angels cannot be. Therefore, pins can be thought of as real in a way that does not apply to angels. From there, it was but a short step to discounting angels altogether. It was not necessary to deny their existence (although many people eventually did), but whether they exist or not, they are irrelevant to our lives. We can talk about them as much as we like but we are wasting our time, because there is no practical result of such a discussion. Thus it comes about that for many people in the modern world, "theology" is a term used to describe pointless debates about artificial issues that practical people would do better to avoid. And from that, it is easy to conclude that theology has no place in an academic environment because it is not a genuine science. Faculties of divinity in ancient universities are now likely to be devoted to

---

22. It is significant that the first pope to be called Francis did not take office until 2013. There has never been a Pope Dominic.

23. It is not certain that this particular question was ever debated in precisely this form, but it has come to stand as a caricature of medieval Scholasticism in modern times.

religious studies, regarded as a branch of anthropology and history, and not as a discipline related to philosophy (and still less to law, medicine, and mathematics as it once was).

The seeds of this later development were sown in the thirteenth century and later, but it was not obvious to anyone at the time. The friars may have been opposed to the ecclesiastical establishment, but they were genuine Christians—in fact, they thought that their way of life was true Christianity in a way that ordinary parish life and monasticism were not. They were constantly in the vanguard of reform, applying it to themselves as much as to the wider church. It should come as no surprise that Martin Luther was a friar, as were many of the first generation of Protestant Reformers. It can even be said that the Reformation was to some extent a battle between the university and the monastery, a battle whose outcome was clearly seen in England, where Henry VIII (1509–1547) dissolved the monasteries and diverted much of their property and assets to the universities of Oxford and Cambridge, which subsequently became the main centers of theological training in the country.

THE (RE-)DISCOVERY OF ARISTOTLE

The emergence of universities in the thirteenth century coincided with a (re)discovery of the writings of Aristotle in Western Europe. Aristotle had never been completely forgotten, because some of his treatises, and in particular his *Categories*, had been translated into Latin by Boethius in the early sixth century and were widely available, though for a long time their importance was not fully understood. This situation changed when Peter Abelard (1079–1142) discovered Aristotelian logic and was captured by it. Before long, he was submitting everything apart from the Bible to searching criticism based on the logical principles he had picked up from Aristotle. As far as he was concerned, this was perfectly natural for a Christian thinker. Abelard knew enough Greek to realize that "logic" derived from *logos*, and that Christ was the true *Logos* who was God himself (John 1:1). It was therefore obvious to him that stressing the importance of logical analysis was a form of preaching the gospel, and he taught his students accordingly.

Like many brilliant people, Abelard was a flawed character. His intellectual arrogance made him enemies he could not afford to have, and in midlife he fell hopelessly in love with a teenage girl called Heloise, by whom he had an illegitimate son. Abelard repented of his affair, but he never really escaped his longing for Heloise and in the end that led to tragedy. Heloise's uncle had him castrated and he was forced to leave Paris for many years. He eventually returned and was still immensely popular with students, but he would never regain the reputation that had originally made his name as the most attractive teacher in France. Instead of that, he provoked the ire of Bernard of Clairvaux (1090–1153), who thought that Abelard's questioning of the church fathers was an impious attack on their authority. In 1140 Bernard had Abelard condemned at the Council of Sens, after which he was forced to retire from public life.

Abelard's crime, in Bernard's eyes, was that instead of using his faith to seek understanding, as Anselm had done, he sought understanding in order to confirm his faith. Abelard did not doubt the truth of the Bible, but he wanted to ground his faith in logic rather than the other way around. Bernard sensed that this was heretical, even if Abelard never strayed into heresy himself, and took preventive action to stop it. He was only partly successful in this, because Abelard's approach would be revived a century after his death, but it is worth noting that Bernard was one of the few medieval thinkers who was unequivocally admired by the Protestant Reformers, who saw in him a kindred spirit.

Abelard did not know it, but there was a great deal more Aristotle still to be discovered. There were two channels by which this corpus of literature came into the Latin world. When the Muslims overran the Middle East and North Africa in the seventh century, they found themselves ruling Christian people who had been steeped in Hellenic tradition. Many of them continued to speak Greek, and those that did not used Syriac, a form of Aramaic that is closely related to Arabic. As time went on, their Arab rulers began to demand translations of Greek learning, either directly from the Greek or by way of Syriac intermediaries. Almost all of this translation work was undertaken by Christians, and it was to have a profound effect on the Muslim world.

For several hundred years Muslim Arabs imbibed the teaching of Aristotle, which they adapted to their own needs. They knew that Aristotle had been a pagan and so they were careful to filter out elements of his thought that did not accord with their own beliefs. One notable example of this was that Aristotle had believed that the world was eternal, whereas Muslims (like Jews and Christians) were obliged to say that it had been created. But once that was done, the works of Aristotle were relatively easy for the Arabs to absorb. Of the three monotheistic "Abrahamic" religions, it was Christianity, not Islam or Judaism, that was the odd one out. Jews and Muslims both believed in a transcendent God who revealed himself to human beings but who remained above and beyond them in his eternal Oneness. Christians did not deny that, but they added the doctrines of the Trinity and the incarnation of the Son, both of which were anathema to the others. Aristotle's concept of the deity was closer to that of the Jews and Muslims, though it lacked the personal and revelatory aspect that the scriptural religions had. Despite that, it was not difficult for them to separate the heavenly from the earthly, giving Aristotle's analysis of the material world a degree of authority that was harder for Christians to acknowledge.

Throughout the Middle Ages, Jewish and Muslim scholars studied and debated Aristotle's teachings, not least in Spain, where the majority of the population remained Christian. As time went on, the Christians of northern Spain, who had never been subdued by the Arabs, began to reconquer the rest of the country, which by the middle of the thirteenth century was once again largely in Christian hands.[24] This created a situation that was the exact reverse of what had obtained in the middle east several centuries earlier. Now it would be Muslim (and some Jewish) writings that would be translated into Latin and these included both Arabic translations of Aristotle and a number of works that had been written by his Muslim admirers.[25]

Foremost among these was Ibn Sina, a Persian polymath better known in the West as Avicenna (980–1037). It was Avicenna who domesticated Aristotle in the Islamic world and produced philosophical treatises that were at least equal to his. Later generations of Muslims would continue to comment on Aristotle, but they did so through the prism of Avicenna,

24. The one exception to this was the Muslim Kingdom of Granada, which was not extinguished until 1492.

25. This fascinating story is outside the scope of this present book, but see Peter Adamson, *Philosophy in the Islamic World* (Oxford: Oxford University Press, 2018), for a thorough and accessible treatment of the subject from the seventh century to the present day.

whom they recognized as the supreme authority on the subject. One of these later commentators was Ibn Rushd (1126–1198), a Spanish Muslim from Córdoba, better known in the West as Averroës. While not as brilliant as Avicenna, Averroës was the right man in the right place at the right time, at least as far as reaching Latin-speaking Christians was concerned. It was during Averroës's lifetime that translations of Aristotle, Avicenna, and Averroës himself were first made in large quantities. Many people were involved in this process, but pride of place belongs to Gerard of Cremona (1114–1187), an Italian Christian who made his way to Toledo in 1140, where he found a precious hoard of Arabic books as well as teachers willing to instruct him in that language. Before long, he was turning out translations at a prodigious rate and managed to produce no fewer than eighty-seven of them before his death. Most importantly, he completed the work of Boethius on Aristotle's logical treatises, making them available to Latin-speakers for the first time.

The other channel of transmission came directly from the Greek world. The Crusades had opened up communications between East and West, and Greek works, preserved in Constantinople and elsewhere, began to circulate in Western Europe, where they were translated into Latin. It was in this way that Aristotle's *Nicomachean Ethics*, one of his most important works, was translated by Robert Grosseteste (1175–1253), who taught at Oxford before becoming bishop of Lincoln in 1235 and was one of the men responsible for establishing the intellectual tradition that would make the university famous. Thanks to men like Grosseteste, it became possible to compare translations from the Arabic with ones made directly from the original Greek, so that Latin Europe was bombarded from all sides—and at the same time.

The Aristotelianism that invaded Western Europe in the thirteenth century was thus a many-splendored thing. Some of it came from Aristotle more or less unaltered, but much of it was filtered either through Islamic thought or through the kind of mixed philosophy that characterized late antiquity. This meant that the writings of scientists like Ptolemy the geographer and Galen the physician were thrown into the mix, as was a hefty dose of Neoplatonism, mediated for the most part through the writings of Pseudo-Dionysius. In addition, as the Muslims before them had done, thirteenth-century Christians picked and chose the elements of Aristotle that suited them, which gave a further coloring to their inheritance. But it was here that Averroës came into the equation. Translations of Aristotle by themselves may not have had the influence they did had they not been supported by an authoritative master of his thought. As a Muslim, Averroës was obviously not a Christian, but neither was he a pagan like Aristotle.

Yet although Averroës might have been expected to keep a certain distance from Aristotle in much the same way as Christians had done, he did not do so. What he found in Aristotle was a thinker who got things right. Within the parameters he set for himself, Aristotle was a virtually infallible authority. He did not need divine revelation to figure out how the world works, and if he could live without it, why could others not do so as well? Furthermore, Christians and Muslims differed about divine revelation, with the former (in particular) regarding the Qur'an as false prophecy. Yet when they came to consider Aristotle, there was no such conflict. They could agree about him precisely because he was talking about things accessible to human logic and reason, and not about a revelation that could only be received by faith. This apparent neutrality was very attractive to many thinkers, not least because it seemed to offer a way to overcome otherwise intractable differences. Averroës did not directly challenge either Muslim or Christian theology, but the implications of his stance were clear, especially for Christians. Aristotle had said that virgin births were logically impossible, and so they did not happen, even if both Christians and Muslims claimed that Jesus had been born in that way. It was not for Averroës to challenge that judgment, which was outside his competence as a philosopher, but he could not logically affirm it either. Similarly, it made no sense to Averroës to say that God made the world out of nothing, even though (once again) that was the teaching of both Christianity and Islam, and he found Aristotle's belief in the eternity of matter and the role of God as the Prime Mover of that matter easier to accept.

Not surprisingly, the church differed from Averroës on questions like these, and eventually he was condemned. Of course, it made no sense to condemn Averroës without condemning Aristotle as well, and so he was thrown in too for good measure. In 1270 and again in 1277, Bishop Stephen Tempier of Paris, which housed the leading theological faculty of its time, anathematized important elements of Aristotelian teaching in an attempt to stop its spread, but by then the damage had been done. Thomas Aquinas, who died three years before the second condemnation but whose works were also caught up in it, had already developed a philosophy that was more consistently faithful to Aristotle than that of most of his contemporaries, but at the same time he had demonstrated that Aristotle could subsist as an autonomous source of truth in conjunction with the Bible.

Aquinas believed that Aristotle and the Bible were in harmony with one another as long as each was properly understood. Aristotle was right when talking about the things of this world—astronomy, biology, etc.—and the Bible was right when it revealed the things of the heavenly order. When either of them strayed into the other domain it was to make connections, but just as Aristotle could not safely be consulted on purely theological matters, so the Bible could not be read as a book of science, either. When either of them departed from their primary sphere, they had to be interpreted allegorically or by analogy, not literally. Thus, if Aristotle talked about the gods, what he said had to be Christianized, often by referring it to angels or some other spiritual movement of God, and when the Bible explained spiritual things in material terms, it was by analogy that it did so. Thus, for example, God is not literally a king sitting on a heavenly throne in imitation of some earthly ruler, but that picture might be used to emphasize his sovereign rule over the whole universe. The same would apply to something like the six days of creation, which were not to be understood as twenty-four (or perhaps only twelve) hours as we would understand them, but as phases or aspects of a process that was much longer and more complicated than the Genesis account would suggest on the surface.

Aquinas was not an Averroist, because where Averroës thought of reason and revelation as completely different ways of thinking that did not connect with each other, Aquinas insisted that they complemented one another as distinct parts of a single overarching truth. Everything ultimately depended on God, of course, but God had created human beings with minds that were adapted to the study of the material universe. That is what Aristotle had done to an extraordinary degree. He was not exactly infallible, in the way that the divine revelation in the Bible was, but near enough as made little difference. Human reason is the tool that we must use in order to unlock the secrets of the material universe, but reason does not stop there. Aided and enlightened by divine revelation, it can rise to the contemplation of God, who is the ultimate source of all Reason—the *Logos* himself.

In this way, Aquinas was trying to harmonize the apparently conflicting positions of Peter Abelard and Bernard of Clairvaux. What divine revelation gave to the human mind was not just an understanding of matters that are beyond unaided human knowledge, like the ranks of angels in heaven, but also of the hierarchy of beings in the material world and the purpose(s) for which they were created. As far as Aquinas was concerned, everything that exists has a purpose. Sometimes that is obvious, but sometimes it is not, and when it is not, divine revelation is necessary so that we can grasp what that purpose is. To that extent, revelation helps us to go beyond Aristotle by filling in gaps in our knowledge that unaided human reason cannot fill.

Aquinas found Aristotle useful when it came to analyzing the concept of sin. As he understood it, sin was a matter of intention as well as of action. If I intend to kill someone, for example, that is a sin, but if I happen to kill a man accidentally (and unintentionally), it is not. Such a murder may still be a crime in the eyes of the law, but it is of a lesser order—manslaughter as opposed to murder—and the punishment will be mitigated accordingly. Aristotle recognized this difference and so do Christians, though Christians go one step further because they introduce the notion of conscience, which was unknown to Aristotle. Conscience is what produces conviction of sin, leads to repentance, and ultimately to forgiveness—all Christian concepts that were essentially alien to the pagan Greeks but that provided a context in which wrongdoing could be properly analyzed and overcome.

Aquinas believed that what Aristotle had discovered and expounded was common to all humanity. He had no exposure to other civilizations and was therefore unable to compare ancient Greek thought with that of China or India, for example, but even if he had been able to do that, it would not have made any real difference. He would have interpreted Confucius or the Buddha in exactly the same terms as he read Aristotle. The outward presentation of their ideas might be different to some degree, but if so, that would be a reflection of their circumstances and not of a fundamentally different perception of reality. Aquinas would have had to say that, because otherwise salvation in Christ would not be universally applicable. The ultimate purpose of the philosophy of Aristotle was to prepare the human mind to receive the gospel of salvation by creating the intellectual framework for understanding what that was and why it was needed. Just as the law of Moses was a schoolmaster leading the Jews to Christ, so the teaching of Aristotle was a guide to the gentiles, pointing them toward the light. It was not the light itself—here Aquinas differed from the Averroists and would have differed from later Enlightenment thinkers as well—but it pointed to the light and prepared the eyes of the mind to receive it.

JERUSALEM UNDER SIEGE

The thirteenth century was the high-water mark of the church's control of the intellectual life of Western Europe, but the signs of decline were already starting to show. The papacy had staked its prestige on the Crusades, which had become an expensive failure. Even the conquests of parts of the Middle East and most of Spain had done little more than open the door to intellectual influences from the Arab and Greek worlds that were undermining the Western church's monopoly on learning. The growth of universities brought education out of the monasteries and introduced students to ideas that challenged the church's official teaching. Secular rulers, who had become more powerful thanks to the papacy's need for troops to conduct the wars against Islam, were gradually asserting themselves and proving to be less willing to accept the church's claims to sovereignty over them. By 1300, a quarrel between the pope and the king of France over the right to tax the clergy was reaching the boiling point, and a few years later the king actually seized Pope Boniface VIII (1294–1303) and carted him off—for his own "protection"! When Boniface died, his successor was not allowed to return to Rome, and the papacy began its seventy years of captivity in Avignon, where it was clearly beholden to the French king. So much so that when the popes finally did manage to return to Rome the result was schism, and for a generation there were two heads of the church (and occasionally even three). A ruler who did not like one pope could always turn to another, and of course the rival prelates did all they could to muster support for their claims. All of that might have blown over given time, but the intellectual currents unleashed by the breakdown of authority could not be easily contained.

The intellectual assault on the church's hegemony is usually associated with the names of William of Ockham (1287–1347) and Marsilius of Padua (ca. 1270—ca. 1342). Though they came from opposite ends of Latin Christendom, they eventually met and worked together at the court of Duke Ludwig IV of Bavaria, who for reasons of his own was happy to support anyone opposed to the Avignon papacy. Ockham is famous for his radical Aristotelianism, which led him to deny the existence of universals like humanity and insist that such a term could only be a mental construct used for convenience to describe the sum total of individual human beings. He also believed that a philosophical problem ought to be solved by relying on as few principles as possible—the more complicated the explanation, the less likely it was to be correct. This has come to be known as "Ockham's razor" and is still widely accepted today.

From the church's point of view, Ockham's most radical proposal was to say that human reason was incapable of fathoming divine truth. He believed in God—indeed, he thought that God was totally sovereign over his creation and the only being that was truly necessary. But God is beyond human understanding, and everything we know about him depends on his self-revelation to us (in the Bible). Human reason, on the other hand, was designed for examining the material world, and it was on that that Ockham urged his colleagues to concentrate. In practice, this made the church irrelevant to the scientific enterprise. The popes might be able to interpret divine revelation (though even that was questionable), but they had no business pronouncing on the natural sciences. Aristotle had managed to study them quite accurately without any such assistance, and that was the right way to proceed.

Marsilius of Padua said much the same thing, though he concentrated more on politics and government. Once again, Aristotle had written about those matters without considering any specifically religious dimension, and Marsilius questioned whether an institution like the papacy served any practical purpose. Although he could not say it openly, it is obvious from his approach that he thought the church was superfluous to society, which could manage quite well without it. The papal claim to stand above the rulers of this world and to exercise jurisdiction over them was false and found no justification either in pagan philosophy or (more importantly) in the NT, either. For both William and Marsilius, the church had overreached itself and its power had to be cut back if secular society was to flourish.

It is against this background that we must understand the writings and career of a man like John Wycliffe (1328–1384). Wycliffe was not an Ockhamist or a radical Aristotelian. He did not agree that faith should be banished from the secular sphere or that it was inimical to reason. On the contrary, he thought it was the foundation of true reason, which is why he insisted that the Bible, and only the Bible, was the true foundation for knowledge. This belief, known in Latin as *sola Scriptura,* would later become one of the hallmarks of the Protestant Reformation, though Wycliffe himself could not see that far ahead. He did, however, realize that Aristotelian principles were of little use in interpreting the Christian message. In particular, he rejected transubstantiation, the idea that bread and wine were material substances that were fundamentally altered when they were consecrated by a priest celebrating Holy Communion (the Eucharist). This made no sense to him, and he rejected it as incompatible with the biblical doctrine of creation. In saying this, Wycliffe was ahead of his time, and nobody, not even William of Ockham or Marsilius of Padua, was more fiercely attacked by the church than he was. But Wycliffe's commonsense approach to matter found supporters, especially in Bohemia, where there was a strong movement against the practice of offering communion in one kind (the bread) only. With transubstantiation, refusing the cup to the laity could be justified, since every communicant continued to receive the body of Christ. But the practice was contrary to the NT, where it was clear that Jesus had shared both the bread and the cup with his disciples, and also clear that said bread and wine could not possibly have been his body and blood, since he was still present with them in his incarnate form.

By the dawn of the fifteenth century, it was becoming clear to European intellectuals that what was by then the traditional teaching of the church could no longer be sustained. Furthermore, it was being increasingly suspected that this teaching was not traceable to the early church. Somewhere along the line things had gone wrong, and the cry went up that theologians had to return to the sources (*ad fontes*) of their belief. This, of course, meant the NT in the first instance, but also the writings of the early church fathers, from which such concepts as papal authority and the sacraments were absent. The quest for authenticity was greatly aided by the appearance of Byzantine Greeks who were starting to bring their manuscripts and their language to Italy. The most famous and influential of these was George Gemistos, surnamed Plethon (ca. 1360—ca. 1452), a latter-day Platonist who had little time for any form of Christian theology, but who was particularly hostile to the forms of it that he encountered in his own lifetime. On the one hand, there was a revival of apophatic theology in the Byzantine world, spearheaded by Gregory Palamas (ca. 1296–1359) and advocated by the monks of Mount Athos, who in Plethon's day were becoming increasingly influential in the Eastern Orthodox Church. It was known as "hesychasm," after the Greek word *hēsychia* (peace, tranquility), and involved spiritual exercises similar in some ways to yoga.

On the other hand, there was the neo-Aristotelianism of the Latin West, which had attracted a few leading Greek churchmen who were opposed to hesychasm and who thought that the Western recovery of Aristotle was the key to rescuing the dying Byzantine Empire. The snag was that if the Eastern church were to adopt that as part of a wider reconciliation with the Latin West, the Roman papacy would demand submission to its jurisdiction and the unique spiritual traditions of the East would be fatally undermined. Plethon rejected both hesychasm and neo-Aristotelianism and proposed a third way—the recovery of pre-Plotinian Platonism. There had always been some Byzantines who had been attracted to Plato, whose works were preserved and studied in Constantinople for their literary value, but nobody had ever dared to advocate pure, pagan Platonism as an alternative to Orthodox Christianity. Even Plethon had to pay lip-service to the church in order to survive, but as time went on he grew increasingly bold in his views and by the end of his life he was openly advocating a return to paganism in a somewhat refined Platonic form.[26]

Plethon made his name in the West when he attended the Council of Florence in 1439, which had been called in order to reunite the Western and Eastern churches. It soon became clear that the West expected the East to bow to its wishes, with only a few face-saving compromises to

26. See Niketas Siniossoglou, *Radical Platonism in Byzantium: Illumination and Utopia in Gemistos Plethon* (Cambridge: Cambridge University Press, 2011); C. M. Woodhouse, *Gemistos Plethon: The Last of the Hellenes* (Oxford: Clarendon Press, 1986).

make it look more like an agreement between equals. Plethon gave up on that but spent his time in Florence giving lectures on Plato to a growing and increasingly excited group of Italian scholars whom he gathered around him. The rediscovery of Plato, as this came to be seen in the West, is often taken as the beginning of the Renaissance, the point at which Western intellectuals freed themselves from the grip of the papacy and branched out on their own.

By coincidence, this was also about the time that Lorenzo Valla (1407–1457), the papal archivist, discovered that the documents used by the papacy to prove that the Emperor Constantine I had given secular jurisdiction over Rome and the Latin West to the pope were later forgeries, which the Eastern church was only too willing to believe. The impact of Valla's discovery was muted at first, but over time it undercut the legal claims of the papacy, and with them the medieval belief that the world contained a hierarchy of powers, of which the pope stood at the apex. It would be another two generations before his authority would be challenged, but when it was, the enemies of the papacy had the upper hand. The return to the sources had produced results that would ultimately lead to the fall of Jerusalem as the medieval world had conceived it and to the sundering of the Western church, from which it has never recovered.

SUMMARY

1. The Christianization of the Roman Empire in the fourth and fifth centuries involved the conversion of the intellectual inheritance of ancient Greece and Rome to a Christian way of thinking. Christians had to develop a systematic theology that could answer philosophical questions without compromising their own beliefs. This led to a series of struggles in which the right way to do this (orthodoxy) fought against various attempts at compromise (heresies). The church often found itself at odds with the Roman state, which tended to prefer compromise, but despite the opposition it faced, it won out in the end.

2. As Christians came to grips with theological questions, differences began to appear among them. The Latin-speaking world

(the West) remained fairly united around the interpretation of orthodoxy put forward by Augustine of Hippo (354–430), who became the leading authority for Christian doctrine in the West. The Greek-speaking world (the East) was more varied and no one form of orthodoxy became dominant.

3. Division occurred after the Council of Chalcedon in AD 451, when the Western church and a large portion of the Eastern one agreed that the incarnate Christ was one divine person in two distinct (and incompatible) natures. This formula, which had strong philosophical undertones, was rejected both in Egypt and in Syria, but in different ways. The Monophysites (or Miaphysites) of Egypt claimed that the incarnate Christ had only one nature, whereas the Nestorians of Syria insisted that he had two, which were not united in the way that the Chalcedonians proposed. The result was that the Eastern church split into three, a division that continues to this day.

4. It was after 451 that Greek philosophy made its greatest impact on Christian thought, especially among the Chalcedonians. In the West, the leading representative of this was Boethius, a Roman aristocrat who translated much of Aristotle into Latin and argued for the compatibility of his ideas with Christianity. In the East, the major influence was that of Pseudo-Dionysius, who claimed to be a disciple of the apostle Paul but who was probably a Syrian monk well versed in Neoplatonism.

5. After 451 Chalcedonian Greek Christians had to refine their thinking in relation to the ongoing controversies with Monophysites and Nestorians, and they did so by making free use of Greek philosophical terms, which they adapted for use in a Christian context. The result of this was a systematic theology composed by John of Damascus, which became and has remained foundational in the Eastern Orthodox (Chalcedonian) Church.

6. The Latin-speaking West was much slower to develop a distinctive theological approach, but when it finally did so, it was more

influenced by concepts derived from Roman law than from Greek philosophy. It came to maturity in the work of Anselm of Canterbury (1033–1109), who grappled with the legal and moral implications of the work of Christ and prepared the way for a great expansion of theological thought in the next two centuries.

7. Medieval Western theology paid great attention to the saving work of Christ and how this satisfied the demands of a holy and righteous God. In the course of this, there developed a sophisticated sacramental teaching that purported to explain how Christians could escape from the power of sin. This eventually produced a crisis, as it became clear that no amount of human effort could overcome the abyss that cuts us off from God. Martin Luther resolved the dilemma by pointing out that sinless perfection is not required of us because we are justified before God by faith in Jesus Christ's work of atonement. This became the basis of the Protestant Reformation, but it split the Western church.

8. Theological controversies about justification became entangled with philosophical questions raised by the rediscovery of Aristotle, whose authority in the secular sphere was taken to be as infallible as that of the Bible in spiritual matters. Thomas Aquinas (1225–1274) believed that the two could be harmonized because each represented truth in a different sphere. The result was the emergence of a tradition of philosophical theology that continues to the present time in the Roman Catholic Church.

9. The authority of Aristotle was widely contested at first, not least in Rome, and the later Middle Ages witnessed a series of theological controversies that owe far more to philosophical differences than to purely theological ones. The rediscovery of Neoplatonism in the fifteenth century complicated matters still further and ensured that the synthesis worked out by Aquinas and his followers would not survive much longer.

VI

THE REVENGE OF ATHENS

The fifteenth century was a time of revolutionary change in Western Europe. Forces that had been slowly at work from the beginning of the Crusades three hundred years before finally coalesced to produce what has come to be known as the Renaissance, or rebirth of the classical culture that had been lost for a millennium. In intellectual terms, it was the rediscovery of Plato, more than anything else, that set the ball rolling. People had always known that Plato had been the master of Aristotle and that Augustine of Hippo had regarded him as the pagan philosopher who came closest to Christianity, but apart from an incomplete and rather inaccurate Latin version of the *Timaeus,* they had almost no direct knowledge of his writings. With the exodus of large numbers of Greek scholars from a dying Byzantium, that began to change. Greeks who settled in Italy and Western Europeans who learned Greek began to translate the Platonic corpus into Latin, and in the process they opened up a whole new world. They did not abandon Aristotle, who in many respects remained the philosopher *par excellence,* but they supplemented him with their new discoveries. To put it crudely, Aristotle had examined the nuts and bolts of the material world to what seemed to many to be an exhaustive degree, but Plato opened up a higher dimension of reality. Plato spoke about universals like beauty and goodness, and offered inquiring minds a framework for constructing a coherent universe. Both in his own writings and in those of Neoplatonists like Plotinus and Proclus, Platonism gave its students a vision of the universe that appealed to a generation that wanted to explore the possibilities of human development in a new and essentially secular way.

Modern observers of this see it most obviously in the realm of art. The famous Italian trio of Raffaello Sanzio da Urbino (1483–1520), better known to us as Raphael, Leonardo da Vinci (1452–1519), and Michelangelo di Lodovico Buonarroti Simoni (1475–1564) are the iconic figures who translated Neoplatonism into high art that is still highly valued and praised today. All three were professing Christians and worked on commissions from the church, but what they produced was a world away from anything that had gone before. Instead of the stylized figures familiar from Byzantine icons, they drew (or sculpted) masterpieces that emphasized the full humanity of their subjects. In a return to pagan antiquity, men and women were often portrayed naked, or almost so, even if they were characters from the Bible. The Virgin Mary was shown breastfeeding the baby Jesus, and OT figures like Adam and David were pictured as larger than life musclemen, as the famous statue of Michelangelo's *David* reminds us. Pagans and Christians were portrayed together, and sometimes, as in the ceiling of the Sistine Chapel in the Vatican, the specifically Christian element was hard to discern. Yet there was no question of denying or abandoning orthodox Christian teaching. The point being made (or claimed) was that noble pagans and OT characters were children of God whose virtues and achievements were crowned with success by the coming of Christ.

A glance at the date when Raphael, Leonardo, and Michelangelo were most active shows that they were the beneficiaries of the Renaissance, not its initiators. For that we have to go back a generation or two and look at the pioneer work that was done by lesser-known scholars. One of the first of these was Giannozzo Manetti (1396–1459), one of the first Italians to master the three classical languages (Latin, Greek, and Hebrew). To the extent that he is known at all nowadays, it is because he wrote a four-volume work entitled *The Dignity and Excellence of Man*, in which he discoursed on the perfection of the human body, the various parts of which were flawlessly designed for the purposes for which they were intended. When discussing deformity, disease, and so on, Manetti ascribed them to the effects of original sin. Human beings were not originally created that way, and in Manetti's opinion it was the duty of Christians to follow their pagan predecessors in affirming the essential goodness of humanity. The heart of that goodness was the human soul, which Manetti claimed was immortal, a view that he derived primarily from Aristotle, though he recognized that it probably went back to Plato, even if he was hard put to find it in Plato's writings.

That was startling enough, but even more unsettling was the fact that Manetti was writing a reply to Pope Innocent III (1198–1216), who, more than two centuries before, had written a gloomy treatise called *The Misery of the Human Condition*. For Innocent III life was a vale of tears relieved only by death and resurrection, whereas for Manetti it was a series of pleasures that even the pains of old age could not completely destroy. Of course, for Manetti to challenge a pope in this way was to reject the teaching of the church, and it was that aspect that made the deepest impression on his contemporaries. Manetti was not entirely wrong, of course, and he had little trouble in justifying his opinions by referring to the goodness of creation as described in Genesis 1. He could also claim that animals, plants, and inert substances like rocks had a perfection of their own, but that human perfection was of a higher order than theirs. It was this that gave humankind the right to have dominion over the other creatures and that constituted the true glory of what it meant to be made "in the image and likeness of God" (Gen 1:26–27). Manetti never went so far as to say that man was God, but he was clearly heading in that direction and those who followed him were not slow to expand on that theme.

One of those who admired Manetti and took his positions further was Giovanni Pico della Mirandola (1463–1494), who by the time he died at the age of thirty-one had produced a body of work that would define Renaissance humanism better than anything else. In a famous *Oration on the Dignity of Man*, Pico made the extraordinary claim that human beings can create themselves in whatever way they want to. Every man and woman is a source of potential that he or she can develop to the best of his or her ability. In most cases, to be sure, nothing much happened, but the gilded youth of fifteenth-century Italy were not bound by the constraints of poverty, disease, and ignorance. On the contrary, the world was their oyster, and they were free to make of it whatever they would. This was not a justification of laziness or hedonism but a call to creativity, which might well require the time-honored virtues of hard work and self-sacrifice. Greatness may come naturally, in the sense that it does not depend on a special gift from God, but it does not come without serious effort. What Pico della Mirandola wanted to do was inspire his readers with a sense of purpose that would lead them to make that effort and realize the dream that Plato had originally had for the philosopher-kings who would rule the world.

Another man who walked in the footsteps of Manetti and was perhaps even more influential than Pico della Mirandola was Marsilio Ficino (1433–1499). Like Pico, but unlike Manetti, he was able to benefit from the new technology of printing, which had been invented in the 1450s and become widespread before the end of the century.[1] More than Manetti, Ficino was unapologetically Platonist and believed that the pagan philosopher's ideas were totally compatible with Christian teaching, to which he also subscribed, at least in theory. Like the Neoplatonists, but more comprehensively, Ficino laid out a hierarchical scheme of reality in which God was at the top, followed by Angel, Soul, quality, and matter, in that order. The first three are recognizably similar to the Plotinian hierarchy of the One, Intellect, and Soul, though Ficino did his best to Christianize them. The One was God, whom Ficino placed above and beyond all intelligible being, but "Angel" is something of a puzzle. Ficino equated this with the Plotinian *nous* ("Intellect") but he had difficulty in making the equivalence stick. For a start, there was only one Plotinian Intellect, whereas there are myriad Christian angels. Ficino tried to harmonize this obvious difference by saying that the angels represented pure minds, rather like the original Platonic forms.

These minds could not play the mediatorial role between God and the world that Christians had traditionally ascribed to angels, so Ficino assigned that to Soul instead. This was convenient, because of course the soul is the element that is present in human beings. Indeed, it is the element that *constitutes* human beings since it is what gives form to matter. Once again, Ficino did not quite say that man was God, but with an immortal soul that partook of the divine, man was about as close to God as it was possible to get without openly dissenting from the teaching of the church. Ficino was clever here—on the one hand, he often talked

1. The revolutionary impact of printing can be compared with the invention of the internet in the late twentieth century, which also had a transforming effect on the production and diffusion of knowledge.

about Soul as if it were a unity, but he rejected the Averroist idea that there is only one Soul that all human beings share. Instead of that, he claimed that every human being has an individual soul that is identical to the one Soul, having the same powers of thought and action without being forced to think and act in exactly the same way as all the other souls in existence. In other words, man was not merely divine (in some sense) but *individually* divine, which made it possible for every human being to develop his or her own potential. Some souls would obviously come closer to Soul than others, and those that did would be closer to the truth. Ficino only had to add that Jesus Christ was the soul who attained the perfection of the Soul in order to (just about) escape the charge of heresy. Instead, he managed to die in his bed—no mean feat for a radical thinker in the fifteenth century.

One theme of particular importance that Ficino touched on was that of love. This was an ancient Christian motif, of course, and was made central to the inner life of the Trinity by Augustine, whose thought dominated the Western tradition ever afterward. But just as the humanists of the fifteenth century secularized the concept of humanity being created in the image of God, so they focused on what earlier generations would have called "carnal love" or "lust." This was largely excluded from medieval thought, and especially from medieval theology, as the numerous allegorical commentaries on the biblical Song of Songs attest. The monastic tradition and the imposition of celibacy on the clergy were further examples of its unacceptability in polite Christian society. But if the human body is perfect and has sexual desires, how can these be wrong? Plato had no problem with carnal love, as his dialogue the *Symposium* makes clear. Not surprisingly, the *Symposium* was one of the Renaissance's favorite texts, and Ficino wrote an entire commentary on it.

Plato started from the premise that human beings are naturally attracted by beauty and that beauty is an aspect of the Good. By falling in love with what is beautiful the philosopher can reach out toward the good, and therefore (in Ficino's estimation) toward God. Beauty of body reflects beauty of soul, because it is the soul that gives form to the body, and so the one who starts with the flesh must penetrate further to the mind that lies within it. Ficino accepted all that, with one slight modification. He did not locate goodness *in* the body but *beyond* it. Contemplation of the beautiful ought to lead the philosopher to a higher level, consonant with the soul and with the Spirit of God. In other words, true love had little or nothing to do with sex. It was from this belief that the expression "Platonic love" derives—it was not the teaching of Plato, but the interpretation put on that by Ficino that would shape later Renaissance perceptions of what "love" is or ought to be. Whether (or how) it accords with Christian teaching is hard to say. If we think of the medieval concept of a purely spiritual love, then Ficino's reading of Plato can plausibly be regarded as "Christian." But the medieval concept in question is highly questionable, to say the least, and from that perspective Ficino would appear to be mistaken. In any case, even the monk seeking the love of God would not have started with Plato's *Symposium*, and in that sense it has to be said that Ficino's attempt to harmonize the two concepts was a failure.

At a deeper level, the Christian idea of love is not rooted in physical beauty but (if anything) the opposite. The Bible contains no description of Jesus, but Christians often apply Isaiah 53:2 to him: "He had no form or majesty that we should look at him, and no beauty that we should desire him." In addition, God's love for the world has nothing to do with its beauty but is an expression of his compassion for human beings who have fallen into sin: "God so loved the world that he gave his only Son, that whoever believes in him should not perish but have eternal life" (John 3:16). It is a far cry from Ficino's conception of Platonic love.

But Ficino's analysis of love did not stop with the desire for beauty. He asserted that human beings are the only creatures who love God because we are spiritual beings, just as he is. Our awareness that we are spiritual beings gives us the power to shape our lives with the same confidence and success as God himself does. In effect, love makes us co-creators with him. Furthermore, the creative impulse in us, which is ultimately a striving after God, is not confined to Christians. It is visible in every human society and religion, so that there is no essential difference between the Christian Bible and church, on the one hand, and the temples and sacred texts of any religion on the other. Ultimately, all religions are the same, because all manifest the same desire to find God and to be united with him as the One. It is a magnificent vision and one that, in different forms, is still commonly met with today in various interfaith contexts. And yet, it is about as far from Christianity as it is possible to get. Christian faith is not a striving after God but obedience to his revelation. It is not an exaltation of human potential but a death to self and a rising again to a new life. Above all, it is not one among many different paths to the ultimate truth. Jesus said, "I am the way, the truth and the life. No one comes to the Father except through me" (John 14:6). The Platonic ecumenist cannot swallow that exclusivist assertion, and his attempts to co-opt Jesus into an international parliament of religions is doomed from the start. The Renaissance humanists would soon find this out the hard way, as the Christian church fought back—not with an alternative philosophy of its own, but with an opposing message that put its finger on the one thing that the humanists could not come to terms with—sin.

The ultimate expression of humanism, and the one that came most directly into conflict with biblical Christianity, is associated with the name of Erasmus of Rotterdam (1466–1536). Erasmus was educated in the classics from an early age, and he became the leading scholar of his time. Though born in Holland, he was not really a Dutchman but a citizen of the world, equally at home in Paris, Cambridge, and Basel, and eagerly sought after throughout Western Europe. Like most of his colleagues and contemporaries, he was a devoted son of the church, but it was his very devotion that awakened him to the deep level of corruption into which the institution of the papacy had fallen. There was no serious doubt or disagreement about this. Virtually everyone recognized that something had to be done to restore the spiritual prestige of the church, which had fallen into the hands of worldly and avaricious popes and their associates. The problem was knowing what to do about it and how to do it.

Erasmus contributed to the general sense of unease with a satirical work entitled *In Praise of Folly*, which he dedicated to Thomas More (1478–1535) and in which he excoriated the church of his time.[2] He did not stop there, however, but determined to do something about it. Erasmus's solution to the church's problems was a full-scale return *ad fontes*—to the sources of the Christian faith and of Western civilization in general. The invention of printing had made textual criticism possible, and he devoted his energies to the establishment of correct texts, gleaned from a comparison of the most ancient and reliable manuscripts he could find. Though

2. The Latin word for "folly" is *moria*, and Erasmus's dedication was a play on words.

he was not the first person to attempt this, Erasmus did it on a scale that made him the true founder of modern philology. In 1516, he published a version of the Greek NT along with a fresh Latin translation that was significantly different from the one Jerome had made 1,100 years earlier. What neither Erasmus nor his colleagues realized was that Jerome had worked from manuscripts that were far more ancient than any that were available to them, and so his translation was by no means necessarily inferior to Erasmus's, which was based mainly on more recent Byzantine manuscripts that had suffered interpolations and corruptions of their own. But what Erasmus did achieve was the imposition of a new requirement in biblical studies—mastery of the original languages, which in principle ought to take precedence over translations, even ancient Latin ones. In this he fell foul of the Roman Church, which later decreed that Jerome's Vulgate was a correct version of the Scriptures and the only one to be used for determining Christian doctrine.[3] It was an absurd decision, but it put an effective end to creative biblical research in the Roman Catholic Church, which did not fully recover for nearly four centuries.[4]

But long before that, Erasmus would be challenged by a very different approach, associated primarily with the name of Martin Luther (1483–1546). It would come from a similar concern for a return to the sources of the Christian faith, but not at the level of textual criticism, where the two men were agreed. Rather, it would be a question of interpretation that would divide them, and here Erasmus would reveal the weakness of his humanistic background and approach. What Luther had to say to him was essentially what Anselm of Canterbury had said to his pupil Boso more than four hundred years previously: "*Nondum considerasti quanti ponderis sit peccatum*—You have not yet considered how great the weight of sin is."[5] That in a sentence sums up the criticism that Christians must make of Renaissance humanism in general, and of Erasmus in particular. Theories of goodness and beauty are all very well, but they do not come to terms with the reality that human beings have to face, which, in

3. This was decreed at the fourth session of the Council of Trent (April 8, 1546), a decade after Erasmus's death.

4. The Tridentine decree was effectively overturned by the papal encyclical *Divino afflante Spiritu*, issued on September 30, 1943.

5. Anselm of Canterbury, *Cur Deus Homo*, 1.21.

the words of the apostle Paul, is that "all have sinned and fall short of the glory of God" (Rom 3:23). No amount of thinking, however clever, and no exertion of effort, however sincere, can alter or mitigate that basic fact. Humanity's alienation from God is not the result of ignorance or the inevitable corollary of finitude, but the fruit of disobedience, a disobedience so profound that it has cut us off from God and made us guilty for the broken relationship that has resulted. Only by restoring that relationship can the problem be overcome, and such a restoration has to be the initiative of the God whom we have offended and whose sovereignty over us we have denied. That restoration can only be effected by what theologians call "justification by faith," and by faith alone. That would be the message of Martin Luther, and it would change the relationship of philosophy to theology forever.

PROTESTANTISM

There is no doubt that the Protestant Reformation of the sixteenth century was the greatest upheaval that Western Europe has ever known, but although it happened during the heyday of the Renaissance, the relationship between the two has always been difficult to determine. Martin Luther cannot be described as a humanist scholar, and although that description is not entirely inappropriate for his close assistant, Philipp Melanchton (1497–1560), or even for John Calvin (1509–1564), it is not the first one that springs to mind for him. Some of the Reformers were interested in philosophical questions, particularly as they touched on theological controversies, but none of them started a school of philosophical thought, and it is possible for scholars to write the history of Western philosophy and virtually ignore the Reformation altogether. Is Protestantism therefore an irrelevance to philosophy?

Luther certainly did not speak up against the humanism of his time or complain that pagan thought was invading the Roman Church and corrupting its message. For him, the question at issue was not one of "nature" but of "law" versus "grace," a difference of emphasis that reflects both the NT and the problems that he perceived in the church of his day. His objections to the sale of indulgences were rooted in the question of jurisdiction—did the pope or the church have any authority over Christians after their deaths? Did they have the right to claim that people could be excused from doing time in purgatory by making a cash payment to the church beforehand? Could the grace of God be sold in this way? Luther's answer to these questions was a series of negatives. No earthly power, however sacred it might claim to be, could affect anything in the spiritual realm, where the sovereignty of God reigned supreme.

Once this principle was admitted, the rest followed on logically. Gradually, Luther came to see that not only was the sale of indulgences a blasphemous impossibility, but the very existence of purgatory was an invention without biblical support. The message of the gospel was that those who trusted in Christ for their salvation would die and go to heaven because they were justified in God's eyes by their faith alone. Sinful acts, like crimes, might be paid for by various forms of punishment, but that did nothing to cure the underlying problem of sinfulness, which remained in every human being from birth onwards. For that, the only cure was death and resurrection, something that was made possible by the atoning death and resurrection of Jesus Christ. No human contribution to that was possible because all human beings are affected by sinfulness, which is the separation caused by a broken relationship with God.

At a stroke, that made all human efforts redundant. The notion that man is perfect and fully able to achieve his divine destiny on his own was anathema in biblical terms. On the contrary, argued the Protestants, human beings are totally "depraved," that is to say, turned away from any prospect of righteousness, because they are cut off from God, who is the only possible source of that. Luther had no time for Scholastic theology and regarded the influence of Aristotle as diabolical, but that was largely because of the way the subject was taught in the universities of his time. The creative generations of Peter Lombard and Thomas Aquinas had long since given way to rote learning that had become increasingly caught up in tortuous arguments that made little sense and that were far removed from the moral and spiritual concerns of most people. That there might be serious underlying questions that would need to be answered tended to escape his notice. The most important of these was the relationship between spirit and matter. Could spiritual power be invoked to produce material change, as supposedly happened in the transubstantiation of the elements used in Holy Communion? Could material things be invoked to prove or predict spiritual truth, as astrologers were wont to claim? Luther generally saw such things in a negative light, but they were side issues for him.

This caused conflict between him and Huldrych Zwingli (1484–1531) over the nature of the eucharistic elements, because Zwingli was more sensitive to the philosophical implications raised by such questions. Luther rejected transubstantiation but he continued to believe that Christ was somehow objectively present in the species of bread and wine. How this was possible he did not know, but he took the words of Jesus to his disciples at the Last Supper ("This is my body"; "This is my blood") literally, even though the context makes such an interpretation impossible (Matt 26:26, 28; Mark 14:22, 24; Luke 22:19–20). Zwingli realized that and insisted that while the Holy Spirit can and does use material things for spiritual purposes, there is (and can be) no change in those material things themselves. As the apostle Paul said to the Romans: "The [Holy] Spirit himself bears witness with our spirit that we are children of God" (Rom 8:16). This difference prevented the Reformers from making common cause, and vestiges of it remain to this day. Unfortunately, it is not often realized that the problem is as much philosophical as theological. To put it simply, can the Holy Spirit work in and through material objects like bread or human institutions like the priesthood, or does he only work spiritually, in the heart and mind of the believer who receives him by faith?

Seen in this light, it can be said that Zwingli and those who followed him (Heinrich Bullinger, Martin Bucer, John Calvin) maintained an absolute separation between spirit and matter, so that those who received the outward signs, like the bread and wine of Holy Communion or the water of baptism, but who lacked the faith that only the indwelling presence of the Holy Spirit could bestow, did not receive Christ. Luther agreed with that but came at the question from what can only be called a theological perspective. He did not believe in transubstantiation but said that Christ had appointed physical substances as means of grace and promised that he would be present "in, with, and under" them when they were consecrated by the preaching of the gospel. Luther thought that Zwingli made the grace of the sacraments dependent on the spiritual state of the recipient rather than on the promise of Christ declared in his word. Zwingli did not deny the importance of preaching but did not accept that it could be tied to material substances in any way. If it was inspired by God, then the Holy Spirit would bear witness with the believer's spirit and the presence of Christ would be felt in that believer's life. Bread, wine, and water might be useful aids to help us understand this, but they were not strictly necessary. Today, most people recognize that the two men were talking past one another and that their respective beliefs were closer than they realized, but that they lacked the conceptual framework they needed to do justice to the unity between the human and the divine in Christ, which both of them confessed.[6]

The Reformed insistence on a clear and necessary distinction between the spiritual and the material was fundamental for the growth of modern science, and indeed for the emergence of the modern world in general. It gradually became clear that astrology was false because it lacked a genuine philosophical basis. Magic and witchcraft, which had long been feared by many, were now discredited as pure fantasy and were gradually banished from respectable society. Wonder-working icons, statues, and "holy places" also fell into disrepute. Superstition, as this kind of thing came to be called, was not eliminated completely, and even today it persists to some extent at the popular level among those who read horoscopes, steer clear of black cats, and regard the number thirteen as unlucky, especially if it falls on a Friday. But none of this carries any weight in academic circles, and for that the Protestant Reformation can take much of the credit.[7]

In political terms, there was a similar effect. Secular rulers, who had previously been regarded as semi-divine because they were anointed with sacred powers (like the ability to cure scrofula) were divested of their aura, and their supposedly God-given authority was transferred to elected representatives of the people who could be dismissed at will. Church officials underwent a similar transformation, as the priest who had been given the power to perform "the miracle of the altar" (transubstantiation) became the preacher and pastor who was essentially no different from anyone else, though he was charged with the special tasks of preaching to and teaching his fellow believers in the congregation.

---

6. See S. D. Paulson, *Lutheran Theology* (London: T&T Clark, 2011), 96–100; Todd R. Hains, *Martin Luther and the Rule of Faith: Reading God's Word for God's People* (Downers Grove, IL: IVP Academic, 2022), 48–49, 164.

7. See Keith Thomas, *Religion and the Decline of Magic* (New York: Scribner, 1971).

It is sometimes claimed that the Reformation set in motion a separation of the sacred from the secular that over time relegated the former to a subordinate place in society and eventually excluded it altogether, but this is a misunderstanding. Protestants certainly rejected the idea that there were distinct sacred and secular realms, but they did so because they believed that everything comes under the sovereignty of God. Every human being has a calling (vocation) from God that sanctifies whatever it is that he or she is called to do. A carpenter or a housewife is no different from a priest or a preacher in this respect. The class system, based on a hierarchy of occupations and the value attached to them, was therefore undermined by this approach, because everyone with a calling was entitled to equal dignity and respect. This did not mean that distinct vocations did not have a character of their own. A master carpenter enjoyed an authority within his discipline that would not be accorded to a biblical scholar, for example, and the same was true in reverse. Ministers of the gospel, in particular, continued to hold a special place of authority in the life of the church, but that was because of their calling and not on the basis of their achievement(s). As these ideas sank in and took hold, societies changed, and the way was opened up to pursue new avenues of inquiry that would eventually lead to what we now recognize as the modern world.

The first generation of Protestants did not create a philosophical system of their own, but they did not break entirely with their inherited tradition either. Despite the controversy between Luther and Erasmus over free will, the Reformers generally accepted humanist principles when it came to textual criticism of the Bible and the need for a thorough mastery of the biblical languages. The methods they used to expound the texts were essentially the same, as was their approach to truth and knowledge. Though they were opposed to Aristotelianism, they tended to follow the system devised by Pierre de la Ramée (1515–1572) or Petrus Ramus, a French Protestant who attempted to reinvigorate Scholasticism by simplifying it and categorizing it in a more comprehensible fashion. Opinions differ as to whether Ramism, as his system is known, can be called a serious contribution to philosophy, but whatever modern commentators may think about it, there is no doubt that it enjoyed great success well into the seventeenth century and beyond.

In systematic theology, the Reformers did make serious efforts to revamp their discipline. Philipp Melanchthon wrote a book of *Commonplaces* (*Loci communes*) in which he set out Lutheran doctrine in a way that would make sense to someone trained in Scholasticism, but the major achievement of the century was John Calvin's *Institutio Christianae Religionis* (*Institutes of the Christian Religion*), which went through five successive editions from 1536 to 1559 and is still in print today in its fifth edition. Calvin structured his presentation in four books, just as Peter Lombard had done four centuries before. A comparison of them will reveal how Calvin tackled his subject and revised what Lombard had written:

PETER LOMBARD	JOHN CALVIN
1. The Mystery of the Trinity	1. The Doctrine of God
2. Creation	2. The Doctrine of Christ
3. The Incarnation of the Word	3. The Doctrine of the Holy Spirit
4. The Doctrine of Signs	4. Church, Ministry, and Sacraments

In both works, books one and four are essentially the same. But Calvin does not have a separate book devoted to creation, and in its place—though after the doctrine of Christ—he puts an entire book on the person and work of the Holy Spirit instead. This reflects the different approach he took to theology, which earned him the title of "doctor of the Holy Spirit." Lombard had concentrated heavily on the incarnation of Christ, which basically forms the overall theme of his work. He started with the Creator, moved on to the Creation, combined the two in the incarnation, and then discussed how Christians have access to the incarnate Christ and his work. Calvin, on the other hand, takes the Apostles' Creed as his framework and expounds how God has revealed himself in three persons, each of whom has his own specific work. In the ministry of the church we meet with God, and most particularly through the work of the Holy Spirit, who is the Creator and Sustainer of God's people.

THE DEATH OF ARISTOTELIANISM

The Protestant Reformers had a negative view of ancient pagan philosophy because it was non-Christian and they rejected any attempt to use it for the construction of their theology. They were less concerned with its impact on other disciplines, but their overall approach made alternative ways of looking at the world potentially more acceptable than they were in Catholic countries, where Aristotelianism, modified to some extent by Platonism, continued to reign supreme. This made Protestants at least marginally more open to new secular ideas, though it must be said that most of these came from people who were themselves professing Catholics.

What happened in the sixteenth and seventeenth centuries was that the dominance of Aristotelianism in the universities was shaken and eventually overthrown by an entirely new approach to the sciences. Aristotle's view of the world was essentially static. There were substances that contained an inner potential that could be activated in order to produce development and change but that remained the same in themselves. There was also a Prime Mover, who (or which) could set other things in motion but did not move himself (or itself). The earth did not move at all, and it was the center of the universe, around which the sun, the moon, and the starts revolved in perfect circles—moving but not really going anywhere. Everything in nature was perfect in itself and remained eternally the same.

As can now be seen, Aristotelianism had its weaknesses, the greatest of which was its inability to explain motion adequately. How could the Prime Mover move other things without him/itself being moved in the process? Why did the movements of the heavenly bodies not always follow the prescribed circular course? These and other questions like them teased scientists, who tried to find out why their observations did not always match the theory behind them—a theory that they never doubted was true because Aristotle had said it. The first person to break with this was Nicolaus Copernicus (1473–1543), a German-speaking Pole who took orders in the Catholic Church and never became a Protestant, even though many of his friends and colleagues did so. It was while trying to solve the puzzle of what appeared to be the irregular movement of the stars that Copernicus hit on the idea that the earth revolves around the sun and not the other way around.[8]

Copernicus discovered that by following that hypothesis, the problems he had encountered appeared to be resolved. But he had no desire to go against the Catholic Church and hesitated to publish his findings, fearing

8. Copernicus may have got this idea by reading the ancient Greek philosopher Aristarchus of Samos (310–230 BC).

that he would be laughed at for doubting what everyone took for granted. He was not wrong about that—one of his greatest detractors was Philipp Melanchthon, who found his theories of planetary motion absurd and said so. Copernicus went to his grave believing that he was mistaken but unable to deny what he had discovered. He was followed by Johannes Kepler (1571–1630), who was a much better astronomer than Copernicus had been, but who adopted Copernicus's theory and demonstrated it by meticulous mathematical observations. In particular, Kepler discovered that the planets moved in elliptical orbits, not in perfect circles, as Aristotle had taught. Moreover, the speed at which they did this varied, making nonsense of Aristotle's theory of motion being guided by the Prime Mover in a fixed and orderly way. Kepler's observations were irrefutable, but he was ahead of his time and Aristotle (or more precisely, Ptolemy the geographer, who had developed his thought with respect to the motion of the planets) retained his hegemony in most places, despite increasing evidence that his theories were misguided. In the end it was left to Galileo Galilei (1564–1642) to put the nail in Aristotle's coffin with his discovery that the heavenly order imagined by Ptolemy was nothing like as perfect as he had imagined. In 1610, he published his findings in a book called *Starry Messenger*, and his reputation as an astronomer began to spread.

Forces in the Catholic Church continued to battle against the theories of Copernicus, but despite their efforts the Inquisition never formally condemned them. Instead, in 1616 it mandated that "corrections" should be made to Copernicus's book, in effect removing any suggestion that the earth actually moved. A few existing copies of the book were corrected by hand, but there was no second edition and most people never found out what the Inquisition had proposed. Galileo was advised by Cardinal Robert Bellarmine (1542–1621) not to publish anything more in support of Copernicus's theory, and he agreed to desist, removing any need for a formal injunction to prevent him, although one had been drafted for that purpose.

By this time, Galileo had gone far beyond Copernicus and developed a theory that the perfection of the universe lay not in its objects or substances but in mathematics, which determined how the universe operates and could lead scientists to make predictions about its behavior even when hard evidence for it could not be produced. It was here that his opponents felt they had their strongest argument. How could a theory be accepted as true if there was no evidence to support it? By what logic could a mental thesis based on abstract mathematical theorems take precedence over common observation and daily experience? Criticisms of this kind rumbled on, but Galileo's reputation remained high. In 1623, Maffeo Barberini (1568–1644), one of his great defenders, was elected pope as Urban VIII and Galileo's position seemed secure, even though the pope had his doubts about Copernicus and did his best to restrain Galileo's determination to pursue his theories as the best explanation of the movements of the stars. In 1632 Galileo finally published his masterpiece, *Dialogue Concerning the Two Chief World Systems*, in which he thoroughly demolished the Ptolemaic (and Aristotelian) picture of the universe. Like Anselm before him, Galileo created a conversation between himself and an advocate for Ptolemy, whom he called Simplicio.[9] The book was an immediate best seller, but it got Galileo into trouble with the Catholic Church, which put him on trial for heresy. Galileo had made the mistake of putting Urban VIII's half-baked cosmic theories in the mouth of Simplicio and condemning them accordingly. The pope saw this as a betrayal and was persuaded to put Galileo on trail, especially when somebody produced the (unsigned) injunction against him that had lain in the Inquisition's archives since 1616.

What happened next came to be seen as one of the greatest scandals in church history, and it has been held up ever since as a prime example of religious bigotry in the face of objective scientific discovery. Ironically, Galileo was not put on trial for his theories but for the fact that he had apparently ignored the injunction of 1616 that forbade him from saying any more about Copernicus, even though that injunction was only a draft that had never been issued and lacked any official status. Galileo defended himself and confounded his critics, who hardly knew what to accuse him of, but instead of being acquitted he was sentenced to house arrest, essentially because the Church could not be seen to have made a false accusation against him. The conditions of his arrest were soon modified, thanks to the intervention of priests in high places, but he never escaped the watchful eye of the Church, which pursued him for the rest of his life. Even so,

9. The name is clearly pejorative, meaning something like "simpleton," but there was a Simplicius in ancient times, whose commentaries on Aristotle were still being widely read in Galileo's day.

he was able to complete a second great work, *Dialogues Concerning Two New Sciences,* but he could not publish it in Italy. The manuscript had to be spirited out and printed in Holland, whose Calvinist rulers admired him for resisting what they saw as papal tyranny.

It was this event that sealed the informal alliance between Protestantism and the new mathematical science of Galileo. Aristotle/Ptolemy and the Catholic Church were now formally bound together in opposition to him, and to reject the one was effectively to reject the other as well. This was to have serious consequences for Christian orthodoxy.[10] The Catholic Church had regarded Aristotle (and his followers like Ptolemy) as infallible in the natural sphere, just as the Bible was infallible in the spiritual realm. But if Aristotle could be shown to be wrong, what would that do to the Bible? This would become a major problem in the seventeenth century and later, but it did not stop there. The dissolution of the Aristotelian worldview meant that concepts like "substance" and "essence" ceased to have any currency. Instead of a hierarchy of beings, the world came to be perceived as consisting only of matter. Matter could neither be created nor destroyed, and in that sense might be regarded as "eternal," but it was constantly being reshaped as it moved and interacted with other matter to form the objects that we perceive with our senses.

Motion was inherent in matter and did not need to be started or kept going by some external force. This did not rule out the existence of God entirely, but it did mean that he was not required to be the Prime Mover or the providential sustainer of the material universe. René Descartes (1596–1650) discovered the principle of inertia, which became the foundation for the physics of Isaac Newton (1642–1727), and both men rested their findings on mathematical principles. Instead of regarding the world as a community of beings interacting with one another, they came to see it as a gigantic machine that operated according to set rules that were innate in its structure and not dependent on God. The idea that nature is governed by a Supreme Mind who could control it at will (and thus, on occasion, produce miracles) was replaced by a completely impersonal

---

10. See J. M. Moritz, *The Role of Theology in the History and Philosophy of Science* (Leiden: Brill, 2017), for an engaging introduction to the Galileo affair and its lasting consequences.

force that human ingenuity might be able to master and control to some extent, but that in itself knew nothing of virtue or grace.

It was a vision of reality that frightened many because it seemed to be heartless in a way that the Christian God (the Supreme Mind) was not, but to men like Descartes and Newton it appeared as the basis of a newfound freedom and certainty. It brought freedom because it put paid to superstitions that had previously chained the human imagination and prevented it from exploring the universe along rational, mathematical lines. It brought certainty because it rested on principles that could be demonstrated by a virtually infallible logic that could not be denied or refuted. We have to say that the logic was virtually infallible, not completely so, because the human mind is incapable of mastering it in all its many subtleties. There is always an element of error or miscalculation in human terms, even if it is very small and decreasing all the time. Newton accounted for these gaps in his knowledge by saying that they were mysteries hidden in the mind of God. What he did not foresee was that over time, as many of these gaps were filled in and explained by further research, the sphere of action that required God to explain it shrank considerably. The "God of the gaps" disappeared as the gaps were filled. God was not a necessary explanation for the way the world works, and therefore he was disposed of—Ockham's razor, in effect, applied to new circumstances.

Newton himself continued to believe in God as a matter of philosophical principle, because even if the gaps were accounted for, there was still the problem of origins: Where did the world ultimately come from? A Creator of some kind was required, though whether this was the God of the Bible was debatable. Even more uncertain was the question of the Trinity. Only one Creator was required, and there was no logical place for three distinct persons. Indeed, the very concept of "person" came under scrutiny because it hardly seemed necessary. All that was required of the Creator was a mind that could (and did) create, but once that was done, the resulting creation could be (and was) left to run on its own. Newton was a deist, not a theist in the Christian sense, and his understanding proved to be very popular in some circles. The doctrine of the Trinity had been questioned since the Reformation, not least because it does not appear as such in the Bible. Anti-Trinitarian writers began to appear; Lelio Sozzini (1525–1562) and his nephew Fausto (1539–1604) formed a heretical movement known as

Socinianism, which taught what we would now call Unitarianism, and managed to establish a base in Raków (Poland). Fausto wrote a short treatise outlining their beliefs, and this *Racovian Catechism*, as it was known, was soon circulating across Europe. Protestant theologians in particular were deeply disturbed by it, and Socinianism became one of the bugbears of the English Puritans and others, who sprang to the defense of Trinitarianism and largely held the Socinians at bay.

The emergence of deism gave new life to Unitarianism, which spread rapidly. By the early eighteenth century it had come to dominate intellectual circles in England, though they could do nothing to change the official teaching of the church, which was protected by law. It was a different matter where the nonconformist, or "free churches," were concerned, and there the effect was devastating. The Presbyterian Church in England opened the door to it in 1719, and within a generation the entire denomination had become Unitarian. Something similar happened in the American colonies, where many leading revolutionaries were attracted to it. In the early nineteenth century, Harvard Divinity School became officially Unitarian, and the established church in Massachusetts, which had survived the American Revolution intact, was torn apart by it and eventually disestablished as a result (in 1833).

But long before the emergence of Unitarianism as an official creed, the dismantling of the Aristotelian worldview had revolutionary consequences in the political realm. For centuries most people had thought in terms of social hierarchy, with peasants at the bottom and the king at the top. Everyone had his or her place in this social order and was responsible to God for living in a way that would fulfill their obligations. From time to time the order broke down, often because theologians questioned it. This was true in the fourteenth century, when John Wycliffe challenged the authority of the church and was condemned by both popes and the Council of Constance, which was held many years after his death.[11] However, the more immediate result of Wycliffe's protest was a peasants' revolt, which briefly paralyzed the English government in 1381 and lost Wycliffe the support that he had enjoyed up to then in court circles. Much the same happened when Martin Luther protested against the abuses

11. Wycliffe died at the end of 1384, but the council met from 1414 to 1417.

he saw in the church—there was another peasants' revolt, which Luther himself was forced to condemn in order to save his Reformation (and probably himself as well).

Order was restored, and for most people that was the way things ought to be. But questions remained, and in the upheavals of the time they had to be addressed. One person who did this was King James VI of Scotland, who wrote a treatise called *The Divine Right of Kings*.[12] This would become notorious in the next generation, but initially there was little adverse reaction. James was not advocating an absolute monarchy, and he was writing in the context of the Calvinistic theology that Scotland had adopted and in which he had been brought up. What he argued for was traditional Aristotelianism. As king, he was responsible to God for his actions, in the same way that his subjects were responsible to him. It did not work the other way around. Later critics would interpret this as the king's desire to lord it over his people, but James did not see it that way. He took his responsibility before God very seriously and was well aware that he had been called to "do justice, and to love kindness, and to walk humbly" with his God (Micah 6:8). Before the throne of eternal judgment, he and his subjects stood on the same level, because each of them would have to answer for his calling. But for a subject to question the king was to go against the order established by God, and that was the problem. James himself was astute in his judgment of men and was careful not to offend the sensibilities of his subjects, but his son Charles I (1625–1649) was not. Charles did not share his father's Calvinism and was caught up in a wider European movement toward absolute monarchy that was gaining traction at that time. His brother-in-law was Louis XIII of France (1610–1643), who shut down what remained of representative institutions in his country, as Charles would eventually try to do in England as well.[13]

The difference between France and England was that in the former country the suppression of popular representation in government went hand in hand with the restoration of Roman Catholicism, with its own

12. He wrote this in 1600, shortly before he became king of England as James I (in 1603).

13. In France, the Estates-General, a kind of parliament, met for the last time in 1614. It was not summoned again until 1789, a move that sparked off the French Revolution. In England, Charles I dismissed parliament in 1629, but was forced to recall it in 1640, a move that had similar revolutionary results.

well-established hierarchy. In England, on the other hand, parliament had been used since 1529 to promote the king's reformation of the church, of which he was "supreme head."[14] This created an unusual theological situation, because the king could not ordain the clergy, nor could he impose a particular theological creed without the consent of the church, which included the laity. In the circumstances of the time, the laypeople could only express their voice in parliament, which therefore claimed the right to share in church government. The bishops were also represented in parliament, but the clergy had their own synods, the "convocations" of Canterbury and York, which deliberated matters of doctrine and church government generally. After 1545 the convocations met in tandem with the parliament, but at first this was a matter of convenience more than anything else. It was only when Charles I tried to govern the church through the convocations alone, which he thought he could control, and ignore the parliament, that the system broke down and contributed to the outbreak of civil war.[15]

It is against this background that we have to understand the way in which relations between church and state developed in England and evaluate the vast amount of political theory that started to pour forth from laypeople who increasingly rejected the Aristotelian presuppositions that had governed popular understanding for so long. Modern historians tend to regard this as a movement toward secularization that was initially non-religious but became openly atheistic as time went on. That, however, is a view from hindsight. At the time, it was not seen that way at all. What the English "revolutionaries" wanted was a return to what they saw as the "old constitution," a situation in which parliament and the king worked together for the benefit of the church, which was identified with the nation as a whole. This "old constitution" had never existed as such—what the polemicists of the seventeenth century were really arguing against was the interpretation put on the divine right of kings by Charles I and the Aristotelian philosophy on which that interpretation was logically based.

At the same time as divine right theory was being debated in England, central Europe was being torn apart by the Thirty Years' War (1618–1648),

14. This title was adopted in 1534 and modified to "supreme governor" in 1558, when Elizabeth I ascended the throne. It remains as such to the present day.

15. This happened in 1640. But the convocations continued to meet in tandem with parliament until 1966, when they were finally set "free."

ostensibly between Protestant and Roman Catholic states in the Holy Roman Empire. That empire was a confederation of polities to which Luther's Wittenberg, Zwingli's Zurich, and Calvin's Geneva all belonged, but it was loose enough to allow them to coexist and even to develop a formula known as *cuius regio eius religio*, which may be translated as "the religion of a local ruler determines the religion of his territory." The emperor himself remained Catholic, though there was an attempt to displace him in 1618, which set off the war in the first place. One of the regions affected by this was the Netherlands, where a Protestant elite had been trying to throw off the yoke of Spanish Catholic rule since 1566. They were eventually successful, and when peace was finally declared in 1648 the *de facto* independence of the Netherlands was formally recognized. It was also the first time that the papacy was excluded from an international treaty, which was meant to be an entirely secular affair.

By then, the world was being influenced by a noted Dutch jurist, Hugo Grotius (1583–1645), whose writings on international law became the foundation of the world order that still prevails today. Grotius was what we would now call a "liberal" Protestant who believed that he could not appeal to church authority for his claims about the law of nations. Instead, he relied on what was known as "natural law," which the Aristotelians and their medieval Scholastic successors believed was both innate in human beings and autonomous, by which they meant that it did not require theology, or even the acknowledgment of the existence of God, for its validity. By working on the basis of what he regarded as universal principles, Grotius believed that he could overcome the divisions caused by the Reformation and secure peace, which he very largely succeeded in doing. What he perhaps did not recognize was that the differences between Protestants and Catholics, serious and deeply felt though they may have been, were nevertheless differences between different kinds of Christians, who shared most of their basic assumptions in common. The result was a secular way of thinking that could nevertheless be harmonized with Christian principles, and that too became a feature of Western society that has remained more or less intact to the present day.[16]

16. This is obvious to adherents of other religions, especially Islam, who see the common "Christianity" underlying Western culture and resist it to varying degrees.

Another important voice in this process was Thomas Hobbes (1588–1679), whose classic work *Leviathan*, published just after the close of the English Civil War in 1651, remains one of the most important works of political theory ever written. As the title indicates, Hobbes took his theme from Job 41:1–34, where the possibly mythical Leviathan is portrayed as a fearsome monster who cannot be controlled by human means, but who nevertheless remains a creature of God. Hobbes used Leviathan as a metaphor for the state, which he saw as monstrous but as a necessary evil, protecting humankind against the alternative, which was chaos and self-destruction. As far as Hobbes was concerned, to live in a state of nature was to court disaster, because the untamed human being was basically no better than a predatory animal. In his famous words, such a condition would produce "continual fear, and danger of violent death, and [make] the life of man solitary, poor, nasty, brutish and short."[17]

Hobbes clearly knew all about original sin, though whether he can be called a Christian has been a matter of considerable debate. What is certain is that he lived in an age that was permeated by Christian concepts and values, and that he wrote for an audience that would be expected to interpret him in that way. He was by no means universally popular, and spend many years in exile in France and the Netherlands, though after the publication of *Leviathan* the Puritan government of England allowed him back into the country, at least for a time. What Hobbes proposed was a new theory of government, quite different from anything like the divine right of kings, which is one reason why he was popular with some people but not with others. However, after the Restoration in 1660 he was supported by King Charles II and protected by the duke of Devonshire, on whose estate he died at the great age of ninety-one.

Hobbes's great contribution to the debate was his introduction of the concept of social contract. According to his theory, human beings have surrendered their autonomy to a higher power, which they recognize as sovereign over them. This entails a loss of freedom, but in compensation comes security, because the sovereign is expected to protect his subjects against predators and enemies of various kinds. In order to do this effectively, the sovereign has to claim authority over every aspect of social

17. Thomas Hobbes, *Leviathan*, 13.9.

life, including the church. This got Hobbes into trouble, because the idea that the church should be a department of the state was thought to be anti-Christian. It was that, of course, but the real problem was something different. The Church of England had been subject to the state, at least to some degree, since the Reformation, but it was a state constituted under God and ultimately subject to him. Hobbes in effect eliminated God from the equation, not necessarily because Hobbes did not believe in him, but because he was unnecessary to the scheme that Hobbes devised for good government. In the mechanistic view of the universe that Hobbes adopted, this made perfect sense, but it is easy to see why a number of people were unhappy with his conclusions. To lose freedom was one thing, but if it was lost to a sovereign that did not acknowledge God, it was a step too far.

This difficulty was addressed by John Locke (1640–1704), who had a much more positive view of natural law than Hobbes had. He did not see the state as a kind of monster made necessary by the omnipresence of sin but as the outworking of God's universal law of creation. According to him, God did not make the world to enslave humankind to a higher power within it but to set people free. The laws of nature were governed by reason, and all people of good will had access to that. Locke insisted that human beings do not surrender their natural rights, as he thought of them, any more than they gave up their capacity to reason. On the contrary, every individual retained his natural freedom, which he used for the benefit of civil society, and that society existed only to protect his ability to do so. In other words, a government that coerced its citizens was a tyranny, and whatever protection it might offer them was essentially a fraud.

It is fair to say that Locke's vision of society was considerably more naive than Hobbes's was, even if it was obviously more attractive. Human beings may be free agents, but there is no guarantee that they will use their freedom responsibly or according to reason. Liberty might be conceivable for those who were so minded, but those who objected or failed to live up to the standards Locke set would have to be repressed one way or another. This was especially true in the case of a sovereign who did not respect the liberty of his subjects. Failure to fulfill that primal duty would mean that the sovereign in question had lost the right to rule and could be overthrown by those whom he was guilty of oppressing.

This was the real innovation in Locke's theory of the social contract. Nobody had ever argued it before, and there were plenty of examples Locke could point to that he saw as ripe for revolt. First among them was the France of Louis XIV (1643–1715), whose reign coincided with Locke's life. As far as Locke was concerned, Louis XIV was a wicked ruler who oppressed his people in order to further his own glory and power—partly by building impressive but essentially useless palaces like Versailles, and partly by eliminating those whom he perceived as a threat to his absolute power, notably the French Protestants (Huguenots), whom he expelled in 1685. Like most Englishmen of the time, Locke was horrified by this, but there was nothing he could do to prevent it. Instead, he confined his activities to what he thought was achievable—toleration of different viewpoints in England and a change of government that would ensure that nothing like Louis's absolutism would ever occur in the British Isles.

Locke was surprisingly successful in achieving these aims, though he may not have realized it at the time. When King James II (1685–1688) tried to emulate his cousin Louis XIV, he was chased off his throne and the sovereignty of parliament was affirmed by its grant of the crown to William III (1689–1702) and his wife, James's daughter Mary II (1689–1694). William and Mary were not sovereigns by divine right but by parliamentary fiat, and the implication was that what had been granted could also be withdrawn if the social contract were not fulfilled. It was essentially on that understanding that the American colonists would later rise up against George III (1760–1820), whom they regarded as a tyrant because his government wanted them to pay taxes for their own defense. It has often been pointed out that the independent American government that resulted from the Revolution was far more tyrannical than George III ever was (or could have been),[18] but to the minds of those who had been schooled in the ideas of Locke, the laws imposing such tyranny were enacted by the consent of the governed, not by an institution still clinging to whatever remained of the "divine right of kings." Locke himself claimed to be a Christian, and one who had reconciled the rationalism (as he saw it) of the philosophers with the superior spirit of Christ:

---

18. For a full discussion of this question see A. Roberts, *The Last King of America: The Misunderstood Reign of George III* (New York: Viking, 2021).

> He that shall collect all the moral rules of the philosophers and compare them with those contained in the New Testament, will find them to come short of the morality delivered by our Savior, and taught by his apostles, a college made up, for the most part, of ignorant but inspired fishermen.[19]

In a curious way, it was a return to the symbiosis of Aristotle and the Bible found in Thomas Aquinas and the medieval Scholastics, though Locke would not have acknowledged any debt to them. How Christian it was, though, was another matter entirely. Nothing in the Bible suggests that government of the people, by the people, and for the people, which is what Locke advocated, was ever seriously considered. The only time when popular opinion in Israel was allowed to dictate the form of government was when representatives of the people asked Samuel to give them a king (1 Sam 8:1–22). They got what they asked for, but only after Samuel had made it clear to the people (and God had made it clear to Samuel) that this was an act of rebellion that would not turn out well. We might perhaps add the Palm Sunday entry of Jesus into Jerusalem, when once again popular acclaim pointed in one direction but the will of God was revealed to be something else altogether (Matt 21:1–9; Mark 11:1–11; Luke 19:19–28; John 12:12–15).

Beyond the social (political) sphere, Locke's other great contribution to philosophy was his analysis of the human mind. In 1690 he published *An Essay Concerning Human Understanding*, in which he denied the existence of ideas innate in our minds and prior to any experience of what they represented. To put it simply, we do not have an idea of a "table" in our heads that we then create or recognize in the material world. On the contrary, we see things that have certain basic similarities among them and give them a common name—in this case, "table." We recognize tables when we see them because we have seen objects like them before and have been taught to use the word "table" to describe them. This is a rational way of proceeding, but it is not infallible. There are things like stools, for example, that share the fundamental characteristics of tables but are sufficiently different from them to warrant having a separate word to describe

19. John Locke, *The Reasonableness of Christianity* (Stanford, CA: Stanford University Press, 1958), 61.

them. Of course, we can also have different words for describing the same thing—synonyms, in effect. A table can also be called a "board," at least in certain circumstances, but the boundaries of definition are porous and both words have a range of other meanings that do not overlap at all.

Locke concluded from this that our knowledge of things, while undoubtedly real, can only ever be probable, not absolutely certain. Observation, backed up by trial and error, shapes our minds to define what we perceive, thereby creating ideas in our minds. To put it a different way, ideas do not shape our experiences, but the other way around. If our experiences change significantly, then the ideas that they create in our minds will change, too. Ancient philosophy was static and uncreative because it started from the principle of fixed ideas, and all observed phenomena had to be classified accordingly. There was no place for change or development—if something new was discovered, it was because until then whatever it was had not been perceived or properly classified. Once it was put in its place, as it were, it went nowhere. Locke opened the mental door to innovation, and it has not been closed since.

On the question of toleration, Locke got much further than anyone could have dared to hope. The monopoly of the state church was effectively broken in England as Dissenters (Nonconformists) were allowed extensive freedom of worship, though not civil equality, which had to wait until 1828. Most importantly, the censorship of publications was abolished in 1695. That led to a flood of books and pamphlets attacking not only the religious establishment but Christianity itself. Jerusalem still occupied a prominent place in society and especially in the hearts and minds of ordinary people, but the increasingly atheistic philosophers had seized the intellectual high ground, from which they would never be successfully or permanently dislodged. Athens had had its revenge, and although complete victory was still some way off, the signs pointing in that direction were unmistakable.

SUMMARY

1. In the mid-fifteenth century a rediscovery of Neoplatonism unleashed creative forces that we now call the Renaissance. There was a new emphasis on humanity and the potential

for educated people to create their own futures. It was not an explicitly anti-Christian movement, but it led to a deep questioning of the church, which appeared to many to be corrupt and out of touch with the new learning.

2. Criticism of the church came both from Renaissance humanists like Erasmus and theology professors like Martin Luther. Luther's attack on medieval theology had the greater impact, at least in the short term, and led to a schism in the Western church that has never been overcome. The result was the emergence of Protestantism, a different and internally diverse kind of Christianity.

3. The Protestant Reformers took a dim view of ancient Greek philosophy, but they did not attack it directly. Rather, they were caught up in a general repudiation of traditional Aristotelian beliefs about the order of the world, much of which was associated with Catholics like Copernicus and Galileo, who fell afoul of the Roman Church because they questioned what had become the traditional synthesis of philosophy and theology.

4. The liberation of the natural sciences from the authority of the Catholic Church was felt more strongly in Protestant countries, where there was relatively greater freedom of thought. But the leading philosophers of the time departed from orthodox Christianity by insisting that theology should be rational. They were mainly deists (effectively Unitarians) who believed in a Supreme Being that was identified with the Christian God in theory, though it differed from him in being impersonal and separate from human affairs.

5. Religious warfare between Catholics and Protestants, and sometimes between different kinds of Protestant, discredited dogmatic theology and allowed rationalism to establish itself as the lowest common denominator among warring groups of Christians. Thanks to the writings of men like Thomas

Hobbes and John Locke, a kind of generic Protestantism took root and became the accepted creed of civil society.

VII

WAR—AND PEACE?

In 1935, the French historian Paul Hazard (1878–1944) began what he intended to be a trilogy of European intellectual history from about 1680 to 1789. The first volume, entitled *The European Mind 1680–1715* in English translation, created a sensation.[1] The second one, published a few years later, continued the story through to the middle of the eighteenth century, but the third was never completed.[2] Hazard's thesis was that the religious and philosophical outlook of Western civilization changed quite suddenly in the years around 1700 and that, despite many ups and downs, that change is still with us today. The German philosopher Immanuel Kant (1724–1804) called it the *Aufklärung* ("enlightenment"), the name by which it is now generally known. Kant's designation was propaganda—he believed, as did those who took part in the movement, that centuries of darkness had been dispelled by a new way of thinking, which for the first time had brought rationality and clarity to our understanding of human affairs. Hazard was more skeptical and tended to avoid the term "enlightenment" as much as possible, but he made no attempt to deny the magnitude of the intellectual revolution that had taken place and chronicled its origins in great detail.

Hazard pioneered the study of a subject that has since captured the imagination of more than one historian of philosophy. Among the more

1. Paul Hazard, *La crise de la conscience européenne* (Paris: Boivin, 1935); ET (London: Hollis and Carter, 1953).

2. Paul Hazard, *La pensée européenne au XVIIIe siècle de Montesquieu à Lessing* (Paris: Boivin, 1946); ET *European Thought in the Eighteenth Century from Montesquieu to Lessing* (London: Hollis and Carter, 1954).

notable of them are two Jewish scholars, Peter Gay (1923–2015) and more recently Jonathan Israel (1946–), whose massive volumes are now the standard works on their subject. It is fair to say that Gay adopted a position not unlike that of Hazard, whereas Israel is a declared supporter of Enlightenment values, which he defends in the face of what he fears are countervailing influences in the contemporary world.[3] What is remarkable about these writers is that, however different their approaches may be in some respects, they are in fundamental agreement about what actually happened. In the space of a single generation, the European mind went from one in which religious questions were of fundamental importance and shaped the framework of discussion for everything else to one in which religion was shunted to the sidelines, to be replaced by the cult of human reason and science (however broadly that might be defined). Old certainties, like the infallibility of the church and/or the Bible, were cast aside in favor of human perception and experience. It cannot be said that this shift went unchallenged, and there have always been Christian philosophers and theologians, both Protestant and Catholic, who have fought against it, but they are the opposition. The mainstream is non-religious and essentially agnostic on matters of faith, which it tends to exclude from serious discussion. This creates a serious dilemma for Christians, who can no longer assume that philosophy is the handmaid of theology, and who often have to fight for a hearing in a climate that assumes that God does not exist, or that if he does, he does not matter.

One of the attractions of Enlightenment thinking is that it embraces the world beyond the bounds of traditional Christendom. In the seventeenth century, Europeans were exploring a world that neither their ancestors nor the Bible knew anything about. The discovery of the Americas was problematic from the start, since there was no mention in the OT of the people who lived there. Where did they come from, and did they belong to the same human race as Europeans did? The ancient civilizations of India

3. Peter Gay, *The Enlightenment: An Interpretation*, 2 vols. (New York: Knopf, 1966–1969); Jonathan Israel, *Radical Enlightenment: Philosophy and the Making of Modernity 1650–1750* (New York: Oxford University Press, 2001); *Enlightenment Contested: Philosophy, Modernity and the Emancipation of Man 1670–1752* (New York: Oxford University Press, 2006); *Democratic Enlightenment: Philosophy, Revolution and Human Rights 1750–1790* (New York: Oxford University Press, 2012); *The Enlightenment that Failed: Ideas, Revolution and Democratic Defeat, 1748–1830* (New York: Oxford University Press, 2019).

and China were another challenge. How could they have produced such a developed culture, complete with a code of moral and spiritual values, if they had no knowledge of Christianity? Europeans were supposed to bring the gospel of Christ to those people and convert them to the truth, but what if they were to find that the people they were preaching to had higher moral standards and a deeper spiritual vision than they had?

Against this backdrop, the quarrels of seventeenth century Europe looked petty and provincial. Why were people being persecuted and even killed just because they had different views of the papacy, for example, or of the sacramental rites of the church? How could so-called Christians be so devoid of the spirit of Christ? Every Christian group thought that it was right, of course, but on what authority? Was it not just as likely that they were all wrong, even if the degree of error varied from one to another, and that nobody was in possession of absolute truth? There were certainly many areas of agreement, such as the sense that murder and theft are wrong, but more often than not, convictions of that kind were common to a wide variety of religions and belief systems. Was this because non-Christians accidentally got it right, or was it because there is an underlying humanity that is shared by everyone, regardless of the form it takes in particular instances? Christians might find the practices of Hindus and Muslims strange and even repellent, but were they just outward expressions of a common inner conviction that all human beings shared, and if so, was Christian dislike of them no more than petty prejudice against the unfamiliar? Has God really spoken only to Jews and Christians, leaving the rest of the world in the dark?

Enlightenment radicals also profited from increasing skepticism regarding such things as miracles, prophecies, and the occult. Protestants had attacked superstitious practices and done their best to abolish them, but in Catholic countries prayers to the saints, pilgrimages to shrines, and a naive confidence in the supposed spiritual power of the sacraments were all strong. Popular superstition was also far from extinguished in Protestant circles, where even King James VI and I kept a court astrologer. Pointing out that a comet was merely an astronomical phenomenon and did not portend some great event on earth was the sort of thing that shook popular belief, but it did not go against the official teaching of the church, which had never subscribed to such notions. The problem for

Christians was that although they were often prepared to recognize that much of what passed for spirituality was fraudulent, they also believed that a spiritual world existed and interacted with human beings. For example, they might doubt whether an angel had appeared to a particular person at a given time, but they did not deny the existence of angels or rule out the possibility that such things could happen, since they were recorded in the Bible. Similarly with miracles. Christians might question whether a particular healing was miraculous or could be attributed to the intercession of a particular saint, but that miracles were impossible they could not accept.

The difficulty was knowing how to distinguish the true from the false. The only way that could be done was by scientific investigation of the facts, but the facts were often virtually impossible to determine, and alternative explanations of what might have happened were always possible and often preferable. Investigations of this kind were a spur to the development of science, and as solutions to various mysteries began to appear, so belief in their supernatural character diminished. In such a situation it was relatively easy for skeptics to claim that with patience and effort, all such mysteries could be solved and a rational explanation be provided for everything. Broadly speaking, that is still the position adopted today—scientists cannot explain every phenomenon that occurs, but when they come across something that they have not previously encountered, they do not think in terms of the miraculous. Instead, they go looking for an explanation and assume that, sooner or later, one will be found. It was this conviction that fueled the Enlightenment. Enlightenment thinkers did not have all the answers, but they had what they saw as the key to finding them, and as that belief gained ground, confidence in traditional approaches to the supernatural declined accordingly.

This change of worldview was gradually creeping into European thought in the early seventeenth century, but it lacked coherent systematization. Men like Galileo, Descartes, and Hobbes were pioneers of what would become the skeptical, or scientific approach to reality, but they never succeeded in freeing themselves completely from the Christianized Aristotelianism in which they had been brought up. That move, as Jonathan Israel has argued, was taken by Baruch (or Benedict) Spinoza (1632–1677), who was the first person to advocate the new science in a way that ensured that there would be open conflict between it and traditionally received wisdom.

Spinoza was a Sephardic Jew whose family had left Portugal to escape the Inquisition and had settled in the more tolerant Netherlands. As a Jew, Spinoza was not naturally sympathetic to Christianity, but he had no time for Judaism either. He was an early disciple of Descartes, and was so insistent that he was thrown out of the synagogue in Amsterdam when he was only twenty-three years old. He did not repent, however, and soon his reputation as a free thinker had spread far and wide, even before he published anything. His views were attacked by Jews, Christians, and Cartesians alike, and most of his opponents downplayed the influence that he had over them, even to the point of pretending that they knew little or nothing about him. But as Israel has convincingly shown, this was all a pretense. In actual fact, Spinoza was changing the mindset of European intellectuals and was the true founder of the Enlightenment as we have come to know it.[4]

Put simply, Spinoza adopted the Cartesian theory that there was a single substance that underlies all material reality. But whereas Descartes had clung to a kind of dualism, claiming that there was also a world of thought that existed independently of matter and worked on it to shape it into the objects that we see around us, Spinoza rejected that. He argued that if there is one universal substance (which Descartes had accepted), then it must be truly one and universal—there was no room for a distinct realm of thought. Descartes had equated that distinct realm with God and therefore allowed for something like the traditional doctrine of creation. But Spinoza said no. He claimed that our thought processes are part of the material world—the mind is not detached from the brain but is part of it. If there was a God, he (or it) could only be a name for the mental process that infused the entire universe—the spirit of matter. Motion, so long thought to have come from outside the material world, was completely enclosed within it. Theology, as a discipline, ceased to exist because there was no place for it in Spinoza's universe. This was a rejection of traditional values so profound that no religious person could possibly accept it, and conflict was the inevitable result.

4. Israel, *Radical Enlightenment*, 159–74.

Whether (or in what sense) Spinoza could be called an atheist is debatable, but it does not matter one way or the other.[5] In his mental construction of the universe, God was unknowable, and what was unknowable was effectively nonexistent. But when theology impinged on the material world it was clearly out of place. A doctrine like transubstantiation, for example, made no sense if there was only one substance. Nobody ever suggested that a priest could turn bread and wine into the physical body and blood of Christ, so the question had no meaning—it was, quite literally, immaterial. The doctrine of the Trinity was more difficult because it dealt with the inner being of God, which was unknowable and therefore irrelevant, even if it was true. But of course, the doctrine of the Trinity had been developed in order to account for the incarnation of the Son of God, something that Spinoza rejected as impossible. This left room for deism, or Unitarianism, which became popular at this time and could to some extent be harmonized with the idea of a "spirit of Nature," but that was as far as it went.

Spinoza's rejection of traditional religious dogmas did not mean that he was indifferent to the moral concerns that were attached to them. It was not for nothing that his great work was called *Ethics*, because his entire intellectual project was built around the notion of virtue, which he conceived of as the power to live in harmony with the spirit of the universe. Because ultimately God and Nature were the same in Spinoza's mind, and Nature was determined by scientific laws, everything that happens in the world is predetermined and absolutely necessary. No other form of existence is possible. But at the same time, everything is in constant motion, though not at an even pace, with the result that some things appear to be stronger or weaker than others. Human beings, like everything else in the universe, have an instinct for self-preservation, but although this instinct is natural, its motions are not always properly directed. Sense perception, the only form of true knowledge, leads most people to grasp at what they see, which may be deceptive. For example, we crave the light and heat

5. See Clare Carlisle, *Spinoza's Religion* (Princeton, NJ: Princeton University Press, 2021). Carlisle points out that Spinoza had a positive attitude toward "religion" and believed that it was possible for human beings to "participate" in the substance of Nature, which was God. Jesus Christ stood out in his mind because he had been more successful at this than other people, but the difference was one of degree, not of kind. In principle, anyone could achieve the same, and Spinoza did his best to try.

of the sun, but tend to think of this only in relation to our own desire for survival. The idea that the sun may not exist solely for our benefit does not occur to most people, and so their perception of the reality is distorted by what amounts to selfishness.

The only way out of this is to train the mind in the disciplines of mathematics and logic, which give us an objective understanding of the world around us and encourage us to adapt our thoughts and desires accordingly. Spinoza did not believe in the objective existence of good and evil—both of these were subjective perceptions determined by our own desires. So what appears as a tragedy to one person may come across as a blessing to someone else—depending on their point of view. Human perceptions are partial and biased toward the will of individuals, but in the real world there was no such thing as "will" because everything was programmed from the beginning and could not change. Happiness could only come by understanding this and by rising above our passions. The essentially Platonic and Stoic nature of this analysis is hard to escape, though of course Spinoza was neither a Platonist nor a Stoic in the strict sense. What made him different from them was his understanding of participation—human beings could enter into the "divine" and share its thoughts by the use of the reason given to them, and that is what he wanted.

Spinoza's theories had greater appeal to Protestants than to Catholics. Protestant rejection of transubstantiation went back to the Reformation, and Spinoza merely confirmed it. There was greater difficulty over the Trinity, but again, the idea that all monotheistic religions were essentially the same held an attraction for people who realized that the endless wars over religious confessions could not continue indefinitely. That Jews, Christians of all kinds, and Muslims worshiped the same God was an attractive proposition, and it was easy for Enlightenment thinkers to claim that they were fundamentally all one. There was, of course, no serious study of these religions themselves, and the philosophers of the time knew that adherents of the different religions thought otherwise. But since all religious believers were victims of what was essentially mythology, their disagreements were only to be expected and could be disregarded as artificial. Few people today would put matters as crudely as that, but there is still a current of opinion that believes it is possible to harmonize the three great Abrahamic religions, and to that extent at least, the Enlightenment vision lives on in interfaith relations today.

Spinoza's great strength was that he conceived of his theories in mathematical terms and worked them out accordingly. In principle, that idea went back to the Pythagoreans, and versions of it had resurfaced in the writings of men like Galileo and Descartes. But Spinoza was more consistent and more thorough in his treatment of the subject, and in his hands the idea of a mechanistic universe reached mature expression for the first time. Ultimately, everything was rational and therefore explicable, and humans could therefore replace God as the ultimate arbiter of their destiny. Confidence in human ability was never greater than it was in the late seventeenth century, and it inspired generations of European thinkers and scientists. At one level we have to accept that there was indeed considerable progress in terms of human knowledge as a result. Medicine, in particular, became a genuine science for the first time, as what had really been no more than quackery gave way to a scientific examination of the human body. There were also great advances in the natural sciences that have stood the test of time and for which subsequent generations have every reason to be grateful. But at the same time, the Spinozist universe was smaller than its predecessors had been, and it left many questions unanswered. For Spinoza, those questions were irrelevant—a distraction from science and reason. But were they?

For all his brilliance, there were important things that Spinoza did not grasp or that he dealt with inadequately. He had no sense of the purpose of being—the world substance was there eternally, and that was all there was to it. Whether it was there for a reason, and what that reason might be, was beyond his understanding. Then, too, his relegation of human emotions and feelings to the level of distorted sense perceptions was not very convincing. It was one thing to preach restraint and self-control, which might be very beneficial if the emotions concerned were essentially negative, like hatred for example. But can we honestly say that a mother's love for her child is the result of a selfish and ignorant distortion of the facts? Can anyone ever truly escape the power of feeling, and is it right even to try?

Spinoza's difficulty with the notions of good and evil is another problem with his system. Even if we grant that there are times when a particular event will appear to be good to some but evil to others, is that universally true? How can there be law and order, crime and punishment, if there is no such thing as evil? But if these things are removed, society will fall apart and the world will be reduced to chaos—it will not be set free to achieve its potential, as Spinoza seemed to imagine. Given that one of the most frequent arguments used to discredit biblical theism was the claim that a good God would not tolerate evil, removing him from the equation was an attractive but dubious line to take. Eliminating God did not destroy evil, but only made it more dangerous because there was no authority to which it was subject, no judge who would eventually condemn it and reward its victims. Spinoza left the whole question of justice hanging in the air with no resolution in sight.

Finally, and most tellingly, if soul and body are one, what happens to the soul when the body dies? Spinoza could not accept that the soul dies with the body, because the soul contains the mind, and the mind contemplates the eternal things inherent in the underlying substance of the world. If the mind is capable of having eternal thoughts then it must be eternal itself, and if it is lodged in the soul, then the soul must survive the death of the body. But how? And where is it? Spinoza had no concept of heaven and hell, no belief in a final judgment, no sense that every human being will be called to account for his or her behavior. Salvation was an alien idea to him because there was nothing to be saved from. In the final analysis, what happened after the death of the body was a mystery that Spinoza could not solve, though it did not prevent him from rejecting what was on offer in the Christian church, or in any other religion for that matter. One way or another, there was a whole dimension of human life and experience that Enlightenment rationalism did not touch but that could not simply be denied or wished away. Sooner or later that dimension would have to be addressed, and when that happened it was by no means clear that rationalism would win the day.

A foreshadowing of what was to come can be seen in the life and works of Gottfried Wilhelm Leibniz (1646–1716). Underestimated in his own lifetime, Leibniz has now come to be recognized as one of the greatest geniuses of all time, a polymath without a serious rival among his contemporaries, who included such luminaries as Isaac Newton. In mathematics, both he and Newton discovered differential and integral calculus, but so improbable did Leibniz's achievement seem that he was accused of having stolen the idea from Newton, a charge that was upheld by a Royal Society investigation and blighted Leibniz's reputation for two hundred years. It is now generally agreed that not only did the two men work independently of one another, but that in some ways Leibniz's solution of the mathematical puzzle was superior to Newton's. Leibniz's genius for calculation was such that it is now said that he was the father of computer science, having been the first person to have devised a machine that could be programmed to compute automatically.

Leibniz was a rationalist in the mold of Descartes, Spinoza, and Newton, but in one important respect he differed from all three of them. Unlike them, he was faithful to orthodox Christianity because he was convinced that both it and the world of nature were created by the omnipotent God of the Bible. At the same time, he also believed that if a theological dogma went against the scientific discoveries of nature, then it was the theology and not the natural science that had to give way. In other words, reason was the ultimate arbiter of truth, even though Leibniz believed that it would always coincide with divine revelation. The notion of the ultimate harmony of all things pervades Leibniz's vision. For example, he believed that if two objects possess identical qualities they must be the same thing. This proposition, known as Leibniz's law, has been questioned in recent times, but it is fundamental to his outlook. He also believed that there are no gaps in nature, so that there is a seamless continuity from one thing to another in an interactive universe. Everything that exists, according to Leibniz, has a reason for doing so, and that reason is sufficient, because it is part of the plan of God.

Leibniz was an optimist in the sense that he believed that God always chooses what is best, thereby introducing a moral element into what might otherwise be no more than logical necessity. He admitted that there might be some situations that would naturally lead to death, say, but that God in his goodness might have decided otherwise. Death might remain a real possibility, but it would not be the only one, and if there was a better option then God would certainly choose it. This sounds rather convoluted to the modern mind, but in the context of the time it was important because it denied the inevitability of certain outcomes.

Leibniz tended to believe that God had created the best of all possible worlds and that nothing better is possible. That, of course, raises the question of theodicy, or the existence of evil in the world, which (on the surface) would not seem to be for the best. Leibniz resolved this dilemma by saying that evil occurs because of human finitude. Our limitations cause us to make bad choices, and the result is both moral and physical evil. The former is sin, the latter is pain and suffering. These things appear to be bad, but they are meant to focus our attention on what lies behind them, the metaphysical evil of our imperfection that causes such things in the first place. Leibniz believed that evil in the world was a wake-up call to human beings who have the capacity to know what is right and to do it. So even apparent evil has a good purpose, which is the overcoming of the limitations of our finitude.

Leibniz sought to find a middle way between the determinism of Spinoza, which he believed was too inflexible, and the libertarianism of Descartes, for whom all choices were equally valid because none of them really mattered. Leibniz believed that moral choices are both possible and real, and sought to find a way of making them logically possible in his system. He was not widely followed in his own time, but he has come back into favor in recent years, especially among philosophers who have felt the need to inject a sense of moral purpose into what would otherwise be a purely mechanistic universe.

THE CRISIS OF AUTHORITY

At the heart of the Enlightenment lay the challenge to traditional authorities of all kinds. No one was spared. The traditions of the ancient past, universal (or apparently universal) beliefs, and claims to divine revelation—all were held up to scrutiny and rejected. In their place came reason, held to be certain because of its base in mathematical logic. Reason was authoritative, but it was authoritative by default, because its conclusions were necessary. Similarly, there was no need to argue about sources because the truth was objective regardless of where it came from. There was no need for an arbiter or mediator to interpret it because its interpretation was self-evident to those who used their reason rightly. To those who met with these assertions for the first time, it seemed as though a great weight had been lifted. From the beginning of the Reformation, questions of authority had dominated both intellectual and political life. All sides agreed that it rested ultimately in God, but how had God revealed it and to whom had he committed it? This was the great question at issue, and it had resulted in wars, bloodshed, and persecution, with no resolution in sight. Did the Enlightenment solve this problem, at least in principle, and should its solution be accepted?

The sources of authority in contention were basically three:

1. The Bible

2. The traditions of the early church, including the writings of the church fathers

3. The Church of Rome, and in particular, the papacy

Of the first of these, there was near universal agreement among Christians. The Bible, consisting of the Old and New Testaments, was the written word of God and therefore unquestionably the supreme authority in matters of faith for the whole church. Protestants and Catholics agreed about that, but Protestants insisted that it was the *only* such authority, everything else being relegated to the level of commentary on the Bible and accepted only to the extent that it was faithful to that.

Of the second, there were traditions that were said to go back to the time of the apostles but that had not found their way into the Bible. Since these traditions were of apostolic origin, they ought to enjoy the same authority as the Bible did. The difficulty, as always, was proving that they were indeed of apostolic provenance. The so-called Apostles' Creed was a prime example of this—it purported to be of apostolic origin but there was nothing to prove that it was, and there were a number of different versions of it. Ancient it most certainly was, but apostolic? That could not be proved. The writings of the church fathers were easier to pin down, but it was not clear what authority they had, or should have, in the church. Medieval scholars had constructed syntheses of their works that were treated as authoritative, but there were many apparent contradictions in what they said, and it was not clear how much of their teaching was still relevant a millennium later. Protestants usually treated them with some respect but did not accept their authority, whereas Rome did.

Of the third, only the Roman Church upheld its authority, which it claimed was supreme because it was supposed to be a living voice from God. If there was something obscure, contradictory, or absent in the other sources, the papacy could supply the deficiency. The papal *magisterium*, as it was called, acted like a supreme court. It was not authorized to introduce new doctrines, but rather to interpret those that already existed, and to decide how they should be applied in any given circumstance. Protestants rejected this because they believed that God had not given the bishops of Rome any such authority, and that said bishops, the popes, had used the claim to impose doctrines and practices that were not only absent from the Bible but in direct contradiction to its teaching.

The thinkers of the Enlightenment were often from a Catholic background, but for political reasons it was easier for them to operate in Protestant countries, where they were much less likely to suffer persecution. The pluriformity of Protestantism made it relatively unnecessary for them to spend much time attacking the Catholic Church, and whatever they had to say about the papacy, for example, could be matched by Protestant propaganda saying the same thing. The Bible, however, was a different matter, and it was here that men like Spinoza came into conflict with their Protestant compatriots at least as much, if not more, than they did with Roman Catholics. Spinoza regarded the Bible as a cultural artifact, a monument to the Hebrew people's sense of collective identity, and he respected that, but it was in no sense a revelation from (or of) God. Reading it was important for understanding Jewish self-identity, but to regard it as a vehicle for establishing eternal truth was wrong. He was supported in this by his friend and colleague Lodewijk (Louis) Meyer (1629–1681), who in 1666 published anonymously a short book called *Philosophia Sanctae Scripturae Interpres* (*Philosophy, the Interpreter of Holy Scripture*). With Spinoza's full support, Meyer insisted that philosophy was the criterion for interpreting the Bible, not theology, which was an artificial and essentially false pseudo-discipline. The book, which many ascribed to Spinoza himself, caused an uproar and was banned in most of the Dutch Republic, the only place where it had circulated more or less freely, but its arguments were picked up and debated far and wide.

So extreme a position was bound to provoke a reaction, and it did, even from people like Louis Wolzogen (1633–1690), a Calvinist of Austrian origin who by 1664 was teaching at Utrecht. Wolzogen attacked Meyer for subjecting the Bible to the inappropriate authority of philosophy, even though his own position was almost as rationalist. But although Wolzogen was censured and put on trial, his views divided the Dutch Reformed Church and he narrowly escaped condemnation. It was a sign that his approach, and along with it the more radical views of Meyer and Spinoza, were making headway among Protestants to a degree that few could have imagined a generation earlier.[6]

While all this was going on in the Netherlands, the skeptical approach to the Bible was reinforced by events in France. In 1685, Louis XIV banished Protestants from his kingdom, and many of them went to Holland. Pierre Bayle (1647–1706) was a French Protestant who had gone there a few years earlier (in 1681) after the closure of the Protestant seminary at Sedan. Bayle was embittered by his experiences and became a radical skeptic, which ensured that he would be persecuted by the Dutch as well. After losing his right to teach in the Netherlands, he set about compiling his *Dictionnaire historique et critique* (*Historical and Critical Dictionary*), in which he presented his radical views to the world. The book was widely read and admired even a century after his death, and Thomas Jefferson wanted it to be included among the hundred works that would form the basis of the Library of Congress.

In this classic work, Bayle took aim at everything that he regarded as irrational in Christianity, and especially in the Bible. He thought it was absurd to believe that God had created the entire human race out of a single couple and then condemned it to eternal damnation because of a seemingly trivial sin they had committed. According to Bayle, God must have foreseen that, and so the question arises as to why he bothered creating them in the first place. He also saw no necessary connection between Christianity and morality—plenty of Christians lived immoral lives, while great civilizations like the Chinese had a highly developed moral system that owed nothing to the revelation of Christ.

Bayle's wrath was kindled by the papacy's misuse of Luke 14:23 ("Go out to the highways and hedges and compel people to come in, that my house may be filled"). It was a verse first used by Augustine of Hippo as justification for coercing the schismatic Donatists back into the Catholic Church, and Catholics saw nothing wrong with re-employing it in the seventeenth century as a divine sanction for forcing the conversion of

6. Israel, *Radical Enlightenment*, 197–217.

Protestants to the Roman Church.[7] It was an egregious abuse of the text, and Bayle had this to say about it: "Any particular dogma, whatever it may be, whether it is advanced on the authority of the Scriptures, or whatever else may be its origin, is to be regarded as false if it clashes with the clear and definite conclusions of the natural understanding, and that more particularly in the domain of ethics."[8]

For Bayle, the question at stake was one of conscience. No secular authority had any right to persecute people on the basis of conscience alone, and those who hold their convictions sincerely, even if they are wrong, must be allowed to do so in freedom. The truth cannot be forced on people; only demonstration and persuasion can achieve the desired result. Of course, what Bayle excoriated in Catholics he could hardly allow among his fellow Protestants, many of whom were just as eager heresy hunters as the Catholics were. That tolerance got Bayle into trouble, but it also gained him sympathy in the wider world, and before long his argument was commonly accepted in intellectual circles. In 1695, the English government suspended the censorship of publications, and the result was a torrent of anti-Christian propaganda. The most notorious book to be published at that time was John Toland's *Christianity Not Mysterious*, a poorly written but passionately argued attack on everything in the faith that smacked of miracles and the supernatural.[9] It was quickly refuted, but the damage was done and Toland (1670–1722) remained a formidable foe of Christian orthodoxy for a generation or more after his death.

The great weakness of Toland and the others of his generation who launched broadside attacks on the truth of the Bible was that their objections were rooted in ideology (or philosophy) and not in serious study of the texts themselves. Miracles were ruled out from the start, not because there was anything in the Bible to call them into question, but because rationalist thinkers had said that they were impossible. Therefore, all mention of them was false to begin with, regardless of any evidence that might

7. Pierre Bayle, *Commentaire philosophique sur ces paroles de Jésus-Christ* (Cantorbéry: T. Litwel; in reality, Amsterdam: A. Wolfgang, 1687).

8. Bayle, *Commentaire philosophique*, 1.1.1; translated as in Hazard, *The European Mind 1680–1715*, 130.

9. John Toland, *Christianity Not Mysterious* (London: Samuel Buckley, 1696). Toland was an Irish Catholic who had converted to Protestantism.

be offered in their defense. Of course, it must be admitted that the defenders of miracles were no better off when it came to supporting the claims of the biblical texts. Nobody in Europe at that time had any access to the original lands of the Bible or knew much about the way ancient societies functioned. Were they more credulous than Toland's contemporaries? There was no way of knowing for sure, and the view that one adopted (and sought to defend) was largely a matter of personal faith, not something based on empirical evidence or a balanced weighing up of the facts.

Serious criticism of the Bible as a divinely revealed text really began with Richard Simon (1638–1712), a French Catholic priest who devoted his life to the study of Hebrew and insisted that strict linguistic criteria should take precedence over theology or traditional understandings when it came to interpreting the biblical texts. It was not long before Simon discovered that many of the books that we now have were composite products of many hands. The Pentateuch, which tradition ascribed to Moses, could not possibly have been produced by him in its present form, because it contained references to laws and customs that postdated his time by many centuries and also because the last chapters of Deuteronomy recorded his death and must therefore have been written by someone else. The historical and prophetic books, not clearly distinguished from one another in the literary tradition, depended on other documents from which our current texts had been extracted, as they themselves tell us. Who wrote those earlier texts? Were they divinely inspired? Who redacted the available material and recast it in its present form? Was this process inspired by God?

Simon took particular delight in attacking Protestants, whose dependence on the written text of the Bible as we now have it he regarded as naive and misplaced. As a Catholic, he could hold up the magisterial authority of the Church as the living voice of the Holy Spirit guiding and teaching the people of God as he had always done in the past. By taking refuge in Catholicism like this, Simon hoped to avoid Rome's condemnation, but he did not escape. When he published his critical history of the OT in 1678, he was expelled from his religious order and was at war with the authorities of his own church after that. He was not silenced, however. On his deathbed, he was reconciled to the Catholic Church he had fought for so long, but the reconciliation was not very deep. Simon never recanted his beliefs, which he claimed were based on solid philological research and not on theological prejudice or tradition. For those looking for an escape from such constraints, Simon's works were a godsend and set the tone for what was to come later. The critical study of the Bible has moved on considerably from his time, but modern readers recognize that much of what he said has been taken on board by all shades of opinion in the centuries since. Simon's views have been modified to some extent and his conclusions have not always been accepted, but his approach is recognizable to a degree that is not true of those who preceded him or of those who persecuted him and did all they could to refute his books. The study of the Bible had been set free from theological or ecclesiastical censorship, and there it has remained ever since.

The expulsion of the French Protestants (Huguenots) in 1685 was intended to bring peace and unity to France, but in spite of what it may have achieved in that respect at the grassroots level, the intellectual climate of the country went in a very different direction. The century between the suppression of Protestantism and the outbreak of revolution in 1789 was one of the most brilliant in French intellectual history, but it was all headed in the same direction. The alliance between the Roman Catholic Church and the French monarchy was condemned as a betrayal of Christianity and a new form of enslavement of the human spirit. The Church was beyond redemption and had to be destroyed, and the monarchy would also have to be completely turned around or else abolished. The British state, a Protestant one, was held up as a model of both religious freedom and social progress, though whether that combination could be reproduced elsewhere was a moot point.

The most prominent of these enlightened philosophers was François-Marie Arouet (1694–1778), better known by his pen name of Voltaire, who was by common consent the leading intellectual of his time. Voltaire fell afoul of the French authorities, but that merely enhanced his status in the eyes of his many admirers. He was thought by many to be an atheist, but he was not. He believed in a deist God and thought that everyone should be free to worship him in his or her own way. He was particularly impressed by the Quakers, whom he met during his lengthy stay in England, and he thought that their non-dogmatic spirituality was the way to go. His contemporary Charles Louis de Secondat, Baron de La Brède et Montesquieu (1689–1755), known to us simply as Montesquieu, was cut from a similar cloth but was more interested in social and political reform. According to Montesquieu, human nature was not to be analyzed in theological terms. It was not the great drama of sin and redemption that defined us, but environmental factors like climate and diet shaped the character of particular nations and provided the right basis for establishing a solid political order.

Montesquieu had a counterpart in Edward Gibbon (1737–1794), whose classic work, *The Decline and Fall of the Roman Empire*, was a broadside attack on Christianity, which he blamed for the collapse of the greatest civilization known to European history. Today nobody would accept Gibbon's analysis, but he was a master of English prose style and is still widely read, with the result that his picture of the past remains familiar to many people today. The idea that a brilliant era of light was eclipsed by the Christian dark ages, which were not overcome until the Renaissance and Enlightenment, is still a powerful force in the Western imagination, despite every attempt by specialists to overturn it.

Another Frenchman who made his mark was Denis Diderot (1713–1784), whose great project was to publish a compendium of human knowledge he called the *Encyclopédie*. In this massive work, he and his colleagues denounced the state of French society and prepared the way for an intellectual revolution that preceded the political one. The astonishing thing about Diderot is that although he had a hard time of it in France, he was lionized across Europe and even supported financially by Empress Catherine the Great of Russia (1762–1796), whose own political philosophy was the exact opposite of everything the French intellectuals stood for. This in fact was typical of the period. The ideas of the Enlightenment were taken up and promoted by despotic rulers, including Frederick the Great of Prussia (1740–1786) and Joseph II of Austria (1780–1792). The courts of these rulers became hotbeds of anti-Christian activity as they emasculated their state churches, and in Catholic countries dissolved monasteries on a scale not seen since the Reformation. Their greatest triumph was in persuading the pope to outlaw the Jesuit order, which had been founded in the sixteenth century to defend the papacy and had been in the forefront of Rome's crusades against the Protestants ever since. Now the Jesuits were regarded as props of superstition and bigotry in an age that had supposedly outgrown such things, and they were cast out—by Catholic kings in officially Catholic countries. Oddly enough, though the main impulse for all this came from France, that country was slow to follow suit, but when it finally caught up the explosion was devastating, not just for France but for the rest of Europe as well.

In Germany, the leading Enlightenment philosopher was Gotthold Ephraim Lessing (1729–1781), who followed in the footsteps of his French contemporaries. Lessing was so taken with deism that he regarded Christianity, Judaism, and Islam as essentially the same, a naive view that had the effect of making theology more or less superfluous. Lessing discovered and published a manuscript of Hermann Samuel Reimarus (1694–1768) in which he denied the divinity of Jesus and claimed that his disciples had created a new religion after his death. Reimarus was the first person to investigate what came to be known as the "historical Jesus," a figure who was assumed to be quite different from the one we encounter in the Gospels. Although he was too circumspect even to attempt to publish his work during his lifetime, Reimarus can fairly claim to have been the founder of modern NT criticism. His particular theories, none of which was based on any real investigation, are largely disregarded today, but his basic orientation remains powerfully present in academic circles, where it is still widely believed that the "Jesus of history" and the "Christ of faith" are two quite different figures.

THE THEOLOGICAL COUNTERATTACK

The emergence of rationalism in the early seventeenth century did not go unnoticed, and it was not long before there were voices raised in opposition to it. Easily the best known of these was that of Blaise Pascal (1623–1662), who in some ways set the agenda for what was to come. Pascal was a Catholic, but a Catholic of a very Augustinian bent. This went against the Jesuits, who were then the dominant influence at Rome as well as in France. Pascal derived his Augustinianism from Cornelius Jansen (1585–1638), a Dutch Catholic who was briefly bishop of Ypres (Ieper) and who authored a major study of Augustine that was published two years after his death. Jansen stressed the sovereignty of divine grace in a way that resembled Calvinism, though he did not exclude the role of human cooperation with God in the divine work of salvation.

Pascal read Descartes but reacted against him because, to his mind, Descartes had championed only one half of the truth. Pascal did not dispute the place of reason and science in our understanding of the universe, but he argued that this was only one side of the story. There was another dimension that was superior to reason: the realm of faith and love about which Descartes had little or nothing to say. Yet, as Pascal argued, human beings are constituted in such a way as to make faith and love central to their self-consciousness, and reason was subordinate to them, even if it could be used to support different beliefs and behaviors. Pascal naturally identified faith with Christianity, though on his principles that particular equation is not necessary.

In some ways, indeed, Pascal was closer to Descartes than he realized, and his justification for faith is not dependent on divine revelation at all. Pascal believed that faith is a risk worth taking, because if there is a God then it will be justified in the end, but if there is not then nothing has been lost. This proposition is known as Pascal's "wager" and has become famous, though he died before he could develop it properly. It is, of course, a rationalist approach to belief in God and not genuine Christian faith, but Pascal's insistence that rationalism must be transcended makes it possible to regard him as a defender of faith over against reason. In that sense, he can be regarded as the harbinger of what was to come.

Another voice that can be heard from this time is that of Nicholas Malebranche (1638–1715), who took a very different approach to that of Pascal and yet was curiously similar to him in some important ways. Like Pascal, Malebranche read Descartes, but instead of reacting against him, he embraced Cartesianism wholeheartedly. At the same time, he agreed with Pascal that Descartes's rationalism was only one side of the story and that room had to be found for faith and religion, which for Malebranche was much more explicitly tied to Christianity. Where Pascal insisted that faith and reason were polar opposites, Malebranche claimed that they were two sides of the same coin. The rationalism of Descartes and the revelation of God's will in the Bible were not contradictory, nor were they completely different explanations of reality that could live side by side but could never be harmonized with each other. Malebranche spent his life trying to reconcile the two, and for many of his contemporaries he was remarkably successful.

Malebranche started by affirming everything that Descartes had to say about reason. He agreed that there was a cosmic order that had been created by God, who had instilled rational principles in it that kept it running and made it possible for human beings to contemplate it with their minds. But at the same time, Malebranche also realized that this cosmic order had faults that could not be overlooked. In a perfectly rational universe, such as the one imagined by Spinoza, there could be no logical place for genuine evil. Yet common experience showed that evil, both physical and moral, does exist and that it constitutes an anomaly in the otherwise perfectly rational plan of God. How could this be explained?

Malebranche solved this dilemma by saying that God is a God of wisdom rather than of pure logic. We can see this, he argued, from what we observe in nature. Rain, for example, falls on the sea as well as on the dry land, but its effects are totally different. When it falls on the sea it does nothing—the sea merely absorbs the water and carries on as before. But when it falls on dry land it can either cause flooding, and therefore potential disaster, or it can bear fruit by irrigating the soil. We all know this and accept it as part of normal life—the rain is neither good nor evil in itself, but it is nevertheless a gift of God. Where it falls and what it does are the result of divine wisdom and are not inherent in the rain.[10]

Malebranche took this kind of analogy and applied it to the grace of God. According to him, God has created a world that functions according to a set of general laws with which he does not interfere. Part of this creation, however, was the gift of freedom; this has been abused, with the result that sin and evil have entered in. In theory, God could reach out to every sinner and offer him or her the grace needed to save them, but that would mean an endless series of interventions that would render the created order dysfunctional and essentially meaningless. So instead of that, God in his wisdom has allowed the world to continue as it is, only occasionally intervening to reveal his offer of forgiveness and restoration to those few whom he has chosen. The supreme manifestation of this occasional intervention came in the life, death, and resurrection of Jesus

10. There is a curious resemblance here to the parable of the sower in the NT (Matt 13:1–9: Mark 4:1–9; Luke 8:4–8), but Malebranche did not make the connection.

Christ, who is now choosing a people for himself by interceding on their behalf with God the Father.

To Christians this all sounds very familiar, apart from the framework of reason and wisdom in which the theology is contained. According to Malebranche, God cannot alter the laws of creation because that would be irrational. In practice, this means that he can neither remove human freedom to sin nor eliminate the results such freedom has engendered. But God cannot go against his wisdom, either, a wisdom that limits his ability to intervene and guarantees that most of his human creatures will suffer eternal damnation. Like it or not, God is constrained by both reason and wisdom, over which he has no control. Without realizing it, Malebranche painted God into a corner from which there was no escape. By distinguishing God's wisdom from his reason, Malebranche makes the divine wisdom both irrational and uncontrollable. The analogy between rain and grace does not hold up because it makes grace seem pointless (and even counterproductive) more often than not. Why that should be wise is far from clear, and some contemporary observers like Pierre Bayle found it absurd.[11] As an attempt to cloak a theological doctrine in philosophical garb it did not work, and in spite of his best intentions Malebranche found himself defenseless against the attacks of the Spinozists and their generation.

Long before Malebranche died, the assaults on Christianity from Enlightenment deists and atheists had become so numerous that they could not be ignored. Most of the attempts to refute them turned out to be short lived, often because they relied on traditional claims that the deists rejected, and they were soon forgotten. Some, however, survived, and a few are still occasionally read today. In France, the most formidable opponent of the deists was Jacques-Bénigne Bossuet (1627–1704), a cultured and kindly bishop who exercised considerable influence at the court of Louis XIV. Bossuet started with the deist argument that the universe was the creation of an intelligent mind, whom he identified (as did most of them) with the Christian God. God had given human beings the capacity to act as his representatives on earth, governing the lower

11. Pierre Bayle, *Réponse aux questions d'un provincial*, 5 vols. (Paris: Reinier Leers, 1704–1707), III, 141.

creation according to the laws and principles that he had established in nature and revealed in the Bible. To make human rule effective, God had further established particular institutions like the church and the (monarchical) state, to which he appointed men responsible to him for their actions. This hierarchy of offices was also a hierarchy of values, because those who had been called to the highest positions also had the greatest responsibility to ensure that their duties were carried out.

Given that there is only one God and one creation, it followed that there must also be one way to govern the latter. This way was revealed in Jesus Christ and confirmed over time by the actions of his apostles and later followers. The king of France ruled by divine right, not because he was a king but because the church, which was God's appointed spiritual authority on earth, had legitimated his rule. To Bossuet, absolute monarchy was not tyrannical but the inevitable outworking of the principle of unity in the universe. To have more than one source of law and order was to invite chaos, which Bossuet believed he saw in Protestantism, whose adherents were constantly arguing about almost everything while claiming to be the one true church. This appeared to him to be a contradiction in terms, and he spent many years doing his best to reconcile Protestants to Rome, which he saw as their divinely appointed destiny.

Bossuet's theory of divine order was attractive to those who accepted its principles, but as with so many theories, it fell victim to reality. Louis XIV was not the philosopher-king of Bossuet's dreams, nor were his designated successors, whom he tutored in their responsibilities—with very limited success. Protestants longed for peace and unity but recoiled from the methods used to obtain them. Bossuet disliked coercion and tried to win them over by persuasion, but his patience eventually ran out and he resorted to force to speed up the process of reconciliation. One of the few people in France who might have been able to bridge the divide between Catholics and Protestants was Madame Jeanne Guyon (1648–1717), whose spiritual outlook and reliance on divine grace for salvation as opposed to any form of human works was Protestant in substance, even though she herself never left the Catholic Church. Unfortunately, instead of seeing her as a possible source of spiritual renewal, Bossuet and his colleagues condemned her as a threat, and she spend many years (1695–1703) in prison for her beliefs. As a result, she became a heroine of conscience for Protestants, who often recognized her as one of their own, and a very bad advertisement for the causes championed by Bossuet. Bossuet won his battles in the short term but lost in the long run because the world he envisaged was simply not true to reality, and his vision of Catholic Christianity suffered as a result.

In England, there was also an outpouring of opposition to the deists, though it took a rather different form. There were certainly politicians of the stamp of Bossuet who held similar beliefs about the essential unity of throne and altar, but they were the Tory (conservative) opposition to what was essentially a Whig (liberal) establishment.[12] The Church of England had its fair share of Whigs who were appointed to senior positions, but they had to spend much of their time restraining the more conservative elements among the parish clergy. But although conservative and liberal forces battled it out in the church, the relative freedom and decentralization of its structures allowed for a significant middle ground that was able to take up the more important struggle against deism. One of the earliest combatants to enter this field was George Berkeley (1685–1753), who published *Principles of Human Knowledge* in 1710, when he was only twenty-five years old.[13] Berkeley denied the existence of matter as an abstract substance. To him, what exists is what is perceived by the mind. Our faculties of perception create ideas in our heads, which in turn assemble these ideas in the form of objects. We cannot imagine something like a table unless we can see one and analyze its various qualities.

This ability to construct objects out of ideas Berkeley ascribes to "spirit," a quality that all human beings possess, although it cannot be directly perceived in the way that ideas can. Every human being has a spirit of his own, which is how Berkeley explains why there are many minds in the world and not just one in which we all participate. God, of course, is the Spirit, the ultimate mind that all other minds resemble, though to a lesser degree. Berkeley's main object of attack was the philosophy of

12. This was associated with the reign of William III (1689–1702) and Mary II (1689–1694). There was a brief change of direction under Anne (1702–1714), when the Tories were in the ascendant, but that changed when the Hanoverian dynasty came to the throne and the Whigs remained politically dominant until the accession of George III (1760–1820), when the Tories returned to government—with unhappy results.

13. Berkeley was an Irishman and ordained in the Church of Ireland, where he became bishop of Cloyne in 1734. The Church of Ireland is an Anglican body in communion with the Church of England.

John Locke, who imagined that ideas had a distinct existence and were of two kinds. There were primary ideas, that is to say, ideas that were necessary to constitute a particular substance, and there were secondary ideas, ideas that were optional or superfluous—not necessary to the existence of a particular substance. By relativizing the whole concept of ideas, Berkeley was able to show that Locke's distinction was meaningless because every idea was contingent on our perception of it. But what if there were nobody to perceive something—would it then exist? Berkeley said that it would, because even if there was no human being to perceive it, God would see it and validate its existence. God was therefore necessary in Berkeley's scheme of things, not to explain the gaps in our scientific knowledge, but to ensure the order of the universe, which cannot depend on limited human perception.

The most successful defender of traditional Christian orthodoxy was Berkeley's contemporary, Joseph Butler (1692–1752), who for some years was bishop of Bristol before being translated to Durham. It was before that, however, when he was still a parish priest, that Butler composed what would become his most famous work and one of the most successful rebuttals of deism in the eighteenth century.

This was his *Analogy of Religion, Natural and Revealed,* which appeared in 1736. Butler argued that it was a fallacy to believe that Nature was always carefully ordered and beneficent. Like the Bible, it was full of mystery and cruelty. Knowledge of both Nature and human affairs can never be exactly predicted, but various patterns of behavior are probable, being based on previous experience. Mechanistic certainty is impossible, and human beings are capable of acting in ways that are sacrificial rather than self-seeking. Whether they will do so in any given instance cannot be predetermined, but the possibility is always there and the way to achieve true happiness is to balance self-love (the desire for self-preservation) with a more general love for creation as a whole. In most cases, these two things will coincide, since the good of the individual is normally tied to the good of the wider community. The impulse for deciding particular cases comes from the conscience, which Butler regarded as a God-given compass that everyone possesses. It is always possible to go against conscience, of course, and some people's consciences have been dulled or corrupted, but in Butler's eyes this is a distortion of God's intentions and will not lead to happiness.

Butler's arguments convinced many of his contemporaries, and his apology for Christianity was widely welcomed by those who believed it already. But to say, as he did, that the Bible was likely to be right because it was an accurate portrait of the failings of Nature was a strange position to take, and we should not be surprised to discover that over time most of the rest of what he had to say was refuted. What remained was his rejection of determinism as the fundamental principle of human life and his conviction that human beings are not robots who can do no more than conform to the world in which they live, whether they like it or not. The mechanistic approach of Spinoza came to be seen as inadequate to describe universal reality, however helpful it might be for understanding certain natural phenomena.

Perhaps the most successful eighteenth-century Christian apologist for natural theology was William Paley (1743–1802), who published *Natural Theology, or Evidences of the Existence and Attributes of the Deity* in 1802 and was still being quoted as an authority on the subject in the mid-twentieth century, despite numerous attempts to discredit his position. Paley famously invented the analogy of the watch and the watchmaker. If you find a watch lying on the ground somewhere and pick it up, you know immediately that it was made by an intelligent craftsman. You cannot tell who that craftsman was, and you know that he would bear no physical resemblance to the watch at all, but that there is a causal connection between them would be beyond doubt. Paley said that much the same thing is true of the universe. The wonderful order and fine tuning we observe in nature cannot have come about by chance; like the watch, it must have been made by an intelligent creator, though we cannot tell from looking at the universe what that creator is like.

Paley's arguments embraced both the traditional cosmological and teleological proofs for the existence of God and were convincing to many people because they made simple and obvious sense. More sophisticated critics objected to him on the ground that the order we observe in the universe is not perfect—there are distorted creatures and failures of various kinds that would appear to rule out intelligent design, especially if the designer is held to be perfect, which the Christian God clearly is.

Interestingly, though, this objection was known to Jesus, and he addressed it in his teaching. At one point, he was confronted with the case of a man born blind, and his critics wanted to know what went wrong. They assumed (or pretended to assume) that his blindness was the result of sin, but they did not know who was guilty—was it the man himself, or his parents? Jesus replied that it was neither. The man was born blind, not because anyone had sinned, but in order that the glory of God might be revealed. He then proceeded to give the man his sight (John 9:1–7).

Jesus recognized that the man's blindness was a physical defect but distanced it from any notion of good or evil. There are cases like this in the world, he said, and implied that somehow or other they are part of God's eternal plan. We cannot know what that plan might be, but whatever it is, God will be glorified. It may be through healing, as it was in that case, or it may be in a life of pious dedication to God, as many disabled people have demonstrated. There is certainly a case for saying that the Paralympics are more impressive than the main Olympic Games, because those who participate in them are demonstrating their ability to overcome handicaps of various kinds and are not just doing what comes naturally to them. We have no way of knowing why disabilities strike some people but not others, but believers in a mechanistic universe have no explanation for that either. What Christians can say, however, is that whatever the physical situation may be, the person subjected to it is loved by God and has a purpose in his plan, even if we do not know what it is.

Paley's great appeal rested to a large extent on his affirmation of this sense of purpose, or *telos* in Greek. Teleology, as this is called, is essentially alien to rationalism, which may be able to explain why things are the way they are but cannot tell us what they are for. Yet human beings are not content with merely existing—they want to know what the meaning of life is, and in particular, what the purpose of their lives is. Paley did not answer that question in detail, but his philosophy left the door wide open for it to be asked and explored. It is interesting to note that after a period in which his approach was virtually eclipsed, it now seems to be coming back into favor, at least to some extent. We live in a more scientifically sophisticated world than Paley did, but we must remember that it is also more sophisticated than the world that the rationalists of the

Enlightenment lived in, too. Their faith in mechanics and their optimism that we live in the best of all possible worlds is no longer tenable, and their readiness to exclude God from the picture now seems to many observers to be naive and simplistic. Paley needs to be revised and updated, to be sure, but his basic instincts cannot be easily dismissed and deserve more of a hearing than they have received until recently.

The work of these eighteenth-century philosopher-theologians was supplemented and supported by pure scientists, of whom the most prominent was Robert Boyle (1627–1691), an Anglo-Irishman who is now regarded as the founder of modern chemistry. Boyle steered clear of the theological polemics of his time, but he had no doubt that the laws of the natural world were the product of the omniscient God of the Bible, who had made everything in accordance with his immutable will. He became a model of the godly scientist, and his reputation has continued to inspire succeeding generations who have followed in his footsteps to the present time. In his will, he left funds to establish the Boyle Lectures, which were intended to defend the coherence of orthodox Christianity. These lectures continued with great regularity until the early twentieth century, but then they petered out until they were revived in 2004, since when they have blossomed.

In a somewhat similar vein, Adam Lord Gifford (1820–1887) bequeathed a legacy to the four ancient Scottish universities (Aberdeen, Edinburgh, Glasgow, and St Andrews) for the establishment of lectures that would defend and develop the principles of natural theology. Though somewhat less focused than the Boyle Lectures, the Gifford Lectures have continued to the present time and several of them have become classics of philosophical and theological writing. Mention should also be made of the Victoria Institute, an association of Christian scientists that was founded in 1865 and enjoyed considerable success before falling on hard times in the early twentieth century. It still exists, though it has never regained the influence it once had. Thanks to men like these, there has always been a stream of believing scientists in the English-speaking world who have given the lie to the Enlightenment view that science and religion are at war with one another, and that religion must be sidelined or even eliminated if progress in our knowledge and understanding of the world around us is to continue.

THE MATURE ENLIGHTENMENT

Bossuet, Berkeley, Butler, and Paley were all orthodox Christian clergymen who were doing what they could to defend their faith in the face of what they saw as devastating attacks from those who did not share it. It therefore comes as something of a surprise to discover that one of their allies in this struggle was a man who was neither a clergyman nor an orthodox Christian—David Hume (1711–1776). Hume is perhaps best understood as someone who shared the mental outlook of George Berkeley but who took Berkeley's assertions much farther and systematized them in a way that Berkeley did not. The similarities and differences between Berkeley and Hume can clearly be seen in the way they understood ideas. Like Berkeley, Hume found no evidence for the existence of a generic material substance. But where Berkeley relied on sense perception to create ideas in our minds, Hume said that what we obtain from the world around us is a set of impressions which in turn create our perceptions.

Hume did not think of the mind as an immaterial substance, which would give it an existence above and beyond the world in which we live. On the contrary, he saw it as no more than a set of perceptions that are forever changing. We may perceive of a thing as hot or cold, we may respond to it with love or hatred, we may be pained by it or take pleasure in it, but the thing in question has no independent existence. It is merely the sum of the perceptions that we have of it. Seen like that, our perceptions would appear to lead to chaos, but they do not because of three factors: their resemblance to one another, their connection with one another, and the principle of cause and effect. Taken together, these factors create the links that enable us to make the connections that give us a sense of identity and even of permanence, though naturally that can only be relative in time and space. We come to expect certain outcomes from our actions because we have experienced a regular pattern in the past, but there can be no guarantee that the same things will always recur. Here we have to rely on probability rather than on certainty. In effect, said Hume, there are no scientific laws, only probabilities, a conclusion that derailed the mechanistic theories of Spinoza and Newton and led to new departures in philosophical analysis.

Hume's theories took a different turn in 1748, when he published *An Enquiry Concerning Human Understanding*. In this book, he included a chapter on miracles for which he has become famous. Hume did not object to the possibility of miracles, which in theory could occur at any time. However, he argued that the common experience of humankind has demonstrated that there is a regular pattern in nature that we can expect to repeat itself. Against this there are numerous historical reports, many of them in the Bible, of miracles having occurred at some time in the past. Should this historical testimony be taken at face value? Hume argued that it should not. His reasons were that people in past ages were less enlightened than we are today, that their understanding of natural processes was inadequate, and that very often they had a vested interest in the "miracles" that they were affirming. To his mind, the common argument made by Christian theologians—that miracles occurred in the past because they were needed in order to back up the claims of Christianity when it was still a new faith, but that now that it has matured miracles are no longer necessary, and so have ceased—was a convenient escape route.

As Hume saw it, historians ought to consider what is most likely to have happened, basing their judgment on what we would normally regard as possible today, and not on reports of uncertain value. The problem with this approach is that it imposes one set of values and perceptions on everything else, whether that is justified or not. Historians can easily adopt an ideological stance that blinds them to large parts of human life and experience—in our own day, Marxists are particularly prone to this. There is nothing beyond their convictions to say that they are right, but they do not hesitate to discredit whatever does not conform to their preconceived beliefs. Such a method claims to be scientific but it is not, and people with religious beliefs are right to complain that their approach has been unfairly written out of the picture. That is not a license for credulity but a reminder that our presuppositions can have a negative effect on our research that must be guarded against.

After Hume's death, his executors published his *Dialogues Concerning Natural Religion* (1779), on a subject that by then was fading from general view but that continued to pose important questions about the existence of God and the nature of his activities. Christians obviously believe that the universe is the product of an intelligent designer and assume from this that it is intended for a purpose, even if we are not always or entirely clear about what that purpose might be. Can either of those propositions be defended on the basis of natural reason alone? It can be argued from observation and experience that there is an order in nature, but we cannot conclude from this that it must have been purposefully designed. We know that machines and houses, for example, have been designed with a purpose in view, but we cannot say the same about the universe because we have nothing to compare it with. We do not know whether the order that we perceive in it is a construction of our minds or whether it corresponds to an objective reality, because there is no other universe that we can examine. We also cannot extrapolate from human intelligence, which we know to have created machines and houses, to a higher one that differs from ours in degree but not in kind.

Even if we posit belief in God, there is no reason that compels us to say that his mind is simply a magnified version of ours. It might be quite different—we do not know. Furthermore, to perceive intelligent design in the universe does not mean that there must be a single intelligent designer behind it. Nor does it imply that this designer, if there is one, is a personal, moral being in the way that the God of the Bible is. It can plausibly be argued that everything that exists depends on something else for its existence—all beings are therefore contingent and interrelated. Our minds can conceive of a self-contained system of contingent beings, but where did that system come from? Would it not be necessary to have an intelligent designer who made it in the first place? Hume argued against that by saying that there is no being that absolutely has to exist. His argument is not a denial of God's existence, but it is not an affirmation of it, either. If God exists, then his being (if that is the right word for it) is totally unlike anything we can experience and therefore cannot be part of reality as we perceive it. The system of interlocking contingencies is the product of our minds and nothing more than that, so there is no need to go beyond what we observe and posit the existence of an intelligent designer who may be equated with the God of the Bible.

Hume also argued that there is nothing in nature to compel us to believe that the designer is necessarily good. If it is, how do we explain the reality of pain and suffering? Leibniz, as we have seen, had an answer to that, but Hume did not regard it as conclusive. As far as he could see, nature seems to be indifferent to matters of good and evil, and if that is true, then it would appear that the designer is indifferent to them as well.

The Christian response to these arguments would be to say that God is not, and cannot be, contingent on anything else. That does not mean that he cannot exist, however. His existence cannot be demonstrated by logical deduction because it is essentially different from the existence of other beings—the distinction here being the familiar one of the Creator and his creation. But if God's existence cannot be proved by logic, it cannot be disproved by it, either. Nor should we expect nature to be moral in itself. Morality is not something inherent in matter but a belief that is activated by minds with a conscience and the power to obey it. If behavior were inherent in the creation, there would be no morality at all because there would be no choice but to follow it. A distinction between good and evil is something that we perceive, and therefore it must exist, and the only way that it can do so is to exist in a spiritual world that lies above and beyond the material universe.

Hume's rational arguments do not support the Christian view, but—and this is the important thing—they do not rule it out, either. To say that there is nothing that compels us to believe in an intelligent designer does not mean that there is no such thing. The Christian assertion that there is a Creator God who made the world according to a plan in his mind is a coherent belief, even if it cannot be proved by natural reason alone. Christians have never argued that we can think our way into belief in the God of the Bible—all we can do, and all we have ever tried to do, is to show that our beliefs are compatible with reason and cannot be disproved by it. Nature cannot be the foundation for morality, but it is not hostile to it either. It is perfectly possible to live in accordance with Christian morality and be at peace with the material universe. Indeed, Christians claim that because the world was made by God and God is himself a moral being, to live in accordance with his nature will ensure that we shall also live in accordance with ours.

Moreover, the fact that morality is not confined to Christians, or even to religious people, says nothing about the truth of Christianity itself. Christians have always claimed that the light of God shines on everyone, and that there is nobody who is totally deprived of it (John 1:9; Rom 1:19–21). We should therefore expect to find it in different forms and to varying degrees in every religion and philosophy devised by human beings. Christianity claims to be the *fullness* of revealed truth, not the *only* truth there is. Christians therefore rejoice to find truth present in other belief systems because, as they see it, that presence confirms the correctness of their own view, which they regard as superior but not unique.

One philosopher who did his best to counter Hume's arguments was Thomas Reid (1710–1796), generally recognized today as the founder of what is known as Scottish common sense philosophy. Reid was an orthodox Christian who thought that Hume's arguments were far too theoretical to be plausible. He relied on things like language, common experience, and an innate moral sense that all human beings naturally share. He argued against Hume's belief that we have no perception of anything but ideas and claimed instead that we have a direct awareness of objects that are real, whether there is anyone there to perceive them or not. For Reid, the human mind does not create external reality but is subject to it. The mind can analyze objects and formulate ways in which they can be used for practical purposes. Reid did not abolish the imagination but tied it to other factors that in effect limited its powers and obliged it to focus on pragmatic realities more than on theoretical constructs. This common sense approach had a limited take up in Europe, but it became popular in the United States, where it could be said to have been the dominant philosophical belief until the rise of Darwinism in the late nineteenth century, and it remained influential long after that. A significant part of its appeal to Americans seems to have been its democratic bias. Common sense, after all, is just that—it is within the grasp of everyone, and looks for solutions to problems that all right-thinking people should be prepared to accept.

Reid believed that our understanding of the world is rooted in sense perception but is not confined to it. Every normal human being is capable of perceiving the same object in similar terms, and denying their validity is irrational. So, for example, if one person sees a large rock, everyone else will see the same rock and attribute the same properties to it. This commonality is what makes science, and ultimately civilization, possible. Reid's belief in objective physical reality naturally led him to extend this to belief in innate moral principles as well. He knew that a physical rock could be used to kill people, but insisted that human beings had an awareness that to use a rock in that way was an abuse of the purpose for which it existed, and was therefore immoral, even if it was possible.

Reid's linking of physical objectivity to moral categories of thought made his philosophy appealing to Christians, particularly to those who, like him, were of a basically Reformed Protestant outlook. Reid was not himself an orthodox Calvinist, but many of his followers were, and they were quite happy to use his principles for their own theological purposes. That the created order should have a moral framework built into it was very attractive to them because it linked their belief in the predestinarian plan of God for humankind to the nature of the material universe in which we live. Someone called and chosen by God could have the assurance that his life and activity in the world was justified in the sight of God because it followed the pattern according to which the world was made. There was therefore a harmony, almost a symbiosis, between man and nature that reconciled the different species of creation to each other and to their Creator.

But Reid's philosophy appealed to others besides those of an orthodox theological outlook. It was universal in scope, because the realities of our physical universe could be perceived in exactly the same way by all human beings, whether they were believers or not. This meant that unbelievers could share the same pattern of thought as believers and that the two could work together in harmony because the objective nature of external reality led them to the same conclusions. This was true, not only in physical terms, but in moral ones as well, because in nature, the physical and the moral are tied together. Thus, in advocating Christian moral principles, believers were not encroaching on the freedom of unbelievers by imposing religious values on them, but merely pointing out that the structure of the world obliges us to think in a certain way about it and act accordingly.

This consensus created a situation in which Americans of all beliefs and none could live together in harmony. Christians could say that their perception of reality was in line with God's revelation in the Bible, while others adopted the same views for purely rational reasons. Of course, it is not difficult to see that this synthesis errs on the side of rationalism, which can be seen in the way that many Christians were tempted to explain miracles in terms of natural phenomena or something else that was not supernatural. For example, Jesus's feeding of the five thousand could be interpreted not as a miraculous multiplication of the five loaves and two small fish that a little boy gave him but as a morally unselfish gesture on the part of the boy that unleashed a similar reaction among the five thousand, all of whom proceeded to produce their lunch and to share it with one another! (Matt 14:13–21; Mark 6:32–44; Luke 9:10–17; John 6:1–13). What really happened cannot now be determined, so this kind of explanation was just as good as any other and perhaps even better, in that it appeared to resolve a problem that would otherwise have remained a mystery and led some people to doubt the truth of the story altogether. It was not a satisfactory solution to the question of miracles and would not be accepted by anyone today, but it persuaded many people at the time, and for a century or more it contributed to the kind of defense of the Bible mounted by superficially conservative Christians.

The fact that Enlightenment thought in the English-speaking world followed a trajectory somewhat different from what occurred elsewhere is largely due to the relatively free intellectual and political atmosphere that prevailed in both Britain and her American colonies. In Britain, religious dissent was disapproved of but it was tolerated, and heresy trials virtually disappeared after 1714. In the colonies, the state churches were generally fairly weak and lacked the institutional apparatus that would have been required to enforce any particular orthodoxy. The pragmatic bent that characterized men like Isaac Newton caught on and was characteristic of people like Benjamin Franklin (1706–1790), who combined deism with scientific inquiry and is now remembered for the latter more than for the former. Thomas Jefferson was another deist who wove his creed into contemporary politics, most notably in the Declaration of Independence (1776), a utopian document that continues to inspire generations of Americans, even though historians never tire of pointing out that it bore little relation to reality—either then or since. Jefferson acknowledged the Creator, but then attributed a number of characteristics to him that have no basis in the Bible, despite many attempts to harmonize what he claimed with traditional Christianity. It was this very ambiguity that allowed both Christians and atheists to claim Jefferson as theirs, and that continues to characterize the United States to the present day. Its clearest manifestation is in the American holiday of Thanksgiving (not a Jeffersonian idea). The initial conception was undoubtedly Christian, but such is the nature of modern American secularism that nowadays God is never mentioned in public discourse and the holiday wanders aimlessly, without an obvious purpose to justify it.[14]

In Britain, at the same time as the American colonies were breaking away, Adam Smith (1723–1790) published *An Inquiry into the Nature and Causes of the Wealth of Nations* (1776). Smith advocated allowing individuals to develop their economic instincts freely, and so is sometimes regarded as the "father of capitalism," though that is an exaggeration. For him, self-interest was the most powerful human emotion and therefore ought to be promoted for the benefit of all. Smith did not think it was necessary for everybody to become a self-made man because if a few people managed to enrich themselves, their wealth would trickle down to the masses and enrich everyone in the end. This analysis reached the public on the verge of the Industrial Revolution, and we know how its principles were applied at that time. It was hardly a Christian vision of the world, and there was great suffering as industrialists and robber barons did all they could to maximize their profits at the expense of human welfare.

It soon became obvious that Smith's theories required moral responsibility if they were to work properly, and there the churches stepped in. Christianity could prick the consciences of the rich and demand honesty and fair play in the workplace. Over time, the relationship between employers and workers was regulated an a virtually universal middle class appeared. For the first time in history, relative affluence for the many became the accepted norm, and it has now spread around the globe. Even Communist China, which is theoretically opposed to the idea, has in practice become a capitalist society and the middle class is expanding exponentially—as is Christianity.

Another one of Hume's admirers was Immanuel Kant (1724–1804), who is sometimes regarded as the classic representative of pietistic Protestant philosophy and quoted as if his views were those of Protestants in general. Kant was an avid disciple of Descartes and Newton, and was fascinated by Hume as well. He accepted Hume's assertion that our knowledge is based on our sense impressions, but wondered what it was that

---

14. Thanksgiving claims to go back to the Pilgrim fathers in Massachusetts, who celebrated it in 1620 in an obviously Christian context. But it did not become an official holiday until 1862, when Abraham Lincoln introduced it as a morale-boosting measure during the American Civil War.

allowed us to connect these impressions with one another. The conventional answer to that was that we must depend on reason to establish the links, but that was not good enough for Kant. It led him to question what reason is and to analyze it in a way that had not been done before. Kant began with the belief that our knowledge comes from experience, but he did not accept that experience alone determined what truth is. From experience we learn that certain things are true in actual fact, but not that they must be true because of some inherent necessity. For example, we might say from experience that a library is full of books, but that does not have to be the case, because the library could be empty. However, if there are books in it, those books will take up room, because all books are space-related objects. This is a necessary truth, in a way that the mere presence of books in the library is not.

It is obvious that if there are books, they will occupy space, but it is not obvious that books should exist. They do not occur naturally but are the result of a series of processes that can be traced back to a beginning, which was probably an idea in an author's mind and not an object at all. In the natural world, rocks and trees are like books in the sense that they occupy space, but where do they come from? They presumably do not have to exist, but like books are the product of a series of causes and effects that have produced them. We perceive them as they now are, as *phenomena* in the world, but we know that they have an origin that can be traced. Did they, too, begin as concepts in a Mind? That we cannot know. Our perceptions are determined by the context in which we live, and that context is governed by things like time and space. But time and space are not objects in the way that books, rocks, and trees are. They are mental concepts that give us a framework for defining the things we see. Because we too are creatures of time and space, we cannot go beyond them, even though we are able to discern what they are.

For Kant, this was the limit to which pure reason can take us. If we analyze an object according to the principles of cause and effect, we can trace its origin to a series of contingent acts that take us progressively back to where it began. Ultimately, we must come to the point where the chain of causes comes to an end—there must be a cause that is not itself contingent on anything else and therefore not caused. That is logically necessary, but it can never be found in practice because in the world of time and space everything is contingent. Our reason points beyond the limits of what it can analyze, and is therefore not the final arbiter of all things. But what lies beyond it is unfathomable because we are not mentally equipped to penetrate that far.

This has great implications for the doctrine of God. God is not bound by time and space and is not contingent. He is the ultimate source of all things, though he did not create the world out of himself and there is no material connection between it and him. For that reason, all analogies and proofs for the existence of God fail in what they are trying to achieve, because our categories of thought are not big enough to embrace the concept of the divine, even if we sense that it must be there. For some people, this conclusion means that theology is impossible, because there is no way that we can measure or define God. This does not mean that God does not exist—that cannot be proved any more than his existence can be—but it removes him from the realm of science. Whether we are believers, agnostics, or atheists makes no difference at this level, because God is beyond our ability to perceive him and therefore beyond our ability to experience him. He may be there, but if he is, we cannot know him because the principles that give us knowledge do not apply to him. This is why so many scientists reject belief in God—it is irrelevant to their concerns, and on the principle of Ockham's razor, it must be abandoned because it is not necessary for explaining the way the world works.

In addition to pure reason, Kant also held that there is such a thing as practical reason, which points us in a different direction. Practical reason is the foundation of ethics because it is the process by which we apply general principles to particular circumstances. It is all very well to speculate about the ultimate origin of matter, as pure reason does, but we all have to live in a world where we engage with one another, and we have to have principles that can govern this behavior by telling us what is acceptable and appropriate and what is not. These principles are not built into our nature in a way that would make us follow them instinctively, as animals do, for instance. We may have a moral conscience, but we can disobey it if we choose to do so—to that extent, we are free from necessity. But at the same time, we have an obligation to act in a morally responsible way, since if we do not we shall destroy ourselves. Once again, that is quite possible, and there are people who have held that suicide is the ultimate exercise of our free will, but although that may be so in theory, it is self-defeating.

There is nothing in the physical world that compels us to act morally, because the concept of morality is alien to it. We may think that the existence of books, rocks, and trees is good, but if we say that, it is because we like what we see, not because the objects in question are capable of being evil. Moral goodness, on the other hand, is a choice, and in order to be able to choose, the subject of the moral action must be free from the necessity imposed by existence within space and time. Therefore, says Kant, human beings, who have this moral freedom, are not just phenomena observable in the universe. There is something about us that makes us more than that, even if we cannot pin it down precisely. We are not just phenomena, but *noumena,* thinking beings with an autonomy in relation to the world that makes moral decisions possible for us.

Where does this autonomy come from? It does not arise from nature, because there is nothing in nature that can cause it. It can only come from another *noumenon,* and that *noumenon* is God. At this point, Kant draws conclusions that are not warranted by his system. If God is the ultimate *noumenon,* then his existence is necessary, but Kant denied this on the ground that no being has necessary existence—all beings are contingent on one another. He did not realize that it is possible to say that God does not exist by logical necessity—in other words, that there is nothing in the universe that would prove that he exists, but that in the world of *noumena* things are different. There his being is necessary because there is nothing that could have caused him. The real question concerning God, therefore, is not whether he exists in the perceptible world of phenomena but whether there is a noumenal world beyond the universe as we perceive it. Kant decided that our rational faculties point in that direction without being able to prove anything because of their inherent limitations. But the need for a noumenal world is justifiable on the basis of our sense that we cannot live in the phenomenal world without input from it—without morality, in other words.

Here we have reached the point where the physical world around us cannot be regarded as an end in itself. Those who have done so may have come to that conclusion on the basis of reason alone, and they may have rejected the claims of religion (especially of Christianity) because they think that the God of the Bible is not moral in his behavior, but their reaction will inevitably lead to an immorality of their own. As the ultimate *noumenon* God is free to determine what he will do—he is not bound by his own laws, a principle that the men of the Enlightenment could not accept. There may be times, and the Bible shows us that there are such times, when God sets aside the laws that he has given to his world for reasons that are best known to him. He may dispense with physical laws in order to perform miracles, and he may dispense with moral laws when he commands people to kill their enemies (as he often did in the OT) or orders a prophet like Hosea to marry a prostitute (Hos 1:2). God can do this because he is sovereign. If it seems unjust to us, we need only reflect that our salvation is also unjust—we deserve to perish, not to be saved, but in his mercy God has reached out to us and gone against his own law of punishment in order to rescue us. His sovereignty over his laws works in many different ways!

At this point, we have reached the limits of where Kant can take us. In his book *Religion within the Bounds of Reason Alone* (1792), which earned him the rebuke of the king of Prussia and his government, Kant recognized that the human will is deeply corrupted, but he was unable to accept the traditional explanation for this. The doctrine of original sin was incompatible with his concept of morality because he believed that morality is only possible where there is freedom, and that therefore people must be free to make the right choices as well as the wrong ones. He did not regard Jesus Christ as divine—to his mind, Jesus was no more than a morally perfect man. As such, he can be a model for others to imitate, but he is not their Savior. So in the end, despite his willingness to make room for arguments in favor of the existence of God, Kant was not an orthodox Christian and his philosophy is ultimately incompatible with the gospel of grace.

ROMANCE AND REVOLUTION

So far, we have been considering the Enlightenment from a scientific and rationalistic perspective, which many Christians (and others) thought was a less-than-adequate analysis of the truth. There were vast areas of human experience, summed up in concepts like "love" and "feelings," that rationalism had great difficulty accounting for, even when it tried to do so. That something was missing from the Enlightenment picture was perceived by Jean-Jacques Rousseau (1712–1778), whose strange philosophy made him at once the darling and the *bête noire* of the movement. Rousseau thought of himself as an artist, and he spent his earlier years writing music and plays that nobody wanted to listen to or watch. He became embittered at his fate, and that might have been the end of it had he not happened to spot an essay competition, which he entered and used to offload all his accumulated frustrations. The subject was one that appealed to him: "Has the restoration of the sciences and arts done anything to improve morals?" Rousseau thought the answer was no, and did not hesitate to say so. Far from improving human behavior, he said, the trends of recent years had made it worse. Whatever improvements there may have been in some ways, specialization and sophistication had created people who were good at certain things but hopeless in the skills required for citizenship. In this respect, Rousseau looked back to the ancient world, and in particular to the Athens of Socrates, who was his particular hero. Somewhat inconsistently, he also praised the Spartans for their rejection of civilization, and the barbarians who overthrew the decadent Roman Empire.

To his great surprise, he won the competition hands down, and his career as a philosopher was launched. Rousseau had written a broadside attack on the intellectual establishment, but although he could not have known it, his timing was good. Plenty of people were starting to doubt the assured results of the prevailing optimism, and Rousseau managed to put those doubts into words. In some ways he might be compared to the modern Jordan Peterson, who has done the same thing with the pieties of our own time. As with Peterson, observers of Rousseau could not agree whether he was a prophet or a fraud—or perhaps a bit of both.

Rousseau chose Plato as his hero and exalted the *Republic*, a book that David Hume denounced as "visionary ranting." By praising Sparta and claiming that the philosopher-king of his dreams would banish both the arts and private property from the ideal state, Plato had provided the key to salvation—a return to the primitive state of nature. The more the individual separated himself from the tribe, the more corrupted he became. The answer was to get back to nature, put the interests of others before your own, and dedicate yourself to a common cause, which Rousseau called the general will of the community. This was the Spartan ideal, and he thought it could be realized even in modern conditions, something that critics like Voltaire doubted. Rousseau thought that the way to achieve his goals was by compulsory education. Every child was to be taught "virtue" as Rousseau conceived of it—love of country, hatred of foreigners who did not share that love, and a willingness to sacrifice oneself for the greater good of the whole. He published this in his best-selling book *The Social Contract* (1761), which became, and has remained, one of the classical works of Enlightenment thought.

Until Rousseau came along, most Enlightenment philosophers had retained a residual respect for Christianity in a greatly diluted form—there was a Supreme Being and Jesus Christ was the perfect example of a truly good man. Rousseau swept all that aside. As far as he was concerned, the church was just as corrupt as any other instrument of civilization, and it had to be done away with. Neither Plato nor the Spartans had had any need of it, and so their modern-day would-be imitators had no need of it either. Instead of that, he advocated a religion of public rituals that would focus its worship on the general will of the nation and unite the citizenry in a common desire to defend it.

To the unprejudiced outside observer, Rousseau's vision seemed both impractical and mad, as indeed it was. But the astonishing thing is the degree to which it attracted the great men and women of his time. Immanuel Kant was an admirer, even though he realized that Rousseau's vision could not be put into practice. Queen Marie Antoinette was another, and was so moved by Rousseau's primitivism that she constructed a peasant farm at Versailles where she could pretend to live the simple life of a shepherdess![15] Hundreds of more ordinary people were seduced by his vision, including many of those who would lead the Revolution after 1789. Indeed, the French Revolution was Rousseau's ultimate revenge on society. Everything that stood in the way of freedom had to be torn down. The Christian religion was proscribed, and a statue of the goddess of Reason was put up in Notre-Dame Cathedral instead. Even the calendar was abolished, to be replaced by a revolutionary version that followed the natural seasons of the year and not the events of the life of Jesus. The ancient provinces of France were dismantled and reconstructed as departments,

15. She called it "Le Hameau" ("The Hamlet"), and it is still there.

which were all supposed to be the same (modest) size and to fit into a country that looked like a hexagon—and was so called.

It soon became evident to the revolutionaries that the moral cleansing of society that Rousseau dreamed of would not easily be achieved. The ingrained habits of centuries could not be overcome in an instant, or even in a generation, and so more radical measures were needed. Those opposed to the Revolution had to be eliminated, as they soon were by mass executions. Foreign enemies had to be confronted and defeated by a citizen army called up to defend the state. This was a new idea at the time and gave France a military advantage that enabled it to conquer most of continental Europe in the space of less than ten years. The revolutionaries created an empire, which soon demanded an emperor—Napoleon Bonaparte (1769–1821), who rose from the ranks of the French army to become the first modern dictator.

Napoleon and his entourage were men of the Enlightenment who sincerely believed that they were spreading freedom and progress across a continent that had long dwelt in darkness. The reforms they had introduced in France were extended far and wide, including such things as a written legal code, the metric system, a decimal currency, and a centralized government in which regional particularities were suppressed. It went too far, too fast, and to some extent it was undone when Napoleon fell, but a surprising amount of it came back and has survived to characterize much of Western civilization to the present time.

In particular, relations between church and state were put on a new footing. Napoleon initially thought of abolishing the papacy and banishing religion from his dominions, but he soon realized that that was impossible, and so he co-opted it instead. In 1802 he signed a concordat with Rome that gave the Catholic Church, as well as Protestants and Jews, civil rights in the new empire. Two years later, he seized the pope, brought him to Paris and ordered a coronation, though in a symbolic gesture at the last minute he took the crown from the pope's hands and placed it on his own head, just to show who was boss now. To ensure compliance with the new regime, clergy of all denominations would be paid by the state, and their places of worship would be officially licensed. The same went for their seminaries and for the public schools, although religious instruction in the latter was carefully controlled by the state and not allowed to fall exclusively into the hands of any church. This system lasted in France until 1905 and is still the basis of church-state relations in several countries, notably Germany and the states of southern Europe. It can even be found in some Latin American countries, and its legacy is seldom far away.

The Christian calendar was restored in 1806, but the celebration of patriotic festivals continued and endures to the present time in almost every country. Flags, military parades, and anniversaries of revolution and/or independence are the stock in trade of modern national feeling and are all but universal in the modern world, not least in the countries created by departing colonial powers after 1945. Until recently, conscription (the famous draft) was also common, even in peacetime, and it still continues in some places, where every young man is forced to serve in the military for a couple of years before returning to civilian life. This is all the legacy of Rousseau, whose influence peaked in the late nineteenth century but is still far from dead.

In most European countries, the creation of a secular state was slow and partial because the heritage of 1,500 years could not be undone overnight. In France, for example, it was impossible to build a new capital city or dispose of all the church buildings in the country. A few were deconsecrated, most notably the church of Sainte Geneviève in Paris, which became the Panthéon, a mock-Roman temple dedicated to the "great men of the fatherland," which is what it still is, though even today a Christian cross sits atop its neoclassical dome. For most of the nineteenth century, France endured a culture war between secularists and Catholics that was embittered by the reluctance of the latter to accept the abolition of the monarchy. That division spread to other countries, notably Spain and Portugal, which suffered similar conflicts that were not resolved until the latter part of the twentieth century. Relations between the churches and the state are much better now than they were, but the legacy of that past is still visible and still capable of provoking strife if there is any suggestion that the secular state might lower its guard against confessional religion, be it Catholicism or anything else.

In the United States, things were rather different. There had always been greater religious freedom in the American colonies than in Europe, and extending that to become comprehensive was not too difficult, since there were few established institutions that needed to be eliminated.

Americans built themselves an entirely new capital city, designed on pure Enlightenment principles as a geometric wonder radiating out from a neo-classical Capitol, the seat of civil government standing where a European would normally expect to find the city's cathedral. The constitution of this new state soon acquired the aura of a semi-sacred document, civic patriotism was focused on the flag to a degree unheard-of elsewhere, and pledging allegiance to it became a national ritual.

God was relegated to the sidelines—not abandoned completely, but restricted to set phrases like "So help me God" or "In God we trust," which were allowed to survive as anomalies in an officially secular society because most people wanted them. Specific references to Christianity were studiously avoided, however, and over time practices like prayer in schools or in public places was banned on the somewhat spurious ground that they violated the constitutional separation of church and state. *Homo Americanus*—the freedom-loving, non-denominationally religious and patriotic citizen—did not appear overnight but by the mid-twentieth century was easily recognizable, not least to foreigners, who often saw him (or her) as brash, insensitive to different cultures, and totally convinced of the superiority of everything American, including belief in God.

This stereotype may be less true now than in the past, but it is still recognizable and has affected American attitudes to both philosophy and theology to the present day. One curious result of it is that many Christian colleges do not have proper theology departments and do not train people for ministry. They are more likely to have a philosophy program, but that is not guaranteed, and the philosophy taught there may not be particularly Christian in nature. There is also a tendency to merge Judaism and Christianity into something called the "Judeo-Christian" tradition, but what exactly that means is not clear. So far there has been little sign that anyone wants to extend it to include Islam, as Lessing would have done, but perhaps it is merely a matter of time before that happens. It also means that the United States can accommodate a wide range of Christian and pseudo-Christian denominations, some of which are quite exclusive, without serious conflict.[16] Each of these groups constitutes a subculture

16. "Pseudo-Christian" would include Seventh-Day Adventists, Christian Scientists, Mormons, and Jehovah's Witnesses, among others.

that is right in its own eyes, but does not necessarily engage much with the wider world. Obvious exceptions to that are Roman Catholics, who have several universities and a lively philosophical tradition alongside their theology departments, and the (Dutch) Reformed churches, who do something similar on the Protestant side. In recent years, many Reformed philosopher-theologians have taught at Roman Catholic universities, so that the historic divisions between them are nothing like as strong as they used to be, and cross-fertilization is common.

It is probably true to say that the idolization of the ancient Greek and Roman past, which was so characteristic of the Enlightenment and of the subsequent revolutionary period, is not nearly as strong today as it once was. Modern research has made it abundantly clear that the ancient world was not the paradise of non-religious freedom that the eighteenth-century philosophers imagined it to be, and there has been a renewed appreciation for the Middle Ages, particularly in France. Nevertheless, the legacy of that era can still be seen in some quarters, as, for example, on American university campuses, where fraternities and sororities still glory in their pseudo-Greek heritage and seek to uphold the social and moral values derived from Rousseau, whether those involved realize that or not.

But perhaps the most curious result of the paganizing neoclassicism of the mature Enlightenment can be seen in the way it affected the country of philosophy's origin. Men like Rousseau adored the ancient Greeks but never dreamt of going to Athens or Sparta, both of which were then ruled by the Ottoman Turks and had been for centuries.[17] This changed quite suddenly in 1821, when the Greeks rose up in rebellion against their Turkish overlords. Apart from a tiny Westernized minority, most of which lived outside the country, the Greeks knew next to nothing about their ancient past and were not particularly interested in it. They called themselves *Romioi* or *Romaioi* (Romans) after their Byzantine ancestors, and that is how the Turks knew them. The word *Hellēnes*, in so far as it meant anything at all, referred to the pagan Greeks of the distant past and was generally avoided. After 1821, all that changed, not because the Greeks themselves began to think differently but because they wanted to appeal

17. Constantinople fell to the Turks in 1453. Athens followed in 1456, and Sparta, or what was left of it, in 1460.

to Western Europe for aid in their struggle, and the Westerners were infatuated with ancient Greece. Only a few years before, Lord Elgin had gone to Athens and carted off the Parthenon marbles to England, where they are now housed in the British Museum, and so philhellenism, as it was called, was very much in the air.

There were many Westerners who volunteered to go and fight for Greek independence, believing that the ancient cities of Athens and Sparta could be resurrected. By far the most famous of these was Lord Byron, who used his poetic skills to promote the Greek cause and eventually even went there himself. What he discovered was a shock to his system. Instead of a sunbathed paradise full of latter-day Platos, what he found was a squabbling band of brigands who wondered what planet Byron and his friends had come from. Byron did not last long—within a few weeks he caught fever and died—but the cause he sponsored lived on and was eventually successful. In 1832, an ethnically Greek state emerged, and it adopted classical Greece as its model. Serious attempts were made to revive ancient Greek as a spoken language, classical names that had fallen out of use were restored to cities, rivers, and islands (for example, Corfu became Kerkyra once more), and Athens was rebuilt to look like a model Enlightenment city, with a grid pattern of streets that resembled the American Midwest more than it did ancient Athens. The Christian heritage of Greece could not be ignored but it was sidelined, something that was made easier because the patriarch of the Greek Orthodox Church continued to live in Constantinople (Istanbul), as he still does. A divide opened up between the real Greece of the people and the imaginary Greece of the philosophically inspired elite that was to dominate the country's culture and politics for 150 years. Only in the past generation has this conflict been overcome, with mixed results. On the one hand, the Byzantine inheritance is now better appreciated than it once was, but the classical tradition is still claimed as the official ancestry of the state. The paradox was most clearly evident during the dictatorship of the colonels (1967–1974), whose slogan was "Hellas of Christian Hellenes," a juxtaposition of ideas that would have seemed bizarre to anyone before 1821. Modern Greece is still very much a creation of the Enlightenment and its neo-pagan philosophy, even though the population remains more than 90 percent Christian.

The Greek experience is a reminder of something else that surfaced during the Enlightenment—nationalism. This too went back mainly to Rousseau and his belief that communities should bond together and fight against their common enemies, as ancient Sparta had done. Sparta was not a "nation" in the true sense of the word, and most of its enemies were fellow Greeks, but in the eighteenth century the principle of group solidarity took on a different coloring. European states at that time were not nations as we understand them today, but either territories united by their dynastic rulers or else small city-states, many of which had a republican constitution. The French Revolution changed all that. France itself was forged into a nation-state by the power of Enlightenment ideas. The French language, in particular, which had long been confined to the northern half of the country, was spread everywhere as the necessary vehicle for the education of the masses. French was already the common language of European aristocracy, thanks mainly to the cultural brilliance of the previous two centuries, and it was widely believed that knowing it was an essential prerequisite for human advancement. The Revolution accentuated this belief, as the French spread their values and culture across Europe.

The advance of French was successful among the elite, where it remained the dominant language of international communication until the early twentieth century, but it also provoked a reaction, especially in Germany. The Germans had never been united politically, but after the French Revolution there developed a national consciousness there that owed more than a little to the theories of Rousseau. The Germans were portrayed as honest, hard-working and uncorrupt—unlike the French. Their language was developed as a vehicle of intellectual expression that could match Latin and French, and it spread across Central Europe. That in turn provoked another reaction, this time from a number of submerged peoples, particularly in the Austrian Empire. Czechs, Hungarians, and Croats began to claim that they constituted special communities with virtues that others lacked. In 1848, these feelings erupted into revolt against the multinational Habsburg Empire, and after that it could not be contained. It took another seventy years and a world war for its power to be clearly manifested, but after 1918 the principle that a nation could claim its own state and achieve sovereignty was generally accepted. Multinational empires were dissolved and a host of new countries emerged, each with its own claims to uniqueness—and in their own eyes, superiority to others.

The idea that a nation was a natural community, bound together by a common language, was essentially racist and anti-Christian in character. Christianity had never been nationalistic, and it was under the aegis of the papacy that an international Christendom had emerged in the Middle Ages, with Latin as its common tongue. A man could travel from Iceland to Italy, or from Portugal to Finland, under the protection of the church and be accepted wherever he went. This freedom was curtailed to some extent at the time of the Reformation, but that was for theological, not nationalistic, reasons. When French Protestants were expelled from their homeland they were welcomed with open arms in Britain, Holland, and the German states and allowed to retain their cultural identity. Eventually, they assimilated into their host countries, but they often retained an awareness of their ancestry and never suffered any discrimination because of it.

After the French Revolution, this changed. The French themselves were not usually nationalistic in a racist sense; for them, being French was a question of language and culture more than of blood, and they sought to spread their universalist Enlightenment philosophy far and wide. If people could learn to speak and think like Frenchmen they would be civilized, and the prejudices inspired by religion and ethnicity would disappear. For the Germans and Italians, who had never had a state of their own, things were more complicated. For them, language and culture were important, but not enough. There had to be something more that would justify the drive toward political unity that their nationalistic leaders desired. It is no accident that both of them achieved their goals at the same time and in a similar way—by defeating France and the papacy, both of which represented a universality that was at odds with their ambitions.

What happened in Europe spilled over into the rest of the world, and in particular to Africa and Asia, which now became the objects of European colonization. In a very short time, most of the planet outside the Americas was occupied by European powers who did not doubt their racial superiority over the people they conquered. It is easy for us to condemn this attitude, but we must try to understand it in context. Europeans were genuinely puzzled by the fact that they had developed a level of civic government and prosperity unknown in other parts of the world. Africans were mostly primitive in their eyes, and even the great civilizations of India and China were sadly lacking in enlightenment. How could Indians burn widows on their husbands' funeral pyre, for example, or allow cows to wander freely in the belief that they were somehow sacred? Why did the Chinese bind their women's feet and practice a feudalism that had long since died out in Europe, to nobody's regret? Above all, why was it that Europeans sailed the world and settled it, while Indians and Chinese (not to mention Japanese and others) were content to stay at home?

We now know that most Asian societies were just as racist as any European ones were, and perhaps more so, but their racism rested on ethnic prejudice and tradition, not on science. It was here that Europeans were different. They were not content to rely on prejudice and tradition but needed some objective basis for their approach. The developing science of linguistics showed that there had once been a people living in or near what is now Ukraine whom we now call Indo-European but were then known as Aryan. These people migrated in different directions and became the ancestors of the Greeks, the Romans, the Celts, and the Germanic tribes. This accounts for the underlying similarity among the peoples of Europe. It was likewise assumed that the Aryans were physically and mentally superior to other peoples, which enabled them to spread in the way they did. There is some truth in this theory, but it is noticeable that those who employed it for racist purposes tended to omit certain inconvenient facts. For one thing, they often omitted the Slavs (Russians, Poles, etc.) who were just as Aryan as the others, and they downplayed the Persian and Indian branches of the Aryan family, too.

They also overlooked most of the non-Aryan people of Europe, like the Finns, the Hungarians, and the Basques, though there was one group that did not escape their attention. This was the Jews, non-Aryans who were branded as "Semites," so called after Shem, one of the sons of Noah.[18] Jews had long been discriminated against because of their religion, but when religion was dismissed as a valid criterion for segregation,

18. Gen 6:10. Shem was the ancestor of the Hebrews, and also of the Arabs. Another son, Ham, was regarded as the ancestor of Africans, some of whom are still called "Hamitic." The Aryans were thought to be the descendants of Japheth, Noah's third son.

some other reason for it had to be found, and racism fitted the bill nicely. To this day, "anti-Semitism" is defined as prejudice against Jews, not against Arabs, Ethiopians, or other Semitic peoples, because these were the only non-Aryans who were present in Europe at the time. The development of race theories also meant that a shared language and culture could not change the objective facts as racists saw them. Thus, for example, African Americans could be just like their white compatriots in linguistic and cultural terms, but they were still inferior because of their race, which justified discrimination against them, particularly in ways designed to prevent interracial marriage, which was regarded as a form of degeneration as far as Aryans were concerned. People who thought like this even devised a pseudoscience called "eugenics," which had a powerful influence on American and European social policies well into the twentieth century.

Pseudoscientific racism was unwittingly reinforced by Charles Darwin (1809–1882), whose theory of biological evolution and the "survival of the fittest" could help to explain—and justify—the mass slaughter of native peoples by white European colonists, and was later employed to bolster the race theories of the German National Socialists (Nazis). It all went back to Rousseau and was deeply anti-Christian, as some people (at least) realized at the time. The missionary movement of the nineteenth century was an implicit denial of racial theories, even if that was not always immediately clear. Christians went from Europe and America to evangelize people around the world because they believed that all human beings are fundamentally the same—created in the image and likeness of God, fallen into sin, and potentially redeemed by Jesus Christ. The missionaries could not overturn racism directly, but by converting and then educating native peoples everywhere they demonstrated the hollowness of the racist claims and prepared subject peoples to take their place among the nations of the world. They were not perfect, of course, and many of them undoubtedly shared the paternalist assumptions of the colonizers, but their actions were nevertheless subversive and, in the end, led to success.

Today, eugenics and racial discrimination are completely discredited, though it must be admitted that there have been some cases where nationalism and racism have co-opted Christianity in support, and that the consequences have been disastrous. We can see this in Ireland, where a pseudo-Celtic purism has mixed incongruously with Roman Catholicism and been used to wage war on supposedly non-Celtic Protestants. We see it also in the former Yugoslavia, where Catholic Croats have fought Orthodox Serbs to the death, even though they speak the same language and share the same genetic inheritance. Above all, we have seen it in South Africa, where a misguided policy of "separate development" was advocated by many in the Dutch Reformed Church there to justify apartheid on theological grounds. These aberrations are a shame on us, but aberrations are what they are, and that must be recognized. The struggle for civil rights in both the United States and in South Africa was very largely a Christian crusade against perceived injustice. It may have been picked up by secular voices as well, but the Christian inspiration is undeniable and has proved to be more effective in the long term, particularly in the avoidance of large-scale bloodshed.[19]

The search for new rituals and even gods to replace a rejected Christianity was nowhere more evident, or long-lasting, than in the sphere of poetry. Most European countries produced a crop of Romantic poets at this time, but England stood out. This was the age of Wordsworth, Byron, Shelley, and Keats, all of whom had a cult following during their (usually brief) lifetimes and whose legacy is still very much with us. Their enduring success was due to their ability to turn what had previously been an external, intellectual creed into an internal feeling that could take the place of traditional Christian piety.

The Romantic poets were all devotees of nature, and both Byron and Shelley were openly atheistic, something that was still rare and scandalous at that time. Shelley was particularly outspoken on the subject and even wrote about it in *A Defence of Poetry*, perhaps the most important book on that subject since the *Poetics* of Aristotle more than two millennia earlier. Shelley's inspiration came not from Aristotle, though, but from Plato, who had Socrates praise the divine nature of poetry: "For a poet is ... holy, and never able to compose until he is inspired and beside himself, and reason is no longer in him."[20] Like Socrates before him, Shelley believed

---

19. That has unfortunately not been the case in Ireland or in the former Yugoslavia, where no correspondingly powerful Christian voice has been able to make itself heard.

20. Plato, *Ion*, 533e,

that poets were the interpreters of the divine to the world of the human, but in fairness to him, he did not limit this activity to what we would call "poetry" today. As far as he was concerned, any creative spirit was poetic, and he was broad-minded enough to include Isaac Newton and Jesus Christ within that definition. What the world needed was an army of such spirits who could discover truth by using their imagination and then sharing that discovery with the population as a whole.

What Shelley had seen, or so he claimed, was a world in which uninspired politicians had preached revolution, only to become entangled in their own lust for power. If the poets could shape things, humanity would enter an age of peace and harmony in which the potential of everyone would be realized. Shelley would not live to see it, but it was a vision that would surface briefly at the end of the First World War, when romantically inspired revolutionaries like Alexander Blok (1880–1921) would capture the spirit of the moment and herald the dawn of a new age, only to see their dreams shattered by a tyranny that made the French Revolution seem pale by comparison.

In intellectual terms, the poetic Enlightenment was naive to the point of absurdity. In his conclusion to "Ode on a Grecian Urn" (1819), John Keats wrote the now famous lines: "Beauty is truth, truth beauty; that is all ye know on earth, and all ye need to know." Compare this with Isaiah 53:2, often used by Christians as a description of the Messiah: "He had no form or majesty that we should look at him, and no beauty that we should desire him." To the idea that beauty is equivalent to truth, the apostle Paul would have retorted: "Satan disguises himself as an angel of light" (2 Cor 11:14).[21] That, for many Christians, pretty well sums up the Enlightenment, but the attraction of the mirage should not be underestimated. In every generation Keats's vacuity reappears in different forms, the most recent one being the "new age spirituality" that brings together every mad idea imaginable and markets it as a way of salvation. As a reaction to a society that is overspecialized and too technical for most people to be able to grasp, that may be understandable, but as a guide to the future it has nothing to offer, and those who chase after it are likely to destroy themselves, as many of the Romantic poets did.

21. "Lucifer" means "light-bearer."

A NEW SYNTHESIS?

Rousseau's vision of the future could not be realized in the vision of the Romantic poets because it was too detached from historical reality. A more substantial framework was needed, and that was provided by Georg Wilhelm Friedrich Hegel (1770–1831), the first truly modern philosopher and the ultimate architect of much of the way in which we perceive the world today. Like a good Romantic, Hegel began his analysis with the Middle Ages, which he saw as a time of moral virtue and spiritual uplift. This was made possible because of the interaction between two competing ideas—sin and salvation. Sin was the lot of the human race and salvation was the promise of the gospel. Unfortunately, what happened in practice was that humanity was repressed and the gospel was confided to a church that became tyrannical. The Renaissance liberated humankind and the Reformation freed society from the tyranny of the church, but the result was half-baked. Instead of resolving the problems inherent in medieval society, the upheavals of the sixteenth century merely unleashed a commercialism that used the new so-called freedom of the human race to introduce a new order of things that allowed for economic exploitation of the masses, unconstrained by the moral influence of anything equivalent to the church.

In order to resolve the problems created by the past, Hegel believed that it was necessary to rethink the nature of reality. As he saw it, previous philosophers, from Aristotle to Kant, had gone wrong by thinking that it was possible to isolate discrete things and examine them independently of anything else. These things could be material objects or they could be ideas, but in either case Hegel argued that they could not be separated from the wider whole. Reality, he claimed, was a continuum, and therefore everything was not only related but contained within itself features that made relations with other things necessary.

Hegel believed that what Kant had said was the unknowable principle of the universe was in fact the Absolute, and that it could be known by the way in which it manifested itself in concrete forms. The Absolute was by definition entirely free, but it had to demonstrate this freedom by creating something outside itself that was also free and independent of it. This was the universe, but the universe was not unrelated to the Absolute. On the contrary, it was the expression of the Absolute's freedom and therefore of its nature. Because of that fundamental connection, the Absolute could not abandon the universe but had to reconcile it to itself. Hegel was writing from a nominally Christian standpoint, and so he could identify the Absolute with the God of the Bible, and many people have accepted his assertion that his philosophy was compatible with Christianity in a basically orthodox form. A deeper examination of his thought will soon show, however, that this is not the case.

Hegel asserted that the Absolute was infinite but that the universe was finite. According to him, finite and infinite imply each other, and it is the historical destiny of the former to be reunited with the latter. In this sense, finitude is unrealized potential, and therefore evil. The infinite, on the other hand, is fully realized and therefore good. Evil was not the result of sin, as Christianity had traditionally taught, but was inherent in creation. This sounds very much like a return to ancient pagan philosophy, but it was not, because whereas the ancients tended to believe that evil was inherent in matter and could never be expunged from it, Hegel saw the created world as a work in progress, heading over time toward eventual perfection. This would happen because the finite world contains elements of the infinite that make connections between them real and open the door to eventual reconciliation. In particular, Hegel said that the Absolute was Spirit, and that human beings, the crown of creation, were also spirits.

The finite could not attain to the infinite by itself, but the reverse was possible—the infinite could manifest itself in the finite. This, Hegel believed, was what happened in the incarnation of Jesus Christ. He was the infinite God revealed in finite human nature, the instrument by which the Absolute reconciled the world to itself. Because Hegel believed that the Absolute reveals itself in history, and that Jesus Christ was a genuine historical manifestation of the divine, he was prepared to accept the uniqueness of that incarnation and to regard Christianity as superior to all other religions and philosophies. As the God-man, Christ took on normal human existence, died a human death and rose again from the dead to demonstrate that the limitations of finitude had been overcome. By being united with Christ in his death and resurrection, human beings could be released from the kind of "freedom" their finitude offered, abandon the selfish individuality that their finitude had imposed on them, and be reunited with God.

The incarnation of Christ was a historical event, but it was not an accident. In the wider scheme of things, it was a realization of the divine nature, making itself visible in time and space. It had to happen, since otherwise the underlying unity of God and man would never have become apparent. Since historical events are all manifestations of the Absolute, the historical death and resurrection of Christ had universal significance. It realized an aspect of reality that had previously been only potential and in that sense it changed the course of history.

Hegel's reconstruction of reality did not go unchallenged for long. If all human beings are spirits, and therefore in a relationship with the Absolute Spirit, why should Jesus of Nazareth be considered unique? If the infinite and the finite are fundamentally one, then all human beings are in some sense divine. It may have been useful, and given human frailty perhaps even necessary, for our minds to be focused on one particular individual, but he could only be a picture of what was essentially true of everyone and not somebody altogether singular and different. This was the view taken by David Friedrich Strauss (1808–1874), whose groundbreaking work *The Life of Jesus* (1835) was a frontal attack on Christian orthodoxy rooted in his rejection of Hegel. Even more radical was Ludwig Feuerbach (1804–1872), whose *Essence of Christianity* (1841) turned Hegel on his head by claiming that, far from Christianity being the manifestation of the Absolute finding its identity in the finite and reconciling it to itself, it was really just the projection of human desires onto a mythical supreme being who was dignified with the name of "God." All religions did the same thing, argued Feuerbach; Christianity only stands out because it is the form most familiar to Westerners. Little though Hegel intended it, it would be these reinterpretations of his ideas that would form the basis of so-called liberal Christianity (Strauss) and modern atheism (Feuerbach).

From a Christian standpoint, the most serious refutation of Hegel's position came from Søren Kierkegaard (1813–1855), whose writings were unfortunately ignored for nearly a century after they were written. Kierkegaard said bluntly that Hegel did not know what Christianity was, and neither did most of his readers. If they had, they would not have fallen for his false analysis. Hegel maintained that Christianity was merely the best outward expression of a truth that was latent in every human being, but Kierkegaard flatly denied that. He said that in fact, the Christian gospel goes against human thoughts and desires. It demands not the expression of a hidden dimension of human nature but a denial of that nature and a complete transformation of our thoughts and actions—a new life, in fact. The challenge we face is to become something different from what we are, and this challenge is not an intellectual construction that we can accept or reject without any real consequences. On the contrary, it is a decision that has to be taken in real life situations on an ongoing, everyday basis. To put it in philosophical terms, it works itself out, not at the level of abstract being but in the concrete reality of our earthly existence. We live one day at a time, called to submit our wills to that of Jesus Christ and to seek his guidance.

For Kierkegaard, the basis of the Christian life was faith, but although this faith could not be measured by assent to various doctrinal statements or philosophical propositions, it was not irrational either. He believed that it was grounded in the recognition of the existence of good and evil and of the consequent need to make a choice between them. He understood that not everyone will think that such a choice needs to be made, but for those who do, there are two options. One of these is to become "religious," by which Kierkegaard meant accepting a series of moral obligations and cultic rituals, fulfillment of which would demonstrate the necessary commitment to the good. But although most of the world's religions, including many forms of Christianity, proposed that solution, it was impossible to make it work. Consistent achievement of the stated goals of such a program is beyond the power of ordinary mortals, and even if it could be realized, there would always be "sins of omission," failings that had never occurred to the person trying to live according to the rules. The only alternative was the gospel of Christ, who offers forgiveness for sin and redemption through what he has achieved and we cannot.

Christians will immediately recognize this as the teaching of Christ, but it is important to remember that Kierkegaard never went beyond practical ethical concerns. He did not venture into the deeper questions of creation, the Trinity, the incarnation of Christ, and so on. There is no reason to suppose that he dissented from traditional orthodox belief, but it was not of central importance to him. His approach to God was one of "fear and trembling" because God is completely different from us and demands behavior from us that may seem absurd, as when he asked

Abraham to sacrifice his son Isaac (Gen 22:1–18). This absurdity merely demonstrates the gulf that separates faith from human reason; it is not irrational in itself, because in a relationship with God, it is obedience that counts above all else.

Kierkegaard's approach was taken up, often without acknowledgment, by various twentieth-century thinkers, including people like Jean-Paul Sartre (1905–1980), who turned it into existentialism. Sartre and those who thought like him abandoned God and faith but retained the notion of moral challenge, in which they saw individuals creating and coming to terms with their own inner reality. They too believed in absurdity, not because God's demands were past human understanding, but because the eternal quest for self-fulfillment can never be realized and so the moral imperative to seek it is ultimately absurd. Kierkegaard never went anything like as far as that, but Sartre demonstrated both that it was possible to adopt his practical position without faith in God and that the resulting tension would produce a dilemma from which there was no escape.

Hegel's views were thus refuted and rejected, but his philosophical reconstruction of history did not disappear. In a tripartite scheme largely borrowed (unacknowledged) from Neoplatonism, Hegel claimed that a conflict between man (*thesis*) and God (*antithesis*) had produced a *synthesis* that combined elements of the two but did it in the wrong way. The conflict should have produced a *crisis* (a word that Hegel used in the modern sense for the first time) that destroyed the old order and brought a new one—the *synthesis*—into being. Man and God had indeed been combined but there had been no reconciliation between them and so society had not been transformed as it should have been. Instead of a new era of harmony and peace, what had resulted was further conflict. This conflict led to revolution, in which the exploited masses cast off the yoke of commercialism by seizing the property of the privileged classes and neutering the influence of the church(es). The resulting synthesis was seen most clearly in the work of Napoleon, a man whom Hegel greatly admired.

What Napoleon did was to create the state as a concept in its own right. There had always been governments of one kind or another, of course, but Napoleon's (and Hegel's) state was something new. The state transcended politics, which could take place within it but not really supplant it. Whatever person or party was in power at any given moment, the state carried on more or less unaffected. This is why Napoleon's state survived his fall and why the political instability of France's Third Republic (1870–1940) or of modern Italy were not particularly problematic. The state institutions and the civil service that ran them carried on regardless, and the political dramas played out in parliament were just that—theater. English-speaking countries generally have a more placid political life, but the principle is much the same. It does not really matter what party is in power at any given moment, because the machinery of government carries on regardless. Politicians who sense that their plans are being frustrated by the durability of the system have been known to complain of what they call the "deep state"—the bedrock institutions that run the country regardless of what politicians say and that can usually fend off their more unacceptable ideas for change.

For the state to function as Hegel thought it should, it had to have control of all the essential factors that make up a modern society. Education was one of them, and during the course of the nineteenth century almost every country adopted a compulsory system that was controlled by the state—if not directly, then through standards and examinations that were applied to everyone as "accreditation." The state also regulated income tax, which was made permanent for the first time, and in return created a network of benefits for the average citizen—unemployment insurance, health care, old age pensions, and so on. Germany (and in particular Prussia) was in the forefront of this development, with the most advanced welfare system in the world by 1900, and the United States, despite the attempts of Franklin Delano Roosevelt (1882–1945), brought up the rear—as it still does—with any progress in that direction being denounced as socialism. Modern conservatives do not usually attack so-called liberals as individuals with their particular ideas; what they want is a smaller state, the institution that they perceive as their true enemy. On the other side, liberals tend to view the state much as Hegel himself did—not as a tyranny but as a protection for the people. To Hegel's mind, the state was the ideal synthesis between man and God. It was made by human beings for their benefit, but it was also the arbiter of rights and freedoms, designed to ensure that everyone received their fair share of society's resources.

Hegel thought of the state as a substitute for God and the church. The word "welfare" does not particularly convey this, but the French equivalent makes it perfectly clear—the "welfare state" is the état-providence, which to theologically attuned minds is a clear reference to the deist God. Hegel never declared himself to be an atheist, but he devised a system that claimed to transcend the need for God and to account for traditional theological virtues by referring to a higher authority. Unlike the God of the deists, Hegel's state was anything but non-interventionist. One way or another, it was involved in every aspect of citizens' lives and there was no escaping from it. Every person owed allegiance to the state, which provided all that was needed and took care of any social or economic inequalities that might emerge. This was Hegel's utopia—a paradise without God, designed for the glory and progress of man.

Whatever we may think about Hegel's analysis, there can be no doubt that countries in the modern world are closer to his model of the state than anything he himself knew. Churches and religious organizations are usually allowed to function more or less freely and often receive special privileges, like exemption from taxes, but it is the state that determines where the boundaries between itself and the churches lie and that reserves the right to alter them as it sees fit. Tax exemption, for example, is by no means guaranteed, and church schools, while permitted, must operate within state laws and (in the United States at least) fund themselves in addition to the support given automatically to schools run by the state. To put it a different way—the state knows who is boss!

REVOLUTION AGAIN

Hegel's theory of the state has influenced the development of Western society ever since, but it was not the last word in the development of Rousseau's vision, nor could it have been. What Hegel worked out was in a sense the very opposite of what Rousseau wanted—his state was a highly organized, and therefore unnatural, creation, even though it purported to give humanity back its freedom. This contradiction was soon noticed, though the moment of truth came many years after Hegel's death. The man who saw where Hegel had gone wrong and who thought he knew the way to remedy it was Karl Marx (1818–1883), and the year of his vision was 1848. It was then that the crisis of the post-Napoleonic European order finally erupted, and as usual, Paris was at the center of the storm. In February, the restored monarchy was overthrown and a republic declared, but there was no revolution on the scale of 1789. Instead, the property-owning classes, or *bourgeoisie* as they were known, seized the initiative and imposed a regime even more conservative and unwilling to reform the system than the one that had been overthrown. That led to a new clash in June 1848, this time between the bosses and their workers.

Hegel's idea that the state would provide for the working poor and regulate the differences between the haves and the have-nots had never been put into practice in France, or anywhere else. Marx went back over Hegel's historical analysis from the Middle Ages onward and rewrote it in an attempt to explain why this had been so. He rejected Hegel's assertion that history is determined by conflicts of ideas that ultimately led to the triumph of Reason, and said that it was really determined by the way that people satisfied their material wants. In the sixteenth century, the merchant class had overturned the feudal agrarian society of medieval times, but they had done so in order to increase their own profits. To put it in later Marxist terms, they had seized what were then the "commanding heights of the economy" and subordinated everything else to them. Later on, this same class developed a form of parliamentary government that looked democratic but was really an oligarchy that was bolstered by claims that appeared to be attractive but that were in fact deceptive. Foremost among these was the belief that private property was the guarantee of freedom and stability, when in truth it was simply an excuse for the ruling class to secure its control of the means of production.

In theory, anyone could make money and join this ruling class, and some people did. A "rags to riches" myth encouraged the poor to hope that they could do so, and that the trappings of liberal capitalism were the way to go. In practice, though, things did not work out that way for the majority. Just as today, when people are encouraged to think they can win the lottery but very few actually do, and most of those who waste their money on this false hope end up poorer than when they started, so the lower classes of the bourgeois state were reduced to a lower economic level even as they were promised better times in the future. In the Middle Ages, this false vision had been propagated by the church, which guaranteed salvation in the next life to those who unfortunately failed to obtain it in this one. The capitalist era that replaced the Middle Ages introduced the Enlightenment idea of progress, typified by John Locke more than by anyone else. But that too was an illusion that was destined to perish when the truth was finally unveiled.

What was that truth? In the Middle Ages, the capitalist bourgeoisie had gradually come into self-conscious existence under the aegis of the church until it was strong enough to challenge the existing order and to overthrow it. Now, in the nineteenth century, Marx claimed that this bourgeoisie was in turn being undermined by the rising working class, or "proletariat" as he somewhat contemptuously called it, because all it did was produce endless children (*proles* in Latin). The events of June 1848 were the first sign of the coming upheaval, but by no means the last. Marx branded it "communism" and wrote *The Communist Manifesto* to explain what that was. He lived to see a similar, but much more protracted and bloody proletarian revolt in Paris in the winter of 1870–1871, when in the famous *Commune* the working class rose up against the bourgeoisie.

The *Commune* was eventually put down, but the ideal of revolution was not. On the contrary, Marx came to believe that it would have to occur on a worldwide scale in order to be successful, and that Germany, which was fast becoming the most advanced industrial society in the world, would be the leader in this. However, the Germans' wily Chancellor, Otto von Bismarck (1815–1898), bought off discontent by introducing a welfare system along Hegelian lines.[22] Marx did not live long enough to see the effects of this, but to him such a move was just one more attempt by the bourgeoisie to stave off the inevitable. What he really did not foresee, and actually discounted, was the possibility that his vision would take root and succeed in Russia, of all places. Russia was economically backward and only semi-European, but its rapid economic development in the late nineteenth century, combined with a sclerotic government wedded to a feudal system that was no longer viable, created ideal conditions for an explosion.

The first of these occurred in 1905, and as had happened in France, it was put down. Cosmetic reforms, including the creation of a parliament, were introduced, but they were never very effective. When war broke out in 1914 Russia was ill-prepared, and despite heroic attempts to survive, the

22. Bismarck was chancellor (in effect, prime minister) of Prussia from 1862 and of imperial Germany from 1871 to 1890.

regime collapsed in a mixture of confusion and idealism. The Germans sensed that they could take advantage of the situation and approached Vladimir Ilyich Ulyanov (1870–1924), better known by his nickname of Lenin, the leader of Russia's Communist Party, who was then living in exile in Switzerland.[23] Lenin was spirited back into Russia, where he took advantage of the confusion and staged his own takeover, the so-called Great October Socialist Revolution, which occurred in Petrograd on November 7, 1917.[24] Its operating mechanism was the worker's council, or *soviet* in Russian, that became the model for the new regime, which was technically a union of soviets.

The Russian Revolution was Marxist in inspiration, but that was about all. It never claimed to be "communist" because the social conditions of Russia were not suited to such a radical leap forward. Instead it was labeled "socialist," a name that endured to the end.[25] "Socialism" in this understanding was a stage on the way to communism, which never actually arrived. The reason for that was simple. True communism, according to Marx (following Rousseau), would lead to the disappearance of the state, because it would no longer be needed. Freed from their economic chains and the illusions that had kept them down, the victorious proletariat would return to the primitive state of nature, in which everyone would put the interests of others first and live for the greater glory of the community as a whole. It caught on to the extent that it did in Russia because it harked back to a semi-mythical Russian past, in which rural communities had been held together by what was called the *mir*, an ambiguous word that means both "world" and "peace." The village *mir* would be replicated on a universal scale, and when that happened, communism would finally appear.

---

23. Originally, Lenin was the leader of only part of the Russian Social Democratic Party, the "majority," or Bolsheviks in Russian. The "minority" were the Mensheviks, but in actual fact, the numbers were reverse. There were always more Mensheviks than Bolsheviks, but they lacked the organization and ruthlessness demonstrated by Lenin and his comrades, and the Bolshevik faction eventually became the Communist Party.

24. Russia was then still using the Julian, or "old" calendar, so the date was October 25 by their reckoning. Petrograd had been Saint Petersburg until 1914, when its German-sounding name had been Russified. It was changed again to Leningrad in 1924, and back to Saint Petersburg after the fall of the Soviet Union in 1991.

25. It was officially known as the Union of Soviet Socialist Republics, established in 1922 and dissolved in 1991.

This vision was theoretically international from the beginning; Lenin himself believed that it had to be extended to Germany, at the very least, and in the chaos following defeat in 1918, that country and a few other places, like Hungary, fell briefly into Marxist hands. However, in these countries the bourgeoisie was too strong and the revolution was put down. It came back again in 1945, but this time it was on the back of a victorious Soviet army, and was most certainly not the result of a proletarian uprising. The social system thus introduced survived for a generation, but only because of a military occupation that became increasingly difficult to maintain. Meanwhile though, it spread to China and to other parts of the developing world, where it still survives, albeit in a greatly modified form.[26]

By the time Lenin died in 1924, the Soviet system was contained in a single country—a complete denial of Marx's theory of international revolution—and quickly degenerated into a reign of terror that lasted, off and on, for the rest of its existence. Far from disappearing as it was supposed to do, the state became ever more powerful, though its formal institutions concealed where the real power lay—with the Communist Party. Lenin's successor, Josef Djugashvili (1878–1953), better known to us by his revolutionary name of Stalin, was never more than General Secretary of that party, and yet he was the unquestioned dictator of the country until his death. It was soon obvious to all but the most easily deceived (whose numbers unfortunately contained many Western intellectuals) that the entire structure was based on a lie, and that the lie had its roots in Marxism itself. Marx never visited a slum or a factory, had no dealings with the so-called proletariat and looked down on people from a working-class background. So too did Lenin, who was from the minor aristocracy of imperial Russia and not from the toiling masses whose cause he supposedly championed. Their propaganda was a fantasy from start to finish, and the only way that they could sustain the illusion they created was by sealing their unfortunate subjects off from the rest of the world. Marxist states were prisons, from which only a few incorrigible

26. "Communist" China is in reality a state-controlled capitalist dictatorship. Other countries, like Cuba, Laos, and Vietnam have their own versions of the Marxist system, but none of them bears much relationship to anything envisioned by Marx himself.

dissidents were allowed to escape. A more complete inversion of the ideal they promoted is hard to imagine.

God and religion, of course, had no logical place in such states, which were declared to be officially atheist for the first time in history. All religions were persecuted, though some suffered more than others. There were even museums of atheism, dedicated to showing how the proletariat had shaken off the superstitions of religion. Ironically, these museums, and the literature that official atheism produced, had to go into the details of religion in quite some depth, ostensibly in order to demonstrate just how pernicious it was, and how hard it had been to get rid of it. The result was that many people learned about religion, and in particular about Christianity, from the very material that was designed to combat it. But as people began to realize that their social system was built on a lie, points of view that the system opposed started to look more attractive and many began to take them more seriously.

This did not necessarily mean that they became Christians, because other worldviews were also given an airing, like Falun Gong in China, an essentially atheistic worldview that is nevertheless severely persecuted by the authorities for its dangerous, anti-revolutionary ideas. But although Christianity was not the only belief to gain a hearing from this inverted approach, it was a major beneficiary of it, so much so that when the Soviet Union collapsed, its museums of atheism could easily be transformed into museums of religion, particularly Christianity, and the church has grown exponentially in China, much to the consternation of the authorities. Tertullian's ancient dictum that the blood of martyrs is the seed of the church has never been more true than in the century since 1917. Marxism survives, but mainly in Western universities where it is cultivated by academics who are as disconnected from real life as Marx was. When asked why communism failed in the Soviet Union and elsewhere, their usual reply is that it was never tried—the future utopia is yet to come! Perhaps there is no better proof than this of the power lies can have to delude even the most brilliant intellectuals—perhaps, indeed, *especially* the most brilliant intellectuals!

PEACEFUL COEXISTENCE

The big difference between Marxism and the ideologies that preceded it is that the Marxists had considerable popular appeal in many European countries. The German Communist Party was destroyed by Adolf Hitler (1889–1945) and the Spanish one was defeated in a bloody civil war (1936–1939), but the French and Italian ones remained significant political forces until the late twentieth century, and they were also prominent in several developing countries. The big exceptions to this were in the English-speaking world. Communist parties existed in Britain, the United States, and elsewhere, but they were never large or popular, despite occasional scaremongering that suggested otherwise. Why was this so?

One reason was that Christianity was not contained within a dominant and authoritarian church as it was in Catholic and Orthodox countries. The upper classes were conventionally religious but seldom aggressively so, and there was plenty of room for dissenting opinions. Potentially subversive groups, like the Irish in Britain or African-Americans in the United States, were themselves highly religious—often more so than their opponents—and there was no space for an atheistic ideology to take root. This feature of Anglo-American life was noted by two prominent French observers whose works remain classics. Alexis de Tocqueville (1805–1859) visited the United States and wrote a remarkably perceptive and prophetic book, *Democracy in America* (1835; 1840), that pointed out how different Americans were from Europeans. De Tocqueville also understood the underlying connection between the United States and the United Kingdom—to him, Americans were what Englishmen would be if left to their own devices, a truth that would later be demonstrated in Australia, among other places. The other man was Élie Halévy (1870–1937), who lived and wrote two generations later but advanced the thesis that it was Methodism that prevented social revolution in the English-speaking world and allowed the working class to come to terms with capitalism.[27] Evangelical Protestantism had little time for ideology, but it was active in social reform, particularly in the campaign to abolish slavery but also in the move to establish decent public hospitals, proper prisons,

27. By "Methodist" Halévy understood the evangelical movement, which was always broader than the Methodist Church as such.

and social organizations like the Young Men's Christian Association (YMCA) that would provide an outlet for youthful energies in a wholesome environment.

But Halévy's interests were not confined to religious revivalism. His principal works were more concerned with what we call Utilitarianism, a set of pragmatic economic theories put forward by men who were themselves atheistic but who avoided serious religious controversy. Prominent among them was Jeremy Bentham (1748–1832), scion of a prominent Tory family, who became the leading radical of his generation. Bentham believed that "the greatest happiness of the greatest number" was the criterion that should govern what was right and what was wrong, and he applied this dictum to his economic theories. Bentham opposed the American Revolution, which he thought was half-baked in ideological terms, but he was initially supportive of the French one, so much so in fact that he was made an honorary citizen of France! But Bentham soon fell out with the French revolutionaries and instead advocated a series of social reforms that could command the support of evangelicals and even of some Tory grandees. He was in favor of a new kind of education and supported the establishment of a university in London that would be much more attuned to the realities of social and political life than the ancient foundations of Oxford and Cambridge were.

Bentham's influence extended to America, where new economic models were all the rage for a time, and even to Australia, though he died before much could be done there. Nevertheless, he was a sponsor of the largely secular educational system that sprang up all over the English-speaking world in which practical subjects, like economics, dominated the curriculum and theology was effectively banished. Bentham was succeeded by a number of disciples, of whom the most prominent was John Stuart Mill (1806–1873), a contemporary of Karl Marx but almost his exact opposite in terms of ideology, apart from their shared atheism.

Mill's father had been Jeremy Bentham's secretary, so he was schooled in Utilitarianism from an early age. There was no concession to human frailty in his upbringing; everything was geared to obtaining the optimum result from the maximum effort, and failure was rewarded with punishment in the belief that pain would be enough to turn the boy away from his errors. But when Mill reached adulthood, he realized that his upbringing had been lopsided. It was geared exclusively to the good of the greater number, which sounds fine in theory, but there was nothing left for him, no satisfaction in which he could rest. He fell into a depression for two years, which was relieved only by an encounter with the Romantic poetry that his father and Jeremy Bentham had no time for. Wordsworth in particular filled a void in Mill's life and led him to see that pure Utilitarianism is not enough.

Mill came to understand that real life demands tolerance of social institutions and customs that may seem to have no practical purpose but that give a sense of meaning to the lives of ordinary people. Studying how these institutions and customs evolved was the key to understanding human nature, and that in turn would lead to a sensitive reassessment of the way we live. Mill read the French philosopher Auguste Comte (1798–1857), who believed that by doing this it would be possible to develop a science of humanity, which Comte called "sociology." To Comte's mind, such a sociology would be just as watertight and infallible as Newton's mathematics appeared to be. Mill's aim was to piece together Comte's sociology and a scientific understanding of nature, which he did in a best-selling book called *A System of Logic* (1843). Mill followed his predecessors—Adam Smith, David Hume, Georg Hegel, and Auguste Comte in particular—in stressing the importance of historical development, but he differed from Hegel and Comte, as well as from Karl Marx, in emphasizing the importance of individual freedom.

For John Stuart Mill, as for the Romantic poets, the freedom of the individual was the key to unleashing the genius of humanity in general. But unlike the poets or Rousseau, Mill believed that this freedom was best exercised in the context of free market capitalism, not in any kind of groupthink or "socialism." He wrote extensively on the subject, but his most influential work was *On Liberty* (1859). This relatively short work remains the ultimate source of liberalism, and of its more recent descendant, libertarianism, in the English-speaking world. In the introduction, he wrote that "mankind are greater gainers by suffering each other to live as seems good to themselves than by compelling each to live as seems good to the rest." It was the exact opposite of what Hegel and Marx believed.

Part and parcel of Mill's belief in freedom was his rejection of the idea that human life had a particular purpose to which history was inevitably heading. For him, the meaning of life had to be seen in the vocation of each individual and not in some collective whole. The result, of course, is that there was an almost infinite number of possible purposes in life, which every person had to discover for him- or herself. In commerce this ought to lead to the expansion of personal choice as different options become available, and that is what Mill advocated. By stimulating freedom of choice, the free market would maximize the potential for individual diversity and encourage merchants to meet the desires of their customers, rather than impose a deadening uniformity on them. The more people were allowed to be themselves, the better life would become for everyone.

Mill recognized, of course, that giving people freedom was risky. Not everybody thought clearly, and crazy ideas as well as outright lies were always likely to surface. The way to deal with them was not by suppression but by argument, said Mill, because that way the nature of the errors would be exposed and right-minded people would be turned against them. The last thing that was needed was dogmatism, which to Mill's mind had been the ruin of history's greatest geniuses. It was when Christ's teaching became church doctrine or when Martin Luther's protests hardened into Protestant confessions of faith that the individual spirit fossilized into ritual assertions and the creative spirit died.

In the nineteenth century, Mill believed, a new breath of freedom was in the air, but there were dangers ahead. Paradoxically, these dangers arose out of the very principles that Mill was trying to encourage. He wanted people to be free, but that meant giving them a voice in human affairs. That in turn led to democracy, but democracy was always susceptible to the herd instinct, which we now call the tyranny of the majority. If the value of an idea was to be judged solely by the number of people who hold it, true freedom and creativity would be lost, and a dangerous form of social conformity would take its place. Mill also feared the growth of Marxist communism, which he saw as the suppression of individuality in the "general will," which Marx equated with the common good. Mill believed in a form of socialism, but it had to be voluntary and not coerced. What was the point, he asked, of being fed, clothed, and looked after, if the beneficiaries were no better than slaves? Far better to be free and responsible, even if there were risks involved. What Mill advocated was the establishment of cooperative societies where people would voluntarily pool their resources and share the profits among them. These cooperative societies actually came into being and survive to this day, but their influence has been much greater than their numbers would suggest. Thousands of small, independent retailers formed associations for their mutual benefit. These associations are not cooperatives in the strict sense, but they perform a similar function in that they encourage their members to maintain professional standards and ensure fair competition, to the benefit of producers and consumers alike.

Mill's approach was not dogmatically atheistic but it was non-religious, because in his mind religion was a form of coercion that would place limits on freedom. In practice, the logic of his position was that churches and religious organizations had to be left alone. There could be no attempt to suppress them, as there had been in the French Revolution and as there would be again under Marxism. This was of considerable practical importance in the early nineteenth century because it enabled the Utilitarians and their allies to make common cause with the Christian churches in the struggle to abolish slavery. The churches had long tried to do that as much as they could, and in Europe at least, slavery died out in the course of the Middle Ages because Christians could not enslave one another.

But as mentioned in chapter 5, the colonial expansion of the sixteenth century and later introduced a new situation. Slavery was tolerated in the colonies if the slaves were not Christian, which explains why they were drawn from Africa, which had not been evangelized at that time. But by 1800 many of the slaves had been converted to Christianity, despite opposition from their masters, and the question of whether the peculiar institution, as it was known, could continue was raised once more. Many Christians took up the abolitionist cause, but the economic arguments for retaining slavery were hard for them to refute. It was here that the Utilitarians entered the fray by claiming that free labor was actually cheaper and more efficient than slavery. As that awareness sank in, economic pragmatism and moral indignation combined to make the abolitionist cause unstoppable. Slavery was abolished in the British Empire in 1833 and in the United States in 1863, though unfortunately it required a civil war for abolition to take effect. Nevertheless, the possibility of cooperation between Christians and others was clearly demonstrated and made it impossible for the non-religious to press for the exclusion of the churches from wider society on the ground that they were supportive of reactionary tyranny.

Another area where religious and secular interests could work together in the English-speaking world was that of sport, and in particular of team games. Sports of various kinds had existed for centuries, but it was in the late nineteenth century that they became regulated and organized in the way that we know them today. Ball games played with the feet were codified as football, soccer, and rugby; games played with a bat became baseball and cricket. There were a number of different codifications, which explains why there are differences among these games today, but all of them originated somewhere in the English-speaking world and all were supported equally by Christians and others. To some extent, Rousseau's dream of collective rituals to replace Christian worship and festivals was taken over by the various sporting leagues that emerged, but these were never allowed to develop in the way that Rousseau wished. To this day, leading sports personalities can express their religious faith and many do, seeing no conflict between the health of the body and that of the soul.

The significance of this can perhaps best be seen if we compare it with what happened elsewhere. Devotion to athletics was also a feature of European liberalism, but it took a different form from what happened in the Anglo-American world. The concentration there was on the revival of the Olympic Games in 1896, a pagan institution that the early Christians had suppressed. There is no religious element in the modern Olympics, and no room for one, either. The Olympics are elitist in the way they tend to focus on the prowess of individual athletes (or small teams), and the state is much more involved in them—so much so, in fact, that several countries have been accused of illegally doping their athletes so as to win medals (and glory) for their country. Constructive cooperation between religious and secular agencies is the farthest thing from their minds.

At the intellectual level, such cooperation was more difficult, because there secular and religious principles came into direct contact—and inevitable conflict. In England, the ancient universities of Oxford and Cambridge were virtually seminaries until the mid-nineteenth century, and the Scottish universities were similar. In the United States, Christian universities were private, and public ones had to be secular in line with the official separation of church and state. Religious revivalism and the influx of European migrants into the United States led to the creation of numerous colleges (and later universities) that reflected particular denominational outlooks, and these continue in operation to the present day. How they could or would relate to the wider pluralist society was a question that was seldom asked at the beginning, but as the emphasis shifted away from the arts and humanities toward the sciences, it became more acute. The natural sciences are not denominationally distinct in the way that theology is, and cooperation between them seemed logical and inevitable. Sooner or later the two quite different streams would have to meet and mingle as far as they could, but quite how that would be done was never very clear and depended on individual circumstances.

In the British world, there was no constitutional separation of church and state, though secularism was powerful, especially in the settler colonies of Canada and Australia. Some colleges and universities were established on a purely secular basis, but religious influences persisted and there was no neat separation between the two. Denominationalism also played a role, but it was less significant than in the United States, and private colleges devoted to a particular church were less common. In Oxford and Cambridge, non-Anglican churches were allowed to set up colleges of their own, but these were always associated with the universities and over time they merged into them in a kind of ecumenical consensus that was essentially, though not explicitly, secular in orientation.

In the United States, the religious affiliation of the old colonial colleges continued, though in some cases it changed complexion over time. Harvard College, for example, moved from being a Congregationalist institution to a Unitarian one, which in the circumstances was really a form of secularization. Yale had already moved from Congregationalism to Anglicanism before the Revolution, but it too was basically multi-denominational. Princeton, on the other hand, was clearly Presbyterian and remained so. In the nineteenth century, it acquired a reputation for strict Reformed orthodoxy, which it retained until the early twentieth century, when more liberal influences began to penetrate it. But those influences came from the church as much as from the academy, and so the Presbyterian character of the university remained more noticeable, even if it was no longer as orthodox as it had once been.

The arrival of European immigrants in the United States created a new situation. Many were Lutherans from Germany and Scandinavia, or Reformed from the Netherlands and elsewhere. They soon established colleges to reflect their particular confessional stances and retained close links with their original homelands. On the whole, they developed separately from their English-speaking equivalents, but there was some cross-fertilization, particularly between the Reformed and the Presbyterians. One result of that was that American academics in the nineteenth century were often more aware of what was happening in Germany (for example) than their colleagues in Britain were. Americans were happy to go to Germany for further education, and as a result were exposed to ideological currents that were largely unknown (or ignored) in Britain. This had a double effect. Some of these Americans were converted to German Enlightenment ideas, but others were led to put up resistance to them, particularly at Princeton. The stage was set for philosophical battles that were to characterize the early twentieth century and that have left an enduring legacy in their wake.

German universities in the eighteenth and nineteenth centuries were more numerous and varied than those in other countries because Germany was not a single state. As a collection of principalities, kingdoms, and free cities, the country found itself with competing jurisdictions, many of which established their own universities in order to enhance their prestige. When the rulers of Hanover became kings of Great Britain in 1714, that state was open to British influence, which became very considerable after King George II (1727–1760) founded a university in Göttingen. Enlightenment ideas that were common in London flooded into Germany by this route and were soon well established there. In the southern state of Württemberg, the local dukes were proud of their university at Tübingen and did all they could to ensure that it would be in the front rank of German higher education. Halle became the home of a university that, although it was fundamentally Lutheran, distanced itself from the more conservative Lutheran institutions in nearby Wittenberg and in Leipzig and soon became known for the degree of academic freedom that it promoted. In circumstances like these, there could be no uniformly imposed orthodoxy in German universities, and students were free to move from one to another. Today we tend to think that they were all liberal in the spirit of the Enlightenment, but that was not so—ideas of all kinds could be found somewhere or other, and the resulting ferment pushed Germany to the forefront of intellectual achievement in virtually every field by 1900.

At the same time, another development was occurring in the Netherlands. There, a liberal surge had gained control of the state in the upheavals of 1848, when church and state were separated for the first time in European history.[28] The public face of the country was Reformed, but members of the Reformed Church were never a clear majority. They had always had to make room for other Protestants and even for Roman Catholics, which perhaps made the transition to a secular state easier and more logical. Even so, it awakened anxieties among Dutch Reformed people, who had to think again how they could present their beliefs in a society in which they were no longer dominant. The solution they came up with was largely due to Abraham Kuyper (1837–1920), who rethought the whole basis of the Reformed Church and virtually invented "Calvinism" as a philosophy of life. How much this Calvinism had to do with Calvin is an interesting question, but whatever the connections were, there is no doubt that Kuyper's reconstruction was in many respects a new departure.

Kuyper's philosophy rested on two basic principles: "sphere sovereignty" (*soevereiniteit in eigen kring*) and "pillarization" (*verzuiling*). According to the first of these, society consists of different "spheres" like the church, the state, the school, and so on, each of which has its own identity and should operate according to its own principles. The state had no business interfering with the church, the family, or the school, just as none of them could impose its principles on the state. Kuyper saw very clearly that that was what the French Revolution had led to, and so he founded his own political party, the Anti-Revolutionary Party (ARP), to combat it. The ARP soon became a significant element in Dutch politics and was able to influence the country in some important ways.

One of the ideas introduced by the ARP and picked up by others was "pillarization." According to this, each church or worldview could develop its own institutions (schools, hospitals, even trade unions) and live within them in accordance with its own principles. It was in this way

28. In a sense they had been separated during the French Revolution, but that separation had been neither complete nor enduring.

that Kuyper was able to found the Free University of Amsterdam, which was designed to develop his neo-Calvinism in every aspect of life. Kuyper was primarily a politician, but his interests ranged far and wide. His brand of Calvinism encompassed the sciences and the arts, on which he lectured to Princeton Seminary in 1898, and those lectures remain the best guide to his thought in the English language.[29] Before long, Dutch society was reorganized along worldview lines, with Protestants, Catholics, and secularists all living in hermetically sealed compartments within a single state. This phenomenon was unique to the Dutch situation and could not easily be exported. It did manage to get to South Africa, where the local Dutch (Afrikaner) population took it up and transformed it in their own way. What was "pillarization" (*verzuiling*) in the Netherlands became "separate development" (*apartheid*) in South Africa, a doctrine according to which each national group was permitted to develop its own culture as it saw fit. The theory sounded good, but the reality, as we know, was quite different. *Apartheid* became nothing more nor less that racial segregation, which led to its inevitable demise and the virtual abandonment of Kuyperian principles in South Africa.

What happened to neo-Calvinism in the United States, though, was quite different. There it was nursed mainly within immigrant Dutch communities to begin with, but it gradually made its way into wider American society, particularly among the theologically closely related Presbyterians. Dutch Americans did not get involved in politics, perhaps because American political life was not ideological in the way that the Dutch equivalent was. But they did invest heavily in education, and also in publishing, which gave their intellectuals an outlet through which they could reach a wider public. Before long, Grand Rapids, Michigan became the hub of a Reformed subculture that reached out across the United States and the world, which it still does. From that subculture there was to emerge a philosophical tradition that remains prominent in American Protestantism, though it has now mostly moved on from its original Dutch roots.

When Kuyper was challenged to explain how Christians could cooperate with unbelievers and what they should make of their undoubted

29. Abraham Kuyper, *Calvinism: Six Lectures Delivered in the Theological Seminary at Princeton* (New York: F. H. Revell, 1899).

achievements in so many fields, he gave two answers. The first was his assertion of the sovereignty of God, a principle derived from classical Calvinism. God is the Creator and Lord of all that exists, and nobody can do anything that is not ultimately under his sovereign sway. Unbelievers do not recognize it, but they too are servants of God, commissioned by him to develop the world in which we live. To the extent that they fulfill this commission they benefit everyone, including Christians, and we should not hesitate to claim their achievements for ourselves, even though we cannot say that they are our own. In connection with this, Kuyper added his belief that all human beings receive what he called "common grace." Christians had always been used to thinking of grace as something given to believers only, but this is not so. Believers receive what is known as "special grace," the grace that leads to eternal salvation. But all human beings receive the grace of preservation, originally given to Noah.

This is Kuyper's "common grace." In practice, it forms a major component of his worldview, because all human beings receive it, including Christians, and for the majority it is the only grace they know. Kuyper did not believe in "nature," at least not in the sense in which it was usually understood. He did not accept the idea that human beings were born with natural gifts that they then had an opportunity to develop. Nor did he believe that the original creation was inadequate or incomplete. What we think of as "nature" is corrupted by sinfulness, and on its own it is incapable of doing anything good. Only by the grace of God can it rise above that and achieve something worthwhile. But because that is a work of divine grace and not of human merit, nobody can claim his achievements as grounds for forgiveness. Those who go to heaven are called and chosen by God, quite independently of their talents or works, and no one can earn his salvation by his own efforts. Indeed, to try to do so amounts to blasphemy because it is a denial of God's grace, and therefore a rejection of his love.[30] Why some people should be saved and not others is a mystery to which there is no answer, but that it is so is evident from history and from what we see around us. Human beings are responsible for

---

30. The equation of grace with love may derive from the teaching of John Duns Scotus (1266–1308), perhaps by way of Robert Bellarmine. Kuyper was more influenced by Scholasticism and even by post-Reformation Catholic thought than most people realize.

their actions, a responsibility that must inevitably lead them to repentance and conversion. If that does not happen, there is no alternative route to heaven, no compensating power to which they can appeal. In the end, we all stand naked before the judgment seat of Christ, entirely dependent on him and on his saving work on the cross.

What was happening within the Reformed Protestant world was that Christian and secular worldviews were achieving a kind of peaceful coexistence. Neither side liked the other, and both did what they could to advance their own cause, but they recognized that they could not displace their rivals and had to live with them. Occasionally, as in the struggle against slavery, they were able to combine forces in what later came to be called "co-belligerence," and in many respects they were often closer to one another in practice than either was willing to admit. On the whole, that peaceful coexistence still survives, despite periodic strains, in marked contrast to what obtained elsewhere, as we shall see.

THE ONGOING WAR

The Roman Catholic Church never came to terms with Protestantism, which it continued to oppose as much as it could, often with considerable success in countries where it was dominant. The Enlightenment, though, was another matter. The Catholic Church opposed it as well, but with far less success. Many Enlightenment thinkers were at least formally members of the Church, which made it hard for it to move against them. They also had the protection of secular rulers who were able to put pressure on the papacy to restrain its own supporters, most notably the Jesuit order. The French Revolution demonstrated where that would lead, but it proved impossible to destroy Catholicism altogether, and in the reaction that followed the Roman Church was able to recover some of the ground it had lost. Even so, the nineteenth century was a time when its influence continued to decline. The remains of the Inquisition, originally set up to combat heresy in the fifteenth century, were finally extinguished, even in the very conservative countries of Spain and Portugal. Anti-clericalism became a feature of political life throughout Catholic Europe and Latin America as Catholics and secularists battled for control of education, social welfare, and so on. In 1870, the unification of Italy put paid to the existence of the Papal States and the popes became "prisoners of the Vatican," as they themselves insisted they were. The occasion was marked by one last act of defiance—the First Vatican Council, called to deal with the crisis, proclaimed the doctrine of papal infallibility, the ultimate challenge to the secular wave and a clear statement that the Church was turning its back on so-called modernity.

The actions of Rome did nothing to stop or even slow down the decline of Catholic influence in Western society. In Germany, there was a "culture war" (*Kulturkampf*) in which the autonomy of the Church was severely curtailed on the ground that it was the enemy of the state. Germany had been united at the same time as Italy, but its ruling class was largely Protestant. It was backed up ideologically by Protestant academics, including many theologians, who advanced the thesis that the early church had been corrupted by creeping "Catholicism," which they interpreted to mean dogmatism and the authoritarian centralization of power. That had been successfully rolled back at the time of the Reformation, and Martin Luther came to be portrayed, somewhat incongruously, as the apostle of free thought. His famous (if probably apocryphal) response to the accusations leveled against him ("Here I stand, I can do no other. My conscience is captive to the word of God.") was understood to mean that the individual conscience was the supreme arbiter of right and wrong, and came to be symbolic of "Protestantism" as a whole.

In effect, Protestantism and the Enlightenment were fused into one in the popular mind. Already, from the restoration of the old European order in 1815, the kings of Prussia had tried to unite the Lutheran and Reformed churches in their kingdom into a single evangelical church, which had the effect of diluting the confessional standards that each of them had previously maintained, and by the end of the nineteenth century those who still thought in those terms were a defensive minority. Many traditional Lutherans refused to accept this move and emigrated to the United States, where (somewhat ironically) they had the freedom to be as exclusive as they wanted.[31] They were fully conscious that they were fighting an ideological battle against liberal elements in their own tradition, which they did their best to reinforce against them.

31. These Lutherans formed what are now the Missouri Synod and the Wisconsin Synod, and they retain a fairly rigid confessional stance.

The Roman Catholic Church, meanwhile, was slower to respond, at least at the intellectual level. Reinvigoration came from an unexpected source—Protestant converts. There were a few of these in Germany, but the most powerful wave came from England, where there was growing disquiet with the lethargic state of the established Church of England and its inability to resist the secularizing tendencies that were apparently leading the country away from its Christian roots. A number of younger clergy at Oxford, led by the charismatic (and enigmatic) John Henry Newman (1801–1890), concluded that those who believed that the secular Enlightenment was the child of the Reformation were right, and that if the former were to be resisted the latter must be overturned as well. From 1833 onward, they made their case in a series of "tracts" (short booklets) in which they outlined their vision of Catholicism. It was not a surrender to the Roman Church, of which they were often quite critical, but in many ways it was an attempt to return to a romanticized version of the pre-Reformation era, which they held up as an ideal. In that sense, it was of a piece with the pre-Raphaelite movement in painting and the neo-Gothic revival in architecture, of which the British houses of parliament, built in the mid-nineteenth century, are perhaps the most outstanding example.

The Tractarians, or the "Oxford Movement" as they came to be known, produced the closest thing that the Church of England had to an ideology, to which they gave the name "Anglicanism." This was supposed to be a theological and ecclesiastical system rooted in the Bible and the teachings of the early church, including the ancient creeds, but without the papacy and the distortions that it had introduced in later times. Newman himself moved on from that to conclude that Christian doctrine had developed over time in order to meet the new challenges that the church had to face, and in the end he persuaded himself that Rome had been the faithful guardian of that tradition. In 1845 he submitted to the papacy, and the Oxford Movement split. Some followed Newman, but others tried to preserve the original Tractarian vision and stayed within the Church of England, which they did their best to decouple from Protestantism.

They had considerable success in liturgical terms, though not without opposition from others in the Church who were not at all sympathetic to them, but despite their efforts, they were never able to capture the mind of the Church as a whole. Their subsequent history has been one of compromise, retreat, and decline. By the early twentieth century, the erstwhile Tractarians had become "Anglo-Catholics," attracted to Rome to a degree that their forefathers had not been, but at the same time infiltrated by a liberal theology that was very different from what Newman and his colleagues espoused. That was ironic, because within the Roman Church, Newman was regarded as a liberal voice, and it was only slowly that his "development of doctrine" thesis took hold. Until then, Rome had affected to believe that all its doctrines, including papal infallibility, went back to Jesus and the NT and had only been articulated (not invented) when circumstances required. It was only as honest historical investigation demonstrated that this position was untenable that the Church began to cast around, looking for alternatives. Newman's thesis was taken on board, but it was not alone. Serious intellectual renewal was to come from another source, apparently rooted in medieval tradition but in fact recycled for the needs of the late nineteenth and early twentieth centuries.

This renewal came in the form of a revival of the Scholastic philosophy of Thomas Aquinas, who in 1879 was proclaimed the Angelic Doctor (*doctor angelicus*) of the Roman Church and held up as the model for modern Catholic intellectuals to imitate. The result was neo-Thomism, a movement that would attack and defeat the creeping tendency toward modernism that was starting to enter the Roman Church and would have made it much more like contemporary liberal Protestantism. In one form or another, neo-Thomism, which drew its greatest strength from French and German sources, would dominate Roman Catholicism at least until the Second Vatican Council (1962–1965) and is not dead yet, though it is much weaker now than it once was. Its greatest representatives were Jacques Maritain (1882–1973), a convert from Protestantism, and Étienne Gilson (1884–1978), both of whom interpreted Aquinas (and Scholastic theology more generally) to a modern audience, but with limited success. More realistic was Maurice de Wulf (1867–1947), who took up the challenge of trying to modernize Thomism but concluded that what the Scholastics had to say about nature and the natural sciences was out of date and had to be abandoned. Given that medieval theology was a superstructure built on that worldview, what de Wulf was effectively saying was that the neo-Thomist project was doomed from the start, even if bits and pieces of it could be salvaged from the wreckage and repackaged for modern consumption.

The basic principles of neo-Thomism (or neo-Scholasticism, as it is sometimes called) were three in number. First, it was stated that divine revelation did not cease with the apostles but has continued up to the present time in the councils of the Church as articulated and interpreted by the papacy. Second, dogmatic formulations are products of their time, couched in the language and thought processes of their contemporaries, and are therefore not immutable. They can be modified and re-expressed as circumstances change, even though their basic content remains the same. Third, the historical-critical method in biblical exegesis is basically correct. It was at this point that the neo-Thomists aligned themselves most clearly with Protestants, and one of the long-term results of their position has been that biblical studies can no longer be subdivided along confessional lines. There are still many different interpretations, of course, some of which are decidedly more conservative than others, but the criteria of judgment are determined by historical-critical principles, and not by pre-existing dogmatic commitments. Roman Catholics can thus agree with Protestants that many of their distinctive doctrines cannot be found in the NT, but can be justified by the principle of ongoing revelation and adaptation to the changing needs of the Western intellectual tradition from which they are derived and which they seek to address.

Neo-Thomism was designed as the Catholic answer to modern philosophical and theological challenges, but although it was embraced in some quarters with enthusiasm and produced a number of good scholars and able exponents of traditional Catholicism, its long-term prospects were never very good. A major problem was that Thomism was irredeemably medieval and could not be plausibly revived in a world where concepts like "substance" and "accidents" no longer had any meaning. They could continue to be used in theology as long as they were reinterpreted to take account of a worldview that was not that of the Bible or of modern society, but of course that merely distanced theology from both its sources and everyday reality.

Outside that rather limited sphere, it was doomed from the start and never really caught on. The permission given in 1943 to employ modern methods of inquiry for studying the Bible was the beginning of the end of it as a coherent philosophical system. Before long, Catholic biblical exegetes were using what had been regarded as Protestant arguments, and their scholarship entered the liberal mainstream, where it largely remains.

But more serious than this was the fact that the natural sciences were fast leaving not only the remnants of Aristotelianism but even the theories of the earlier Enlightenment behind. The key development in this was the emergence of biological evolutionism, which will forever be associated with the name of Charles Darwin. Like his contemporary Karl Marx, Darwin has the dubious distinction of having given his name to one of the most controversial theories of all time, and one that, like Marx's, has usually been associated with opposition to religion in general, and to Christianity in particular. But while Marx was a convinced atheist, Darwin was not. His disillusionment with Christianity is said to have been due mainly to the agonizing death of his daughter, which he could not come to terms with, and not with anything he discovered in the scientific sphere. Be that as it may, his theories of biological evolution provoked a reaction in church circles in a way that Marx never did.

Darwin's discoveries and theories did not come out of nowhere. There were already scientists who were exploring and cataloguing the natural world, and Darwin inherited their achievements. One of the most remarkable was Carl Linnaeus (1707–1778), a Swedish biologist whose system for classifying plants and animals is still in use today. Another great forerunner was Alexander von Humboldt (1769–1859), a German explorer who penetrated the Amazon and Orinoco rainforests in South America, discovering thousands of species that were completely unknown in Europe at that time. But Humboldt did more than simply explore the world. He also sought to turn biology into an exact science in a way that nobody had previously thought possible.

Skepticism with regard to biology went back to people like John Locke, who argued that the life sciences could never be truly scientific because they could not be reduced to mathematical precision. As far as he could see, there was no way of telling how or why plants or animals grew and developed in the way that they did, nor could it be explained what their interrelationship might be—if indeed there was one. Individual species might be isolated and examined, but whether or how they were connected to each other was unknown and seemed likely to remain so. Humboldt wanted to change that, and he began with the human race. His explorations had taught him what the Bible had always affirmed, which was that all human beings belong to a single species, regardless of their different characteristics or stages of development.

Humanity, according to Humboldt, was the physical manifestation of a natural order of things, with the difference that it alone possessed both the desire and the ability to reorder the natural environment to suit its own tastes and desires. In one sense there was nothing new about this—it had all been said by Thomas Aquinas, and indeed by Aristotle, centuries earlier. Humboldt, however, did not see humankind as being above the natural order but rather as part of it. The human desire to improve nature was therefore part of the natural order of things itself, and not something imposed on it by an essentially alien source.

The man who seized this insight and ran with it was Erasmus Darwin (1731–1802), grandfather of the more illustrious Charles. Far more than his grandson, however, Erasmus Darwin was a declared atheist who believed that humanity's place in the universe was due to its inherent rationality, which led people to work to improve their lot. This inner drive was part of nature itself, not a gift of God, and Erasmus Darwin gave it the name "evolution," which his grandson later inherited. Erasmus went even further and claimed that the whole of nature followed a similar evolutionary path, even though he could not explain it. That would be the work of his grandson.

Charles began his academic career studying theology, but he was soon distracted by the accounts he read by Humboldt and John Herschel (1792–1871), an astronomer who turned to biology during a trip to South Africa, where he found fossil evidence of the existence of species that had since become extinct. He corresponded with Charles Lyell (1797–1875), a Scottish geologist who had made similar discoveries, and the two men came up with the idea that Humboldt's classifications could be developed into a complete system of natural cause and effect that would explain the process of evolution and make sense of the order of the universe. Charles Darwin imbibed the thinking of these men, and of others like them, and embarked on his own voyage of discovery that would take him around the world and introduce him to species in the wild that he had never come across before.

At first, Darwin had no idea what to make of the mass of information that he was gathering, but sometime in 1837 the penny dropped. He had wanted to know why it was that some species almost died out but somehow managed to produce just enough offspring to survive. He had wondered why it was that those offspring were like their parents in most respects, but sometimes subtly different in others. He had asked himself why some species were similar to others, and why it was that some had died out altogether. Putting all these thoughts together, he concluded that the world had not been an act of special creation, in which each species would have been specially designed for a particular purpose, but rather a process of development by which species mutated and adapted to their environments. As evidence to support this theory, he cited what to him were examples of survivals from an earlier stage of evolution that had somehow failed to disappear when they were no longer needed. The classic example for Darwin was the fact that men have nipples, which they do not need. When he asked himself why this was so, he concluded that it was because at some earlier point in time they had served a purpose that evolution had subsequently made redundant.

In some respects, Darwin's theory was harking back to Aristotle, who had conceived of a great chain of being leading from the lower to the higher creatures, but whereas Aristotle had seen this chain as eternally fixed and immovable, Darwin claimed that it was moving all the time, usually upward and onward but occasionally in the opposite direction, which would cause the species in question to die out. It was even possible, given enough time, for one species to produce another one. As Darwin looked around, he began to make connections—lizards, crocodiles, and mammals of all descriptions, including human beings, ultimately derived from a common ancestor.

Somewhat ironically, the capstone to Darwin's thinking was provided by a clergyman, Thomas Malthus (1766–1834), who argued that the human race was multiplying so fast that it would run out of resources and that the result would be a struggle for existence that would see large numbers die off. Darwin read that and applied it to animal populations, which to his mind accounted for the destruction of certain species when conditions for their survival were unfavorable. This was the essence of what Darwin called natural selection, and it became for him the key to understanding the whole of life, including human life.

Darwin arrived at this understanding around 1842, but it was not until 1859 that he was forced to publish it because others were coming to the same conclusions. His book *On the Origin of Species* caused an immediate sensation, and the reaction has not died down since. It was clear to most people at the time that Darwin's theory of evolution contradicted the creation story in Genesis, but although that was problematic for Darwin's opponents, it was not decisive. The real question at issue was the distinctiveness of humanity, created "in the image and likeness of God" (Gen 1:26–27). In Darwin's evolutionary scheme, there was no place for divine intervention of that kind. Human beings were perhaps more highly evolved than other animals, but they were not essentially different. Gorillas, chimpanzees, and orangutans were our closest living relatives, so close (as later investigations demonstrated) that only minor changes in our genetic codes would be enough to make us identical. Or so it seemed.

What Darwin did was refocus the attention of the world on the greatest question of all: Where did it come from and how did it come to be what it now is? This had been the chief battleground in ancient times as Christians fought the pagan idea of the eternity of matter with their own belief in divine creation. The opening chapters of Genesis had been the most commented on part of the Bible in the early church, and Darwin brought that issue back to the forefront once more. Christians were alarmed by what he claimed, but on the whole their reaction to his thesis was naive and inadequate. It began with the interpretation of Genesis 1–11, which most Christians in the nineteenth century took to be historical in the usual sense of that term. In other words, they were inclined to believe that God had created the world in six twenty-four-hour days about six thousand years ago. Evidence to the contrary, from fossils for example, was simply dismissed.

This kind of interpretation, which is nowadays generally labeled as "fundamentalist," can still be found in some quarters but it is not taken seriously by the scientific establishment or even by a very large number of Christians. It is now generally recognized that the opening chapters of Genesis must be read as something other than straightforward history, though quite what they are is hard to say and remains controversial. Many scholars call them "myth," but that is a difficult word to use because in popular speech "myths" are regarded as false, and that is going too far. Whatever Genesis 1–11 is, it is not to be regarded as "false" in the usually accepted sense of that word. What it is doing is expressing truth in terms that unsophisticated people can understand, and it is from that perspective that it must be interpreted. The men who composed the texts as we now have them were not eyewitnesses to the events that they described, all of which had taken place centuries before them. Whether there were oral traditions handed down over time, or whether those men received a direct revelation from God, may be debated—perhaps it was a bit of both. In any case, what we have is not chronicling in the way that history is, but a conceptualizing of how things that now exist originally came to be.

Seen in that way, the six days of creation are not so much periods of time as aspects of the cosmic order laid down by God. Many things are left out entirely—there is no mention of the creation of insects, for example—and the account knows nothing of dinosaurs or other prehistoric creatures. Mankind (*homo sapiens*) is said to have been formed out of the dust of the ground, and in Hebrew the two words are closely related, "man" being *adam* and "ground" *adamah*.[32] As far as science is concerned, that could imply anything, including some form of biological evolution. Suffice it to say that the Bible affirms the connection between the human race and the rest of the material creation, however that connection is to be understood. But the emphasis of the Bible is not on that. Rather, it is concerned to explain how and why the human race is different from the rest of creation, and it is here that the conflict with Darwinian science becomes acute. Whatever happened at the beginning of time, the fact is that *homo sapiens* is unique in the created order, and it is this uniqueness that matters more than anything else. What the Bible is concerned to point out is the following.

First, all human beings belong to the same species. There is no difference between a sophisticated European or American, on the one hand, and a jungle dweller in the Amazon rainforest or New Guinea on the other. This view is universally accepted nowadays, though it was contested until quite recently, and in the form of racism traces of that still survive. On the whole, though, it can be said that on this point the Bible, modern science, and public opinion generally coincide.

Second, male and female are both members of the same species, which cannot propagate without them. Again, this is now all but universally

32. There is a similar connection in Latin between *homo* ("man") and *humus* ("ground").

agreed, although notions of female inferiority could still be found in the nineteenth century, when it was seriously claimed by some people that women were less rational than men and should not be allowed to vote or to enter certain professions. Today, if anything, we have gone to the opposite extreme and are inclined to deny any real difference between male and female, regarding them as effectively interchangeable. That is an overreaction, which the Bible does not support. Male and female are "equal" in the sense that both are fully human, but they are also different, and Christians believe that that difference must be respected. Here there is a conflict with much modern thought, but in purely biological terms the Christian position is hard to dispute.

Third, human beings are made "in the image and likeness of God." Here there is genuine disagreement between Christians (and theists generally) and those who adopt a non-theistic view of the world. But it is hard to deny that humans have characteristics that are not found in the animal world, even in our closest biological relatives. Animals do not have consciences, they do not have a moral sense, and they do not worship a higher power, which virtually all human beings do and have always done, however unsophisticated that worship may have been. Animals do not ask questions, they do not philosophize, and they have no concept of right and wrong. Some of them have social organization of a kind, but none of them has produced anything like a civilization in the human sense. Anthills and beehives are remarkable in their own way, but they can hardly be compared to pyramids or great works of art. Animals are not creative in the human sense—they do not write books, paint pictures, or compose complex works of music. In all these ways, human beings stand out and resemble the biblical picture of God more than they look like their fellow creatures.

Fourth, human beings as they are now are not what they are meant to be. Here again, Christians and secularists agree up to a point, but the explanations they give for this are totally different. Secularists will usually argue that humanity, like everything else in the world, is on a path toward future evolution. Right now, our finitude and incompleteness mean that we make mistakes and suffer the consequences, but over time these will disappear. Christians, in contrast, say that the human race has fallen away from its original state and will not be restored or improve. There will be an end to this present world, when it will be transformed into something even greater than it was originally meant to be.

Fifth, the world is enslaved to sin and evil, the consequence of which is death. Secularists find this very difficult to accept in any form. To the extent that they have a concept of evil, it is usually identified with finitude and its limitations, which lead to wrong decisions being taken. These wrong decisions correspond to what Christians would call "sin," but secularists generally avoid using that term. Christians, on the other hand, regard sin as an act of disobedience to God that originated in the spiritual realm when an angel called Satan rebelled against his Creator. Satan then tempted the human race to follow his lead, which caused humans to sin and brought evil, the consequence of sin, into the world. Evil can sometimes be contained and even eliminated in particular cases, but it will never disappear because it is the result of sin, which cannot be eradicated in this life.

There, broadly speaking, are the points of agreement and disagreement that characterize Christians and secularists in the post-Darwinian world. For Christians, the main difficulty is knowing how to relate the principles outlined here to historical events. To put it simply, was there a first human being whom we call Adam, did he have a wife (Eve), and did they sin in a way that implicated the entire human race? These are extremely difficult questions to answer satisfactorily because the evidence is patchy and inconclusive. We are told that there were once proto-humans, or hominids who somehow evolved into *homo sapiens* as we know him today, but the details of how, when and where that may have happened are unknown. Nor can we say why hominids disappeared. Were they all transformed into *homo sapiens*? We do not know. There is an intriguing passage in Genesis 6:1–4 that may give us a clue to this:

> When man began to multiply on the face of the land and daughters were born to them, the sons of God saw that the daughters of man were attractive. And they took as their wives any they chose. Then the LORD said, "My Spirit shall not abide in man forever, for he is flesh: his days shall be 120 years." The Nephilim were on the earth in those days, and also afterward, when the sons of God came in to the daughters of man and they bore children to them. These were the mighty men who were of old, the men of renown.

Were these "sons of God" *homo sapiens*, and were the "men" and their daughters hominids? Who were the Nephilim? These are questions to which we have no answer, though there has been plenty of research and speculation into the possibilities that exist.[33] As far as a historical record is concerned, it has long been known that tracing the OT chronologies back will take us to about 4000 BC.[34] The world is certainly much older than that, but perhaps the date is not as odd as one might think. For if we look at the great civilizations of Egypt, Mesopotamia, and even China, it was around that time that they began to develop. Does the biblical record reflect this? Did something happen about that time that led to this great leap forward in human history? It may be that the Genesis chronicler was not concerned to tell us the age of the earth but to look back to the dawn of civilization and focus our attention on that. This suggestion must remain tentative, but it makes sense of the data and may provide the key to interpreting the pre-Abrahamic era outlined in the first book of the Bible.

But the difficulties that Christians face, though real, pale in comparison with the problems that confront secularists. They are less concerned with the origins of the human race, to which they claim to have an answer, but they cannot explain sin and evil in the context of evolutionary theory. To explain evil by ascribing it to the limitations of finitude is to trivialize it—people who are murdered, for example, are unlikely to be comforted by the assertion that their killers will one day give birth to descendants who will behave differently. If the twentieth century has taught us anything, it is that despite the great advances that we have made in science and technology, there has been no improvement at all in the character of the human race. On the contrary, if anything, human beings are worse now than they have ever been. Moreover, it is not primitive tribes in tropical forests who are guilty of committing crimes against humanity, but some of the greatest scientists in the most developed countries, who have dreamed of becoming "supermen" and who have used their knowledge to create weapons of mass destruction. So far, those weapons have not been used, but they are there, and it is hard to believe that they will stay

33. For a recent attempt at this, see W. L. Craig, *In Quest of the Historical Adam* (Grand Rapids: Eerdmans, 2021).

34. James Ussher (1581–1656) calculated the date of creation as 4004 BC.

unused forever. The awful truth is that the human race is now capable of destroying itself in a way that it never was before, and that it is far likelier to do so well before any eventual evolution can occur.

We should perhaps add that this in no way prevents secularists from denouncing evil in the world or demanding justice in the form of retribution for wrongs that have been committed. In practice, they may be more insistent and more demanding than Christians would normally be because they have no concept of repentance and forgiveness. For that, God is required, and if he is taken out of the equation there is no reason why the punishment should not be just as merciless as the crime. The hope must be that severity will extirpate the evil, but so far there is little evidence to suggest that that is what actually happens. Like Anselm's companion Boso, modern secularists have not considered how great the weight of sin actually is, and therefore they have found no satisfactory way of dealing with evil, which has become more of a problem in a world without God than it ever was before.

IMPLOSION

As the nineteenth century drew to a close, the battle lines between Christianity and secularism were hardening and it seemed that everywhere Christianity was in retreat. Hegelianism, in one form or another, was all the rage in Germany, and Germany was increasingly recognized as the center of Western intellectual life. The world's leading scientists, philosophers, and even theologians all seemed either to have come from there or to have studied in one of that country's universities. That Germany would proceed to self-destruct was unimaginable. There were certainly many people who opposed German ideas, but they were fragmented. Dutch Calvinists, Catholic neo-Thomists, and Anglo-American empiricists all dissented from Germany's intellectual hegemony, but they did not—and could not—make common cause with one another.

The defeat of German liberal secularism would not come from without, but from within, and from an unexpected source. The man chiefly responsible for this was Friedrich Nietzsche, a highly controversial figure whose reputation and influence continue to be subjects of lively debate today. Nietzsche began his career as a professor of ancient Greek philosophy in Basel, where he chose to specialize in the fragmentary thoughts of the pre-Socratic philosophers, in particular Heraclitus. Not much was (or is) known about them, but enough has survived to enable us to get some idea of how they thought, and Nietzsche was only too willing to fill in the gaps and to make connections between them that the evidence itself does not necessarily justify.

Nietzsche's main point was that Plato and Aristotle, usually regarded as the founders of the Western intellectual tradition, had gone wrong by putting their emphasis on reason as something above and beyond the world that they were studying. The pre-Socratics, according to Nietzsche, had not made that mistake. To them, reality was not an abstraction in the mind but something concrete that can be perceived in the world around us. Nietzsche claimed that all the pre-Socratics thought more or less the same way, but he reserved particular approbation for Heraclitus, whose intuition enabled him to grasp the meaning of life in a way that reason and logic never could. Heraclitus's famous statement that *panta rhei* ("everything flows"), which had long been dismissed as a formula for instability and ignorance, became for Nietzsche the key to intellectual liberation. Nothing in the world was fixed and immutable, and so the conceptual oppositions that the later Greek philosophers had introduced—between mind and matter, body and spirit, good and evil—were meaningless and did not exist.

Nietzsche directed his philosophical ire at Socrates, whom he regarded as the chief culprit of the decadence that he believed characterized Western civilization after the eclipse of the pre-Socratics. Socrates was the one who elevated reason to a higher level than instinct, who introduced the harmful notion of "conscience" as a guide to behavior, and who pointed toward a spiritual source as the arbiter of truth. Nietzsche even went as far as to claim that Socrates was rightly put to death for having corrupted the youth of Athens by depriving them of their natural, hedonistic sensuality. That was the ultimate heresy in terms of classical philosophy, but Nietzsche did not stop there. Christianity, which he saw as nothing more than a vulgarized form of Platonism, was even worse, and the entire history of Western civilization was a conspiracy to repress human freedom, with only occasional relapses during the Renaissance, when a spirit of human freedom was supposedly recaptured (however briefly) in the works of men like Leonardo da Vinci and Michelangelo. Looking at his own time,

Nietzsche saw the much-vaunted progress of the nineteenth century as the latest, and probably terminal, phase of the collapse of civilization. Hegel and Marx he denounced as false prophets, and he opposed virtually everything that might be considered progressive—democracy, women's rights, international peace movements, and so on.

If the West was ever to regain its proper spirit, it would have to return to the primitivism of the pre-Socratic age, briefly repeated in the barbarian invasions of Rome centuries later. This was characterized by the will to seize power at any price. Murder, theft, rape, arson, and so on might seem to be immoral to the decadent, but to those who are pure in heart and mind they are the vigorous activities of the truly free spirit, the Superman (Übermensch) who would inherit the earth. Darwinian evolution and the rapid progress of the natural sciences had eliminated any need to believe in God, who, in Nietzsche's notorious phrase, was "dead." Cut adrift from God, man was free to become his own deity. Self-restraint, humility, and hard work were condemned as evil because they sapped humanity's essential vitality. Once people could be brought to accept that reality is constant motion, but that it recurs in endlessly repeating cycles, they will have achieved their freedom. Knowing that there is no such thing as progress, that everything repeats itself, and that all we can do is choose from the options available what most appeals to us, is the way to a new world order, which (true to its essentially cyclical nature) would at the same time be a return to the age of Heraclitus.

Nietzsche published his philosophy in his most famous book, *Thus Spake Zarathustra*, supposedly the wisdom of the Persian sage Zoroaster (of whom Nietzsche knew virtually nothing) but in reality the meanderings of his own increasingly warped mind. By the time the fourth and final volume of the work was published in 1892, Nietzsche had gone literally insane, but that did not stop his books from becoming immensely popular. So much was this so that foreigners were taking note. In his final lecture on Calvinism at Princeton Seminary in 1898, Abraham Kuyper pointed this out, but perceptively added, "What else is his demand for the Übermensch but the cry of despair wrung from the heart of humanity by the bitter consciousness that it is spiritually pining away?"[35] From

35. Kuyper, *Lectures on Calvinism*, 6.

his Calvinist perspective, Kuyper was able to put his finger on the problem—humanity without God was longing for a substitute deity that they hoped to create in a new, improved human being. Given that Nietzsche was still alive, though insane, when Kuyper spoke these words, and that hardly anybody outside Germany knew who he was at that time, his revelation was astonishingly prescient, and he would live long enough to see his nightmare scenario start to come true.

Fascination with the pre-Socratics was not unique to Nietzsche, however. In France it was shared by Henri Bergson (1859–1941), who came at them by way of Zeno of Elea. Bergson came to believe that Aristotle and his successors had always thought of time as the measurement of motion, but that Zeno and the pre-Socratics had seen it as an aspect of human consciousness, which he called "duration." According to Bergson, the mind sees time as a series of separate moments, each of which can be isolated and labeled as past, present, or future. But in reality, time is the creature of intuition, which assembles these discrete moments into a compact and coherent whole, which constitutes "memory," a dimension of awareness quite distinct from reason. What is more, intuition connects us to the vital force (élan vital) that makes us living beings and that reflects the animal instincts that we have inherited from our evolutionary past. Bergson was a convinced Darwinian and saw the vital force inherent in nature as a process that led inexorably from the fount of life to the most sophisticated forms of human consciousness. In this respect, intuition opposes and complements the natural sciences. Science encourages us to study matter, which points us downward to the ground from which we originally sprang. But intuition leads us ever upward, giving us the perspective to contemplate the whole of reality and bringing us, in the end, face to face with our Creator.

Bergson's acknowledgment of a Creator sets him apart from Nietzsche and made his thought attractive to elements in the Roman Catholic Church, who saw in his philosophy a possible way of reconciling modernity and Catholicism. The Church itself did not see matters that way, and tried to ban Bergson's books, though toward the end of his life Bergson declared that he was very close to Catholicism and might have converted had it not been for Hitler's persecution of his fellow Jews, whom Bergson did not want to abandon in their hour of need. Unfortunately for Bergson, the sorts of Catholics who were attracted to his ideas were not typical of their Church. Some were Modernists, espousing an approach that the papacy had officially condemned, while others were what might be called "Christian nationalists," who saw in Bergson's "vital force" an idea that might regenerate a France that had abandoned its ancestral faith.

Bergson's impact cannot be fully understood unless we take into account the work of his contemporary, Georges Sorel (1847–1922), who absorbed his ideas and transformed them into something Bergson never contemplated. Sorel was an early convert to Marxism, and when he listened to Bergson lecture on the transformation of consciousness, he realized that he could adapt this concept to a Marxist vision of the future. As Sorel saw it, Bergson and Marx both believed that by adopting their perspective, humanity would be delivered from its present limitations and raised to a higher level of freedom. Like Nietzsche, Sorel saw Enlightenment values as decadent and believed that they had to be destroyed before the power of Bergson's "vital force" could be unleashed. That would never be achieved by argument alone. People needed a vision of the future for which they would be prepared to die, and that would be put to the test in a violent insurrection, which was the only way the necessary cleansing of society could occur.

The construction of the motivating vision was inevitably a work of fiction because nobody could really predict the future. The fact that the "vital force" rose above conventional oppositions between things like truth and falsehood meant that it was perfectly OK to tell lies as long as people were prepared to believe that they pointed to the final goal—the end justified the means. Sorel lived long enough to witness the beginnings of the violent overthrow of the established order that he desired, but he died before he could see the consequences. The Marxist revolution in Russia was forced to compromise with the social structures that already existed—complete destruction was impossible. But without that destruction, the promised ideal could never be realized. As a result, the totalitarian society that emerged from the revolution was in constant need of "reactionary saboteurs," as the remnants of the old order were called, because their (presumed) existence justified ongoing repression and the otherwise inexplicable delay of the paradise that their propaganda had promised.

Sorel's views had limited success in Russia, but they were by no means confined to a Marxist dictatorship. His principles could be applied equally well elsewhere, by ideologues whose socialism was not Marxist at all. He did not live to see it, but the potential link between conservative Catholic Christianity and national regeneration in France was aided and inspired by the rise of fascism in neighboring Italy. In 1922, the year Sorel died, Benito Mussolini (1883–1945) seized power there and instituted a state modeled on Hegelian lines. He took as his emblem the *fasces*, a bundle of sticks surrounding an ax that was one of the symbols of ancient Rome, and used this as an emblem of what he wanted Italy to become—a new and better Roman Empire. It was an absurd vision, but one that appealed to a country that was still only a generation old in political terms and far from united. Mussolini despised Christianity, but he was clever enough to see that his power would be strengthened if he could make peace with the papacy. Since the unification of Italy in 1870, the popes had shut themselves up in the Vatican and refused to recognize the Italian state. Mussolini grabbed that bull by the horns and in 1929 concluded a treaty with the pope, granting him full sovereignty over Vatican City, which thus became technically independent.

This success effectively neutralized the Church as a political force opposed to his regime. In 1936 Spanish fascists rose in rebellion against a secular republican government that threatened to persecute the Catholic Church in that country, and their victory in the subsequent civil war established a second fascist country in Europe. Even before that, Portugal had gone in a similar direction, though without a war and therefore with considerably less brutality than in Spain, making it effectively a third fascist state. In all three countries, closely tied together by their common Latin heritage and Catholic religion, national regeneration was the order of the day, and the role of the Church in achieving this was taken for granted. In France, where church and state had been separated since 1905, things were less straightforward, but after the country fell to the Germans in 1940, a similar regime was introduced in the part of the country that was not officially occupied. It was centered at Vichy, from which it acquired its name ("Vichy France"), and the Christian national ideal became its semi-official ideology.[36] Bergson lived long enough to see that, but his Jewishness ensured that he never became a fascist himself.

36. Never truly official however, since the Catholic Church was not re-established.

Things worked out rather differently in Germany, where just over a decade after Mussolini seized power in Rome, Adolf Hitler was voted into office in Berlin and set about transforming the country into another fascist state. It lasted only just over twelve years, compared with twenty-one in Italy, but its ruthlessness and brief success have left a permanent mark on Western consciousness. Hitler became, and for many has remained, the incarnation of evil in the world. What is often forgotten is how many intellectuals, children of the Enlightenment and faithful followers of Marx, Darwin, and Nietzsche, bought into the totalitarian systems that Sorel's vision created. An exception was Benedetto Croce (1866–1952), who was briefly attracted to fascism before realizing what its true nature was and becoming one of its fiercest opponents. But Croce was rare. For the most part, his fellow Italian intellectuals fell into line with the new regime and stuck with it as long as it seemed to be a success. The most prominent of these was Croce's onetime friend and ally, Giovanni Gentile (1875–1944), who became the acknowledged philosopher of fascism and never deviated from it, even after Mussolini was overthrown in 1943.[37]

Much the same happened in Germany, though a number of prominent intellectuals emigrated after Hitler took power. Most prominent among those who supported Hitler was Martin Heidegger (1889–1976), a philosopher who was a faithful disciple of Nietzsche and saw in German National Socialism (Nazism) the realization of Nietzsche's dream of a neo-barbarian takeover of a decadent civilization. Remarkably, Heidegger survived the Nazi regime relatively unscathed and returned to teaching in 1950, consolidating his reputation and acquiring numerous disciples, even though he never renounced his Nazi past.[38] More clearly than many others, Heidegger couched his views in the language of the ancient struggle between Athens and Jerusalem. He was notoriously and consistently anti-Semitic, regarding Jews as the source of Western decadence. At the same time, he exalted the pre-Socratics in true Nietzschean style, and rather inconsistently, from Nietzsche's point of view, quoted Plato in defense of Hitler.[39]

37. Gentile was assassinated by Italian communists in the closing phase of the Second World War.

38. Heidegger was removed from teaching by the French occupation authorities in 1946, but in 1949 he was excused because he had supposedly been no more than a "fellow traveler" (*Mitläufer*) of the Nazi regime. It was clearly a whitewash.

39. See Victor Farías, *Heidegger and Nazism* (Philadelphia, PA: Temple University Press, 1989), 108.

In Russia, support for the new regime was more uneven, and in 1922 the Soviet government forcibly exiled a large number of academics, including several who were (or who were becoming) Christians. These exiles regrouped in Berlin, Prague, Belgrade, and above all Paris, where they spearheaded a remarkable religious renaissance that had already begun before the revolution but that was to become a significant force in Russian culture for most of the twentieth century.[40] Among the exiles in Paris were Sergei Bulgakov (1871–1944), Nikolai Berdyaev (1874–1948), Nikolai Lossky (1870–1965), and his son Vladimir (1903–1957), all of whom were to make major contributions to Russian philosophy and theology. Left behind in Russia, but equally important as a philosopher-theologian was Pavel Florensky (1882–1937), a victim of Stalin's purges whose work only became widely known in the dying days of the Soviet regime.

What is remarkable, though, is not the degree of support these totalitarian regimes had in the countries that they dominated, support that can be explained by many factors other than philosophical conviction. Rather, it was the attraction of their perverted ideals *outside* their countries of origin that is truly astonishing. Dozens of French, British, and American intellectuals made pilgrimages to the Soviet Union, convinced that it was paradise in the making. A few, like George Orwell (1903–1950), discerned the truth and wrote about it—Orwell's *Animal Farm* and *1984* became and have remained classic critiques of a system built on lies and perverted idealism. But there were others, including such luminaries as Pablo Picasso (1881–1973), Louis Aragon (1897–1982), Bertolt Brecht (1889–1956), and others who never did. Brecht was so smitten that after the Second World War he emigrated to the German Democratic Republic (East Germany) and through his plays became one of the regime's most noted propagandists. Fewer people were attracted to fascism, but some were, like Louis-Ferdinand Céline (1894–1961), Pierre Teilhard de Chardin (1881–1955), and even William Butler Yeats (1865–1939) for a time. What became increasingly clear as time went

40. The trend away from Marxism toward Christianity was first noticed in *Vekhi: Sbornik Statej o Russkoj Intelligencii* (Moscow: V. M. Sablin, 1909), translated into English as *Landmarks: A Collection of Essays on the Russian Intelligentsia—1909* (New York: Karz Howard, 1977). In addition to Berdyaev and Bulgakov, the contributors were Mikhail Gershenzon (1869–1925), Aleksandr Izgoev (1872–1935), Bogdan Kistyakovsky (1869–1920), Semyon Frank (1877–1950), and Pyotr Struve (1870–1944). Frank and Struve made their way to Paris after the revolution; Izgoev died in Estonia.

on is that the strongest and most determined opposition to these regimes came from people with Christian convictions. There were not as many of them as there should have been, and the official churches were by no means always supportive of their efforts, but they made their mark nonetheless. The anti-fascists among them came to public notice mainly after the collapse of most of the fascist regimes in 1945. The anti-communists, on the other hand, were recognized from the 1960s onward, and some of them, like Aleksandr Solzhenitsyn (1918–2008), became famous long before the regimes they condemned were finally overthrown.

Turning to Christian influence in the West, the Catholic Church had long been something of an outsider in Germany, where it claimed no more than a third of the population, so it was somewhat wary of the state, but it managed to strike an agreement with Hitler (himself baptized as a Catholic) that seemed to offer it roughly the same kind of status that it enjoyed in other fascist countries. The Protestants, however, were a different matter. Most of them were loyal to the state out of habit and acquiesced in the new status of "German Christians" that was imposed on them. However, German Christians were far from orthodox in theological terms. For one thing, they were expected to deny that Jesus was a Jew, even though that was clearly nonsense. They were also expected to venerate the state and its leader (*Führer*), Adolf Hitler, and participate in rituals that were neo-pagan both in origin and in feel.

It was inevitable that some Protestants would object to this, and in 1934 they banded together as the "Confessing Church," signing a document at Barmen that clearly denied the pretensions of Hitler and his state. They suffered persecution as a result, but with one notable exception. This was Karl Barth (1886–1968), who although he was teaching in Germany and signed the Barmen Declaration, was a Swiss national and therefore could be deported back to his homeland. There he sat out the war and became one of the most outspoken opponents of the Hitler regime. Others were less fortunate. Some, like Martin Niemöller (1892–1984), who initially supported Hitler, were alienated by his extremism and turned to opposition. Niemöller was arrested in 1937 and spent the next eight years in prison. Another colleague, Dietrich Bonhoeffer (1906–1945), managed to escape arrest for a long time but was implicated in the plot to assassinate Hitler in 1944, and was executed only a few days before the end of the Second World War.

But unlike both Niemöller and Bonhoeffer, who may be described as somewhat late converts to anti-fascism, Barth's claim to that designation went back to the very beginning—indeed, it even antedated Mussolini's coup in 1922. Barth opposed Christian nationalism as early as 1914, when he objected to the fact that his former professors in Berlin all supported the German war effort. Barth was in Switzerland at that time, so did not suffer for his views, but spent the war years writing a commentary on the Epistle to the Romans. It was not published until the war was over, but then it caused a sensation. Barth launched a broadside attack on the liberal tradition that had grown up in German theology over the previous century, claiming that it had moved away from traditional Christian teaching about sin and salvation and adopted an Enlightenment view based on natural theology. He rejected that completely, insisting that God cannot be known by extrapolating human conceptions based on our study of the created order and applying them to him. In his essence, God is "wholly other" and can only be known through revelation. Barth did not return to the classical Protestant belief that the Bible was that revelation, but he did agree that the texts bore witness to it, so it made little difference in practice. His hesitation on this point made more conservative Protestants wary of aligning themselves too closely with him, but there can be little doubt that his approach did much to reinstate traditional Protestant dogmatics as a viable option in academic circles.

Known as "neo-orthodoxy," Barth's approach continues to attract theologians from a conservative background, though it has elicited criticisms from the more philosophically minded among them. Catholics have accused him of lacking a doctrine of creation, though Barth strenuously denied that and devoted the last part of his life to refuting it. A similar criticism has come from Dutch Calvinist circles, with which Barth had little sympathy. The Dutch insistence that Calvinism is a biblical philosophy that applies to every aspect of life sounded to him to be too much of a compromise with natural theology, and his experience of Germany in the 1930s made him understandably wary of political involvement, not least because some of Kuyper's successors were sympathetic to fascism, even if the movement as a whole kept its distance from that.

Perhaps the fairest thing to say is that in the early twentieth century theology and philosophy of all kinds had gone their separate ways and were no longer in regular dialogue—or conflict—with each other in the way that they had been before 1900. The era of "war and peace" had given way to a new situation, in which it would become necessary to defend the relationship between the two disciplines, if indeed there was one. In that context, Barth's proclamation of the "wholly other" being of God could be used to justify the separation that had come about. It is to a consideration of that, and the consequences it has had for modern thought, that we must now turn.

SUMMARY

1. Around 1700, the mindset of European civilization changed from being essentially "religious" to becoming increasingly "secular" in a movement known as the Enlightenment. Dogmatic theology was marginalized and increasingly rejected, even though the institutional churches retained their official status and people were expected to belong to them.

2. The leading proponent of the Enlightenment was Baruch or Benedict Spinoza, a Sephardic Jew who rejected religious dogma and tradition, whether Jewish or Christian. His followers and imitators launched concerted attacks on the authority of the Bible, the church(es), and the theological tradition in general, which they regarded as steeped in ignorance and prejudice. In place of these, they advocated an approach grounded in reason, which became the secular equivalent of God. Miracles were a particular object of attack because they seemed to go against the laws of natural science.

3. Many Enlightenment thinkers were from Catholic countries, especially France, where the superstitions of an unreformed Catholic Church were regarded as sacrosanct and dissent was punished by the state with death or exile. Protestants sympathized with the victims of such persecution and, in rejecting what appeared to them to be irrational dogmatism, they often became more open to their unorthodox opinions than they might otherwise have been.

4. Enlightenment thinkers were often extreme in their accusations against Christianity, and that provoked a reaction both in Catholic and Protestant countries. The reaction was of two kinds. There was an intellectual pushback in which Christian apologists sought to demonstrate the weaknesses of Enlightenment rationalism, and a spiritual revival that endeavored to transcend the sterility of abstruse theological debates by emphasizing the importance of religious experience. This revival took both Catholic and Protestant forms but was particularly strong in the English-speaking world, where it led to the development both of a lively tradition of intellectual defenses of Christianity and a series of religious awakenings that produced a renewed and largely interdenominational form of Protestantism known as evangelicalism.

5. Evangelical Protestants were hostile to Enlightenment rationalism but they supported philosophical inquiry, scientific research, and social reform. They also sponsored missionary work in the non-Christian world that would have far-reaching effects.

6. Enlightenment rationalism was countered by theological conservatives but not defeated. It remained particularly influential in France, where it contributed to the revolution of 1789, an event that is generally regarded as the beginning of the modern world. At the same time, the newly independent United States of America established a secular government that was essentially deist in character. It allowed all religions to compete on an equal footing but removed theological questions from political life.

7. In Protestant countries, rationalist philosophy flourished but usually without causing a rupture with the churches. Thomas Reid, David Hume, and Immanuel Kant were classic examples of this, and are still important philosophical voices today. In Catholic countries, conflict between philosophy and theology was more frequent, especially in France, where Jean-Jacques Rousseau and Voltaire were open enemies of the Catholic Church.

8. During and after the French Revolution there was a revived interest in Greek culture, which most Europeans claimed as their own. This gave them a sense of superiority over other nations and contributed to the development of pseudoscientific racism in the nineteenth century. It also contributed to a wave of Romanticism and idealism, represented by poets and philosophers like Georg Wilhelm Friedrich Hegel, the first truly modern philosopher. These men were often openly atheistic and their beliefs denigrated traditional Christianity, which was seen as barbarous.

9. The nineteenth century saw a concerted attack on Christianity from pseudoscientific sources, often rooted in somewhat superficial interpretations of Darwinian evolution. The moral and ethical demands of Christianity were highlighted by Søren Kierkegaard in what would become known as "existentialism." By the late nineteenth century, traditional Christianity had largely been rejected in philosophical circles and replaced by secular visions of progress and development, of which Karl Marx was the leading exponent. Marxism was adopted by Russian revolutionaries, who eventually made their country the first officially atheist state in the world and tried to abolish religion altogether.

10. In the English-speaking world, secular materialism was pragmatically atheistic but avoided open conflict with the churches. It was represented by men like Jeremy Bentham and John Stuart Mill, who developed what became known as "utilitarianism," a practical philosophy designed to solve the world's problems without recourse to metaphysics.

11. In the course of the nineteenth century, most European universities became secular institutions, even if many of them retained theology departments. In the United States, public universities were all purely secular, but private colleges with Christian roots were numerous and influential. They ensured that there would be space for a Christian philosophy to flourish in spite of general secularization.

12. In the Netherlands there developed a unique form of Christian philosophy, rooted in the Dutch Reformed tradition and claiming the name of "Calvinism." Something similar appeared in Catholic countries with an attempted revival of the philosophical theology of Thomas Aquinas (neo-Thomism).

13. Toward the end of the nineteenth century there was a renewed interest in human origins, sparked by Charles Darwin's theory of evolution. This led to a real conflict between some natural scientists and theologians because it appeared to deny the creation stories of Genesis. The debate continues to the present time, though most people now accept that Darwinian evolution is not necessarily atheistic in nature.

14. The most important philosophical voice of the late nineteenth century was that of Friedrich Nietzsche. Nietzsche regarded the civilization of his time as hopelessly decadent and urged a return to the pre-Socratic era, which he popularized for the first time. Nietzsche had a profound impact on European culture, inspiring both the neo-barbarism of fascism and a renewed fascination with spiritual forces that Nietzsche saw as fundamental to human life.

VIII

THE TWO CITIES TODAY

Has the Enlightenment come to an end? Like the Renaissance, the Enlightenment has left a deep mark on Western culture, and in many respects its principles are still very much with us. But if we think of the Enlightenment as a movement dominated by men like Spinoza, Locke, and Newton, then there is a sense in which we have moved on. This is not to say that their ideas no longer have any currency, but that in many respects they have been supplemented and even supplanted by subsequent developments. This is particularly true of Newton, whose understanding of physics has been superseded in recent times, with effects that go far beyond the natural sciences.

The Enlightenment promised to bring light to what its proponents saw as the darkness of Western culture. Their aim was to abolish superstition, to put reason at the heart of everything, and to reform society and its institutions so that they would function on a rational basis that would have a positive effect on everything else. It is therefore particularly appropriate that it was the very question of the nature of light that helped Western thinkers to move on to another stage. Historical periods seldom begin and end at particular times; there is usually an overlap or transitional phase in which older ideas remain current while newer ones appear and develop beneath the surface. In the late nineteenth century, there was a feeling abroad that something was about to change, and in the work of a man like Nietzsche we can see how that played itself out.

With the benefit of hindsight, we can see that the years from about 1880 to 1914 were a time of transition as more and more people were growing uneasy at the way things were developing and predictions of an apocalyptic catastrophe became more frequent. There was a growing taste for dissonance in music, for the macabre in literature, and for distortion in art that seemed to portend the demise of a civilization, even as outwardly it was reaching new heights in science and technology. After the cataclysm of the First World War, there could be no more doubting. A world had vanished, but nobody could yet say what would take its place. We now know that the years 1919–1939 were a kind of interlude between two phases of a conflict that did not come to a definitive end until 1945. The explosion of two atomic bombs on August 6 and 9 that year, in Hiroshima and Nagasaki, respectively, brought the Second World War to a sudden end and at the same time revealed that entirely new forces were being unleashed. What they were and how they would affect the future were still largely unknown, but that a page in human history had been turned, and that there could be no going back, was now plain for all to see.

The events that led up to the dropping of the first atomic bombs can be traced back to 1867, when James Clerk Maxwell (1831–1879) published a series of computations that he had made. Maxwell began by asking a question that had puzzled physicists since Newton's time: Is light a wave or a particle? Maxwell decided that it was a wave, and from there he went on to look at electricity and magnetism, two other phenomena that had interested scientists for generations. What Maxwell concluded was that all three—light, electricity, and magnetism—were different aspects of the same thing. He argued that light was an electromagnetic wave and that what we can see is only a small part of a much larger range of invisible radiations, which could be either long or short.[1] Maxwell was even able to calculate the speed of light at 186,000 miles per second, a figure that remains constant regardless of other circumstances.

Maxwell had in fact predicted the existence of a series of phenomena that are invisible to us but follow exact mathematical formulas. He then applied his theory to his study of gases and heat, taking up the theory of Rudolf Clausius (1822–1888) that heat was the product of the

1. In 1888, long after Maxwell's death, Heinrich Hertz (1857–1894) established the existence of very long waves, now known as radio waves, and in 1895 Wilhelm Röntgen (1845–1923) discovered very short ones, which we now call X-rays.

kinetic movement of atoms inside the gases. These atoms are too small to be visible and too numerous for their motions to be easily or exactly calculated. Maxwell concluded that the most we can hope for is statistical probability—some atoms move faster than others and some slower, but there is a kind of "average" speed. This spectrum of flexibility was a scientific breakthrough of the first magnitude, so much so that Maxwell could not really believe it. Ever since Aristotle, it had been assumed that science was about discovering exact results, and that mathematics was the best means of reaching that goal. But if mathematics produced probability instead of certainty, either it was not scientific or science itself would have to change its parameters of judgment. This was the dilemma that confronted Maxwell and his colleagues when they tried to calculate the movement of light waves. If light waves moved, they assumed, they had to move through something, because all matter must occupy some space. Various theories about what that something might be were produced, but none seemed to be satisfactory, and so Maxwell's theory remained no more than that until long after he was dead.

The man who solved the puzzle was the Austrian physicist Ludwig Boltzmann (1844–1906), who made a careful study of Maxwell's theory at the behest of his tutor, Josef Stefan (1835–1893). Stefan not only understood the importance of Maxwell's discoveries but was also convinced of the truth of Clausius's theory of atoms that Maxwell had used in his analysis of gases. This seems perfectly normal to us today, so it is hard for us to appreciate just how unsettling Stefan's views were. As a theory, atomism could be traced back once again to the pre-Socratics, this time to Democritus and Leucippus, but it had never been more than a guess, and Aristotle's assertion that the world is made up of material substances effectively sidelined it for two thousand years. Clausius revived it, albeit within a limited range of possibilities, and Maxwell's theory of electromagnetism lent further weight to it, especially when Clausius replaced the quest for exact certainty with Maxwell's theory of statistical probability.

It was Boltzmann who combined Clausius and Maxwell by tying their theories to the question of thermodynamics. Clausius had already discovered that every time something moves, the available energy in the system that permitted the motion loses something of its capacity. Over time, this loss of energy multiplies to the point where the system eventually runs down completely. Clausius called this progressive loss "entropy," which would eventually lead to the disintegration of everything, including the universe. Here Boltzmann came to the rescue. By applying Maxwell's theory that heat was not a substance that was forever losing energy but a random movement of atoms from an orderly state to more disordered one, he saw that nothing was actually lost. The atoms could regroup and retain their energy, though that was not guaranteed. Boltzmann concluded that some did and others did not, though the general tendency was for them to move from a high-energy state to a lower one, making the latter more common in practice. It is when energy is out of balance that it can be used—as when water flows over a dam, for example. In that case, the disequilibrium creates electricity, and it is atoms that determine what the invisible properties of matter, like electrical conductivity, are. Once that is grasped, the entire nature of matter is called into question, because it is no longer to be seen as a fixed substance with immutable properties but as a constantly moving and changing interplay of atoms that can be predicted by mathematical calculations but not exactly determined, since the movement of those atoms is essentially random.

Boltzmann's discoveries would be epoch-making, but he was ahead of his time. He was opposed by Ernst Mach (1838–1916) and Henri Poincaré (1854–1912), both of whom were leading physicists of the time. Mach discovered the ratio of speed to sound, and his calculations are still in use today, so his opposition had to be taken seriously. Mach was also one of the founders of the so-called Vienna Circle of philosophers, which advocated the principle of logical positivism (discussed later in this chapter). This was not primarily an attack on Boltzmann, and still less on Christianity, which many logical positivists held in high regard, even if they were not particularly active believers themselves. Their target was Hegel, whose philosophy was then dominant in the German-speaking world. The logical positivists wanted to avoid abstract theories and concentrate on observable facts, and so to them it seemed natural to oppose Boltzmann, whose theories could not be verified. Poincaré thought that entropy was an irrational idea, because in a closed system of atoms, if such a thing existed, each atom must eventually return to its original condition. Poincaré did not realize that in a world made up of atoms there can be no closed system, but by the time that awareness came it was too late for Boltzmann.

To make matters even worse, Max Planck (1858–1947) was using Boltzmann's theory about the decline of energy but replacing the concept of atoms with electromagnetic waves, thereby driving a wedge between Maxwell and Clausius that threatened to derail Boltzmann's entire life's work. When Boltzmann realized that Mach and Poincaré were the established purveyors of scientific truth against whom no opposition was possible, his despair led him to commit suicide. The real tragedy is that this happened almost at the very moment when he would be proved right after all, and when Planck would turn against Mach and denounce him as a "false prophet," which in a sense he was.

That something would have to give in the generally accepted physics of the time was vaguely realized by Albert Michelson (1852–1931), who was convinced that he could develop a mechanism for detecting variations in the speed of light. Following the dictates of Newtonian physics, Michelson believed that the speed of light would change depending on the way it traveled. Michelson was an important and influential man in his day, the founder of the American Physical Society and a winner of the Nobel Prize in physics (1907), but try as he did, he could find no way of altering the speed of light from what Maxwell had decreed was 186,000 miles per second. He went to his grave believing that he had been a failure because it never occurred to him that it might be Newton's physics, and not his own experiments, that got it wrong.

Meanwhile, Michelson's many experiments had attracted the curiosity of Albert Einstein (1879–1955), who was already questioning Newton's belief that time and space are a fixed system within which everything must fit, including the speed of light. Einstein calculated that if he could travel that fast he would outrun time. Everything depends on our perspective, not on some predetermined grid pattern that cannot be altered. Once he had established that, Einstein altered the way natural science was understood. No longer was it a question of objective, immutable facts. Instead, it was all a matter of observation, which could vary according to our starting point. This did not mean that science was unpredictable, however. Mathematical measurements would still be valid within the parameters established by the perspective adopted—this was what we now call the theory of relativity.

At this point, Einstein heard about the work of Boltzmann and was persuaded by it. He accepted that statistical probability, rather than absolute certainty, could explain many aspects of nature, including electromagnetism. Boltzmann had wanted to divide the energy of an electromagnetic wave into small units, which he called *quanta*. Max Planck had also followed Boltzmann in this, but was unpersuaded that these small units actually existed because he rejected the theory of atoms. Einstein read Planck, but he did not reject Boltzmann's atomic theory. On the contrary, he showed that if every quantum of radiation energy was considered independently, the result would tally exactly with the observations of standard thermodynamics. Einstein demonstrated that quanta were atoms of energy that constituted light. Light was not a wave, as Maxwell had thought, but a stream of quanta ("photons") that moved at their own speed, regardless of any other atoms that might have got in the way. It was for that reason that the speed of light never changes, something that Michelson had already discovered but could not explain. Einstein went still farther—in his formulation, light was the only thing that stayed the same. Everything else was subject to the laws of quanta and the atoms of which they consisted, including time and space.

The next stage was to work out the relationship between the quantum and the atom. That was done by the Danish physicist Niels Bohr (1885–1962), who had been converted to atomic theory during his studies in England. Guided by Ernest Rutherford (1871–1937), Bohr learned to think of atoms as if they were a mini-solar system, with a nucleus (equivalent to the sun) encircled by electrically charged particles he called "electrons." In mathematical terms, Rutherford's theory worked, but Bohr realized there was something missing. If Rutherford's atoms were allowed to go unchecked, the energy they contained would eventually wind down and disappear. Bohr resolved this dilemma by appealing to Planck's *quanta*. As long as an electron stays within its own orbit, it releases no energy, but when it changes orbits it gives off a *quantum* of energy, not in a continuous stream but as distinct lines that reflect the nature of the element concerned. Hydrogen, for example, lets off three lines—one red, one green, and one blue, each of which testifies to a release of energy as the electrons move from one orbit to another.

Bohr published his findings in 1913. A year later, European civilization would be plunged into a war that destroyed the old order forever, but Bohr had effectively done that already. His findings both overturned Newtonian physics and the concept of "matter" that had been held by everyone since the time of Aristotle. Instead of being a concrete substance, matter now turned out to be no more than bundles of energy. Electrons generate electricity when they move from one orbit to another, and in doing so they can trigger other electrons to follow suit. With the right amount of *quantum* energy, electrons relate to one another rather like musical tones and can bind atoms together to form molecules. In this way, atomic theory lies at the heart of chemistry, as well as of electricity. All this could be measured mathematically. Instead of stable, constant matter there was now only a field of energy, a range of probabilities that suggested where the electrons might be at any particular moment, but with the speed of light as the only fixed reality.

The next stage in the development of atomic theory was reached by Werner Heisenberg (1901–1976), who established that it was impossible to measure both the position and the momentum of a particle simultaneously. This leaves a degree of uncertainty about what will happen next, which overturned the mechanistic determinism of an earlier era. Heisenberg's uncertainty principle did not meet with universal approval—Albert Einstein, for example, was one of those initially opposed to it. It is important to remember that "uncertainty" in this case applies to human perception and does not necessarily reflect the underlying reality. It is perfectly possible that there is a more complicated series of movements that is (so far at least) beyond the powers of human calculation, but nevertheless not uncertain or random in the true sense of the word. If that is so, then it is an argument for the operation of a higher mind, which both Christians and secularists have labeled "God." How long our knowledge will remain at this stage is impossible to predict. Perhaps further research and experiment will remove the lingering uncertainty and give us a deeper understanding of the way that quantum mechanics operates. If that happens, the God of the secularists will be eliminated from consideration, but it will make no difference to believers. On the contrary, it will merely demonstrate yet again just how complex and profound the mind of God is. There will always be more to discover, and we must not fall into the trap of using the word "God" merely to account for what we have not yet managed to figure out. This "God of the gaps" is not the God of the Bible, and Christians cannot restrict their belief in God to an explanation of problems that human beings have not yet resolved.

Between them, Einstein and Bohr had reshaped human understanding of the physical universe, but that was not all. Every power and ideology that had been built on traditional assumptions about matter came crashing down, at least in the minds of those who understood what was going on. Marxism's dialectical materialism, for example, was discredited even before an attempt was made to put it into practice in Russia. Classical imperialism, which had been based on the idea that to be great, a country had to control as much territory and as many natural resources as possible, was shown to be false—the really great powers would in future be those that knew how to harness atomic energy. As with all new ideas, it took time for this one to sink in. Those who were heavily invested in the old order had no desire to give it up, and it was not clear, even to Einstein and Bohr, what their discoveries would amount to in practice. They would find out, as would the rest of the world, in the course of the Second World War. It was then that the potential of atomic energy was explored seriously, and the result was the atomic bomb. Only when that bomb had been detonated over Japan with devastating results did it become clear what could happen, and the result was a moral and spiritual crisis through which we are still living today.

The scientists who worked on atomic energy were not particularly religious, nor did they give much thought to the moral implications of what they were doing. In the summer of 1945, it was clear that Japan would lose the war eventually, but the question was when. Germany had already been defeated, but the Japanese were in thrall to a warrior ethic that exalted suicide, and their army thought nothing of literally fighting to the last man. In terms of conventional warfare, that could have taken a long time, and the temptation to cut it short—and potentially save thousands of lives—was hard to resist. If atomic bombs were dropped, Japan would be given such a fright that it would surrender immediately, sparing further carnage, and that is what happened. But no sooner had the dust settled than doubts began to arise. Did the adoption of the lesser of two evils amount to something justifiably good? Was it right to annihilate thousands of innocent people in the way that had been done? What about the aftereffects of radiation, which might cause harm to victors and vanquished alike? Once the atomic genie was out of the bottle, who could put it back?

Before long, these questions and others like them, were taking away whatever satisfaction there was in the recent victory. Campaigns for nuclear disarmament became commonplace. Peaceful uses for atomic energy were certainly found, but the danger from misuse was always present, and getting rid of it was a constant objective of campaigners. The disaster at Chernobyl in 1986 stands out as the classic example of what can happen, and it played an important role in the subsequent disintegration of the Soviet Union, which had shown that it could not control its own science. The danger of proliferation also became apparent. It was bad enough that a few developed countries had a nuclear arsenal, but what might happen if the technology that supported it were to be exported to unstable countries, some of which were eager to get their hands on it? The threat of a nuclear Iraq turned out to be exaggerated, but it was enough to provoke a war in 2003, the consequences of which are still with us.

While all this was going on, research into the origins of the universe was proceeding apace. Initially, most scientists were convinced that the material world was eternal, that it had no beginning and no end, despite the problems that this traditional theory caused. For example, it was not clear how the universe avoided collapsing in on itself under the weight of gravity, and when Einstein developed his theory of relativity he felt obliged to balance it with a kind of uncertainty principle of his own that would counteract the force of gravity and preserve a steady-state universe. He later rejected that compromise, but by then a different model of the universe had emerged to deal with this question. The man chiefly responsible for that was Edwin Hubble (1889–1953), who studied the way in which other galaxies were drifting apart from ours. The farther away from us a galaxy is, the faster it was moving still farther away. If this observation was correct, it suggested that if we could reverse time, we would discover that at some distant point in the past all the existing galaxies were in effect one. What that was like is unknown, but something happened to set the universe as we know it into motion—the Big Bang, as it is now called. It is hard to put a date on this, but most cosmologists now think that this occurred about fourteen billion years ago.

The Big Bang theory does not answer every question. In particular, we cannot (yet) say whether the tendency for the galaxies to distance themselves from one another will one day be reversed and a process of regrouping, perhaps back into the original one, will begin. But what we can say is that the Big Bang has put paid to any idea that the universe is eternal. It had a beginning, and the question must be asked: How did it start? There is no scientific answer to that. In the words of Robert Jastrow (1925–2008):

> At the moment it seems as though science will never be able to raise the curtain on the mystery of creation. For the scientist who has lived by his faith in the power of reason, the story ends like a bad dream. He has scaled the mountain of ignorance; he is about to conquer the highest peak; as he pulls himself over the final rock, he is greeted by a band of theologians who have been sitting there for centuries.[2]

Jastrow's observations do not prove the existence of God, but they do open doors that for many secular scientists had been either closed or nonexistent. That the natural sciences are a closed system that can potentially explain everything is no longer a tenable position. It is now necessary to look further and consider possibilities that had previously been dismissed. Among these possibilities is theism, and in particular, the revelation of the God of the Bible, who is not "dead" as some rather too hasty critics of the late nineteenth and early twentieth centuries were so eager to claim.

Even if the Big Bang theory stood on its own it would be a powerful challenge to a secular or atheistic philosophy, but it does not. To believe that the universe started in one particular place from a single set of elements implies that the now diverging galaxies have essentially the same characteristics as far as their material composition is concerned. Does this mean that there is likely to be life as we know it on other planets, of which we are unaware? There is obviously no answer to that question, and the time that it would take to find out what is going on millions of light years away makes looking for such life impractical. But the possibility that it exists cannot be dismissed out of hand, and it has led to a much closer examination of the conditions that have permitted life to flourish on

---

2. Robert Jastrow, *God and the Astronomers* (New York: W. W. Norton, 1992), 107.

earth. What this investigation has shown is that our life is only possible because several factors have coalesced in what scientists call "fine tuning." This is so exact, and the margin of error is so narrow, that it is extremely difficult to maintain that it has come about by accident. It is far easier to believe that the current order of things was fashioned by a superior mind, that may be identified as "God." It is particularly interesting to note that atheists, who are determined to oppose any mention of "God," are often reduced to arguing their case by citing apparent anomalies in the system, like the existence of disease and various kinds of physical handicap, which they claim would not be there if God were really in control. But even they cannot deny that fine tuning is a reality, since the concept of anomaly is dependent on it to begin with. Exceptions to the rule do not prove that there is no rule but the exact opposite, because without a rule the exceptions would not be recognized as such.

The argument from fine tuning was enough to persuade the eminent atheist and critic of religion Antony Flew (1923–2010) to abandon his earlier unbelief in favor of a kind of deism, which some observers mistakenly regarded as a conversion to Christianity. Flew never went that far, but the fact that he gave up his atheistic certainties in the face of the evidence was enough to provoke a furious backlash from his fellow unbelievers, a sure sign that they realized just how weak their position actually was.

One of the spin-offs from the fine-tuning argument has been the realization that the world as we know it was not an immediate result of the Big Bang. Fine tuning took a very long time to mature to the point where it could support human life. Even the sun and our solar system are no more than five billion years old, and earth was not ready for human habitation until long after that. *Homo sapiens* did not exist, and could not have existed, in the age of the dinosaurs, for instance, and there had to be major modifications in plant and animal life, as well as in the climate, before humans as we know them could survive. Furthermore, it seems at least possible, if not probable, that the emergence of human beings was foreseen from the start. As Stephen Hawking (1942–2018) put it, "It would be very difficult to explain why the universe should have begun in just this way, except as the act of a God who intended to create beings like us."[3]

---

3. S. Hawking, *A Brief History of Time* (New York: Bantam Press, 1998), 144.

Hawking lived and died as an atheist, unpersuaded even by his own argument, but that he made it at all is revealing. The suggestion that the world was prepared in order to receive human beings is precisely what Genesis 1–2 claims, albeit without the sophisticated detail that we find in modern scientific research. In spite of himself, Hawking came surprisingly close to the most ancient explanation of human origins, a coincidence that in its own way is almost as revealing as the fine-tuning argument for the existence of a Creator God.

As might be expected, most theologians and philosophers have been slow to adjust to the new situation in physics. Theology had long worked with the Aristotelian concept of "substance" and found it hard to abandon. The Roman Catholic doctrine of transubstantiation, for example, which had divided the Western church in the sixteenth century, became utterly meaningless once substance had given way to energy, but to abandon it would mean cutting loose from traditional sacramental theology, not just for Catholics but for those who opposed them, too, because they had formulated their opposition in terms that also presupposed Aristotelian categories of thought. Denying a change of substance became just as untenable a position as transubstantiation once the concept of "substance" itself was brushed aside. The sea change in conceptual thinking that adapting to this new situation demanded was too much for most theologians to absorb. There was also the problem of traditional confessions of faith that had been formulated according to the logic of an earlier time and that might now have to be abandoned, or at least modified in ways that might prove disconcerting. For example, the rise of existentialism and of "situation ethics" might lead to a position where things that had always been considered evil, like murder or adultery, could be justified on the ground that absolutes do not exist and that people have to make up their own minds about what to do according to circumstances. There were voices on the fringes of the churches that were saying more or less that already, but the mainstream was not prepared to follow in their footsteps, and so the questions that had to be asked were mostly avoided.

One movement that did try to get to grips with the new situation was what is known as process theology. This rested on the philosophy of Alfred North Whitehead (1861–1947), who embraced the break-up of the

Aristotelian worldview and replaced it with a theory more in tune with the atomic age, though in many respects it went back to the pre-Socratics, and especially to Heraclitus's idea that everything is always in flux. To Whitehead that was reality, and his theory was taken up by Charles Hartshorne (1897–2000), who gave it a Christian gloss. Both men were opposed to what they called "classical theism," that is to say, a doctrine of God rooted in Aristotle's concept of the Prime Mover that is itself unmoved. Such a being, if it exists, cannot have relations with anything else, because relations involve engagement, and engagement will bring about change. If God cannot change, then he cannot be in relationship with the world. But the God of the Bible clearly does have relations with the world in which he is deeply involved. This leaves only one of two possibilities—either classical theism is wrong and God is not immutable, or it is right and we must live without God in the world. Whitehead was not particularly interested in choosing between these options, but Hartshorne, as a Christian, was bound to opt for the former solution. God had to be found in the ebb and flow of real life as a force in process, not as a fixture in some transcendent mind.

Whitehead returned in many respects to the beliefs of the pre-Socratics, and in particular to the view of Heraclitus, that the world was in constant flux. He found room for God, insofar as he did, by saying that the world of flux had no natural boundaries and that, left to itself, it could go anywhere and in any direction. To the extent that it was directed in one way rather than in another it required a principle of limitation, and that principle was "God." In this respect, Whitehead borrowed from Plato's *Timaeus*, which makes his philosophy look like a very traditional response to what was supposedly a challengingly new worldview. Be that as it may, Hartshorne took up the framework of Whitehead's ideas and extended them in a more obviously Christian direction. For Hartshorne, God was part of the flux, to be sure, but he was also a constant, guiding principle working within it. Moreover, Hartshorne saw Christians as believers who were caught up in the flow because their minds were attuned to the Mind that controlled it. Those who were not so attuned were still caught up in the divine movement, but they did not understand it and were inclined to resist it—they were "reactionaries," to use the political term for it, and they suffered the consequences of swimming against the tide.

Process theology never really caught on because at root it was thoroughly pagan. Its God was not a transcendent being but only the spirit that animates the universe. This spirit has supposedly been set free from the immutability of the God of classical theism, but in reality it is just as immutable because it is ever changing. It never rests, as the God of the Bible did on the seventh day of creation, because rest is alien to its nature. There is no sin and no judgment because there are no constant factors to make such categories meaningful. There is also no individualism or personal responsibility, both of which are subsumed in the flow into which we are absorbed. Of course, there can be no dialogue with God, no prayer, and no real relationship with him, though it was precisely in order to provide this that process theology came into being in the first place. It continues to find a few defenders, but as a movement of theological thought it is now virtually dead.[4] But although process theology is mistaken in most of its conclusions, the circumstances that brought it into being are still very much with us and demand a response. To put it a different way, if process theology must be discarded, it must also be replaced by something that appreciates what it is asking and provides a more satisfactory answer to the questions it raises.

If this is to happen, it is incumbent on theologians and biblical scholars to come to terms with the opening chapters of Genesis. Naive assumptions about the supposed historicity of the six-day creation have to be abandoned—creationism in that sense is not a viable option in the face of overwhelming evidence to the contrary. But at the same time, the broad outlines of the biblical story have received some interesting support from scientific research and are quite compatible with the Big Bang theory and its derivatives. There is no reason at all why anyone should find an irresolvable conflict between what the Bible says and what science can affirm. But to do this properly, theologians have to rise above the concerns of biblical scholars who are mainly interested in such things as the origin of the texts and their composition and consider the philosophical validity of the worldview that underlies them. This is not to deny the importance of the groundwork being done on the texts themselves, but to put it in context and to give it a purpose. For that, something more than an analysis of the

4. See Bruce Epperly, *Process Theology: A Guide for the Perplexed* (London: T&T Clark, 2011), for a good overview of the movement from one of its few defenders.

physical universe is required—we must also consider the meaning of life, for it is life that the Bible is primarily interested in, and the need to preserve and enhance life that lies at the heart of the story that it has to tell.

THE LIFE OF THE WORLD

The revolution that occurred in physics in the early twentieth century has been paralleled by similar developments in the life sciences. It is often forgotten today, but Charles Darwin's theory of evolution by natural selection was widely criticized in his own time, and not just by people who objected to it on religious grounds. Darwin can be credited with having done a great deal to put biology and what we now call "paleoanthropology," the study of human origins, on a scientific basis, but he was working from a small fossil base and was unable to demonstrate the truth of his hypotheses by producing actual examples of the processes whose existence he conjectured.[5] Subsequent research has filled in many of the missing pieces, but it has done so in a way that has gone beyond Darwin and his immediate followers. They tended to think that the human race evolved in linear fashion from pre-human ancestors, many of which are now extinct but some of which continue to exist as apes and so on. That idea has now been overturned by multiple fossil discoveries that demonstrate the existence of numerous species of what are called "hominins," that is to say, creatures that have characteristics similar to those of modern humans but that cannot be classified as *homo sapiens*.[6]

The number and variety of these hominins is astonishing, and the relationship between the different "species" (if that is the right word for them) remains unclear. What now seems to be decided, though, is that hominins that were once thought to be proto-humans from which we are descended actually were not. The most famous case of this is "Neanderthal man," known from the discovery of a skull in Germany in 1856 and since traced in many other parts of the world. The Neanderthals, and the similar *homo heidelbergensis*, who was more recently identified, also in Germany, were almost human in physical makeup but apparently lacked minds capable of

5. For an excellent introduction to this subject, from which must of what follows is drawn, see Kostas Kampourakis, *Understanding Evolution* (Cambridge: Cambridge University Press, 2020).

6. See Ian Tattersall, *Understanding Human Evolution* (Cambridge: Cambridge University Press, 2022).

abstract thought. It is also usually claimed that they lacked the facility of language, though how this can be proved is uncertain. Still less can we tell whether they possessed what we would call consciousness, a conscience, or emotions as we understand them. Perhaps they demonstrated mutual affection and attraction in the way that some animals do, but if so, that is still a very long way from what we are used to as human beings.

The result of all this is that the ancestry of *homo sapiens* can no longer be traced with confidence to these hominins. Even if intercourse between some of them and early *homo sapiens* was possible and may have occurred to a limited extent, the overall picture suggests that hominins, if they continued to exist after the appearance of *homo sapiens*, became extinct fairly quickly. Certainly there are none around today, nor have there been any for a long time. Of course, "long" is a relative term—in this context it means something like forty to fifty thousand years ago, which in biological terms is no time at all. Hominins, not to mention earlier creatures like dinosaurs, are reckoned to have lived millions of years before that. What happened to them is unknown, though one frequently mentioned scenario is that *homo sapiens* killed them off. That may or may not have been the case, and we shall probably never know one way or the other. But whatever emerges from the research being conducted by paleoanthropologists today, and it seems certain that a great deal of further knowledge will be forthcoming in the years ahead, the overriding result will be that *homo sapiens* will be clearly distinguished from every other living creature, whatever underlying similarities there may be. In the words of Ian Tattersall (1945–), one of the leading authorities on this subject today:

> We modern human beings have an astonishingly recent origin, and a sudden one. In evolutionary terms, we acquired our extraordinary symbolic reasoning capacities virtually overnight, and we did so *ex*aptively (*i.e.*, not in the context familiar today) rather than *ad*aptively (within that symbolic context). What this most importantly tells us is that we cannot have been fine-tuned by natural selection over the eons to be the kind of creature we are today: there was simply not enough time.[7]

7. Tattersall, *Understanding*, 148.

Tattersall then goes on to add that "Nature" has unintentionally "given human beings almost unlimited freedom to become the kinds of creatures they individually choose to be. We can only express this freedom, however, by using some rather jury-rigged cognitive equipment that was most certainly not optimized by evolution to respond to the demands we routinely place upon it."[8] This is an extraordinary statement from someone who bases his thinking entirely on scientific evidence. What is "Nature," and why is it capitalized? Is it anything more than a cover term for a series of things that have no governing principle beyond themselves? And what is "almost unlimited freedom"? I might want to become an elephant, a giraffe, or a stone monument, but am I free to realize those desires? Would they not go completely against Nature and therefore be impossible? Yet—and here we must agree with Tattersall—we humans have the capacity to *imagine* such things, even though we can never realize them in practice. How is that possible?

At a more practical level, human beings can go against the dictates of Nature in some ways, and often do. Our instinct is for self-preservation, which is a form of self-interest, and that is natural to animals as well as to humans. But in certain circumstances, I might be moved to sacrifice my own well-being for the sake of someone else. If that someone else is my child (or other close relative), such a reaction may be understandable, and is indeed found in the animal kingdom as well. But what if the person concerned is a complete stranger? What would motivate me to go to the rescue, even if there is no conceivable benefit to myself, and every prospect that I might suffer as a result? Perhaps a purely rational person would refrain from such an action, but the fact is that many people perform such acts of heroism and kindness, and nobody thinks of them as irrational. Why not? True freedom, after all, must mean the freedom to walk away from such situations, and why would anyone think of me as cowardly or irresponsible if I were to do so? Yet the fact is that they might well do—and that I might also feel guilty for shirking my duty. What duty? Why would I feel that way? These are questions that Tattersall's statement raises but does not—and cannot—answer. This is where religion comes in.

8. Tattersall, *Understanding*, 148.

Tattersall makes no mention of religion and discusses the evidence entirely within a secular scientific framework, but his conclusions are remarkably consistent with a Christian worldview, especially when set next to the firmly atheistic views of people like Richard Dawkins (1941–). No doubt Tattersall would not want to see his conclusions used in defense of a Christian (or other religious) position, and they certainly do not prove the existence of God, but that is not the point. What is significant here is that if traditional religious claims have been swept away by modern discoveries (and they often have been), then traditional secular claims have also been shown to lack compelling supportive evidence. In other words, nothing that scientists have recently discovered invalidates the Christian worldview. On the contrary, much of what has been recently concluded goes at least some way toward supporting it, and nothing in the purely scientific sphere proves either atheism or theism as an incontrovertible philosophical position.[9]

One of the more extraordinary findings of recent research is that while it took millions of years for life on earth to evolve, and there were many ups and downs along the way, the emergence of *homo sapiens* was rapid and apparently complete. Sudden change cannot be ruled out, but when it occurs it is usually destructive. For example, dinosaurs are supposed to have disappeared about sixty-six million years ago following a cataclysmic event like the crashing of a meteorite into Earth, and similar extinctions in rapid (and often unexplained) succession are often invoked as explanations for the disappearance of particular life forms. We might even go so far as to say that the biblical story of Noah's flood belongs to this category, though it should be pointed out that one of the lessons of the flood was that God would never again destroy the earth in that way—and so far, nothing has happened to make us revise that opinion.

But here again, Tattersall reveals something extraordinary: the rapid rise and universal dominance of *homo sapiens* is most unlikely ever to be reversed. He claims that the rapid transformations of the past were facilitated by (if not due to) the fact that our hunter-gatherer predecessors lived nomadic lives in sparsely populated conditions. According to

9. This is also the position taken by Kampourakis, *Understanding*, who explicitly distances himself from the views of Dawkins, though without embracing theism.

him, the invention of sedentary agriculture changed all that. Instead of remaining few and far between, human beings started to multiply and in his words are now "a single huge interbreeding population within which the probability of incorporating significant genetic innovations is negligible." He assures us that in these conditions, "it is highly unlikely that a new and improved version of humankind will emerge."[10] The only way that could happen would be if there is another cosmic disaster, something that he does not rule out, but regards as highly undesirable—and therefore improbable! So we are stuck with our imperfections—evolving toward a better state of being is not really an option for us, unless we are prepared to face unprecedented mass destruction. That might be good for whatever was to come afterwards, but as Tattersall himself admits, it is unappealing to us, who would certainly perish in the maelstrom.

None of this offers much comfort either to theists or to atheists, but it is remarkable how close it comes in some ways to the Christian vision of the future. Like Tattersall, Christians see no chance of human improvement in this life, even if the reasons we give for thinking that are different from his. Like him, we can easily picture mass destruction—the Bible calls it Armageddon, a word that is frequently picked up in secular discourse (Rev 16:16). Like him, we also believe that out of the catastrophe will come a new heaven and a new earth that will be a great improvement on the one we now live in—with the important difference that we shall be there to share in it. In sum, Tattersall's vision is really no different from that of John the Divine in the book of Revelation, or from that of the apostle Paul in 1 Corinthians 15. It is not even expressed in significantly different language! Is it not surprising that speculation based on scientific research should lead somebody to almost exactly the same conclusions as the Christian church has all along borne witness to in the form of divine revelation? And that without the aid of modern science!

Speaking of modern scientific research, the great discovery of our times was that the DNA molecule is the means by which inheritance is passed from one generation to another, and that this molecule is the same in all forms of life. For hundreds of years, scientists and philosophers were enthralled by what Aristotle called the "final cause" of events—the purpose

10. Tattersall, *Understanding*, 149–50.

for which things happened or were designed. This was what lay at the heart of William Paley's illustration of the watch and the watchmaker. He saw that a watch had to have been designed by a being capable of doing so, and that it came into existence for a purpose. He then extrapolated from that observation to the universe, which (he argued) must have been similarly designed and intended to serve particular purposes. More recently, this way of thinking has been discredited by distinguishing artifacts (like a watch) from organisms (like a human being).

In the case of artifacts, which are things made by humans, it is perfectly reasonable to suppose that they have been made for a reason, which can usually be deduced from considering what function they have been designed to perform. But organisms are different. It may be true that an artifact like an airplane has been designed with wings to allow it to fly, and that this design was at least partly inspired by birds, which also have wings. But while most birds use their wings to fly, and all flying birds have wings, there are some that are different. Penguins, for example, have wings that help them to swim, but they cannot use them to fly. Ostriches have wings that apparently do nothing at all. So if we extrapolate from an airplane (an artifact) to birds (organisms), and assume that the same processes are at work in both, we shall have to conclude that "nature" is imperfect, which would appear to rule out a Creator God, since most people (and certainly most Christians) would assume that if such a God exists he must be perfect and would not have designed an imperfect world. This assumption is then used to disprove the belief that God is an intelligent designer, since no such being would have acted in this way.

But the Bible never says that God made a perfect world—only one that was "good" in his eyes. Indeed, the text of Genesis 1 specifically allows for the development of the created order by human beings, which would be impossible (or counterproductive) if the world were perfect to begin with (Gen 1:28; 2:15). What could humans have done with it other than make it less perfect? Nor is there any suggestion in the Bible that God designed the world in such a way as to give everything a fixed purpose from the start. It may be true that virtually all creatures are adapted to their environment, which is why they continue to survive, but it is not obvious that they were designed with a particular function in view. What are roses for? Or hedgehogs? They may have their attractions, but are they necessary to the functioning of the world? Similarly with ostrich wings. Perhaps they did have a function at one time, or were meant to have one but somehow the original plan did not work out. But what if there never was such a plan? What if ostriches have wings simply because God wanted them to be like that? It is not the Bible but the proponents of a mechanistic universe who insist on purposefulness and who go looking for it. The Bible is content to say that everything in the world exists for the glory of God. Nor is it worried if human beings find this incomprehensible. As God said to the prophet Isaiah:

> My thoughts are not your thoughts,
> neither are your ways my ways. ...
> For as the heavens are higher than the earth,
> so are my ways higher than your ways
> and my thoughts than your thoughts. (Isa 55:8–9)

Christians are not disturbed by the fact that there is much about God and his ways that we do not understand. In fact, it would be much more worrying if we did have the key to all knowledge, because then we would be reducing God to our level and depriving him of his sovereign uniqueness. None of this is meant to disparage scientific discoveries. On the contrary, such discoveries help us to see more clearly just how complex the mind of God is, and how unsearchable his judgments ultimately are (cf. Rom 11:33). The irony, from a Christian point of view, is that science seeks certainly but can never find it, whereas Christians accept the limitations of their capacity for knowledge, and do so with certainty, because they accept that God knows what they do not and are content to leave it at that.

The discovery of the centrality of DNA and its consequences may be less dramatic than the dropping of atomic bombs, but it is no less significant. The great breakthrough came in 1953 when James Watson (1928–) and Francis Crick (1916–2004) discovered the inner structure of DNA and effectively founded the new discipline of molecular biology. Both men were convinced atheists, Crick more aggressively so, and Watson made links between genetics and race that caused him to be ostracized in academic circles in the United States. They were also accused of using data taken from colleagues without their permission, which cast a shadow over their achievement.

Be that as it may, the study of DNA has progressed ever since, especially after it was realized that there is another molecule, known as RNA, that acts as a messenger that can copy information stored in DNA and translate it into protein, which can then be transferred to other cells. Very small mutations in particular DNA can have major consequences and are often responsible for various diseases and disorders that occur in different human beings. By working on repairing these mutations, it is now possible to find cures for many of these problems, and medicine is being revolutionized as a result.

The vast complexity of DNA, combined with the usefulness of being able to treat its anomalies when they are detected, made it desirable to construct a complete picture of DNA as found in the human genome. The mapping of the genome, which began in 1990 and was finally completed in 2022, promises to alter our understanding of life almost beyond recognition. It has already proved to be of immense value in helping to treat cancers, and its medical importance is only just beginning to be felt. There is every prospect that previously incurable diseases or genetic disorders may be treatable and scourges that have plagued humankind since the dawn of time may finally be overcome and eliminated.

The magnitude of this task is hard to appreciate, and from the beginning there were competing forces at work. Some wanted to patent the discoveries being made and restrict their use, while others, including those who established the Human Genome Project in 1990, believed that all the research should be made available free of charge to anyone who wanted it. James Watson, the first director of the Human Genome Project, resigned from it over this question—he was in favor of universal availability at a time when financial constraints were pressing the project to go for the private funding model. He was succeeded by Francis Collins (1950–) who, unlike Watson and Crick, is a believing Christian and has been a staunch advocate for the compatibility of science and religious faith. It is notable, however, that Collins, who was once an atheist, was not converted to Christianity by his scientific work, but by observing and experiencing the living faith of very simple people that culminated in a personal experience of God.[11] This is not to say that nobody can ever be converted by

11. See Francis Collins, *The Language of God: A Scientist Presents Evidence for Belief* (New York: Simon and Schuster, 2007), 11–31.

philosophical arguments, but that true profession of Christian faith goes beyond them, a principle that Collins endorses and makes central to the reconciliation of science and religion for which he is widely known.

Collins believes that God works through the evolutionary processes discovered by modern scientific research and rejects theories of human origins that do not take these on board. He understands why some Christians reject modern scientific theories that appear to contradict their faith and that are often advocated by atheists for that reason, but he rejects their approach to the question. He believes that the discoveries of modern science reveal something of the mind of God in creation, and that Christians should embrace them with gratitude for his goodness toward us. We have been given minds with the ability to examine the world around us and should not be afraid of what we discover, though of course we must use whatever gifts we have with wisdom and discretion.

At the same time, Collins insists that the realm of natural science and the teachings of the Christian faith, while they overlap to some extent, are also addressing quite different issues. Here DNA is a particularly important witness. It has a complexity that makes it far easier to believe that it was created by God than to suppose that it evolved by random selection, but at the same time it is common to all life forms. Human beings, on the other hand, are significantly different from other living creatures, however much we have in common with them. We have conscious self-awareness, we have minds that can think "outside the box" in the sense that we can imagine things and create new realities like books, paintings, plays, and music, which other animals cannot do. Above all, we have a moral sense rooted in a concept of good and evil that helps us determine what is right and wrong. The precise details of this may vary to some extent from one group of humans to another, but the range is actually quite small. Different tribes, cultures, and religions may prescribe certain activities as "good" and others as "bad," and some of these may appear strange to outsiders, but underneath we find that they all have many of the same goals—a desire to preserve human life, to protect those whom we love from harm, and to promote the interests of the community, even if this means making sacrifices ourselves.

The uniqueness of humanity in these respects is obvious but it cannot be accounted for by referring to our physical makeup, since that is closely connected to the rest of the animal world. If moral awareness, for example, were part of our DNA we would expect to see it replicated, to some extent at least, by all living creatures who share the same genetic structure. Since this is not the case, we are obliged to find some other explanation for it. This is where religion comes in. Collins does not distinguish between the different religions of the world in the way that a theologian must do, but as a Christian himself, he starts with the teaching of the Bible. As he sees it, all human beings are morally responsible agents and this can only mean that they are distinguished, and bound together, by a relationship and a consciousness that goes beyond the material world of which we are a part. That moral awareness is not a logical consequence of biological evolution is brought out very clearly by Richard Dawkins, one of the most vocal and best-known advocates of atheism today. Dawkins writes: "The universe we observe has precisely the properties we should expect if there is, at bottom, no design, no purpose, no evil, and no good, nothing but blind pitiless indifference."[12] Leaving aside the question of how it is that we could expect anything at all from such a universe, it is clear that most people instinctively rebel against this caricature. No good or evil at all? Not even Dawkins goes that far—for him, religion and all its works are "evil," and if they did not exist he would have nothing to complain about!

It is at this point that the Bible really begins. The texts say very little about the physical creation and nothing at all about biological evolution. They are not concerned with how we are like the animal world, but with how we differ from it, because that is what really matters. Collins agrees wholeheartedly with this—the fact that we have uncovered so much about the workings of the natural order and that we have ways of using it that were unknown even to our recent ancestors does not liberate us from our moral and spiritual inheritance. On the contrary, those things become even more important to us now that the decisions we take concerning them may very often be matters of life and death.

People who lived in biblical times knew about deserts, for example, but climate change was not something they had to worry about. We, however, are in a very different position. We can contemplate deserts just as our

12. Richard Dawkins, *River Out of Eden: A Darwinian View of Life* (London: Weidenfeld and Nicolson, 1995), 133.

ancestors did, but we can also observe them spreading in ways that are potentially harmful, and we have the means to do something about it. It is our spiritual service to God and our moral duty to our fellow human beings that drives us to think in this way, not changes in our genetic structure or any form of biological evolution. But virtually nobody would say that our behavior in this respect does not matter. Indeed, it is often the case that those who are the most aggressively atheist are also those who press most strongly for action in areas such as these, even to the point of accusing Christians of negligence and hypocrisy for failing to be as concerned about them as they are.

Furthermore, this reaction, although it may be tainted with an element of self-interest, is not exclusively selfish. It has an altruistic dimension that is often foregrounded in discussion—we want to save the planet, not just for ourselves but for one another, and for generations not yet born. This concern is shared by believers and unbelievers alike, but it is not shared between humans and chimpanzees (our closest natural relatives). Why not? The atheist has no real answer to this, and the reasons he might give have a strongly Christian ring to them—we do this out of love for one another, out of the value we attribute to human life, and so on. Christians, of course, agree with these sentiments, but they know why—we think this way because we are created in the image and likeness of God, because we have a mandate from him to govern the world around us, and because we seek his glory in all things.

Certainly, there is an element of self-interest in this, but that is not confined to survival in this world, which Christians know can only be for a time. Rather, it is the hope of eternal life with God in heaven. But Christians will immediately add that life is not something that we can earn. Those who go to heaven are not the deserving, because there are no deserving. Heaven is populated by sinners who have been saved by the grace of God poured out on the cross of Calvary by his incarnate Son, who came to this earth in order to die for our sins and make it possible for us to live in union with him. In this context, self-interest becomes self-denial, a concept that makes no sense to those who do not believe in God and that is completely unknown to other living things.

It is true, of course, that Christians have not deduced the way of salvation from a study of the natural order, nor is such a deduction possible.

"Natural" theology, if it can be called that, is not totally impossible, but it has its limitations. Psalm 19 tells us that "the heavens declare the glory of God" and goes on to explain what this means in astronomical terms. But then the psalmist moves subtly from the order of the heavenly realm to the law of God that speaks to the heart of every human being:

> The law of the LORD is perfect,
> reviving the soul;
> the testimony of the LORD is sure,
> making wise the simple;
> the precepts of the LORD are right,
> rejoicing the heart;
> the commandment of the LORD is pure,
> enlightening the eyes. (Ps 19:7–8)[13]

The "law" here is clearly the moral awareness written on the conscience of every normal human being, but it is also the Law contained in the OT—the two things, while not identical, are closely related. The apostle Paul makes this point in his letter to the Romans, where he praises the law of Moses given to the Jews, but adds that non-Jews (gentiles) also have a law written on their hearts, by which they will be judged. The outward forms are different but the inner content is basically the same (Rom 2:1–16). But Paul goes on to say that the law, holy and righteous though it undoubtedly is, has no power to save anyone. Its purpose is to reveal the nature and seriousness of sin, something that it is very good at, and that is necessary if salvation is to mean anything (see John 16:8–11). The cure must follow the right diagnosis, and that is what the law is for. But while the law can (and does) diagnose the problem, it lacks the mechanism needed to provide the answer. For that, divine intervention is necessary, and divine intervention can only be discerned by revelation. This is because God and his ways are not susceptible to the analysis of human minds, which were not designed for that purpose.

It is noticeable, however, that divine intervention, when it occurred, happened by what a doctor today might call "non-invasive surgery." By

---

13. The capitalization of LORD in the OT tells us that the original Hebrew word is YHWH, the unpronounced name of God.

this is meant that God did not reach down from heaven, point out the problem, and then surgically remove it from the world. Instead of that, he sent his Son to become a man, to live our life, to die a human death, and to rise again from the dead. That was not just a demonstration of his power to do such things but the means by which he paid the price for our deliverance. In Paul's words, the Son became sin for us even though he had no sin in him, and by taking our place before the judgment seat of the Father, pleaded, as he still pleads, for our forgiveness. Forgiveness is not an amputation of something inside us that is diseased but a healing obtained through the restoration of the relationship with God that we were meant to have from the beginning. To the outward eye, there is no sign that we have been operated on, but in the sight of God everything about us has changed forever.

When we look at the wider world, we discover that almost every religion and philosophy ever devised recognizes the basic problems that afflict our common humanity, and that most of them provide some way of dealing with them, ranging from resigned acceptance, to restrictive and coercive legal codes, to alternative pathways to self-improvement. But interesting as these things are, their chief value is that they bear witness to the needs of the world without offering a solution. It is here that Christianity stands out—the diagnosis has been met with a cure. What the men of Athens discussed endlessly was finally resolved on a hillside outside Jerusalem, and it is that solution that forms the basis of Christian faith.

IN THE BEGINNING WAS THE WORD

Students of philosophy today, especially in the English-speaking world, may be surprised to discover how important mathematics and the biological sciences have been in the history of the discipline. Until about 1800, this connection was taken for granted, but sometime in the nineteenth century perceptions of philosophy began to change. The result can be seen in bookstores, where the philosophy section is usually quite small and dominated by historical studies of people like Plato and Aristotle, not Karl Marx and Charles Darwin. Marx might be found under politics, economics, or history, and Darwin under some branch of science or perhaps social studies, but not in philosophy. This does not mean that philosophy has ceased to exist, but that it now tends to be more restricted in its range.

Even theology is now often perceived more narrowly from the way it was in the past. Once again, bookstores are a good indication of this. In most of them, there will be a section for "religion," but the books in it, apart from Bibles, will probably be mostly about church history or works of popular devotion and spirituality. It is unlikely that there will be any systematic theology, which tends to suffer from neglect. There is a certain market for books on creationism, but they are something of an exception and are of variable quality. Most of them are polemics against Darwinian evolution that rely on data culled from different scientific sources rather than philosophical studies. The closest we usually come to that are books written to defend the existence of God against the attacks of atheists like Richard Dawkins, but (with some exceptions) they tend to be responses to particular questions rather than philosophical studies in their own right. During the nineteenth century and later, mainstream philosophy and theology retreated into separate compartments that had little to do with one another, despite their overlapping interests. To the extent that they coincided, it was largely in the context of Kierkegaardian existentialism, though, as we have seen, Kierkegaard was not an existentialist in the later sense of the word.

Existentialism developed a secular dimension that was largely indifferent to religious questions, because for its proponents, like Jean-Paul Sartre, God did not exist. Existentialist theologians could not go that far, but they too were preoccupied with what they saw as the need to confront the world as it is and develop their own approach to it. Somewhat ironically, many of them were inspired by Martin Heidegger, who was not himself a believer in any religion and had little to say about God. His influence on theology was due to his book *Being and Time* (1927), in which he claimed that there is such a thing as Being that lies behind the beings that we perceive in the world. For Heidegger, the uniqueness of humanity lies in the fact that we are aware of our own being and can question it from the standpoint of our existence. We can sense that there is something more than what we see and feel in this life, and that we have the ability to become something other than what we are. In this, Heidegger was opposed to Hegel and was closer to Kierkegaard, though he lacked the latter's faith in God.

Heidegger believed that human beings are troubled by the awareness of their own finitude, and that they have different ways of realizing their existence. They can either choose what they will become because they possess a freedom that he called "authentic existence," or they can go with the flow of society and conform to prevailing norms, which for him was "inauthentic existence." His own career, it must be said, was hardly consistent with his beliefs. When Adolf Hitler came to power in 1933, Heidegger was one of his more enthusiastic supporters, which hardly suggests independence of mind, but that did not seem to matter in the academic world, perhaps because his basic ideas were taken up and developed differently by others.

One of these pseudo-disciples was Paul Tillich (1886–1965), who was more consistent and rational than Heidegger. Tillich identified Being—or as he preferred to call it, the "ground of our being"—with God, though it would appear that his theology, if that is the word for it, was little more than a form of self-examination. His Being was not to be encountered in some kind of supernatural revelation but in the inner depths of our own souls, which are a superficial manifestation of absolute underlying Being. We ought to come to terms with that and live accordingly, but we can choose not to do so, and most people do. Authentic existence, as Tillich understood it, is rare, but that is what Jesus supposedly taught his disciples to pursue and what constitutes "real" Christianity.

Others who followed a similar existentialist approach include the Jewish philosopher-theologian Martin Buber (1878–1965), who claimed that our reality is expressed in dialogue, not in dogmatic statements. This introduced an element of relativity into theology, because dialogue is not the same as submission to authority, but whether that is really appropriate for our relationship with God can be questioned. God does allow his people to speak to him, but he also expects them to obey him. Prayer is not an attempt to change God's mind but to understand him better by opening ourselves up toward a deeper and more demanding obedience. Another existentialist theologian was Gabriel Marcel (1889–1973), who saw faith as a participation in mystery, which he believed lies at the heart of the world. That view would have a profound impact on Eberhard Jüngel (1934–2021), among others, and has had a significant influence on the growth of mystical theology in recent years. Finally, mention should be made of Karl Jaspers (1883–1969), who believed that religion and philosophy promoted myths that, if properly understood, can connect us with nature, as well as with history and our own experience.

Tendencies of these kinds dominated much theological thinking for most of the twentieth century, but they were a long way from the concerns of most secular philosophers. Martin Heidegger was a colleague of Edmund Husserl (1859–1938), but Husserl, who was a generation older than Heidegger, moved in a very different direction. To him, logic and mathematics were rooted in the human mind and were therefore a branch of psychology, about which there was nothing mystical at all. Husserl was deeply influenced by Gottlob Frege (1848–1925), who is often credited with having invented, or at least developed, the theory known as phenomenology. Philosophical discussions of "phenomena" went back to the eighteenth century, but Frege approached the question differently from his predecessors. To him, everything depended on how a phenomenon was perceived. He agreed with his contemporaries that only sense perception was valid, but claimed that our senses start with what Aristotle would have called the "accidents" of a thing. For example, we see a white table as white, in the first instance, and by combining other accidents like size, shape, and so on conclude that the object in front of us is a table. He claimed that science had limited itself to a few criteria that did not include such things as "whiteness," and that this has limited our knowledge of the objects we see around us.

As a result, our minds are in crisis. We are conscious of our surroundings, but all consciousness, according to Frege, is intentional, since otherwise we would not be aware of it. A dog sees what we see but it lacks consciousness and therefore passes by without registering what it has seen. Human beings, on the other hand, start with the intention of seeing something, which Frege called *noēsis,* that resulted in a defined object, which he called *noēma.*[14] This kind of phenomenology led to the conscious development of a school of logical positivism, originally based in Vienna but spreading out from there in conscious opposition to Hegelianism, which dominated Germany. Logical positivism reached the English-speaking world thanks to the writings of Alfred ("Freddie") Jules Ayer (1910–1989), who published his best-selling *Language, Truth and Logic* in 1936.

14. Here Frege was relying on the Greek parallelism between "active" nouns ending in -sis and corresponding "passive" nouns ending in -ma, which runs through the language. Compare *thesis*, the act of making a proposal, with *thema* ("theme"), the result of that act. English, following Latin, does not recognize this distinction but (in this case) would use "proposal" for both the act and the result.

Like phenomenology before it, logical positivism was based exclusively on sense observation that can be verified or falsified by experiment. If a concept could not be judged in that way, it was meaningless. For the logical positivists, this effectively meant that metaphysics does not exist outside the imagination. Antony Flew, one of Ayer's disciples, was therefore able to claim that a phrase like "the love of God" has no meaning because it cannot be proved or disproved. Theologians might claim that God is love, but in the face of suffering and evil they have to qualify that statement to such an extent that it is no longer recognizable. If a loving God can allow people to experience pain and death in the way that he apparently does, how can he be said to be "loving"? It seemed to Flew that the word had been twisted so much that it no longer conveyed anything at all, and therefore a loving God did not exist. Even when he became a theist in old age, Flew never abandoned that conviction—his "God" was the unmoved mover of Aristotle, not the God of the Bible, and he always firmly rejected any suggestion that he had been converted to Christianity.

This kind of reasoning can also be found in the writings of Bertrand Russell (1872–1970), who was greatly influenced by the logical positivists and helped to perpetuate their influence in the English-speaking world long after the presuppositions on which their thinking was based had been discredited by the physical sciences. The man who more than anyone else moved on from logical positivism to something more flexible, and therefore better able to adjust to the changing scientific perception of the world, was Ludwig Wittgenstein (1889–1951), an Austrian who spend most of his adult life in England. Wittgenstein pointed out that there is more to reality than what can be said on the basis of sense perception alone, but he added that what cannot be said is more important in the long run than what can be. He made that claim on the basis of the nature of language, which in his mind has many functions, not all of which can be reduced to descriptions of phenomena.

In Wittgenstein's understanding, words get their meaning from the context in which they are used. Taken in the abstract, "white" cannot become dirty, but a white table can. What we mean by the word "white" therefore depends on the context—if the table is dirty, its "whiteness" will appear differently from what it would be if the table were clean. Religious language must also be understood in this way. To say that God is "love" in the abstract has no meaning, but in the context of a personal relationship with him it does. Here we can sense that Wittgenstein is building a bridge to the existentialism of people like Martin Buber, even though he was apparently unaware of it. What Wittgenstein was doing, whether he knew it or not, was opening the door to hermeneutics, the science of interpretation, which ultimately depends on language and on the context in which language is used.

Interest in hermeneutics can be traced back at least as far as Wilhelm Dilthey (1833–1911), who distinguished natural science from what he called "human" science. Human science was the lived experience of every human being as worked out in and through history. The mistake of the logical positivists was to apply the techniques of natural science to the human variety, which does not work, because human beings are more than what can be understood entirely by sense perception. Language is a uniquely human trait, and cannot easily be regarded as an offshoot of biology, but it is obviously of central importance. Without language, a book like this could not be written, nor would life as we know it be possible. But where does language come from, and how important is it for our understanding of reality?

Students of language have to start with the languages that actually exist. Many of these can be traced back to a common ancestor, though some of them, like Basque, have no known relatives. It is possible that the human race originally spoke a common language, which then diversified—that is the story of the tower of Babel in Genesis 11—but if so, that happened long before written records existed and we are not able to retrace the history that far back. In a few cases, we can follow a particular language's development for about three thousand years, but that is as far back as we can go. Yet even in that relatively short space of time we can observe a process of evolution that is infinitely faster than anything comparable in the plant or animal world. In the well-documented case of Latin, for example, we know that it evolved into the modern Romance languages in historical time, though even there the precise steps are not always recoverable.[15] What we can say, though, is that the modern Romance languages

15. The most important Romance languages are Catalan, French, Italian, Portuguese, Romanian, and Spanish.

are more like each other than any of them is like Latin, which we could not reconstruct if it did not already exist. In other words, linguistic evolution in this documented case has followed a pattern, even if it has not been uniform and could not have been predicted in advance.

As with biological evolution, its linguistic equivalent retains anomalies that cannot be logically explained. An obvious example of this is the preservation of the ending "(e)s" in the third person of the present tense of English verbs. Nobody ever says "he love" or "she give," although there is no logical reason why that should be so. The presence of the ending adds nothing to the meaning and its absence would make no difference, but its use remains universal and grammatically compulsory. The only explanation for it is that it is the residual survival of an older ending in -eth (e.g., "he loveth," "she giveth"), which has been eliminated as a separate syllable, but that does not help us much, because that extra syllable is not necessary, either.

All this does is support a generally observed phenomenon that most languages simplify their structures as they develop, usually becoming more analytical and less synthetic. Latin, for example, had noun and verb endings that made it possible to say *caput hominis* (synthetic), whereas Spanish has "simplified" this to *la cabeza del hombre* (analytic). In this case, English has retained both possibilities—"the man's head" and "the head of the man"—but generally speaking it is more like Spanish than it is like Latin. When new verbs are created in English, they all take the same form, with the past tense ending in "-(e)d"—thus, "telephoned," "xeroxed," "emailed," etc.[16] It is generally assumed that these "weak" forms are the wave of the future, whereas the corresponding "strong" forms, where the past tense is indicated by internal vowel change, are now fossilized and uncreative. But if you read the King James Bible, you will discover words like "digged" and "kneeled," which were once used as past forms of the verbs "dig" and "kneel." Today, everybody says "dug" and almost everyone uses "knelt" instead of 'kneeled," a development that appears to be counterintuitive. What is more, this process is still going on. "Speeded" has now generally given way to "sped," and many people say "pled" instead

16. This is also true of the Romance languages and even of Latin, where newly created verbs end in -are (*baptizare*) or their Romance equivalents (-ar, -er, etc.).

of "pleaded." Even "snuck" seems to be driving out "sneaked," although educated speakers tend not to go that far—yet. Nevertheless, the trend is clear—linguistic evolution, even within the parameters of a single language, is ongoing and not always straightforward.

When it comes to expressing meaning, it is the English habit to put adjectives before nouns, making it necessary to wait for the full phrase to be stated before we know what is intended. For example, I could say "the clear blue [something]," but unless or until I added a word like "sky" or "sea" nobody would know what I was talking about. We might even say that this procedure, which is common to most European languages, accords well with phenomenology, where the accidents are logically prior to the substance.

In the Romance languages, however, the noun being qualified usually comes first. In French, I would have to say either *la mer claire et bleue* if I was speaking about the sea, or *le ciel clair et bleu* if I meant the sky. Speakers of Romance languages can make a good case for saying that they are more logical than English is, but that does not mean that we can simply manipulate our grammar to fall into line with their logic. We do occasionally do this, as in words like "governor-general" or "attorney-general," but this is because such terms have been borrowed from French, and the "general" has almost lost its original meaning. Certainly nobody would think that an attorney-general was no more than a general attorney! It is a mystery to Romance speakers, but somehow English (and most other European languages) manages this kind of mental suspense without noticeable difficulty.

There is a further complication about most other European languages that often puzzles English-speakers. In spoken French, the adjectives sound the same (at least in this case), but in the written form they reflect a difference of gender—*mer* is feminine and *ciel* is masculine. To complicate matters still further, in the parent language (Latin) both *mare* and *caelum* are neuter! The modern Romance languages have dropped the neuter, which means that those words have been reallocated, though it is by no means clear why one should have become feminine and the other masculine.[17]

17. In most of the other Romance languages, the word for "sea" is masculine, but Spanish *mar* can be either masculine or feminine!

English has dispensed with grammatical gender altogether, except when it is related to biological sex. That has led to confusion, in that "gender" is now often (and mistakenly) used to mean "sex," as in terms like "gender identity," a concept that is difficult to express in most other European languages. For example, the Latin word *persona* is feminine, but nobody has ever suggested that a person is exclusively female. Indeed, so elastic is the concept of gender that in some cases a feminine form can be used as if it were masculine. This happens in French when *personne* is used to mean "nobody" rather than "person," as in a phrase like *personne n'est présent ce matin* ("nobody is present this morning"). To use the feminine form *présente* might appear to an English speaker to be more logical, given that *personne* is technically feminine, but it would be a mistake. In this case, transgenderism is not just a possibility—it is obligatory!

From what has been said so far, it will be apparent that individual languages have a certain structure to them, but none is fully logical. They all contain anomalies that may be due to redundancy, as in the case of the final "-(e)s" in English verbs, or to grammatical gender unrelated to sex. This may not seem to matter very much, but in fact it does, because language is the only means we have of communicating our thoughts. If we expect our thoughts to be entirely rational when the language in which we express them is not, there is a problem, which is further aggravated when we try to translate from one language to another. If a particular thought that is pure and logical in itself is inevitably distorted in some way by the language in which it is expressed, would translation into another language not simply increase the risk of distortion and take us even further away from the original thought?

How meaningful is talk about God, even if it purports to be a revelation from him? Can human language, governed by rules that have been shaped by our time-and-space environment, speak about someone who is not confined by those limitations? In the twentieth century, this question acquired a new urgency as some linguistic theorists claimed that the human brain is structured in such a way that all languages follow a certain pattern. There can be no doubt that all human beings perceive the same phenomena—an American who sees a tree and an Indonesian who sees the same tree are seeing the same thing. The claim of linguistic structuralism is that, although they might speak different languages, their thought processes are governed by the same principles and they will express their observation according to a preset pattern.

Discoveries in the realm of DNA and the human genome have called this theory into question because there is no evidence that a particular thought pattern is hardwired into our genetic makeup. If our genes are shared with all living things, then we might ask why it is that only human beings have language—would this ability to reason and to speak not have to come from somewhere else? Further investigation of the world's many languages has merely confirmed this observation. It may be true to say that European languages exhibit similar characteristics, but this is mostly due to a common culture going back centuries. If they derived from the structure of the brain, those characteristics would presumably be replicated everywhere but, as translators have discovered, they often are not.

This is the basic dilemma faced by philosophers of language, and it is of great importance for those who base their beliefs on written texts they claim have been inspired by God. To what extent do those texts reflect what God actually said, and if we read them in translation (as most of us do) is it even more difficult to hear him speaking to us? Furthermore, do the texts distort the message only because they are finite representations of an infinite mind, or is there something more sinister at work—has the message been tampered with by people who have used language as a means of conveying their own ideas in the guise of simply recording what God has said? This is essentially what the discipline of hermeneutics is about, and it has become the main battleground between philosophy and theology today. Compared with this, arguments over Darwinism or Marxism are fairly trivial because they are debates about the merits of various theories, whereas hermeneutics goes deeper and questions the meaning of anything and everything that we say.

In premodern times, the problem of language was often approached in a pseudo-historical way. People believed that humanity originally spoke a single tongue, and Christians (in particular) were inclined to believe that it was Hebrew. Indeed, some even suggested that Hebrew was God's language, the one that the persons of the Trinity used to converse with each other.[18] But those who suggested that never bothered to learn Hebrew

18. The risen Christ spoke to the apostle Paul in "Hebrew" (i.e., Aramaic). See Acts 26:14.

themselves. The ancient Jews evidently did not think like that, because long before the coming of Christ they were already translating their sacred texts into Greek.[19] The task was made somewhat easier because Hebrew is a relatively straightforward language, with few irregularities and very little abstract technical vocabulary. Both it and Greek used particular words in many different senses, and so the translators did not have to choose which one to prefer. A good example is the Hebrew word *basar*, which the Greeks translated as *sarx*. In English, this word is usually rendered as "flesh," but *basar/sarx* has levels of meaning that "flesh" does not normally have. They can both refer to the meat on our bodies, to our material humanity in general, to the entire human being, and even to the sinful state into which we have fallen.

All of these meanings are now possible in English because of a long tradition of translation that has allowed them to enter our language, but understanding them properly is often difficult. For instance, we can speak of "the sins of the flesh" and think we know what we mean ("the actions of a person who is cut off from God"), but this is not necessarily clear to everyone. There is a long and unhappy tradition that interprets this phrase to mean that our bodies are somehow evil and must be subdued by rigorous asceticism. Can we maintain this linguistic tradition, in spite of the misunderstandings to which it might lead, or should we try to repackage the message we are trying to convey in language that is more meaningful today and that avoids such errors as much as possible?

Let us take another example. The apostle Paul spoke of his hope that his "bowels would be refreshed" by Philemon (Phlm 1:7, 12). What did he mean? Most commentators concur that what Paul was hoping for is that he would be encouraged and made happy by Philemon if the latter would take back the runaway slave Onesimus, but the phrase sounds odd and we would not use it today. Obviously, we cannot translate it literally as something like "my constipation will be relieved," but is it faithful to the text to abandon the metaphor altogether and just say something like "I will be very happy if ..."? That may well be what Paul meant and what we would normally say now, but it misses the psychosomatic element

19. Contrast this with the Muslim approach to the Qur'an, which they believe was revealed to Muhammad in Arabic and cannot be authentically translated into any other language.

present in the original. We do occasionally speak psychosomatically in English, as when we talk about our "gut feelings," for example, but that does not fit the context here. So what do we do? Opinions are divided between those who prefer to stick as closely as possible to the original wording, even if the meaning is obscure, and those who insist that what we need is "dynamic equivalence," that is to say, a modern phrase that says what was originally intended, even if it does so in totally different words. There is no easy answer to this question, but the option we prefer is very likely to reflect how we think about language in the first place. Should we discipline ourselves to submit to the mindset of the original text, or do we have the freedom to express the thought that lies behind that text in a way that suits us better now, even if it means losing something of the flavor of the original? If words reflect a thought world that lies behind them, as most modern linguistic philosophers claim, can that thought world be discarded without altering what the words drawn from it were originally meant to convey? In other words, what is communication, and what is it that we are trying to communicate?

Edmund Husserl came up with the idea that voices from the past, transmitted to us almost exclusively in literary texts, operated within a horizon of their own, which both their authors and their audiences shared. Thus, for example, people in ancient times had no trouble believing that there were supernatural beings, like angels or demons, who interacted with humans on a fairly regular basis and could be regarded, as they are in the Bible, as intermediaries between God and humanity. Supernatural interventions were accepted as a matter of course, especially in cases of unexpected healings or victories in battle. What really happened on those occasions is now unknowable, but modern man cannot accept the records of those events at their face value. This is not because there is evidence to disprove them, though perhaps there is in some cases, but because our horizon today is different. We no longer believe in supernatural interventions, or in the existence of angels (or demons), so an alternative narrative has to be found.

Rudolf Bultmann (1884–1976) called this "demythologization" and claimed that it was essential if the word of God is to be heard today. The process involves a transposition of ideas from one frame of reference to another, and so the question arises as to how far this is really possible.

Bultmann himself doubted whether demythologization was enough, because the only thing left would be a moral framework that had no room for God, which is essentially what many philosophers had ended up with. As a theologian, he recognized that there was a need for what he called "remythologization"; in other words, the principles of an earlier age had to be restated by inventing new stories, or new myths, to replace the old.

An example of what that might mean can be seen from the identification of the crucifixion of Christ with the sacrifice of the Passover lamb. That imagery was taken over from the OT, but it is no longer readily understood. Animal sacrifices are now regarded as semi-barbaric and totally unsuited to the moral climate of our times. The idea that God would want the blood of bulls and goats to appease his wrath is far too primitive to be acceptable today.[20] To some extent that was also true in NT times, and it can be argued that by transferring the language of such sacrifices to the death of Jesus, the way was clear for getting rid of the sacrifices themselves, which the Christian church promptly did. But now the sacrifice of Christ cannot meaningfully be explained in terms of OT law, because our horizon has changed. We have to see the death of Christ, not as the fulfilment of a divine command enshrined in the law of Moses, but as a loving response to the plight of humanity today. Jesus's self-sacrifice thus becomes a model for our self-sacrifice; we are meant to give ourselves for the life of the world just as he did. To a Christian this sounds blasphemous, because it suggests that we are setting up ourselves in the place of God. But to anyone who thinks our image of God is basically self-projection anyway, following in the steps of Jesus is a logical and responsible thing for us to do. We can forget about the traditional picture of heaven (above the earth) and hell (below it)—these are somewhat simplistic attempts to portray a reality that we can only experience on earth.

From the standpoint of traditional Christianity, demythologization, or the two horizons, involves a massive reinterpretation of the meaning of words and language—it is (as it has been called) a "new hermeneutic." How valid is it? Here we have come to the nub of the matter. If God exists, then the only way he can communicate with us is by self-revelation, and that self-revelation will have to be adapted to our capacity

20. In fact, this was understood by the ancient Israelites as well. See, for example, Ps 50:7–15.

for understanding it. That will inevitably involve some kind of "distortion" because our finite minds cannot fully grasp the infinite. Christian theologians have said this, one way or another, for a very long time. Our knowledge of God, such as it is, proceeds by way of *analogy*. That is to say, when we call him "Father" we are using a relational term familiar to us that gives us a picture of how we relate to him without being an exhaustive description of him, or even a particularly accurate one in objective terms. God is our "Father" because he has created us, because he preserves us in being, and because he invites us to share in a relationship with him that is modeled by his Son, Jesus Christ. It does not mean that we share the same material substance or that we are organically connected to him in some way.

The history of Christian theology can be written in terms of becoming more precise in our definition of what words like "Father" mean in relation to God, but that presupposes that we are dealing with an objectively existing being, not with something we have conjured up in our imaginations. We sense when somebody says something about God that is either not true or is misleading, and we try to correct it, but we do so on the basis that we know what has gone wrong, and why. This process has been going on for a long time and has been more or less continuous since the beginning of Christianity, which raises questions for the concept of two "horizons." As stated by philosophers like Husserl and those who have followed and developed his thought, like Hans Georg Gadamer (1900–2002), Ernst Fuchs (1903–1983), and Gerhard Ebeling (1912–2001), all of whom have been influential theologians, the impression is given that there has been a rupture between one horizon (the ancient biblical one) and the other (the modern one). But when and how did this rupture take place?

The usual answer to this question is that it happened during the Enlightenment, which occurred a generation either side of 1700. Everything before that time is lumped together as "premodern," and everything since is thought to be in immediate continuity with the thought patterns that are dominant today. There is no doubt that the Enlightenment did bring about many changes in Western thought, but whether it was as dramatic a shift as has been made out is open to question. Similarly, it is by no means clear that all premodern thought can be classified together, as if Homer and John Milton (both of whom wrote epic poetry) had more in common with each other than either of them has with us. The boundaries of the horizons are far from clear and may be contested from many points of view, including the Christian one.

For Christians, the great break with the past did not occur around 1700 but much earlier. It was Jesus whose teaching and life broke the mold of what had gone before and ushered in a new era, which the NT calls "the last days" (Heb 1:1). This meant that the OT laws and rituals were either swept aside or so drastically reinterpreted that they led to the founding of a new religion. Christians were always something other than sectarian Jews, and if it took some time before the synagogue and the church were clearly separated, the direction of travel was present from the beginning. Put simply, Christianity differed from Judaism in that it was primarily internal, not external, and universal, not confined to a single nation. The struggle over the internal/external relationship can be seen in the NT, where Jesus and his followers rejected the purity laws of Moses and put inner spiritual conviction in their place (Matt 15:19). This dimension was by no means absent from the OT but it coexisted with external practices that could not be put to one side. The circumcision of the heart was important, but it did not displace the circumcision of the flesh, which remained compulsory (Deut 10:16). The NT broke with that duality and at the same time extended the meaning of the "circumcision of the heart" to both women and gentiles.

This change did not affect the way in which people viewed angels, heaven, or hell, so in that sense it can be said that a premodern horizon continued to exist unimpaired, but to focus on that is to misunderstand the nature of biblical religion. Most of the OT, and in particular the law of Moses (Torah), is not concerned with such matters at all. The law is very much a manual of instruction for this life that governed everyday activities. Nothing much is said about going to heaven (or hell) after death, and when it is compared with surrounding pagan religions, it can be claimed that the Israelites practiced their own form of "demythologization." God was not to be found in rocks, rivers, and trees; indeed, idolatry was the worst of all sins because it denied the majesty and distinctiveness of the Creator. In that respect, the ancient Israelites were far more modern than their pagan contemporaries were, including the ancient Greek philosophers. Yet modern critics who reject the Bible because of its supposedly premodern worldview seem to have no trouble with Plato or Aristotle, who if anything were less enlightened in this respect than the OT writers were.

This matters, because while nobody today would use Plato's *Republic* or Aristotle's *Nicomachean Ethics* as a detailed guide to everyday life, Jews and Christians both treat the Bible in that way. Even for Christians, the OT remains the word of God. It must be interpreted in the light of Christ, to be sure, but it cannot be discarded as no longer relevant. The NT, of course, can be taken as read, because it assumes that Christ has come and speaks to the world accordingly. A case can perhaps be made for saying that the NT is more spiritual than the OT, in the sense that it is more exclusively concerned with the quality of a believer's understanding of nonmaterial things than the OT is, but it is hardly a book of mythology. In its own way, the NT is just as worldly as the OT is, putting equal (if not more) emphasis on the way we live our lives here below and seeing the consummation of all things as the resurrection of the body and the appearance of a new creation. The old (current) body and creation will not be so much destroyed as transformed into something better, but no less material for all that.

Can this self-revelation of God be taken at face value and applied in our lives today? Those who have adopted the principles of the "new hermeneutic" say that it cannot, because the worldview undergirding it is no longer accepted as valid. Traditional Christians say that it can, because there is no new hermeneutic—the words of the Bible are plain and meaningful as they stand. Admittedly, there are times when certain practices commended in the NT can be dispensed with for cultural reasons, but the principles underlying them cannot. The classic case of this is the command given to women to cover their heads while praying, "for the sake of the angels" (1 Cor 11:10). This would appear to be a prime example of the premodern worldview that is now rejected. Perhaps it is, in a way, but if so, that has little or nothing to do with reason or the Enlightenment. Women were told to cover their hair as a way of honoring God by not exposing themselves to the sexual desires of men. Today, relatively few men (at least in the Western world) pay much attention to a woman's hair, but they may well be attracted to other parts of her body, and the same principle of modesty applies. In other words, it is the spirit of the law that counts, not the letter, and in that respect Paul's directions to the Corinthians are in full agreement with the basic teaching of the NT.

An example like this one is relatively trivial, but the implications of the "new hermeneutic" can be much more serious than that. In some cases, it can lead to an interpretation of the biblical text that inverts its original meaning and practically cancels it out. This can be seen most clearly in the way that a phrase like "God is love" is now often understood. In the Bible, God's love is very demanding, both of him and of us. It involves sacrifice—God so loved the world that he gave his only-begotten Son in order to die for us (John 3:16). It involves obedience—the friends of Jesus are those who obey him, an odd definition of friendship in any other context (John 15:14). It can involve correction and punishment—the Lord chastens those whom he loves, in order to make them more acceptable to him (Prov 3:12; Heb 12:6). Today, however, many people reject such interpretations as being unkind and judgmental. For them, the love of God means accepting other people as they are and not telling them that they need to change their lives. This is especially true in the realm of sexuality—anything goes, including homosexual behavior, and it is those who criticize this who are branded as unloving. Curiously though, this definition of "love" appears to be of somewhat restricted application. A doctor who tells his patient that he will refuse treatment if the patient does not stop smoking is not considered to be unloving, nor is a policeman who insists that a driver wear a seatbelt. In those cases, telling other people what to do is not only acceptable but expected, and is regarded as a clear act of love.

Only when it comes to God does it seem that his commands can be ignored or reinterpreted to suit the desires of whoever is doing the reinterpreting. From a traditionalist point of view, this might be seen as a new kind of Pharisaism, tailoring the law to make it fit what people want. But it is really more like a new Gnosticism, in which a spiritual fantasy is applied to material reality, leading in the end to a justification for immoral behavior of all kinds. Augustine of Hippo saw this centuries ago in the practice of the Manichees, who claimed to be a spiritual elite but who lived lives of great moral depravity. The purveyors of sexual freedom are the Manichees of our time, claiming to transcend the material world spiritually but in fact degrading themselves and their bodies by using them for purposes for which they were never intended. That such people can claim to be following the precepts of the Bible shows just how far the "new hermeneutic" can be used to pervert God's revelation of himself. Once again, a philosophy has been used to corrupt theology, and people are as deceived by that now as they were when they fell for Neoplatonism centuries ago.

So far, we have been considering revelation only with respect to the Jewish and Christian Bible, which make the claim to be God's word and have been accepted as such throughout the history of the Western tradition. But there are many claims to divine revelation, and Christians have to justify their belief that the Bible's credentials are superior to those of others. Verification of the Bible's claims is not possible in the strict sense, but there are good reasons why they can and should be taken seriously.

We must start with what the Bible says about itself, because if the Bible does not claim to be a revelation from God then there is no point in trying to turn it into one. Here the evidence is plentiful. "Thus says the Lord" is a frequent refrain in the text and must be our point of departure. Did God say that or not? Jesus certainly thought he did, and did not hesitate to quote the text accordingly (Matt 4:4, 7, 10; 5:17–19). The same is true of the NT writers (2 Tim 3:16; 2 Pet 1:21). The NT does not make the same claims about itself, but the apostle Paul was confident that he had the mind of God when he was writing to the churches and they appear to have agreed (1 Cor 7:40).

The second point is that the books of the Bible were received in the churches and taught as God's word to them from the beginning. That does not prove that their claim to be divine revelation is correct, but the fact that it was made spontaneously and more or less independently across the Christian world for many centuries before any final decision about them was made by the church suggests that there is more to this claim than mere tradition or wishful thinking. In reading them, the early Christians heard the voice of God speaking, and this hearing continued over time. Equally significantly, the large amount of literature produced by Christians of later generations was never regarded as divine self-revelation, even if it was sometimes claimed that the writers were inspired by God. There was always a clear distinction made between the Bible and the secondary literature, and that distinction goes back almost to NT times.

The third consideration to bear in mind is that the biblical texts have been examined for their historical and cultural accuracy far more than any comparable works, ancient or modern, and that they have passed every test. It is true that there are some things in the Bible that cannot be verified by independent research—the careers of David and Solomon being outstanding examples—but nothing has ever emerged that would *disprove* the biblical accounts. The fact that no extrabiblical record of Solomon has survived does not mean that Solomon never existed or that the biblical stories about him are false. All it tells us is that so far archeologists have not found anything that would corroborate what the Bible says. This is not a big problem, however, because archeological evidence does exist for many other things, many of them far more obscure, and nothing has ever turned up that would contradict the biblical account. One day material evidence of Solomon's existence may be found, and the case for believing the Bible will be strengthened all the more.

Finally, the Bible's ability to convert people to its message has been demonstrated time and again. Countless individuals have picked it up and been convicted by reading it, while tribes who have no connection to Israel have heard it and believed. Their lives have been transformed by it, despite the vast differences of time and space that separate them from the horizon of the original human writers, of whom they know virtually nothing. This has happened so often and in so many different circumstances that it is hard to believe it is merely coincidental. As with the points made above, none of this proves that the Bible is the word of God, but that it has an extraordinary power to transform people's lives for the better is undisputed. It is certainly not a book just like any other book, and divine revelation, while not proved beyond any possible doubt, is at least one plausible explanation for this.

When compared with other books that are said to be divinely inspired, the Bible comes out quite well. The Qur'an and the Book of Mormon both claim to be revelations from God, but they are very unlike the Bible in some crucially important ways. First of all, both of them are supposed to have been revealed to a single prophet (Muhammad and Joseph Smith, respectively) and in precisely the form that they have been transmitted to us. God spoke Arabic to Muhammad and Tudor English to Joseph Smith, which makes translation of their writings strictly impossible, though attempts must be made for the benefit of those who profess the religion but who cannot comprehend the language in which the revelation was given. It is obvious that in these circumstances, the scope for deception is high. Who is to say that Muhammad and Joseph Smith were not deluded, or did not consciously make up what they have written?

For Christians, the question is further complicated by the fact that we regard non-Christian claims to revelation in much the same way as secularists regard ours—as wishful thinking at best and outright deception at worst. We may object to secular critics of *our* sacred texts, but at least we can easily understand where they are coming from because we share their skepticism with respect to texts that we do not regard as having been truly given by God.

To a Christian observer, the Qur'an makes no logical sense. It is arranged in 114 *surahs*, or "chapters," according to length, with the longest one coming first and the shortest one last. That is a handy arrangement, to be sure, but it is completely unrelated to the content of the messages, which the prophet supposedly received at different times, and not in that order. The texts contain specific references to historical figures, including some found in the Bible, but what they say about them is sometimes demonstrably false. For example, Jesus is said not to have been crucified, and many Muslim commentators have inferred from this that it was Judas who was put to death in his place.[21] Muslims resist the kind of critical scrutiny of the Qur'an that has been applied to the Bible, and understandably so, because it would be unlikely to survive serious scientific investigation. As for the Book of Mormon, it is pure fantasy, couched in the language of the OT to be sure, but with no historical foundation whatsoever. How can such things be regarded as a revelation from God?

Christians are much less rigid than either Muslims or Mormons are in their understanding of the Bible. The biblical revelation was given to many different people, many of whom are anonymous, spread over time and over different languages. Translation is not only possible, it is present in the original records themselves, since most of the Gospels (for example) are translations of what Jesus really said. Many Christians believe

21. *Qur'an* 4.157.

that the Bible is verbally infallible and inerrant, but this does not mean the same thing to them as it means to Muslims or Mormons. What is infallible and inerrant is the message that the words convey, and it is for that reason that the words must not be tampered with.

There is also a certain open-endedness about the biblical revelation that is absent from its competitors. Christians generally agree about the canon of the NT, but there are serious differences about the OT, where there are disputes about whether certain books, now extant only in Greek and not in Hebrew, are part of God's self-revelation. Uncertainty on this point has produced a variety of responses ranging from full acceptance of them to complete rejection. Today there is something of a consensus, which says that they are an important witness to the period between the two testaments but that they should not be used to establish points of doctrine, a compromise that leaves their status as revelation unclear.

TIME AND ETERNITY

Language can be complicated is in its relationship to time, and although linguists are well aware of that, most theologians and philosophers have not fully grasped the implications of this for their disciplines. We think that English verbs are rooted in time, but this is mistaken. English verbs have only two simple forms, like "come" and "came," which are generally understood to refer to present and past, respectively. All other tenses of the verb are expressed by using compounds—"have come," "will come," etc. Why is this so? It is because the simple English forms are not really tenses, even though we think they are. In fact, they are "aspects," which are determined by whether what they describe is a completed action. Generally speaking, a completed action will be "past" and an uncompleted action will be ongoing (present) or future, but that is not always the case.[22] Consider the following:

If I come tomorrow, will you be at home?

If I came tomorrow, would you be at home?

22. Linguists call these aspects "perfect(ive)" and "imperfect(ive)," but as these terms are often used for different kinds of "past" they are avoided here.

Both of these sentences are correct in English and have essentially the same meaning, though the second one suggests a more remote possibility than the first. But look at the way "come" and "came" are used. Both refer to the future in real time, but neither is "future" in form, and in fact it would be wrong to say "If I shall/will come tomorrow." In the first case, the action of coming is left open—it might or it might not happen. In the second case, the action of coming is logically assumed to have already occurred (though in fact it has not), which is why the "past" form is used. The difference is not one of time but of aspect, the second one being more precise, though seemingly less probable, than the first. This difference of usage is residual in English, but it remains common in the Slavic languages, in Greek, and above all in Hebrew, which gives it a particular relevance for theology. The name of God, written without vowels in Hebrew as YHWH, is said to be derived from the Hebrew verb "to be" and is usually translated as "he who is," or (if God himself is speaking) as "I am."

Occasionally, some translators will try to capture the force of the incomplete (imperfective) aspect in Hebrew by translating it as "I shall/will be" or even as "I am becoming," but such forms sound artificial and have not caught on. They are also theologically incorrect, as we can see from the NT, where the verb form is rendered by the Greek present tense, something that is lacking in Hebrew, or occasionally by the present participle, which is closer to Hebrew usage.[23] One text that is of particular interest is Revelation 1:8, where the glorified Christ is described as "the one who is (*ho ōn*), and who was (*ho ēn*), and who is to come (*ho erchomenos*)." The order is significant, in that the present comes first, followed by the past and what purports to be the "future." Given the usual structure of ancient triadic formulas, it is the first of the three that governs the other two—in other words, the present defines both the past and the future.[24]

Modern theologians appear to have overlooked the significance of this, but it indicates to us that it is possible to speak about God beyond the confines of time and space, because our language itself transcends those

23. In modern Hebrew, the participle is the basis for the construction of the present tense.

24. This pattern is also found in the Trinity, where the Father defines both the Son and the Holy Spirit, in the sense that the Son is begotten of the Father and the Spirit proceeds from him.

categories.[25] It is obvious that John's use of the present tense is meant to convey a sense of the eternal, but it is not always appreciated just how appropriate that is. One of the main criticisms of theology is that human language is bound by the finitude of time and space and is therefore incapable of expressing anything that lies beyond that, as God is supposed to do. Some theologians, like those who developed process theology, have tried to resolve this problem by conceiving of God within a time-and-space framework, but that denies the fundamental outlook that governs the biblical revelation. Others resort to the category of "mystery" and claim that it is impossible to speak about God at all. The most we can do is to recognize out limitations and accept that silence in the presence of the divine is the only viable option. That leads to various forms of mystical theology that have enjoyed considerable popularity in recent years, but are inevitably a reaction against the Western theological tradition and inimical to any suggestion that theology and philosophy might be able to connect with each other.

There is, however, a third way, one in which it can be shown that human language is capable of expressing things that go beyond the limitations of time and space and is therefore capable of grasping truth about God, even if that truth can never be exhaustive. In our everyday speech, the default position is the present: "I am." We take this everywhere we go, and it is our conscious response to everything we experience. We move through time, of course, but our sense of the present never leaves us. The remarkable thing about this is that the "present" does not exist in time—it is a supratemporal category by which we define the past and the future. We cannot live in the past, even if we know that we have experienced it to some extent, and if we try to do so (as many people do) the result is incongruous. John had to invent a non-grammatical form to express it, which gives us a picture of how awkward it can be.

Whether we like it or not, we always subordinate the past to the present, and cannot do otherwise. Our perception of it is partial and filtered according to what we remember or choose to remember. Very often this leads to a distortion of one kind or another. When we are bereaved, our

25. The Eastern Orthodox iconic tradition does not do that, however. Icons of Jesus invariably have the words *ho ōn* ("the being" or "he who is") inscribed around his face.

memory tends to forget the bad or difficult times that we had with the person who has died and retains only (or mainly) what was positive and good. Occasionally, our memory goes the other way and exaggerates the bad, but this only happens in order to justify our present attitude toward whoever or whatever it is that we are condemning. A balanced picture is very hard to achieve, and probably only possible (to the extent that it is) if we are distant from the events we remember and do not care about them one way or the other. Past experience can certainly help us when it comes to making decisions that will affect our future, but it has to be examined and used with care because it belongs to a reality that has passed away and cannot be recovered.

When we look toward the future, we are inevitably forced into conjecture. Our predictions of what can happen may be soundly based and probable, but they can never be certain. The plans we make are always subject to change from factors that we are unaware of and can do nothing to control. We must be ready for anything but accept that what will happen will be only one of many possibilities, and possibly not one that we have considered. This is why languages are always fairly vague when speaking about the future. In English we have two traditional ways of expressing it, and these two ways, which were originally distinct, have now fallen together in practice because it is impossible to be definite about what has not yet taken place. This means that "I shall come" and "I will come" are synonymous, though "shall" and "will" did not originally mean the same thing. The difference can still be heard in the subjunctive forms "should" and "would." "I should come" implies that I am subject to some obligation, and means "I ought to come," but "I would come" expresses only desire without any external constraint. We can also express future intention by saying things like "I am going to come," but whether this counts as a future tense or not is hard to say.[26]

John uses the present participle *erchomenos* ("coming") for the future, which is significant, because the ancient Greek verb *einai* ("to be") possessed a future form he could have used instead. He did not do so, perhaps

26. The Romance languages have generally replaced the Latin future by adding the verb "to have" to the infinitive, but this is concealed to some extent by the fact that the forms of "to have" have been attached to the verb, creating the appearance of a separate tense, even though it is not.

because that form suggests that what it refers to has not yet begun, which is not true of the Son of God. Jesus is on the way, in John's vision, but he is already in being and his coming will involve no change in his relationship to us, nor will it signify any development in the Godhead. Like future time, his coming is open-ended from our point of view and impossible to predict (Matt 24:36). To him, of course, it is eternally present, an integral part of his reality.

When we speak of God as he is in himself, we do not do so in time-bound categories but in the present, which is our window into eternity. This is why we can say that our relationship with him never changes despite the ups and downs of time-and-space existence. There was a time when we did not know him, but there was never a time when he did not know us. The apostle Paul makes this clear in his epistle to the Galatians. He first refers to his "former life" when he persecuted the church, but then goes on to speak about God "who had set me apart before I was born and who had called me by his grace" (Gal 1:15). Paul's experience of God is one that is common to all Christians. Before we came to know him personally, we had no idea about his purposes, even if we held some kind of belief in his existence. But when we met him and received his transforming grace in our lives, then everything became clear and we realized, as Paul did, that his hand was on us even before we were born, because in his eyes we are part and parcel of his eternal reality.

One day we shall be set free from the bonds of time and space and shall know the fullness of that reality ourselves, but even now we experience its "firstfruits," as the Bible calls them, in our lives (Rom 8:22–39). These firstfruits of the Spirit guide us in our earthly pilgrimage, and at the same time they open up for us a world of which we have no direct knowledge—the kingdom of God. When we pray, we do so "with angels and archangels and with all the company of heaven," as the Book of Common Prayer so eloquently expresses it. These are not mythological creatures devised by our imaginations but companions on our journey who are guiding and protecting us as we move toward our destination. Christians do not claim to have the answer to every problem, but we know the One who does and are confident that one day he will reveal the mysteries of our life to us. Neither the philosopher nor the theologian has attained this goal, but the Christian knows what to expect and interprets what happens along the way in the light of the glory that in God's good time will be revealed.

In light of all this, what shall we say of Athens and Jerusalem? Athens has a glorious past that continues to inspire people today. Seen from afar it is magnificent, but the closer we get to it the more we see that it is in ruins, its achievements memorialized in museums and marketed to tourists. In the present it is much like anywhere else, and its future is unlikely to be very distinguished, even if it continues to survive and prosper in its own way. Jerusalem also has a past, but so contested has it been that little of it can still be seen. We know where its temple was, but we cannot see it today. All that is left is the outer wall of a building that, although ancient, was not the original. Other faiths, other traditions have come in, giving it a life of its own but at the same time obscuring the foundations on which it was built. This Jerusalem is also marketed to tourists, but most of these are worshipers in a way that visitors to Athens are not.

From the Christian point of view, neither Athens nor the earthly Jerusalem is of eternal consequence. We are forced to choose, to be sure, and our choice will inevitably fall on Jerusalem, but it is not the city that we see here on earth. As the Bible puts it: "I saw the holy city, new Jerusalem, coming down out of heaven from God, prepared as a bride adorned for her husband. And I heard a loud voice from the throne saying, 'Behold, the dwelling place of God is with man. He will dwell with them, and they will be his people, and God himself will be with them as their God'" (Rev 21:2–3).

This is our future, the final revelation and realization of the promises of God given to his people in ancient times, preserved through centuries of turmoil and suffering, and finally consummated in the great wedding feast of the Lamb and his bride.

SUMMARY

1. Modern philosophy has developed into a number of different schools of thought that often have little to do with one another. For example, few people today think of the history of science as part of philosophy, despite the fact that before 1800 the two things were intimately connected.

2. Modern science has been deeply affected by studies of the speed of light and its nature. For the first time, atomic theories of matter came into their own and finally overturned the philosophical tradition that traced its origins back to Aristotle. The notion that the universe was basically static gave way to the belief that it was in perpetual motion, and several theories of its origins were proposed, of which the Big Bang theory is currently the most persuasive.

3. Scientists explored the complexity of the universe with a new thoroughness, leading at least some atheistic philosophers to reconsider their opposition to the existence of God. Few atheists were converted to a theistic worldview, but the latter became more respectable among the uncommitted.

4. Some theologians responded to the new developments in physics by attempting to reconfigure traditional Christian theology. Process theology was an important result of that attempt, but its materialistic secularism discredited it in the eyes of many theologians and it is no longer taken seriously by most of them.

5. Discoveries in biology have led to a reappraisal of all life forms, particularly as it is now known that the genetic structure of DNA is common to all of them. This research is still a work in progress and there is much that remains to be discovered, but it is significant that many of the most prominent researchers in the field are practicing Christians.

6. Modern atheism continues to exist, but its intellectual dominance can no longer be taken for granted. The collapse of communism in the political sphere and the inability of atheistic critics of Christianity to provide a viable alternative have eroded their confidence, though the popular mind continues to believe that "science" will eventually solve all human problems.

7. Another branch of philosophy, with which the discipline is now usually identified, concentrates on linguistic analysis and the nature of logic. Many philosophers of this type have claimed that theological assertions are meaningless because they cannot be proved, but language itself extends beyond mere logic and allows for the possibility that there are realities that reason alone cannot explain.

8. Some theologians have tried to come to terms with logical analysis by agreeing that theological language is largely "mythical" and that a new form of "mythology" is required for the modern age. This has led to the development of what is known as a "new hermeneutic." However, professional biblical scholars have proved resistant to this, and it is doubtful whether any of these new ways of reading the sacred texts will become standard.

9. Human language is capable of expressing concepts that transcend time and space and frequently does so. Divine self-revelation is neither meaningless nor incomprehensible and cannot be dismissed on linguistic grounds alone.

IX

WHERE DO WE GO FROM HERE?

Athens (philosophy) and Jerusalem (theology) are inescapably different, both in their origins and in their respective methodologies. Theology is dependent on divine revelation and is an interpretation of that. That is true even of so-called natural theology. The investigator who reads the "book of nature" in the expectation of finding God is still thinking in terms of revelation because he assumes that God reveals himself in his creation. Whether that is true will ultimately be a matter of faith, since the material world does not compel us to say that it has a divine origin. Furthermore, although Christians accept that there are different ways of approaching theology, its subject matter is the one God of the Bible. That gives theology a focus that always comes back to the same starting point, even when courses in it are expanded to include the study of church government, worship, and so on. These ancillary disciplines arise because of the way in which biblical theology is applied in the life of God's people, but they have no independent existence and would be superfluous if God had not revealed himself.

Philosophy is completely different from this. It begins in the human mind and tries to make sense of the world around it, but it has no predetermined focus in the way that theology has, nor is it defined by a single principle that restricts what it can legitimately include. The mental constructions that can claim the mantle of philosophy are almost boundless in number, and new philosophies can appear at any time and in any religious or cultural environment. The human mind is capable of very diverse forms of inquiry, which are not necessarily bound to any objective reality. We can easily imagine worlds that do not exist and sometimes do so. Many people delight in such inventions as Middle-earth (in J. R. R. Tolkien's *Lord of the Rings*) and love to explore the inner coherence of this fantasy, but it has no basis in fact. Similarly, it is possible to construct artificial languages like Esperanto or Klingon, and to use them for communication with those who have bought into the same intellectual game, but games are what they ultimately are.

Even in the real world, it is possible for our minds to invent theories to explain different phenomena that turn out to be misconceived, as the history of philosophy demonstrates. To take but the most obvious example of this, Plato's idealism has frequently reappeared in different guises and it still attracts people today, but is there any truth to it? In the end, it is a mental construction that allows us to read the universe in a particular way, which some people find congenial, but it is always open to objections, and these have been just as frequent as the reincarnations of Platonism have been.

Divine revelation is not necessarily static and unchanging, but because it focuses on God, it is fixed in a way that philosophical speculation is not. Christians believe that God revealed himself to the prophets of ancient Israel and made certain promises to them. Israel had a long and eventful history, much of which is recounted in the OT, but the promises remained the same. They were essentially fulfilled in the life, death, and resurrection of Jesus Christ, who remains the touchstone for interpreting what divine revelation is. There remain some divine promises for which we are still waiting, but we believe that they will be fulfilled by the return of Christ and the subsequent end of the world. Jesus will not be superseded, and in that sense divine revelation is complete. Muslims, Mormons, and others may claim to have received further disclosures of God, but Christians reject these. Whether we are right to do so is ultimately a matter of faith, but those who have met Christ and who have his Holy Spirit dwelling in their hearts are in no doubt about that. They live their lives on the assumption that the divine self-disclosure in Jesus Christ is God's final revelation, and they are prepared to die for that belief, which they would hardly be if they thought that other options are possible or that there is more to come. This does not mean that theology is a fossilized or moribund discipline, because although God, as its chief subject matter, stays the same, the circumstances in which our knowledge of him is expressed are changing all the time and demand new and creative ways of thinking in order to ensure that the same message is communicated afresh in each generation.

In contrast to this, philosophical speculation has no fixed point of reference and is changing and developing all the time. Even those who identify with a particular school of thought are seldom so wedded to it as the final answer to life's mysteries that they are prepared to die for it. Philosophers may find a particular analysis of reality insightful and attractive, but they know that it can always be overturned or superseded. All philosophical ideas, including scientific theories, are inherently falsifiable, and one of the tasks of the good philosopher is to seek to do just that, not in order to destroy confidence in the truth, but to go more deeply into the nature of things and open up avenues of thought that were previously unknown or obscure. To put it a different way, whereas theologians doubt whether new revelations can be true and reject them if they contradict what is already known, philosophers welcome new ideas that open up pathways to explore and demonstrate that what has been accepted in the past is false.

This difference of perspective is fundamental and is enough to ensure that philosophy and theology cannot walk together side by side. But are they complementary perspectives that can meet in the middle? Some theologians like Tertullian have denied this, but most of them have looked for complementarity, even if they have conceived of it in different ways. Philosophers have often done the same, though in the centuries when the Christian churches wielded secular power, they had little choice. Even if they were basically atheists, philosophers of the seventeenth and eighteenth centuries had to pay lip service to Christianity, so whether their attempts to harmonize the two disciplines was genuine may be questioned.

Nowadays, that constraint has been removed, and many philosophers have distanced themselves from Christianity, and particularly from its theology. They have often thought that metaphysics, on which theology depends, is a kind of mythology that tries to impose a fantasy onto the world of material reality. They claim to be able to liberate themselves from what they see as supernatural myths and confine their speculations to the real world, although somewhat paradoxically that world is not necessarily material. This is because central to modern philosophical and scientific research is mathematics, which is the least material of the intellectual disciplines, but also the one that is most capable of achieving internal perfection, and therefore the one most likely to serve as a benchmark for knowing everything else.

The importance of mathematics for the development of modern science is beyond dispute, and for many modern philosophers it is the key for unlocking the secrets of the universe in a way that dispenses with any need for God or religion. At the same time, there are others who claim to see the mind of God revealed in mathematical equations and the like. These are the so-called believing scientists whose data and methods may be the same as those of their unbelieving colleagues, but whose interpretation of the phenomena they encounter is radically different. Theologians are naturally attracted to them and are grateful for their witness within the scientific community, but believing scientists are not necessarily theologians. For example, while they may be convinced that there is a God, they may hesitate to affirm the existence of the Trinity, while others deny the existence of hell and eternal punishment, to take but two well-known examples. This is possible because, while mathematical science can be understood as a product of the mind of God, it is essentially impersonal and amoral. Believing scientists are persons, of course, and almost all of them have a moral sensibility that is compatible with Christianity, but these factors are imported into their scientific worldview and not derived from it, which means that complete congruence between their science and their faith is not to be taken for granted.

If metaphysics is to be excluded from the discussion, then it is obvious that there can be no connection between philosophy and theology, even if the existence of God is accepted as possible. But can metaphysics be discarded? The truth is that all philosophy, and especially every philosophy of science, relies on certain metaphysical presuppositions that they take for granted whether they articulate them as such or not. Among the more important of these basic beliefs are the following six.

First, there is a universe that is orderly and rational. This means that there are scientific laws that are valid everywhere. Matter, or the atomic structure on which traditional concepts of matter have been based, is the same wherever it is found, making scientific exploration possible.

Second, the human mind is able to understand the workings of the material universe. This does not mean we have immediate knowledge of everything—some things remain a mystery because the rules governing them are not obvious and have to be worked out. But such mysteries are in principle soluble, and scientists spend their time trying to solve them. If they fail to do so, this is because they have not yet cracked the code needed to understand what is going on, not because the mystery is beyond the capacity of the human mind to unravel.

Third, the order of the universe is determined by contingency, not by absolute necessity. This means that there is a chain of cause and effect that produces change. Whether that change is desirable or not is another matter, but that can only be decided by the application of moral and/or spiritual principles that must be imported from outside the system. The universe is not fixed and immutable, because if it were, no human effort to develop it would be conceivable and everything would be static. Furthermore, the only way to find out how the world works is by trial and error, a process that is itself contingent.

Fourth, the universe has an objective existence outside the human mind. This means that when we investigate it, we must be prepared to change our assumptions if the evidence points us in an unexpected direction. No preconceived theory is immune to challenge. In other words, the structure of the universe can change our way of thinking about it, but not the other way around.

Fifth, in resolving the mysteries of the universe, researchers prefer solutions that are simple and "beautiful." The former of these goes back to Aristotle but has come down to us most famously as Ockham's razor, named for William of Ockham, who insisted that problems should be solved in the simplest way possible. The desire for beauty is also ancient, although beauty is notoriously difficult to define. Even so, there is a strong tendency among scientists to connect it with simplicity. If that is the case, we may say that simplicity is objective fact, whereas beauty is a subjective value given to that fact and not intrinsic to it.

Sixth, most scientists and virtually all philosophers distinguish between what is objectively possible or real (fact) and what is desirable (value). Very few people would say that we should (or must) do something—like blow the world up—merely because we can; almost always people agree that there ought to be a reason why a particular possible action should be taken. This involves taking a decision that does not impose itself by the nature of the subject but is determined according to a system of values that has been imported into the situation from outside. That decision is determined by the values held by those who take it, which may be derived from any number of sources that are unrelated to the action in question.

The Christian theologian who looks at these metaphysical assumptions soon sees parallels with his own beliefs that can hardly be accidental. Even a superficial reading of Genesis 1–3, the creation narrative in the OT, makes the following four points crystal clear:

1. The universe is orderly and rational because it has been created as such by God. It is coherent because there is only one Creator. This produces a difficulty when it comes to explaining the origin and existence of evil, which is opposed to God and not directly caused by him. At the same time, it avoids dualism, which is the belief that there are two (or more) different powers that have made the world and whose differences account for the incompatibilities that we observe in it.

2. The human mind has been given the ability not only to understand the universe, but also to exercise dominion over it. This is symbolized in Genesis 1 where it is stated that human beings have the right to name the animals (i.e., classify them), to till the soil, and to multiply their own species.

3. The contingency of nature is inscribed in the laws that govern it. There is a regular pattern of cause and effect that allows for change and that to some extent can be guided and controlled by human agents.

4. The universe has an independent, self-contained existence. It was created by God out of nothing (*ex nihilo*) and is not an extension of his own being. It can therefore be examined by human beings without incurring the danger of transgressing

into the realm of the divine. It also excludes the worship of anything in creation (idolatry).

It should be stressed that these Christian beliefs did not emerge to accommodate scientific discoveries, which they long predated. If anything, the reverse is true—Christian convictions about the nature of the world made the scientific enterprise possible, and it is a matter of historical fact that it has been in traditionally "Christian" countries that modern science has developed. This will not persuade atheists or doubters to become Christians, but at least they ought to acknowledge that science relies on metaphysical presuppositions, that those presuppositions are fully supported by Christian theology, and that the latter cannot be dismissed merely because it goes beyond the limits of the physical. Christian beliefs limit the possibilities of philosophical speculation about the nature of the universe, but those limitations fall within the boundaries of the natural sciences and are fully compatible with them.

THE LIMITATIONS OF OUR KNOWLEDGE

All human intellectual activity is subject to limitations placed on our knowledge by our inescapable finitude. For the theologian, those limitations have been determined by God, though whether we have fully exploited what has been revealed to us is another matter. God knows everything, but we do not. Our nature as creatures prevents us from having the perspective that he (as an infinite being) can have, and we have to respect that. That there are many things we cannot know does not bother Christians, because we know the One who does know them and we trust him to make sure that we are not unjustly disadvantaged by our ignorance. This conviction is based on faith, of course, but it is not blind, because we trust in the God who has made us, who has saved us from our sins, and who has promised to keep us safe, whatever happens. Our faith is not an excuse to avoid asking questions and seeking answers insofar as they can be had, however. Some of the most penetrating researchers have been guided toward their discoveries by their faith in an almighty Creator God, not limited or blinded by it. For Christians, belief in God is not a form of obscurantism—on the contrary, it is a spur to investigation, because we can rest assured that if there are answers to be had, we can be led to find them. We may not discover everything we are looking for—life is too short and often too complicated for that. But we believe that one day we shall go to be with our Creator and that then we shall know, even as we are known (1 Cor 13:12).

The situation of the philosopher is quite different. He cannot put boundaries on the possibility of his knowledge, since there is no telling how far his researches and speculations might lead. Whether this activity will bring him to the "truth" is impossible to say, because how would he know when he has found it? He might make discoveries that turn out to be illusions, or speculate on matters that sound logical but turn out not to be correct. He can never know for sure, because even what he thinks he knows is not beyond question. The history of philosophy is full of attempts to prove that nothing ever changes, that motion does not occur, that time does not exist, and so on. Logical arguments to support this kind of conclusion have been proposed and debated for centuries, but common sense tells us they are wrong. We may not be able to explain what time and space are, but we know from experience how they affect us, and we find attempts to deny their existence bizarre, if not comical. The philosopher may accuse a theologian of building metaphysical castles in the air, but he is building his own house on sand, and however impressive it may look, it will crumble and be washed away if challenged by a better theory.

The practical importance of this can be seen most clearly when we look at the problems that face theologians. Why does evil exist? How can a good God allow innocent people to suffer? What allows the wicked to prosper but denies justice to those who deserve it? Questions like these are staples of atheist critics of Christianity, who insist that if God is who we say he is, things like these would never happen. As Christians, we have to admit that we do not know why the innocent suffer. We cannot say why God tolerates the existence of evil, nor do we know precisely when the judgment of the unrighteous will come. When bad things happen to us, we may be blown off our feet and doubt the goodness of God toward us—the Psalms are full of laments and complaints to a God who seems far away, and in many respects the psalmist speaks for all of us.

Those who do not believe in God are quick to pounce on these unanswerable problems and to use them as sticks to beat believers with. As often as not, their pleas for atheism are rooted in moral dilemmas of this kind and not in any scientifically objective fact. But what alternative do they propose? What else can they suggest? There is nothing. They cannot deny what they see in front of them any more than Christians can, and their sense of the wrongness of these things may be even stronger. Yet they have no solutions to offer. They may claim that science and human progress will eventually eliminate all such problems, but that is an act of faith with no objective basis. The exponential growth of modern science in the past two hundred years has solved none of the classical dilemmas posed by the existence of suffering and injustice. On the contrary, they have become even worse, as weapons of mass destruction have been invented for the sole purpose of destroying human beings. An objective consideration of this history would suggest that further discoveries will produce still more devastating possibilities. Science cannot prevent this on its own—only judgments based on other criteria can do that. Seen in that light, the Christian message is more relevant and more necessary now than it has ever been.

The optimism of so many humanist thinkers has no objective justification. In our age of supposed progress and development, creative minds portray disorder and destruction. For over a century now, the novels of Fyodor Dostoyevsky (1821–1881), Franz Kafka (1883–1924), William Golding (1911–1993), Paul Auster (1947–), Cormac McCarthy (1933–2023), and others have told the same story of human depravity and despair. Painters like Pablo Picasso and Salvador Dalí (1904–1989) have portrayed a world of chaos and disorder and most modern art echoes the same themes. Great musicians like Igor Stravinsky (1882–1971) and Modest Mussorgsky (1838–1881) have reveled in disharmony, which is the sound of our time. What is true of the highest levels of modern culture is true also lower down the scale, where notions of harmony, beauty, and love are constantly perverted. The God-free *Brave New World* of Aldous Huxley (1894–1963) is not a paradise but a hellhole bent on self-destruction. Theologians contemplating this expect nothing else—without God the world is lost in sin and depravity, chaos and disorder. Philosophers may speculate about how to achieve a better future, but they cannot deliver it because they are caught up in the very depravity that they protest against.

The terrible truth is that whether we like it or not, we are living in the first generation that has the capacity to destroy the entire planet. Never has there been a time when human wisdom has proved to be so inadequate, and yet the hearts of modern people, especially of modern Western people, are hardened against God in a way that they have not been for generations. In our secular world, every problem can be exposed and every fantastic solution can be put forward, but it is virtually taboo to speak about the God of the Bible and his Son Jesus Christ in public. It is almost as if there is a conspiracy of silence in the public square, where media commentators and others habitually declare themselves to be atheists (or at least agnostics) and perhaps feel they have to do so in order to get a hearing.

In a world that appears to be in thrall to an aggressive secularism that has precious little time for theology or religion, especially Christian religion, it is necessary to remind ourselves that this tendency, dominant though it may seem to be, is not the only one represented in the realm of contemporary philosophy. Christians of various persuasions also manage to find a voice, and some have become prominent exponents of various philosophical positions. Among Roman Catholics, Charles Taylor (1931–) has contested the secularization theories that have shaped so much modern sociology, and John Rist (1936–) has probed the depths of traditional Augustinian and Thomist thinking. The Dutch Reformed tradition continues to be creative, especially in the United States, where the names of Cornelius Van Til (1895–1987), Nicholas Wolterstorff (1932–), and Alvin Plantinga (1932–) have continued and expanded the work of an earlier generation that includes Herman Bavinck (1854–1921) and Herman Dooyeweerd (1894–1977).

Others who have made notable contributions to the defense of a Christian worldview are Richard Swinburne (1934–), Oliver O'Donovan (1945–), and William Lane Craig (1949–). Special mention must be made of John Lennox (1943–), not himself a philosopher but a scientist who has taken on prominent "new atheists" like Richard Dawkins, Christopher Hitchens (1949–2011), and Sam Harris (1967–) and demonstrated how shallow their thinking actually is. Particularly interesting, and potentially important for the next generation, is the work of Peter Adamson (1972–), not himself a professing Christian but someone who believes that religion, including Christian theology, is important for understanding philosophy and who has undertaken a massive project designed to explore and expound every branch of that discipline "without any gaps."[1] Also of great potential importance for the future is the work of Christopher Watkin (1980–), who applies a strongly Christian (and evangelical Protestant) critique to modern philosophy of all kinds.[2] It is too early to say whether (or how many) others will follow in their wake, but the appearance of such material may be the harbinger of a more fruitful dialogue between philosophy and theology, and a greater understanding among the general public of the importance and intellectual integrity of the Christian tradition.

The unreality of the God-denying world we are living in cannot continue forever. Sooner or later it will implode, and the danger is that it will drag our civilization down with it. The signs of social breakdown are everywhere—uncontrollable gun violence, drug abuse, environmental pollution, massive corruption in high places, and so on. Yet so far the collective will to do something about it seems to be lacking. No philosophy is capable of resolving these problems, and none is being tried. Churches and religious organizations seem to be afraid to speak up or are hesitant to do so because of a misplaced devotion to secularism. There is no magic formula that will solve every dilemma. The great ideologies of the past—Platonism, Marxism, and so on—have invariably failed when attempts have been made to put them into practice, and we should not expect anything better from their current reincarnations. History tells us that only when religious revival has occurred—in fourth-century Rome, for example, or sixteenth-century Europe—has there been lasting change for the better. Can this happen again? Will it? We cannot tell. Here we have reached the limits of our knowledge, and if we are Christians, we can do no more than cast ourselves on the grace and mercy of God, who may yet spare us from the wrath to come.

---

1. Adamson has a podcast, *History of Philosophy without Any Gaps*, that he eventually turns into a series of books. See the bibliography for a list of those already available.

2. C. Watkin, *Biblical Critical Theory* (Grand Rapids: Zondervan, 2022).

FOR FURTHER READING

The resources available for the study of philosophy and its relationship to theology are almost boundless, and no one person can hope to master the entire field. The list of books for further reading can only be a guide to introductory literature, and serious students will need to pursue the subject much further. Nevertheless, we must begin somewhere. The volumes listed here tackle the subject from different angles and offer different approaches to it, but all are informative and useful for beginners who wish to look into these matters more deeply.

Adamson, Peter. *Byzantine and Renaissance Philosophy*. Oxford: Oxford University Press, 2022.

———. *Classical Philosophy*. Oxford: Oxford University Press, 2016.

———. *Medieval Philosophy*. Oxford: Oxford University Press, 2022.

———. *Philosophy in the Hellenistic and Roman Worlds*. Oxford: Oxford University Press, 2018.

———. *Philosophy in the Islamic World*. Oxford: Oxford University Press, 2018.

Allen, Diogenes. *Philosophy for Understanding Theology*, 2nd ed. Louisville, KY: Westminster John Knox Press, 2007.

Boersma, Hans. *Five Things Theologians Wish Biblical Scholars Knew*. Downers Grove, IL: IVP Academic, 2021.

Carlisle, Clare. *Spinoza's Religion*. Princeton, NJ: Princeton University Press, 2021.

Collins, Francis. *The Language of God: A Scientist Presents Evidence for Belief*. New York: Simon & Schuster, 2007.

Craig, William Lane. *In Quest of the Historical Adam*. Grand Rapids: Eerdmans, 2021.

Dawkins, Richard. *River Out of Eden: A Darwinian View of Life*. London: Weidenfeld and Nicolson, 1995.

Dodson, Joseph R., and David E. Briones. *Paul and the Giants of Philosophy: Reading the Apostle in Greco-Roman Context*. Downers Grove, IL: IVP Academic, 2019.

Epperly, Bruce. *Process Theology: A Guide for the Perplexed*. London: T&T Clark, 2011.

Farías, Victor. *Heidegger and Nazism*. Philadelphia: Temple University Press, 1989.

Gay, Peter. *The Enlightenment: An Interpretation*. 2 vols. New York: Knopf, 1966–1969.

Grayling, A. C. *The History of Philosophy: Three Millennia of Thought from the West and Beyond*. London: Penguin, 2019.

Hawking, Stephen. *A Brief History of Time*. New York: Bantam Press, 1998.

Hazard, Paul. *The European Mind 1680–1715*. London: Hollis and Carter, 1953.

——. *European Thought in the Eighteenth Century from Montesquieu to Lessing*. London: Hollis and Carter, 1954.

Israel, Jonathan. *Democratic Enlightenment: Philosophy, Revolution and Human Rights 1750–1790*. New York: Oxford University Press, 2012.

——. *Enlightenment Contested: Philosophy, Modernity and the Emancipation of Man 1670–1752*. New York: Oxford University Press, 2006.

——. *The Enlightenment that Failed: Ideas, Revolution and Democratic Defeat 1748–1830*. New York: Oxford University Press, 2019.

——. *Radical Enlightenment: Philosophy and the Making of Modernity 1650–1750*. New York: Oxford University Press, 2001.

Jastrow, Robert. *God and the Astronomers*. New York: W. W. Norton, 1992.

Kampourakis, Kostas. *Understanding Evolution*. Cambridge: Cambridge University Press, 2020.

Kołakowski, Leszek. *Main Currents of Marxism*. 3 vols. Oxford: Oxford University Press, 1978.

Kuyper, Abraham. *Calvinism: Six Lectures Delivered in the Theological Seminary at Princeton*. New York: F. H. Revell, 1899.

Novak, David. *Athens and Jerusalem: God, Humans and Nature*. Toronto: University of Toronto Press, 2019.

Siniossoglu, Niketas. *Plato and Theodoret: The Christian Appropriation of Platonic Philosophy and the Hellenic Intellectual Resistance*. Cambridge: Cambridge University Press, 2008.

Tattersall, Ian. *Understanding Human Evolution*. Cambridge: Cambridge University Press, 2022.

Watkin, Christopher. *Biblical Critical Theory*. Grand Rapids: Zondervan, 2022.

SUBJECT INDEX

NAMES AND PLACES INDEX

SCRIPTURE INDEX

Old Testament

New Testament

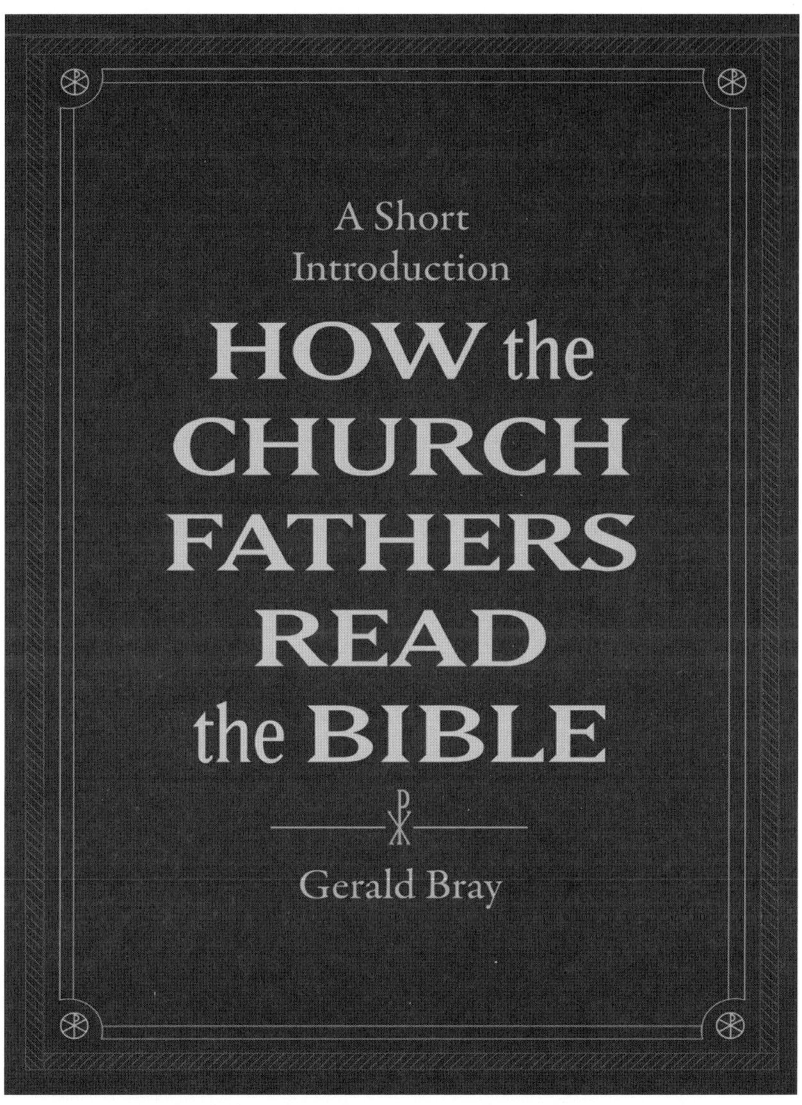
A Short
Introduction
HOW the
CHURCH
FATHERS
READ
the BIBLE
Gerald Bray